Life in

ISTANBUL

A Family's Odyssey

Alice Ketabgian

Avid Readers Publishing Group

Lakewood, California

Life in Istanbul   *A Family's Odyssey*

Avid Readers Publishing Group

http://www.avidreaderspg.com

ISBN-13: 978-1-61286-312-2

Printed in the United States

In Loving Memory of my Parents

Ardashes and Wilhelmina Lafdjian

&

Dedicated to our Grandchildren

Beatrice, Noah, Lydia

Table of Contents

CHAPTER I: Life in Istanbul

CHAPTER II: Life in Istanbul

CHAPTER III: America

CHAPTER IV: Great-uncle Abraham's Memoir

x

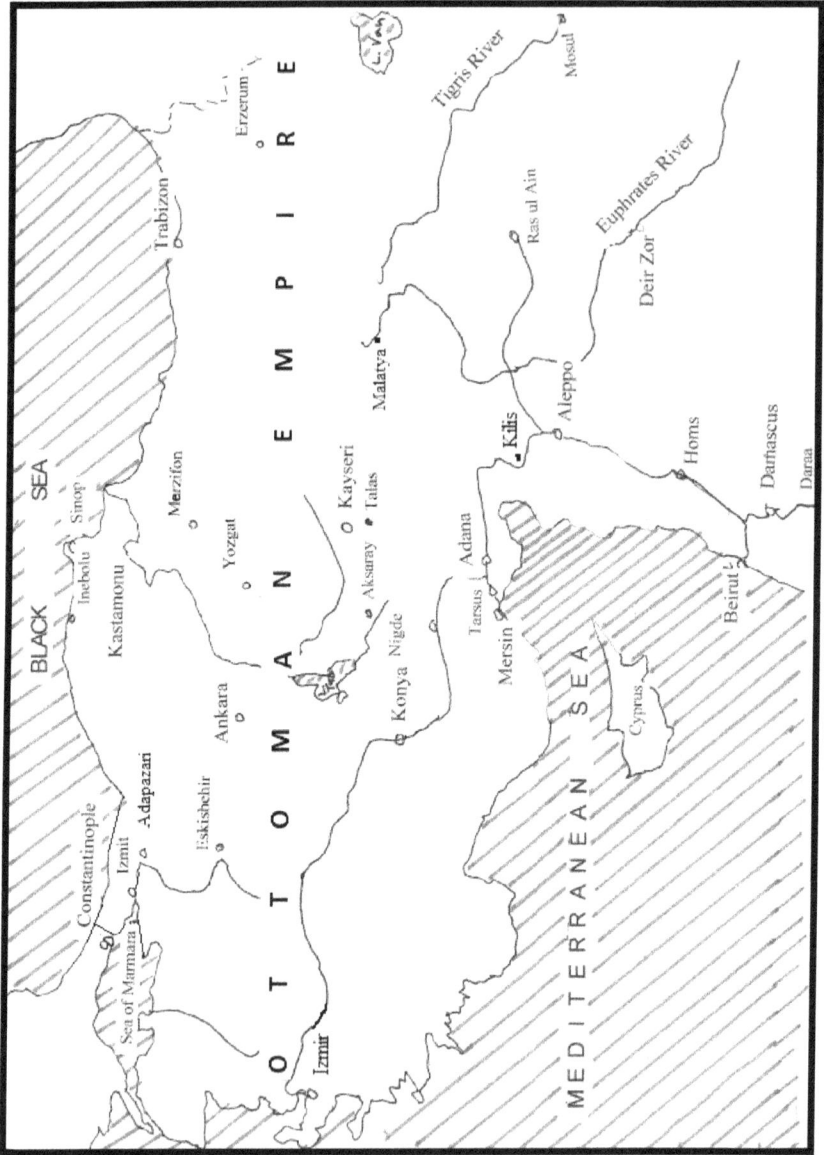

Map of Ottoman Empire

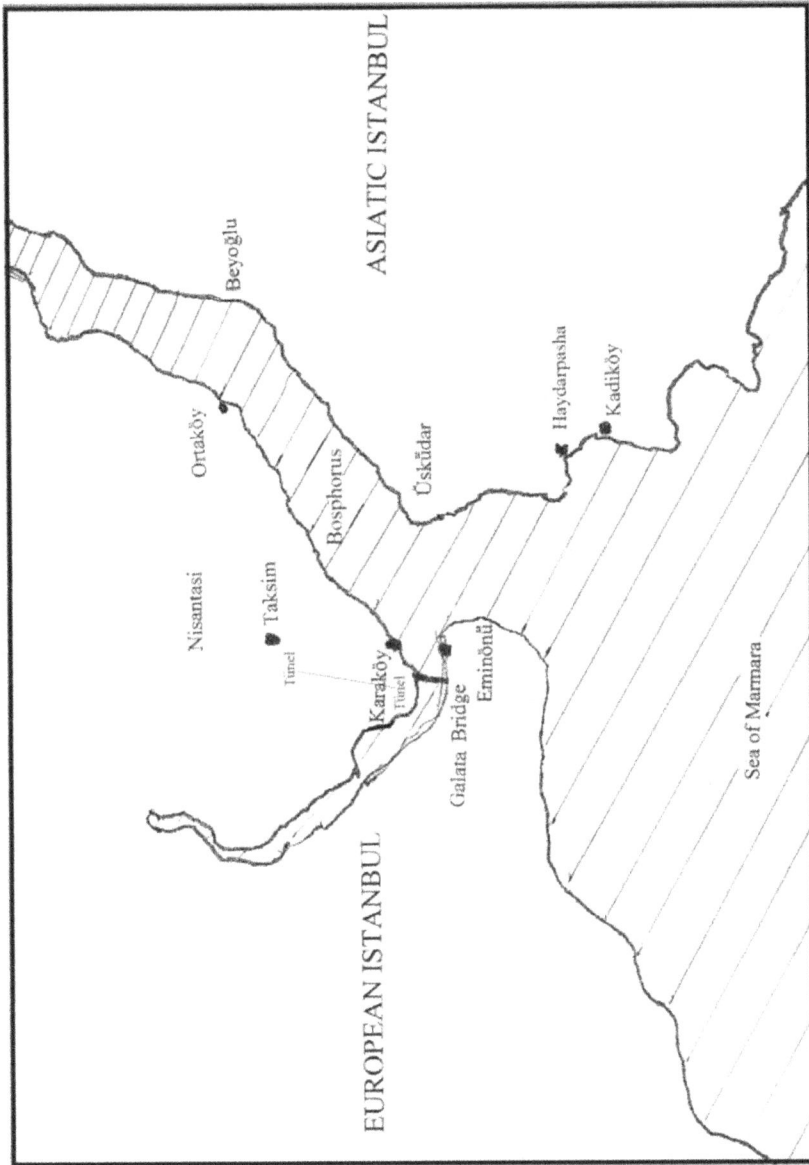

MAP OF ISTANBUL – REGIONS COVERED IN TEXT

PROLOGUE

There are a number of reasons why I felt compelled to write this memoir. Perhaps the principal one was that on occasion of the commemoration of the 50th anniversary of the Armenian Genocide in 1965 when I watched the documentary at UCLA and found out for the first time what had really happened to my people, I felt betrayed and angry because I had been kept in the dark regarding the true history, as were the rest of students in Turkey attending history classes; instead we had received a distorted, sanitized version of history.

Another motivating factor was that after finding out the true history about my people starting with the Hamidian Massacres of 1894-1896, followed by the Armenian Genocide of 1915-1922, I realized that those guilty of the criminal acts had never received the punishments they deserved; therefore a moral lesson was never learned by the aggressors. Consequently, these terrible events kept happening in different stages at unpredictable intervals. They were: *Varlik Vergisi*, the unaffordable Wealth Tax on the minorities of Istanbul and Izmir of 1942, and the Cyprus Crisis of 1955 which was accompanied by pogroms. I personally witnessed the latter during which the wealth and properties of minorities were stripped from them, enriching Turkish citizens, in an effort to create a homogeneous Turkey. As long as we Armenians lived in Turkey as a minority, we always lived with the fear that tomorrow might be the day we could lose what we owned, perhaps even our lives.

An additional reason for writing this memoir was to inform the future generations that our forefathers had a colorful past and came in contact with a number of notable figures of their time. My Great-uncles Abraham and Parsegh had closer connections to Sultan Abdul Hamid II and the 3rd and perhaps least malicious of the triumvirates of *Ittihad ve Terakki*, Jemal Pasha, than most people of their time. In the generation following them, my father's cousin, Jacob, suffered throughout his life the deleterious effects of the way he had handled a previous university cheating incident by Ömer, the elder son of the 2nd president of Turkey, Ismet Inönü.

Another reason for writing this memoir was my father's dangerous profession, because during the years that I lived in Turkey I was constantly worried about him, and wished he had a different profession which did not involve covertly transferring the funds of desperate Armenians out of Turkey. My attitude changed radically after the Cyprus Crisis and the pogroms of 1955. They helped me realize what a critical role my father had been playing in the lives of Istanbul's Armenian population by ensuring that their funds reached the destinations they were heading to, placing him in harm's way in the process. I now view what he did as: a heroic service framed by quiet modesty.

The Cyprus Crisis, and the pogroms of September 6-7, 1955 I witnessed must have had an indelible effect on my psyche at the time because upon graduation that year from elementary school, and with my mother's extraordinary drive and invaluable help, they encouraged me to be a highly-disciplined eleven-year-old, willing to try to accomplish the nearly impossible.

Later at age seventeen, venturing on my own to cross the Atlantic to attend college in the States under the guidance of my father's savant, but uncommunicative cousin Jacob, there came another challenging test for me in academic and emotional survival, not to mention the culture shock. In spite of the mixed blessing his guidance provided for me, I was still most thankful that he was there for me.

The final and perhaps most precious part of the book is my Great-uncle Abraham's own memoir in Turkish, utilizing the Armenian alphabet, which I translated fulfilling my father's wish. It was against great odds that my father had personally managed to save and transport this document through our moves, first to Üsküdar then to Nisantasi and later to the States in 1968, as he and my mother were getting ready to leave the country for good. If this document was discovered at any point and the Turkish government happened to get a clue as to its content, the punishment my father would suffer could be deadly. My Great-uncle Abraham's memoir, which commences with the depiction of life in Talas in Historic Armenia in the second part of the 19th century and points out the necessity of their move to Aksaray, paints an authentic picture of the saga they endured during the deportations and the Armenian Genocide of 1915 against the historical background of the times. Finally by 1922, he gives a most realistic account of the survivors of the genocide within his extended family, whose status by now had been transformed from riches to rags, and whose members had been scattered throughout the world, unlikely to see each other again.

It was during our visit to Istanbul in 2006 that I unexpectedly happened to come across the doomed love story of my aunt's sister, Verjin, set against the backdrop of the Armenian Genocide, related to me by my cousin Sona. I found out how the kind Turkish mayor of tiny Inebolu, the port of Kastamonu on the Black Sea, fell in love and married Verjin, helping save her extended family, my six-month-old mother being among them.

Mostly however, I wrote this memoir to pay tribute to my mother and father who began their own odyssey of survival. As we were growing up, they were undaunted in making enormous sacrifices so we would prosper and be able to transport ourselves to a country where fear no longer was expected to raise its ugly head with regularity. Once settled on my mission of familial discovery--not to mention my curiosity and insistence on ferreting out the truth--I pursued it with dogged resolve, which included visiting my father's hometown of Aksaray. I wanted to save the history that emerged for my children and children's children so it would not be forgotten.

CHAPTER 1
LIFE IN ISTANBUL

Observing the Destruction from my Bedroom Window

I was eleven, when a thunderous humming rudely awakened me around midnight on September 7, 1955. As I built up the courage to open my eyes in the dark, I was surprised but also pleased to recognize the silhouettes of my parents nearby. Standing by the bay window, my father was carefully studying the street four levels below us to find out what the commotion was all about. My parents must have rushed to my room from their bedroom across the corridor to make sure I was safe and not frightened, since by now I had been sleeping all alone in that room for almost a week. My sister had been gone for an extended vacation to my maternal grandparents who lived in Üsküdar. My parents' voices sounded alarmed and perplexed, although they were trying not to show it to me.

In just a few minutes, I could hear the chanting growing louder and louder. The racket was that of a mob howling and advancing down our street like a relentless stream of lava led by the waving red Turkish flag with the white star and sickle moon that one of them was carrying. As it approached our house, its haunting hum increased in intensity and became more threatening. Now I could distinctly hear wild voices and shouting coming from the street below, as if hundreds of coyotes had gathered for an evening hunt. The changes in their pitch and yelps sent a chilling uneasiness in me. The yelps were followed by the smashing of store windows and steel shutters, as plate-glass came crashing down amid the screams of the mob. In spite of being four stories above the street level, I felt as if the whole thing was taking place right next to me because the uproar was so deafening. It sounded as if the smashed glass from the store windows was cascading down like a waterfall. At times the noise was so loud that it drowned out the cries of the unruly mob that kept on moving relentlessly down our street. As I would later find out, the mob was systematically plundering Greek, Armenian, and Jewish possessions while trying to grab as much of the loot as possible.

Horrified and huddled next to my parents in the dark, I joined them to peek cautiously through the old wooden shutters that looked gray with age, to find out what was going on at the street level. From the limited exposure they allowed me, I could see groups of wild men approaching in waves, with clubs, crowbars, and wooden sticks in their hands. Many were chanting, *vurun, kirin* in Turkish, meaning "hit them, break them." They were breaking into the stores of Greeks, Armenians, and Jews, whose lists and whereabouts it appeared had been previously provided for them. They were wasting no time in destroying and vandalizing the unlucky stores on their path until at the end they all looked as if they had been through a hurricane. There were even more vicious ones among them chanting the slogan, *bugün maliniz, yarin caniniz*, meaning "Today, it is your goods; tomorrow, it will be your life…" As I looked more carefully, I noticed among the demonstrators the municipal night-watchman directing traffic and leading sections of the mob to the targeted businesses and institutions. A number of policemen were laughing loudly, sounding not too different from hyenas. They were not restoring the order; instead they were cheering and assisting the raging mob flooding the street.

I soon realized there was a certain plan to the destruction going on in front of my eyes. Eventually I could distinguish, more or less three waves of attacks. The first one must have had the task of breaking down the doors and shutters of the stores to prepare the way for the second wave to pillage and steal everything that could be moved away. The third wave was totally destroying whatever remained.

Further down our street and to the west, but still quite visible from my bedroom window, was a small store belonging to Master Krikor. He was in his late sixties; he only sold cigarettes, candy, water, and newspapers. He was a widower and lived alone on the floor above his store. Several times the mob had attempted to break in, but his Turkish neighbors had not allowed it. However, the last persistent unruly bunch, not listening even to their countrymen, had managed to break in. They looted his store. They shredded everything in sight to pieces. The poor man had no choice but to view the entire calamity from one level above through his drapes with a somber gaze. Who knows how many earlier calamities of this sort he had already witnessed, somehow triumphing over adversity. But how long could he continue doing it?

As my eyes adjusted to the darkness of my bedroom, where the only source of light was from the street lamp outside, I noted my parents' caution. They had carefully avoided turning on the dimmest light or making the slightest audible sound. So far they had not made a single remark about the violence at the street level or about the misfortune of the minority shopkeepers. Yet the agitated look and the worried tone of my father's voice, often dotted with long silences, conveyed volumes even to an eleven-year-old little girl. It covertly conveyed the message, "Beware, here comes a repeat performance of earlier dreaded days from our history! I remember living through these sorts of terrifying times before…"

Across the street from our house and to the east was the Greek-owned general store, *Koperatif*, from where pots and pans, pressure-cookers and china along with massive wheels of imported cheese, long sticks of salami and sausages, suddenly had become airborne. They were being tossed to carefully aim them at the *Soorp Takavor*, Holy King Armenian Church, less than fifty feet away. Members of the mob, as if it were a contest, were trying to clear the massive eight foot wall surrounding the church as well as its iron gate. I had often wondered why church walls had to be so tall! During the funeral processions held there, I would get an eerie feeling each time I heard the church bells toll to announce the eternal departure of a loved one from amongst us. Now at 2 AM in the morning, witnessing the atrocities four stories down at the street level from my safe bedroom window, and comforted by the presence of my parents, I wished the church bells would mysteriously start tolling as an act of God to protest the injustice and brutality in front of my eyes.

Across the street from us and slightly to the west was the Greek appliance store with brand new washing machines and refrigerators, quite unaffordable for the average citizen. At this unearthly hour of the morning, every existing appliance in that store was being punished with blows from heavy metal rods in the hands of what seemed to be village youth. It was as though they were instructed to destroy with no reverence to ownership. They seemed to be taking pride in the vandalism and devastation they were participating in.

The three of us continued viewing the street until close to dawn, in spite of the daunting schedule we had to face the next day, not to mention the alertness it would require of us. After what we had thus far observed, we were too anxious and scared to sleep. Just before sunrise, when the work of the mobs was completed, and its participants were exhausted from the strenuous activity of the night, they hauled their instantaneously acquired riches and were now ready to resume their regular activities of the day. It appeared as if there were some officials from our district who were overseeing the situation. Upon finishing their "work," the mob disappeared into a government vehicle in the region in front of the *Soorp Takavor* Armenian Church where four streets crossed each other. My parents and I, who until then were huddled together inconspicuously in front of the bay window of our ancient, wooden five-story house whose wood now had acquired a drab-gray color with age, decided we should go to bed for a couple of hours so we would have the energy to face the new day.

As a child I felt fortunate that in contrast to the violence four stories down at the street level, I was safe and close to my parents. However, all the destruction had left me scared and perplexed. As far back as I could remember I had known the neighborhood to be safe and friendly. Was I mistaken? Was there a duplicity all along that I had failed to detect? What I observed seemed to be from a violent movie or a page from the history books. It was no different than the pillaging of a city, for that matter Constantinople by the Ottomans when they conquered it in 1453 from the Byzantine Empire. I was at the time too young to know that what I had just witnessed was an act of government-engineered ethnic cleansing which would searingly replay in my memory at some of the most unexpected times in the years to come. As an unspoken visual image, it was engraved in my memory and would assume a life of its own.

Chapter I

An Attempt to Gain Admission to the American Girls' School

During the events of the Cyprus Crisis in early September of 1955, the British had left the island, while both Greece and Turkey claimed ownership to it. I was alone in the bedroom I normally shared with my younger sister Arminé. While she was having an exciting time visiting my grandparents, I was on another mission undertaken by my mother. She had always been a tireless, devoted, and persevering parent, constantly in search of ideas--hers as well as those of others in different social circles. After she came across an idea which she interpreted as having merit, she would never leave it on the back burner, but would go full force to implement it. I am convinced she made up in drive what she lacked in higher education and self-confidence. Fast forward some thirty years, by which time my husband Greg had gotten to know her well, on more than one occasion he had remarked about her perseverance:

"In my 37 years of medical practice in internal medicine, she was perhaps one of the very few people I encountered who out of her own free will radically and permanently altered her lifestyle and eating habits. She shed some sixty pounds by diligently walking and exercising and controlling her portion sizes, never to regain the weight she had lost."

When I graduated from the *Aramyan Ounchiyan Armenian Elementary School* in Kadiköy, instruction was in Armenian and Turkish. A rudimentary course of French was taught starting in third grade with emphasis on rote memory and grammar but not on practical conversation. I remember learning the conjugation of numerous verbs without a clue as to how I would use them in everyday conversation. Consequently, in three years' time I had not made much progress in improving my language proficiency in conversational French.

A day early in June of 1955, when numerous hopeful prospective students were tested for admission to the American High School would remain in my memory forever. It represented my first exposure to testing, where I was handed a pamphlet-sized book of numerous questions on myriad subjects with little boxes to mark my choices. I had never seen such a huge study hall before, nor had it occurred to me that tests could exist with timed multiple choice questions. I was quite disappointed when I was ordered to turn my paper in after I had not even had a chance to answer a third of the word problems. This was also the first time I was confronted with mathematics word problems in Turkish rather than in Armenian. Needless to say, I was not among the lucky few to gain entry to the *American Academy for Girls in Üsküdar*. This was my mother's alma mater all the way from elementary school to the 11th grade. It was a highly regarded private institution of superior quality where English was taught by American teachers young and old, in cooperation with the Turkish Ministry of Education. I could tell our entire family was sad and disappointed. Deep down they were hoping that I could gain entry to this school, learn perfect English, and someday be able to attend a respectable college in the United States. This was the dream of all minorities in Turkey, but especially that of Armenians.

From my parents' show of enthusiasm in tackling this school issue, I realized that in due time, just for us in the younger generation, my parents would be willing to leave behind a lifetime of memories, prized possessions, their precious circle of friends and relatives, and travel across oceans in search of a new life. The U.S. quota of immigrants to the United States from Turkey for the year 1963, as I later found out, was 225 with a waiting list of 16,551! In the light of this extremely low probability of entering the country as an immigrant, attending college in the United States on a student visa seemed a more viable choice.

Commute across the Bosphorus on the Ferry

Since for the time-being seriously studying English in middle school did not seem to be in the cards for me, my parents and I thought I should start improving my French, my second language of choice. For the fast approaching fall semester, my mother had already enrolled me at *St. Benoit*, a French middle and high school across the Bosphorus in Karaköy; she had even paid a good portion of the tuition to guarantee a space for me for the 1955-56 academic years, starting on the 1st of October. Simultaneously she had registered me for a preparatory summer course in French so that when the regular academic year resumed in the fall, I would be better prepared to meet the challenges of tackling this foreign language.

To improve my French, early each morning I would hike the fifteen minute distance from our house in Kadiköy to the ferry landing; I would pass by grocery stores, a bookstore and bakeries where my sense of smell would be enriched with the aroma of their freshly baked pastries. In spite of having had breakfast, I must admit when I smelled the bouquet created by the union of unadulterated butter, flour, sugar, almond paste, thinly shaven freshly toasted almonds combine with the aroma of fresh cherry or apricot jam infused in the air, it made me forget that I had already had my hasty breakfast! This early morning experience would never fail to sharpen my sense of smell and ultimately my longing to taste these exciting baked goods. It had also convinced me that in the culinary world there could be instances where just the right combination of ingredients expertly put together could result in a finished product infinitely better than just those ingredients. I would also pass by *Haji Bekir*, the famous, century old Turkish delight establishment where one could buy this treat plain, with almonds, hazel nuts or pistachios; one even had a choice of buying a small block of *helva* which was a confection made of sesame flour, sesame oil and honey with its many flavor-enhancers including nuts and chocolate.

I had to be careful not to get carried away so I would be on time to catch the ferry to cross the Bosphorus to arrive on the European side. If I was early and lucky enough, I would get a seat on the ferry. Otherwise I had to stand up for the entire trip, either inside or outside. On foggy mornings, the foghorns of the larger commercial ships passing by and Russian tankers heading to and from the Black Sea would interrupt the silence of the serene sea air. They would also remind me of my whereabouts. When I got off the ferry at Karaköy, I passed by the old Galata Bridge on foot to arrive at St. Benoit. Towards the end of summer, I had figured out all the possible shortcuts since I had been traveling this route every day for over two months.

Mother's Novel Idea

Late in August that summer when I was least expecting it, thanks to her buoyant energy, my mother came up with an alternate and totally novel plan. Earlier that day she had been conversing with my elementary school classmate Irma Odabashian's mother who had told her, "Irma's score on the entrance examination was not good enough in getting her admitted to the American Girls' Lycee in Üsküdar, either; but she has been studying English throughout the summer to try her luck one more time using a different method. On September 15th she will be taking an English language proficiency test. If successful, there is a chance she can be accepted to the 2nd Special grade at the very same school."

In looking back, I now realize Irma's mother must have been a good-hearted and moral woman to present this window of opportunity to my mother; or perhaps she was unaware of my mother's unusually high level of energy and enthusiasm for projects she wanted to accomplish. Knowing that there were only ten spots available for this type of an admission to the school, I could be reducing her daughter's chances of being accepted.

Then my mother informed me of the remaining important details. She told me there were only three weeks left to prepare for this special type of admission. Later continuing in the same calm and collected tone, perhaps intended not to unnecessarily make me nervous, she casually mentioned the most essential detail of it all, "In three weeks you are expected to have learned the equivalent of an entire academic year of English." She said the reasoning behind all this was that if successful, I would be placed with the fifteen students from the previous year who had been unsuccessful in mastering the English language to the school's satisfaction during their first year of exposure to it.

The Teachings of my Mother and Mrs. Alexanian

There were some phenomenal advantages to making use of my mother's latest discovery. One was that my mother was a bottomless source of energy when she put something in her mind; during her academic career she had attended the very same school I now had my eyes on, starting with their first grade when the school even had an elementary section; she knew the mechanics of English quite well although she had not spoken it much at all within the last forty years! She had told me that during her years as a student there, Armenian was taught regularly in the curriculum until she was in third grade, at which time it was discontinued due to a surge of incoming Turkish students during the Atatürk years. The teacher who my mother instantly thought she should contact was Mrs. Alexanian who had been her very own extremely capable English teacher at the very same institution. When my mother contacted her by phone early the very next morning, her response was lukewarm at best:

"Go ahead and bring your daughter to our next scheduled teaching session this afternoon. I want you to know that the girls I have been currently working with have been attending my classes for at least two months. The exam is scheduled in three weeks. I am unable to give specially tailored sessions to your daughter; however, if you are willing to undertake most of the teaching and catching up, I am willing to have your daughter join my classes."

By most measures this was not a very encouraging response, but it was not an emphatic "No" either. Understandably, Mrs. Alexanian had no clue about the indefatigability of my mother. She did not know that in this type of endeavor my mother was in a class of her own. However, having started so late, I could conceivably hold her class's progress back and make the teaching of English unnecessarily difficult for her. I was so lucky she was willing to give me a chance! I think she did not want to deny my mother the slightest quiver of hope, especially when she recalled the diminutive cute blond Wilhelmina with her green eyes and prominent well-pressed ribbon as her student of some thirty years ago.

Mrs. Alexanian must have also realized that if anyone could accomplish this practically impossible task of instant language instruction translated into instant learning of the new tongue, it would have to be my mother. She had the necessary background in English and was going to be guided during the entire process by her, the master teacher. Besides if it worked, it surely would make a number of people extremely happy. Mrs. Alexanian herself would gain further respect in the eyes of Miss Martin, the principal, in addition to performing a much needed service at the moment for her former student who now was in a bind. If her random act of kindness somehow produced its intended result, she would simply feel good for being a Good Samaritan and having exponentially improved my prospects for the future.

With my mother's help and Mrs. Alexanian's guidance, I was willing to accept the grueling challenge of learning numerous words and phrases, as well as the conjugation of many irregular verbs. However unlike my previous French instruction at my elementary school, I had to acquire a practical conversational and comprehensive knowledge of the language. Then there was the matter of constant drilling. The whole thing had sounded like an intricate game to me at the time. Yet for a change, there was a slight chance that this new language with its novel assortment of words, verbs, phrases and rules, which had meant nothing to me until the end of August, could suddenly and magically become part of my everyday vocabulary at the end of the following three weeks! I should also not neglect to mention that during these three weeks I would be getting the undivided attention of my mother, something a child of any age wants more than anything.

Will it be English or French?

Because my mother and I still had serious doubts about our undertaking, during the first week of classes with Mrs. Alexanian, I attempted to learn French and English simultaneously. In the mornings, I would take the ferry from the Kadiköy quay to cross the Bosphorus to make it to Karaköy and from there would walk to reach *St. Benoit* to learn French. Then, in the afternoons, this time accompanied by my mother, I would take the ferry again. We would walk through the passageway leading to the tunnel, which was one of the world's oldest subterranean transit lines. It was a two-stop subway built by French engineers, having begun its operation in

1875 to link Karaköy Square and the embassy district in central Beyoğlu. The subway would deliver us in close proximity to the bus we needed to take to arrive within walking distance to Mrs. Alexanian's teaching corner in Nisantasi. One day towards the end of the first week I must have by mistake responded, "Yes," to my French teacher instead of, "*Oui.*" To this, her emphatic and frank response to me was, "Dear child, one cannot fit two watermelons under one arm. You have to make a choice and pursue only one language at a time!"

It was my great desire to learn English under my mother's guidance so I could one day continue my studies in the United States and avoid the routine oppression at random intervals by the Turkish government that had made me decide to discontinue my French lessons. I knew I was taking a very big chance; but I also knew I had a capable, caring, and unwavering mother who within the next three weeks was not going to spare any effort to transfer her knowledge of English to me.

Thereby started what seemed like unending days of intensive study on my part, and constant drilling on my mother's. It took place at all times of the day except for my sleeping hours, in all sorts of locations, even on the ferry where most people would be socializing or leisurely reading the daily paper while they crossed the Bosphorus. It would even take place under the dim illumination of the tunnel which took us deeper into the European quarter of Istanbul to Taksim, and in the bus which eventually took us to Nisantasi where Mrs. Alexanian lived. They all had their special functions in the grand scheme of things. I would take along lists of the conjugation of verbs, idiomatic expressions, and their translations virtually everywhere during these three weeks. Free time was practically non-existent. However, because of my mother's infinite enthusiasm, confidence in me and complete dedication to the task on hand, at some point I also had decided to take the endeavor as an exciting challenge. I had resolved to give it my unwavering support and was totally cooperating with my mother's and Mrs. Alexanian's efforts.

Travel during the Cyprus Crisis

We were well into the second week of classes with Mrs. Alexanian when the destruction and plundering of the shops and residences, as well as the abuse of Greek, Armenian, and Jewish communities associated with the Cyprus crisis raised their ugly head. Anyone with some sense of the risk involved would not have left the safety of their home that afternoon of September 7th to take the daunting trip through the hustle and bustle of downtown Kadiköy; they certainly would not have wanted to increase their risk by crossing the Bosphorus to take the subway to Taksim, the hub of the disaster. The agitation in the air felt like static electricity, ready to ignite anytime; however, by now I was totally familiar with my mother's nature. There was nothing that could stand in the way of her giving me that additional chance of one more day of exposure to expert instruction which would later translate into myriad questions in my mind as to how to use these new words and expressions in sentences.

My mother and I were walking down the narrow sidewalks of Kadiköy toward the ferry landing like sleepwalkers after our sleepless night of watching the pillaging from my bedroom window. I could hardly recognize Kadiköy anymore. The usually busy street leading to the ferry landing, the same street my favorite pastry shops were located on, appeared practically deserted. The sidewalks were littered in many places with shattered glass and smashed metal from the destroyed store windows belonging to Greeks and Armenians. My mother and I were quietly conversing with each other in Armenian when suddenly the harsh staccato voice of a young Turkish man interrupted us with, "Citizen, you should be conversing in Turkish." We bent our heads, as if we were guilty children and kept on walking.

Being part of a non-Muslim minority had not been easy in Turkey. As Christians, Armenians faced a number of problems which were not dealt with adequately by the government. Christians and other non-Muslims often faced persecution by the Sunni Muslim extremists as well as the ultra-Nationalists. A century ago in 1915 during the waning days of the Ottoman Empire, Constantinople, the Istanbul of today, was home to a large number of non-Muslims including Greek and Armenian Christians as well as a sizable Jewish community. These minorities used to comprise as much as 20% of the population of Turkey. This number had consistently been dwindling since then, until now nearly one hundred years later, only about 120,000 Christians remain in the entire country. Today Christians and other non-Muslims add up to less than 1% of the Turkish population.

After recovering from the unjust reprimand my mother and I had received, we managed to get on the ferry, crossed the Bosphorus to the European side; we took the subway and boarded the bus that took us to Nisantasi, traveling along the Istiklal Blvd. However neither one of us could recognize the boulevard which had been the pride and joy of all of Istanbul. From my window seat on the bus, I had difficulty locating the sidewalk because it was covered with shattered glass. The thoroughfare itself was even less recognizable because yardage from multiple bolts of fabric was lying on it in a haphazard fashion, completely hiding the cobblestones underneath. The day before, myriad cars must have been instructed to attach the first few yards of their loot of coiled fabric to their trunks and let the remainder of the bolt unroll as they drove along this boulevard. On that particular afternoon, Istiklal Boulevard to me appeared as if it were an upholsterer's workshop in utter disarray. As traffic got heavier, numerous vehicles were driving over the existing layers of fabric, spoiling them for good.

Our bus had to travel slower than usual to avoid the many obstacles on its way. Among the heaps of items on the street, I could detect clothes, carpets, burned and mangled cars, overturned refrigerators, washing machines, bicycles and piles and piles of broken china having landed there from the elite stores on Istiklal Boulevard... From time to time on the fabric-lined streets I could detect a tank which must have arrived to the scene too late to secure the peace and order. It seemed an intensified nationalistic sentiment had once again swept the city the night before, as it had done with regularity at unpredictable intervals in the past. This merchandise had come from the stores of Greeks, Armenians, and Jews. Were these poor people once again going to find the strength and the determination to pick up the pieces of their shattered lives to start all over again? By now both my mother and I had tears in our eyes. It is true the administration was trying to hurt the minorities, but ultimately it was hurting Turkey which at the time was running a significant budgetary deficit. To this very day, that heartbreaking and out of character image of Istiklal Boulevard has remained in my memory, testifying to a much darker day in the life of this famed thoroughfare of Beyoğlu.

My father must have faced similar disappointing sights on the morning of September 7th in an effort to reach his office in *Vakif Han*. Although he had preferred to remain mostly silent about it, I had read the following day in the *Cumhuriyet* newspaper that his workplace district of Eminönü was among the areas where rioters had hit the most. Being on the second story of a commercial building, his office must not have been as readily exposed to the vandals as some of the other minority businesses in Eminönü at the street level had been. I knew *Vakif Han* had a doorkeeper and was normally locked after hours, which must have presented an additional level of security for my father's office.

The entire conflict regarding Cyprus had started because in 1955 the British had left the island. As Greece was preparing to take the entire island over, an agent of the Turkish secret service had thrown a bomb into the birthplace of Atatürk in the Greek city of Salonika. Istanbul newspapers had exaggerated the incident claiming the bomb was thrown there by Greeks, further intensifying the already existing highly nationalistic feeling. Mobs hostile to the city's non-Muslim inhabitants had gathered in Taksim Square and after they had burned, destroyed and plundered all the minority-owned shops in Beyoğlu, they had spread to all parts of the city to continue to do more of the same.

Mendes France's Pun

A mob had headed towards the nearby Park Hotel which was owned by an Armenian, Mr. Aram Hdryan with whom my father had done business through the years. As soon as the mob had arrived at Park Hotel, they had smashed the windows of its pastry shop, ruining all of its pastries. At the time this hotel was providing lodging for the former French minister and the present governor of *Banque de France*, Pierre Mendes France, while he was attending an international conference in Istanbul. After Mr. France had acquired enough of a distaste for the violence going on in the neighboring streets, a Turkish guest at the hotel pointing at one of the omnipresent *"Kibris Türktür,"* Cyprus is Turkish, emblems had asked him, "Your many years as a politician must have given you plenty of insight. What are your honest thoughts on the Cyprus conflict?" Mendes France had initially made the sardonic remark that knowledge of French was indeed useful in interpreting the conflict. Then, with a sly smile he had responded in French: *"Qui bruise et Turque."* The interrogator was elated with the Frenchman's response and had instantly cheered, "Look, even Mendes France agrees that Cyprus is Turkish." In reality, his reply was a pun on Mendes France's part and was far from being complimentary. What he meant covertly was, "He who breaks is Turkish!"

A number of churches were destroyed during the 1955 riots and a number of priests were murdered.[1] The violence had started against the Greeks, but soon Turkey had decided it was an excuse to expand its reach to include the Armenian and Jewish minorities as well. One thousand stores, 150 homes, three churches and four schools belonging to the Armenian community were targeted, while the Jewish community had 500 shops and 25 homes vandalized and one synagogue damaged.[2] Throughout the night, any non-Muslim who ventured to the streets where the rioters were, would face bodily harm if not death. Finally on September 7, martial law was declared and no one was allowed to venture out of his house after dark. Turkey knew that although these three minorities were long marginalized, they still presented considerable strength in the business world. The Turkish government, as well as the majority of the Turkish people, resented this. Only a few kind Turks, who against all odds extended a helping hand to the oppressed minorities, were the exception.

Rioters Hit Ortaköy

The rioters hit Ortaköy, on the European side of the Bosphorus, especially hard because it had a large Greek and Armenian population. Dr. Asher was a Jewish physician who had lived in this town for years and had been a long time neighbor of my friend Aida Bedrosian's parents.[3] On that fateful day in 1955, Dr. Asher's young sister-in-law from Paris was visiting him and his wife. After the pillagers had broken into his house and helped themselves to its contents and destroyed whatever they could not carry, they would not leave before kidnapping his young sister-in-law. They forced her into a car, dragged her up the hill and savagely raped her.

After the young woman's traumatic experience, when the rioters finally descended down the hill to deliver her back to Dr. Asher in a bloodied, shaken up, and sobbing state, they grabbed his small Frigidaire brand refrigerator and tossed it down his third floor balcony, so deliberately aiming it at his pride and joy, the Desoto brand automobile parked down below, that they managed to completely demolish the vehicle as well as the appliance in minutes. Hence Dr. Asher's young sister-in-law was so repulsed and horrified with the barbaric treatment she had received that the very next day she lost no time in taking the first flight back to Paris, vowing never to return to Istanbul.

There was another event that evening in Ortaköy my friend Aida was unable to erase from her memory in spite of the passing of some sixty years. After destroying most of the classrooms and contents of the Ortaköy Greek Elementary School, the rioters next turned their attention to the nearby St. George Church Cemetery where a number of Greek high-ranking priests were buried. They went through great pains to dig up their long-resting bones at the unearthly hour of 2 AM. Subsequently starting a bonfire, they tossed in and burned all the bones of the patriarch and the high priests they had so far unearthed, just to desecrate these poor souls whom the Greek Church held in high regard.

The nearby high-class eatery, the Lido Restaurant, had its own misfortune of being on the rioters' path of destruction. They shredded to pieces the red leather upholstery of its stylish chairs, using razor blades. After the demonstrators finally had left, the Lido Restaurant could no longer claim to have a sizeable supply of its signature huge lobster and choice fresh fish, because they were now lying haphazardly on the highway, having been dumped there by the rioters.

Istanbul was famous for its long cosmopolitan and multi-ethnic history. The Armenian Patriarchate was established there all the way back in 1461, only eight years after the Ottoman Turks had conquered the city. After generations had called Istanbul their home, in the aftermath of the Cyprus Crisis, a substantial number of Greeks, Armenians and Jews felt compelled to leave the country and emigrate. Thus Istanbul, which once was such a rich mix of diverse people, languages, cultures, and religions--like a lovely Byzantine mosaic--was gradually denuded of its multicultural wealth.

It later came out in the open that throughout these tragic events, the organizers had the state's support and blessing, just as they had for previous ones in the past: "During the court hearings in Yassi Ada in 1961, it was determined that the Secret Service under the command of Prime Minister Adnan Menderes had given the orders to plant the bomb that damaged the revered Turkish leader's birthplace in Salonika."[4]

Turkish Government Retaliates against Yanikian

During the ensuing years, minorities in Turkey, especially Armenians, suffered a number of turbulent years. In the Diaspora when an elderly despondent Armenian Genocide survivor Gourgen Yanikian's logic disintegrated, he killed two innocent Turkish consular officials in Santa Barbara, California in 1973. He thought it was the only way he would turn Turkey's, as well as the rest of the world's attention to the great injustice of failing to recognize the 1915 Armenian Genocide, the first genocide of the 20th century. In retaliation, to punish the perpetrators for the assassination of a number of its consular officials throughout the world, Turkey resorted to a new strategy with some of its tactics taken straight from the motion picture *The Midnight Express,* which depicts the horrific experiences of a young American student in a Turkish prison. Turkish authorities overzealously resorted to the imprisonment and torture of the innocent heads of Armenian philanthropic organizations of Istanbul. Heeding baseless allegations that some of these benevolent associations could be funneling funds to aid Armenian extremists throughout the world, Turkey jailed their innocent administrators and treasurers. Without any concrete evidence, they tortured them to get them to confess.

The treasurer of the historic Karagözyan Orphanage in Istanbul was my friend Arpie Dalian's elderly father, Mr. Haig Chilinguirian. Just like the rest of the codefendants, he was arrested and crowded in a dark room. The shirt, pants and undergarments he had on during the first day of his ordeal remained the very same ones throughout the week that the torment continued. The room he eventually got shuffled into had a limited number of wooden chairs to sit on. As the day progressed, he realized the same chair with the stiff seat he had sat on during the day, would have to suffice for a makeshift bed for him after dark. Each meal consisted of slices of dry bread with some water to drink. During the interrogations, he was ordered to wear black patches to cover his eyes, so he would not be able to identify his interrogators. In addition to being apprehensive because of not knowing what was in store for him, he developed extreme discomfort due to his chronic constipation, which was exacerbated by his circumstances as well as the Spartan diet of white bread and water he was being served. It was then that he realized he was still quite fortunate compared to some of the younger colleagues in his group. In an effort to get them to confess, the interrogators had subjected the soles of their feet to *falaka,* "bastinado or a severe thrashing," and their testicles to the painful electric shock.[5]

Meanwhile government officials searched the headquarters of the various philanthropic organizations and the residences of their administrators, turning the furniture upside down in a hunt for secret lists. They labored over their books in an effort to unearth concealed lists of individuals to whom they allegedly had forwarded funds. Countless mattresses and sofas in buildings where they lived and worked were knifed and thus rendered non-salvageable. The lists the government officials were searching for were never found, because they did not exist in the first place. Furthermore, to avoid having to pay for any of the resulting damage, the Turkish government was careful to have the philanthropic organization heads sign a prior agreement stating, "They are thereby waiving their rights to recover any of their material losses resulting from these searches."[6] There seems to be a curious similarity between the way these investigations were conducted in 1973 to the way the unfair Capital Tax, *Varlik Vergisi*, was enforced in 1942 when the cost of printing the notices for the auction of the seized properties from the minorities, as well as the defaulters' cost of food, clothing and shelter, were ordered by the government to be borne by the deportees. You try to forget the past, but so many events from the past ultimately lead you back to difficult crossroads which are impossible to forget.

Red Crosses on a Street in Kinali

Throughout history, among the Princess Isles on the Sea of Marmara, Kinali maintained a significant Armenian presence. A number of Armenian families lived on the island year round; others used it as their summer retreat. Kinali even had its very own historic Armenian church where services were held every Sunday. Mr. Chilinguirian, a close acquaintance of my friend Arpie's father but no relation to him, had a number of Armenian neighbors in Kinali he had gotten to know closely, because he had lived in the same neighborhood with them for many years. They each could easily recall celebrating several happy events together, as well as consoling and helping each other when sad and troubling ones had taken place.

Shortly after Armenian extremists had overreacted and killed a number of Turkish diplomats in the U.S. and few other countries, Mr. Chilinguirian noticed on one of his leisurely hikes that every dwelling in his Kinali neighborhood where an Armenian neighbor lived, except for one, was inexplicably marked with a red cross.

There were so many things belonging to this country that they had treasured for so long. They liked the Princess Isles, the Bosphorus; they liked its warmhearted people. They had spent a lifetime here. It did not matter in which direction they turned; they would have a flashback to some precious memory. Some of these priceless recollections went back many years. However every minute of the time that they had lived on Turkish soil, an element of fear always had clouded even their happiest moments. They could never completely relax and get rid of this apprehension. Hence when Mr. Chilinguirian and his Armenian neighbors tried to explain the mysterious appearance of red crosses on certain buildings on their street and not on others, they could not immediately come up with a logical explanation.

Then an idea flashed through their minds taking them back several decades: They recalled that on repeated occasions in history, this type of conspicuous symbol on Armenian residences during times of political upheaval was nothing new. It almost always preceded some form of foul play involving destruction of property and occasionally, loss of lives. The close-knit Armenian neighbors in Kinali realized they should not lose another moment but strategize while time was still on their side. Their unanimous decision was: "Let us all get together in the home of the neighbor bearing no mark of the Red Cross."

They all brought with them some food, candles and their pajamas so they could spend the night together in what they presumed would be the "safe house." Furthermore to remain inconspicuous, they carried out their activities in candlelight in an atmosphere of fearful anticipation. To an outsider who had never lived in Turkey as a minority, all of these seemingly extreme safety measures may seem unjustified. However, these neighbors in Kinali came from generations of Armenians who had to pay close attention to the smallest unsettling signs. Thus far, their survival instincts had served them well, while their less observant friends had not prevailed. This was the reason they thought, "It is better for us to be early rather than be late and sorry."

Early the next morning, with a high level of apprehension when they cautiously parted the drapes to observe the street down below, they spotted the all too familiar municipality truck. It was unloading its workers on their street for a routine maintenance job! To their great relief, they realized that on this occasion they had misinterpreted the red crosses which marked the residences that would be getting new pipelines installed to connect them to the central water main.[7]

Living on the Asian Shores of Istanbul

Ever since the fall of the Ottoman Empire, it seemed a dark cloud had descended on its one time capital, Istanbul, the captivating cosmopolitan city with a glorious past. Besides its role in the evolution of numerous civilizations, it boasted an extraordinary geographical location. It was situated where the continents of Europe and Asia so harmoniously communicated with each other. There were not too many cities in the world where, during a routine ride on a ferry along the Bosphorus or on the Sea of Marmara, you would see verdant landscapes against the indigo waters of the sea, historic buildings dotting not one but both of its shores. Most of the time, you would be quite unaware that you are actually crossing continents. This is where a previous knowledge of geography or having looked at a map would prove helpful. On both its Asian as well as its European shores, the Bosphorus was full of subtle reminders at each of its wharfs by the special smell of the sea and the moss against the beautiful scenery murmuring and reminding us, "Beware of what you are taking for granted each and every day; it is nothing short of a miracle!"

Unfortunately by the 1950s when I lived there, in spite of its infinite charm, the facades of the majority of Istanbul's multi-story buildings had lost their once distinctive color. The paint had faded; the structures had slowly darkened with dust, soot, poverty, and neglect. The city's one-of-a-kind proximity to the incredibly beautiful bodies of water seemed to have come at a price. The constant presence of salt water had subjected the structures to the adverse effects of mildew. Budgetary constraints brought on by unwise policies, which had caused the recession in the first place, prevented restoration or even just repainting. Sadly, all of these factors had degraded the appearance and condition of these once so well-liked period buildings. Endless excavations of the cobblestone streets for the maintenance and upgrade of utilities and sewers were facts of life inhabitants of Istanbul had to learn to live with. Nevertheless a brisk ten minute walk straight north from where we lived in Kadiköy, would take us to the Sea of Marmara to enjoy the solitude and the unforgettable smell of the fresh sea air.

My Father's Morning Routine

My father had once told me that when he was in his thirties, bright and early on most summer mornings he would routinely run this course on the streets of Kadiköy that eventually took him to the seashore, clad only in his swimming trunks and wearing an absorbent cotton shirt on top. When he reached the Sea of Marmara, he would boldly dive from one of the boulders to swim in the chilly waters. This offered him solace from his unusually demanding profession of money-changing and the transferring of funds; it also helped him extend his exercise routine for the morning. Returning home ever so refreshed, he would rush through his breakfast, skim through the Turkish newspaper *Cumhuriyet* as he psychologically prepared himself to face the challenges of his brand new business day. He would cover the half a mile distance on foot between our house and the Kadiköy wharf to catch the ferry to reach Karaköy, on the European side. He would walk across the shimmering Golden Horn via the landmark Galata Bridge, often hearing the bold fog horn of a Soviet tanker as the remainder of his brisk morning walk would lead him to the older section of Istanbul. Continuing his pace for an additional ten minutes, he would finally reach his humble and dimly lit office on the second story of *Vakif Han* in Eminönü.

Chapter I

The Busy Streets of Kadiköy

While living in Kadiköy, only two doors down from our house, the eroded marble stairs leading to the charming but somewhat aged classic stone building were claimed by a beggar most afternoons. Her name was Eminé. My sister and I had to hold our breaths as we hastily passed through the stretch of narrow sidewalk in front of her so we could drop our coins into her collection dish. If we were not speedy enough, the potent stench of urine was sure to hit our nostrils!

When living in Kadiköy during the summer months with our windows open, we would recognize the loud voice of the junk dealer with a burlap bag on his back, willing to offer an insignificant sum for any item ranging all the way from a genuine antique to an old piece of discard. I think one of these junk dealers called *eskici* got to be the beneficiary of even some of our most irreplaceable treasures as my parents were gradually disburdening themselves with the wishful thinking that one day they may be able to leave the country for good. Among these treasures were my paternal grandmother's ancient and extremely heavy leather-bound Bible and my mother's two massive antique enameled navy blue vases.

Among the relics of the past distinguishable on the Kadiköy streets was the tinsmith all too willing to recoat our copper pots and pans to render them safe for cooking for yet another year. Even though my mother prepared her own homemade yogurt, one of our neighbors was the customer of the yogurt dealer. Her wicker basket at times dangling on its way down, would descend by rope from the topmost floor with her money and a bowl for the peddler to place some very concentrated and tasty yogurt for her to pull up. I could not hear the street porters readily; however, they were an integral part of the community. I would usually see one approaching me in slow motion bearing a massive load on his back and torso. His job was so intense that I would often see him wiping his forehead so the droplets of sweat would not obscure his sight.

Desire to Dramatize a Victorious Past

Uncertainty about the future and the continuous recession since WWI had hindered new construction and major renovations in the city, curtailing growth. It was quite apparent these neglected buildings had seen better days. The government had placed a moratorium on the construction and even repair of all minority and foreign schools, churches and hospitals. The conclusion I derived from reading my Turkish history books was that Turks had a burning desire to keep hearing and reliving their victorious past up to the sixteenth century. This was their way of lifting the sorrowful mood they had never snapped out of once their empire started crumbling. What I had studied in my history books was so emotional and one-sided that many a time, as an outsider, I would feel sorry for the Turks and would wish I could give them a helping hand!

The Sad State of Present-Day History Texts in Turkey

Fast forwarding some 55 years from that time, I was hoping that by 2015 the Turkish history textbooks would make more of an effort to be impartial. Unfortunately this has not happened. According to the present law, textbooks to be used in schools in Turkey have to be approved by the Ministry of Education as well as the government. The conclusion reached by the Turkish scholar Taner Akçam, Chair of Genocide Studies at Clark University in Massachusetts, after researching what is taught to the children and teen-agers in history classes in elementary and middle schools in Turkey, including Armenian schools, on the subject of the Armenian Genocide of 1915, is "both shocking and saddening." This is because the textbooks characterize Armenians as: "People who are incited by foreigners, who aim to break apart the state and the country, and who murdered Turks and Muslims." In the same textbooks for middle school, the Armenian Genocide, which is referred to as *"the Armenian matter,"* is described as "a lie perpetrated in order to meet the above goals," and is defined as "the biggest threat to Turkish national security, urging Turkish youth to be vigilant against this threat." Dr. Akçam accurately concludes that these falsehoods in the textbooks of the future generation only contribute to feelings of hatred and enmity towards this specific citizen group, Armenians, for the present as well as the foreseeable future. Since these textbooks are required reading in Armenian schools as well, these youngsters are taught that they are *traitors*, which as Taner Akçam rightly points out, is an attempt at *identity destruction* by the Turkish Government. Additionally, the section for the Middle School that deals with 1915 alleges that Armenians committed massacres against innocent Turkish women and children, while Turkish men were fighting on the fronts, which is the reverse of what has been recorded in the numerous testimonials and eye-witness accounts, which scholars of genocide believe play the most crucial role in forming our understanding of what life was like and what truly transpired during those turbulent times. The textbook also claims that: "Armenians who were deported were then able to return to Turkey unscathed and were able to reclaim their properties," to which Dr. Taner Akçam's response is: "We all know this to be untrue."[8]

During my high school years in Istanbul I had often observed that minorities, especially Armenians, were always an easy target. Whenever the outcome of an election was not to their liking, in spite of our insignificant numbers, we were often blamed for it. This type of sentiment was more accentuated in times of national crisis; on these occasions we tried to be especially quiet and innocuous. These were times we would have loved to be invisible, because we would be blamed to some degree no matter what we said or did. Conceding defeat graciously, whether it was a political party losing an election or a sports team losing a game was not in the nature of Turks, at least during the years I lived there. We often feared facing the conclusion of these events because of the inevitable exchange of unsavory remarks quickly escalating into big fights where people got hurt.

Life in ISTANBUL
Clues that Actual History might be Different

There were a few clues here and there, mostly expressed through silence, which made me wonder if things were quite different in reality from the everyday version I kept reading and hearing about. Going back to my early childhood years, I will always envision my paternal grandmother Verkin Menee, as we lovingly called her, hiding the worn-out, muted photographs of her beautiful twin sister Mariam and that of her two young handsome sons, in her ancient leather-bound Bible. This time-worn Bible, with its two aged and faded photographs tucked painstakingly inside it, were probably the only mementos that had survived in our household from the period of the deportations and the Armenian Genocide of 1915. My grandmother's twin sister had married into a prominent Armenian family in Talas, the sought after summer resort of Gesaria, today's Kayseri, at the base of the Erciyas Mountain. After moving his family to Merzifon in the southern region of the Black Sea, her husband had prospered as a prominent merchant. Unfortunately in relation to deportations and massacres, visibility and prominence meant increased vulnerability. My grandmother would from time to time remove these precious old photographs from her place of safekeeping; she would carefully study them with tears in her eyes; she would caress and kiss them one by one and gingerly place them back in her bible, murmuring *"mesim,"* meaning "my dear loved ones" in colloquial old Turkish.

In Merzifon, Dr. George White, who had returned to the city as an American Near East Relief officer and reopened Anatolia College, had reported that: "Of the 40,000 Armenians in the region in 1914, about 10,000 remained alive. Of the 14,000 Armenians in Merzifon city, 1,100 prominent businessmen, doctors and able-bodied men had been taken out of the city in batches of 250 at a time and killed outright, after which the general deportations and massacres had begun. No more than 1,000 had escaped death by converting to Islam or through other means."[9]

My paternal grandmother knew only Turkish and not Armenian, because in those days Turks had scared young and old Armenians alike, especially around Afyon Karahisar in South

Central Anatolia, slightly west of Talas where she had lived as a young girl. My grandmother had told me that a ruling official in this area had at one time decreed that an Armenian could speak his native language only at the risk of having his tongue torn out. This must have been the reason why entire generations of Armenians, including my paternal grandmother learned to speak only Turkish.

As a state policy of the post genocide period, Turkey has officially denied the Armenian Genocide. Misrepresenting history in an effort to hide the crime is a continuation of the genocide mentality. Having been born and brought up in Turkey and having lived side by side with the perpetrator of the crime, I know for a fact that we as Armenian residents of Istanbul often had no choice but to normalize the crime in order to survive in that country.

Our House in Kadiköy

Until I was thirteen, we lived in Kadiköy, on the Asian side of the continent, not far from the wharf where the Bosphorus commenced. The cobblestone streets leading to our imperfect but cherished abode would get muddy during the rainy winter months.

Unlocking our heavy metal front door required some expertise but most of all quite a lot of strength. The key that worked best was bulky; it was made of iron and weighed at least two pounds. It reminded me of the key to medieval castles I had read about in storybooks; but that is where the similarity ended!

Each of the three floors of our rented house on Mühürdar Ave. had two modestly furnished, medium-sized rooms at each end of a dim corridor which led to a staircase. I can clearly visualize the wooden stairs because each morning I would hear the tapping sound my eighty year old paternal grandmother's 12X6X½" sheet of marble made against them. She would have warmed it the previous evening on our coal burning stove upstairs and would have taken it down with her in its special cloth bag, to make her otherwise chilly bed more tolerable. Noticeably short of breath, each morning she would climb up the three flights of stairs with determination, as she clung to the base of the banister with her right hand and to the bag containing the sheet of marble with her left. From the smile on her face, I could tell she felt triumphant when she finally reached the fifth floor to join us for breakfast.

Each of the floors was covered with dull green and light brown linoleum with non-offensive lines in its pattern. Every other floor also had an old-fashioned and rudimentary "*a la Turka*" bathroom with standing room only for our two feet. Slightly to the back and centrally located, was a sizable hole. Fortunately it was connected to the sewer lines, one of the advantages that came with living in a large city. Even including the wash basin in the adjoining area, the entire bathroom was not even large enough to be an ordinary closet. I have to admit our house did possess a couple of desirable features. The first one of these was a well-lit marble entryway that led to four marble stairs and boasted a distinguished looking alabaster lampshade hanging down from the lofty ceiling. However the pride and joy of our entire house was our fifth floor balcony with a northern exposure and a million dollar view facing the azure-blue Sea of Marmara all the way to where the Bosphorus commenced. Unfortunately, its uneven aluminum floor detracted somewhat from the benefit of having such an exceptional view.

Our Den with a View

The only room in the house which took advantage of this amazing view was our rather narrow den. If you happened to sit on the sofa in this room by the window, you could observe the many moods of the Sea of Marmara throughout the day, each one advancing towards the Bosphorus with an unpredictable urgency. On rare occasions, this sofa doubled up in function to serve as a bed. Across from it in the corner was a square multifunctional table with a couple of comfortable chairs standing against it. A mahogany china-cabinet stood at the opposite end of the room from the window, whose wood and marble-inlaid countertop accommodated our telephone, that very important device for my father's business.

Chapter I

For about three days each year, this room would serve as a workshop for my mother's paternal aunt, Sirarpie, who was a widowed seamstress. She would travel to our house from a far-away location on the European side of the Bosphorus, to cut out and sew new outfits for all the women and children of our family, from different textiles of varying dimensions, textures and colors my mother would have previously bought for this occasion. My sister and I had some say in what our final outfit would look like, since she often showed us pictures of some possibilities from the fashion magazines she brought with her.

When we were young children, the occasion had always been one to cause merriment for my sister and me; this was because after a couple of fittings, we would each be the proud recipient of a brand new outfit. As we got older, Aunt Sirarpie's visits to us as a seamstress started becoming a mixed blessing because she started feeling sorry for herself due to her limited income and wished she were in our shoes, making it difficult for us to relax while we were in her presence. My mother thought we were already doing her some good by paying appropriately for her services as a seamstress. However being aware of Sirarpie's somewhat unpleasant character, she did not feel comfortable recommending her to others she knew, although her execution of each project for us as a seamstress had been spotless. Aunt Sirarpie had a competent daughter who regularly contributed to the family's income each month, but it was her son she was always worried about. Although he looked like the most handsome and eligible bachelor in town, he was socially inept, making him incapable of holding a steady job. I finally remember feeling relieved after my father had kindly introduced Sirarpie's daughter Vartoog to a young male colleague of his. His well-intentioned effort had paid off for the family. My father's bachelor colleague and Vartoog had enjoyed each other's company well enough to join their lives and form a happy and prosperous family with two young children. As was his nature, with his random acts of kindness, my father had once again managed to bring some lasting happiness to a family that otherwise would have faltered.

Our Tiny yet Resourceful Garden

Our 5th floor balcony facing north overlooked a toy-sized garden, no more than twenty feet in length and even less in width. However, in spite of its size, it boasted a fair sampling of a number of fragrant bushes, including honeysuckle and philadelphus. It certainly has acquired a more profound meaning in my memory with the progression of the years. My longing for its contents and appreciation for family members who cherished it has increased immeasurably. My paternal grandmother Verkin Menee had succeeded in enhancing the color of our hydrangeas, rendering them a more vivid blue by simply adding indigo, washing blue, to their soil. In those days, this chemical, packaged for one time use in wrappers, was utilized instead of bleach. It helped rid the white sheets and underwear of the undesirable yellow shade they acquired after multiple washings. Grandma Verkin must have figured, "If indigo can perform such magic on the color of clothes, why not try it on our hydrangeas?"

Every Friday I would observe my mother extending clotheslines from the bushes on one side of the garden, crossing and extending all the way to the loquat tree. As I look back, her arrangement of the laundry that would hang up on it with wooden clothes-pegs showed an extraordinary degree of precision, if not obsession from smallest to biggest, starting with children's socks and underwear sorted by color and finally would proceed to a sequence of ever-larger shirts, hung upside down with sleeves outstretched.

Among the vegetation of our small garden was a lone pink rose of the most fragrant variety, called *okka gülü* in Turkish. This was my paternal grandmother's favorite flower. Whenever she was presented this type of rose in sufficient quantity as a gift, she would not waste any time in making rose petal jam from it. It would taste heavenly and it would exude a special rose fragrance as we spread it on our slice of whole-grain bread on top of freshly purchased cream. Our mini garden's pride and joy was a beautiful and mighty loquat tree planted in 1927, marking the year my cousin Sona, the first child in the family, was born. By the time I was elementary school age, this loquat tree had almost reached our fourth story bedroom window. Its fruit, especially when left to ripen on the tree, in spite of its sizeable seeds was my favorite among fruits. My parents had given me strict orders not to climb this tree to pick the ripe fruit because descending it was quite an undertaking. I remember being adventurous and attempting it once when my parents were not home. I had encountered so much difficulty in making my way down without breaking an arm or a leg that I never tried it again.

My Father's Profession

I can still picture my father seeking respite in this restful and protected little garden after returning from his risky job across the Bosphorus in Eminönü, where he was in harm's way nearly all of the time. While I did not realize it then, I know now that someone had to perform the challenging and outright dangerous job of assisting the traumatized surviving Armenians who were trying to emigrate from Turkey to friendlier havens. Their hard-earned money had to somehow catch up with them. This was only if they were lucky enough to get away from harm's way at the right time with some of their savings.

What my father experienced firsthand during the deportations and the Armenian Genocide of 1915 had changed him irrevocably. He had become a person with a great deal of empathy. He had also learned to recognize impending danger.

Up until 1915, in Aksaray he was living the last years of a normal childhood where nothing threatened to disturb the tranquility of his day. Then at age fourteen, when curiosity about romance and sexuality had just started making his life seem different and new, he suddenly found himself stepping into a chaotic and lawless landscape. In this new world where bartering got you places, people had to literally do anything to avoid being murdered or raped if they had not already been a casualty of starvation or disease. While driving his family's oxcart through the dangerous passes of the Taurus Mountains, he had to grow up in a hurry to deal with the serious questions of survival, endurance, and responsibility. Many a time he had to make a split-second intelligent decision for his family and for those following his lead. The Armenian Genocide of 1915 had suddenly interrupted and twisted my father's life out of shape.

In Istanbul they called my father's profession *sarraf,* meaning money-changer. However, in Turkish this word had an additional and very fitting connotation: *appraiser of mankind.* It took many years, and the wisdom those years brought with them, for me to realize this. My father had no visible scars; but the stressful experiences and burden of prematurely serving as the family's breadwinner due to his father's death resulting from typhus during the deportations had robbed him of his precious teenage years. As a result, unlike his cousins John and Jacob, he had to forego schooling and instead was pressed to grow up fast to guide his family and those around him out of danger, in addition to trying to make a living. Throughout his life he could never completely get out from under this monstrous legacy. However, it helped make him the conscientious, trustworthy and vigilant person that he was, always weighing all the pros and cons before taking his next step.

My father did not have the flair for diplomacy and the polished language his uncle Parsegh had. Neither did he have the brilliance to sail through engineering problems his cousin Jacob did; however, he was able to help me with my rather complex algebra word problems in elementary school more often than my mother, in spite of the fact that he had never formally studied mathematics beyond the 1st grade level. The other day while putting on my hiking boots, I suddenly remembered watching him lace the eyelets of my boots when I was five and had just started kindergarten. I also remembered the brown shoe polish he had previously applied to them with care. To finish them off, he would brush them with a rather large soft brush until they acquired a certain luster, so he could extend their life and make them fit for another week. As I progressed through high school, he became a source of inspiration for me in his quiet unassuming way as I saw him tackling a few of his clients' finances in their quest to emigrate to the diaspora.

View from our Fifth Floor Balcony

Our small garden in Kadiköy overlooked a medium-sized lettuce field with a rich dark brown soil. The field was irrigated by pumping water from a well with the help of a blindfolded horse going in circles as in a merry-go-round, the neck collar of the horse being attached to an axis revolving the waterwheel. As I travel back in time, I can envision and almost hear its noise and feel its coolness, as that of a waterfall.

When I glanced north from our balcony on the fifth floor, before my eyes lay the bright blue almost luminous Sea of Marmara in all its glory. At times it almost hypnotized me as I watched its shifting colors; it was as if I was watching a rainbow of blues dictated by the sky and the sun. On a spring day a gentle breeze would be wafting through the balcony as I viewed this shimmering sea. On short notice with the wind from the north picking up, I would view it in an angrier mood crowded with whitecaps.

Clearly visible above the rooftops and to the east was a minaret with the muezzin's voice full and throaty. It was audible five times a day starting before dawn, all the way until dusk when he would be calling the faithful to prayer. Istanbul being a cosmopolitan city, all of this felt strangely comforting, almost possessing a soothing quality; it must have felt even more so to the devout. By then I had learned to expect it just like I anticipated hearing the tolling of our own *Soorp Takavor* Armenian Church's bells across the street from us before mass.

To the northeast, I could see the civic center building and its courtyard. This is where the Independence Day celebrations and the fireworks displays were held every October 29th. After pleading with my mother many times, when I was eight years old I finally had succeeded in convincing her to take us there to participate in the Independence Day celebrations. It was late fall and the evenings being somewhat chilly, we had our favorite woolen green coats on. Whoever was in charge of the fireworks display and flares that evening, must have failed to aim one of them accurately. The still flashing flare startled me by coming frightfully close. Limited in my ability to flee due to being surrounded by the crowd, I could not prevent its unavoidable collision with my body. It landed squarely on my left chest scorching my coat and leaving a great big ugly brown spot on it. I was so lucky it had not hit my left eye because if it had, it could have easily blinded it. I remember leaving the civic center courtyard in a hurry with my mother and sister, vowing never to attend such an event in the future!

The combination of the sights and sounds from this fifth floor balcony had an everlasting quality about them. As a run-down house in a central neighborhood, our home gave us a bird's eye view and enabled us to feel the pulse of the entire neighborhood with its eclectic history, culture, religion, architecture, and social class.

Our Fifth Floor Window with Western Exposure

The lone small window on the fifth floor with a western exposure, which only opened vertically, brings to my mind recollections all the way to the time I was barely three years old. Acquaintances of my mother, two middle-aged single sisters, were visiting us about a year after my sister was born. I must have expressed to them my displeasure about my parents' bringing home this "new person" who, while small was getting in my way. I must have confided in them, thinking they would understand and try to help me. Instead, out of the blue the uglier-looking sister, Sirvart posed me a question I had never expected to hear from an adult: "How would you like me to toss your baby sister out of this window right now, so we can get rid of her forever?" To further prove that she was earnest about it, she opened the window for me to see how scary and far away five stories down looked. Then she grabbed my baby sister Arminé, being as realistic as possible, to find out what my reaction to her outrageous proposal would be. To this day, thinking about it gives me a chill. I ran to Sirvart in desperation in an effort to stop her, the whole time sighing, *meghk é* in Armenian, meaning, "it is a pity." Shortly after that scary episode, as I learned the new person can't be returned and is on the way to becoming more responsive every day, I realized a good companion could make toys more fun for me, and nighttime a little less scary.

Chapter I

Our First Toys

Around this time I received my first purchased toy from a visitor with prospects of becoming a relative. My cousin Sona was engaged to a surgeon by the name of Shahan. My uncle Dikran was rightly proud of her because she was smart and attractive and had recently graduated from the American Academy for Girls in Üsküdar. She had several suitors asking for her hand in marriage; however, my uncle had found some fault with each one. One worthwhile gentleman who owned a sizable and thriving industrial plant producing *Pastirma and Sucuk,* cured beef and sausage, was rejected simply for being in the "cured meat" business. It was unfortunate that uncle Dikran had not taken the time to deliberate upon his decision and ask for the informed opinions of others he could trust. If he had, he surely would have reconsidered. At the time it did not seem to matter to him that these two delicacies, *Pastirma and Sucuk* were favorite mainstays for most of Turkey's population. The prospect for growth of such an industry, even just within Turkey, was phenomenal considering Turkey's population was increasing at a fast pace with practically every family willing to make room on their table for these two delicacies.

As a three year old child I barely can recall Dr. Shahan, except for the fact that he had finally passed muster to become Sona's fiancé; he looked handsome and always had a smile for me and my sister. However more importantly, he may have persisted in my memory all these years because he had gifted my sister and me two brightly painted toy wooden carts whose wheels kept turning for a long time without breaking down. When we first received them, they were overflowing with hard candy in multicolored wrappers. Because money was scarce at the time, these toy vehicles remained our lone purchased toys for quite some time. Neither one of us voiced an objection to my mother when she informed us that "it was not wise to spend money on non-essentials," when my father described the days we were living as "times of uncertainty."

Throughout my early elementary school years in Istanbul, I very rarely felt disadvantaged for not owning the latest toy.

Instead, it encouraged me to stretch my imagination to cooperate with my younger sister to create our own novel toys, from ordinary household items. My mother's colander got transformed into a hill for our carriage to climb over and our houseplants became the enchanted forest when our imagination was given free reign. We could do this because we felt confident we could always return home when we were ready.

At other times, the cylindrical four foot pole of the colorful soft linoleum used as our primitive tablecloth, when we were too young to observe table manners, was our toy of interest. My sister and I had already invented an alternate function for it. It would be our stage-coach with me as the driver, and my sister as the demanding passenger. By installing French windows in the hallway of our top floor during his spare time, my father had used his ingenuity and resourcefulness to create a very functional bonus room at minimal cost. However, my passenger had ordered me to speed up as we approached the French windows, prompting me to shatter a number of them into myriad pieces, leaving me in search of an apologetic explanation to give to my father when he returned home from work at night.

The comfortable and cozy armchair by the window from which Sirvart had threatened to toss out my sister, had a function of its own. We would get up on this kid-friendly armchair and jump up and down on it as if it were a trampoline. During the entire stress test for the armchair, which it always passed with flying colors, we would sing Armenian songs and recite poetry we had recently learned; but we would always conclude our performance with the announcement in Armenian: *Somiyenere gavruin*, meaning, the springs are getting worn out. We must have heard this comment repeatedly. Our own acknowledgement seemed to provide us with poetic license to repeat this ill-conceived, nonetheless pleasurable activity yet one more time. Sometimes we would hug our favorite doll or even our cat Pompon briefly to jump with us. Pompon knowing full well what was likely to follow, would mysteriously disappear and hide in the nearby closet for a while to avoid what to her was a strange and scary ritual.

Not too far away from this improvised trampoline was a dark closet with many shelves where my mother stored her vacuum-cleaner, brooms, dustpans and dust clothes, in addition to other items. It was here that before I was ready to attend elementary school, my sister and I had enjoyed conducting a harmless scientific experiment on our cat Pompon. We had noticed that her pupils were thin straight lines in bright daylight. Were we surprised to discover they became much larger, darker and spherical when we were in the dark closet with her! Not knowing the physiology involved, we were at a loss; but the significant change in Pompon's pupils seemed like magic to us then, longing for a scientific explanation. I had often wondered as a child if this closet had a hidden entryway to the attic and if anything of significance might be hidden there; but for now that adventure had to wait until I was older and stronger.

An Unexpected Visit from the Secret Police

I was in 4th grade and had just returned home from school, working on embellishing the preliminary maps I had previously drafted of Iran and Iraq with multicolored ink, when I heard the loud ringing of our doorbell. It had caught me by surprise because we normally would not be expecting anyone at that hour. When I rushed to our fifth floor balcony facing the street to bend down and see who it was, I saw two formally dressed men I did not recognize. I was ready to race down the stairs to open our front door to see what they wanted, when my mother promptly stopped me, saying: "I will handle this. You two run along and start working on your homework." The previous evening my father must have alerted her with: "Two secret police officers may be coming here soon to conduct a search of our house, since they have already done the same in my office in Eminönü."

The fact that the two men ascending our stairs were wearing ordinary street clothes had put my mind at ease to some degree; however, when they started searching each one of the rooms of our five story house methodically, I knew something must have been wrong. It took the two officers close to two hours to complete a thorough search of our house. When they were done, the officer with the darker features ascended the stairs to the fifth floor to let my mother know that they were leaving; in passing, I even remember his complementing me on the map of Iraq I had been working on as part of my homework for the next day.

The worried expression on my mother's face and the rapidly increasing number of wrinkles on her usually smooth forehead had always been accurate predictors of imminent danger for me. This is when I had a sudden flashback to the strange phone calls my father would receive some evenings around dinnertime about the kilograms of wheat and barley being shipped. These were from Hüseyin, the Kurd, who my sister and I had nicknamed *Metz Por,* meaning "big-bellied" in Armenian. He was a giant dark-featured man with a protruding belly who had been to our house previously and was from Kilis, a city on Turkey's southernmost border with Syria. He called my father *Mösyö Kardash,* meaning "Mr. Brother" in a mixture of French and Turkish, which rhymed perfectly with my father's abbreviated name, Ardash. After a while, my sister and I had been able to figure out that it was the number of gold bullions and coins that were being communicated on the phone covertly as kilograms of wheat and barley.

After the officers had left, I was curious if the money belt which used to be inconspicuously stretched out underneath my parents' wardrobe was still there. I rushed to their bedroom; stretched my arm under their wardrobe to find out. I took a deep breath when I could still touch it. It was for the first time then that I picked it up to examine it. I discovered it had special compartments for the bullions, a cylindrical section for the gold coins and a whole row of compartments for the paper money. Neither one of my parents had remembered to remove this money belt from its precarious location under the wardrobe; however at least for the time being, it had escaped the officers' attention. Thank goodness lady luck had smiled our way one more time on that fateful day! I was only in elementary school at the time, but I had already started to comprehend why my father was so secretive about his profession, especially regarding the transfer of funds out of the country, and how difficult it was for him to make a living in Turkey, having to conduct his business under such constant scrutiny. It was because the existing law clearly banned the transfer of the funds of minorities abroad resulting from the sale of their businesses or properties. If he was ever caught performing this service, the monetary and physical punishments were severe and archaic.

My Father's Necessary but Dangerous Profession

My father's profession as a money changer was a very dangerous one, yet very essential for the Armenian families living in Istanbul. It seemed as if this community was in a constant state of flux, especially after the September 6 and 7, 1955 incidents, also referred to as the *Cyprus Crisis.* Families who could afford to emigrate were exiting the country in significant numbers. Meanwhile, Armenian parents were making every effort possible so their youngsters would learn a foreign language, preferably English. Attending an American high school in Istanbul was the best preparation; however these schools were few in number and very selective.

It felt as if most of the financially secure and motivated Armenians were in a constant investigative mode exploring where they could emigrate and how they could exit the country, while they caused the least amount of harm and inconvenience to themselves as well as the next generation. They were already confused and heartbroken knowing that they would be venturing into the unknown as they were leaving behind this jewel of a city they had called home for so many generations. They knew that moving away also meant giving up an intricate support system they had painstakingly established with their friends and neighbors. It had taken them years to set up these safety nets due to having suffered similar hardships and reversals of fortune in the past.

After years of serving their communities with honesty and integrity, they finally had earned the respect and trust of their peers. Was it worth starting all over again as a novice at a more advanced age in an unfamiliar environment? Then without exception there was a new language they were expected to know. Could they somehow master it at this more advanced age if they were not already proficient in it? Their labor over the years, which they had converted into the country's currency, was the only insurance they had and they were willing to trust my father with it.

My Father's Previous Clients

Sixty years into the future from the day the two secret police officers had paid my childhood home in Kadiköy an unexpected visit and a number of years after we had lost my father, I recognized the names of two of my father's former clients as I was glancing over *Marmara,* one of the two Armenian newspapers published in Istanbul. The two brothers whose names I recognized, had been the sole proprietors and producers of the highly sought after brand of *pastirma* and *sucuk,* cured beef and sausage, in Turkey. One of the brothers, who still resided in Turkey at the time, had been apprehended, tried and was indicted for having transferred the money from the sale of his business abroad. He had been sentenced for a long prison term in Ordu, on the Black Sea coast. Other than having to reimburse the government a significant portion of the transferred sum, he had to pay a hefty fine and additionally was subjected to an archaic form of torture in his prison cell. The interrogators had instructed their subordinates to forcefully retract his nails out of their nail beds, in an effort to get him to confess and disclose the names of additional individuals who may also have been involved in the transfer of his funds. My heart bled for him and his family; however, once again I totally appreciated how difficult it must have been for my father to maintain the confidentiality of his clients while conducting similar transactions covertly throughout the many years he lived in Istanbul.

Mrs. Alexanian and her Family's Exemplary Credentials

After I had made the decision to go along with the fast-paced English lessons of Mrs. Alexanian, facilitated yet made more demanding for me with my mother's ongoing drilling sessions, life had suddenly changed radically for me. I knew I was still the same youngster, but one now who no longer had the luxury of any carefree time. However, after having observed Beyoğlu's main thoroughfare, Istiklal Boulevard, in its worst state ever from the bus with my mother only a few days earlier, I felt if anything I should count my blessings for being given such an amazing second chance in life. In spite of the long distances we had to travel to get there, my mother and I had been arriving consistently on time at Mrs. Alexanian's special teaching corner in Nisantasi.

Mrs. Alexanian shared her plain 4th story apartment with her physician sister Dr. Kavalciyan, who had earned her medical degree in the United States, but was unable to practice medicine in Turkey since the government had refused to issue her a license to practice. Therefore, just like Mrs. Alexanian, she had been teaching the science courses in the American Girls' School including biology, physiology and chemistry, until both sisters had retired in 1951.

These dedicated Armenian teachers, including Mr. Alexanian who was Mrs. Alexanian's late husband, and her sister Dr. Kavalciyan, had devoted loyal service to the school for nearly fifty years in Adapazari, Izmit and Üsküdar.[10] It was discovered only recently by Turkish journalists in late August of 2014 that Dr. Zarouhi Kavalciyan had the distinction of being the first woman medical doctor in Ottoman Turkey. She had graduated from Boston University Medical Faculty in 1903. She had returned to Ottoman Turkey to be close to her relatives since her father Dr. Serop Kavalciyan was a famous physician practicing in the Izmit and Adapazari areas.

Mrs. Alexanian had taught music and had directed the school choir, which was so well-known in the community. However, most importantly, she was a master in teaching English to beginners in what was called "the Specials' Class." It is claimed she aroused such enthusiasm and eagerness for learning English that even with a class of 80 or 90 students in the Study Hall, not a sound was heard as each little girl listened with attention to her every word. It is also said that, not only did she give a good foundation in English, but she also taught lessons of honesty, self-control and good conduct. What a spectacular accomplishment for a diminutive but determined woman to succeed not only in one but several difficult undertakings she was simultaneously attempting!

Mrs. Alexanian's Teaching Corner in Nisantasi

From the first day I met Mrs. Alexanian as a somewhat shy eleven-year-old attempting to learn English for the first time, it did not take me long to realize that she was quite an exceptional teacher. She had a scholarly style that often challenged me and demanded my undivided attention all the while I was in her presence. However, she managed to get this with her unselfish interest in her students' welfare, her vast experience in teaching English as a second language, her organizational skills, her precise translations, and her clever and no-nonsense style in which she delivered everything always with a healthy dose of enthusiasm. Her love and caring for her students was most noticeable in the way she treated us. Since she had no children of her own, we felt we were her children.

After her husband's passing, she had dedicated herself completely to teaching. Even though she had retired from the American Academy for Girls in Üsküdar four years earlier due to her advancing age and for health reasons, she had such an impeccable reputation as a teacher of English for beginners that she was constantly in demand. Her long wavy gray hair was gathered in a neat bun in the back of her head. Her outfits which fit the contours of her body perfectly were flawless and always in good taste; it was obvious much reflection had gone into their selection. It seems there was nothing haphazard about her life or her teaching. It seemed she had the ability to coordinate every detail to make the end result picture perfect for us, her students. In doing all this, she somehow managed to keep the elements of humor and suspense unscathed. She wore the appropriate pin or necklace, possibly a belt, to match each one of her outfits to complete the ensemble. However in making her selections, she made sure that there would not be anything to detract our attention from what she was teaching.

We, her students knew she cared about us, but she certainly would not ever spoil us. She somehow could inject enthusiasm into the most rudimentary task of teaching a foreign language. We really wanted to please her and did not mind going through the lengthy preparation it took.

In addition to her chair, there were three additional seats around a very ordinary table in a relatively plain, smallish room of an apartment building in Nisantasi. The window occupied one end of the table and the light that entered through it gave us a ray of optimism, whether deserved or not.

After about a week and a half of rigorously and resolutely delving into learning English, what was wonderful was that I no longer had to coax myself to live up to what I initially thought was an unrealizable challenge. With my mother's help and Mrs. Alexanian's guidance as I started making a dent in unraveling more and more of the puzzle of the English language each day, to my surprise I started liking it! Of course, I also enjoyed the attention bestowed upon me by my mother, with the exception of a few rare humiliating remarks uttered in her moments of desperation, such as *tetoom klough,* meaning, "squash head" in Armenian. I learned to interpret them as humorous outlets of tension and frustration built up in her, since she was a better judge of the impossibility of the task we were embarking on than I was.

"I am going to go around the room and give each one of you an irregular verb; be ready to give me its past tense and its past participle," Mrs. Alexanian would say with the enthusiasm of a child anticipating to play hide and seek.

After years of experience, she really knew how to teach this language to a beginner like me, starting with the simple concepts first and building upon them, until I could comprehend the more complex ones. She knew where I would be most likely to lose ground; she would patiently go over the more intricate concepts, always giving examples as they applied to everyday usage. In instances when I got the idea of what she was driving at, her dark brown eyes would sparkle with excitement mixed with satisfaction in a way I had never seen it happen in any other teacher before. She must have enjoyed teaching; otherwise she would not have continued doing it after her retirement at age 76 and in spite of the diagnosis of breast cancer, which in those days almost always carried a stigma of fatality about it.

My Mother Makes All the Difference

In all fairness, much of the credit is also due to my mother, who in her infinite enthusiasm had managed to convert the entire learning experience into a meaningful game for us. Although this type of enthusiasm existed in our group, it seemed my mother was responsible for my possessing a healthy dose of it. It seems she had already benefited from and was now putting to use some of the principles we had learned from my unsuccessful entrance examination earlier in June. She would dream up these stimulating contests. Sometimes they were against time, to see how fast I could translate from Turkish to English key words and phrases and idiomatic expressions. At other times, they were how fast I could make the transition from the present tense of an irregular verb to the past tense and ultimately to the past participle. Of course the secret to success depended on my registering numerous irregular verbs and how they were conjugated into my long term memory. On other occasions, the secret to success depended on recalling the plurals of nouns that neither looked nor sounded like their singular counterparts. Looking back, the experience certainly made me an advocate of teaching a foreign language to children early on, when their brain cells are most equipped to absorb, retain and recall all of this information at a faster rate.

For another week, our trips to Mrs. Alexanian's far removed domain and special teaching corner in Beyoğlu continued with no more unexpected violent interruptions such as that of September 6th and 7th and life tended to very gradually return to normalcy; or so it seemed. I am sure it did not appear that way to those unfortunate souls who had felt the oppression physically, financially and psychologically. This was a violation of their civil rights, just for being part of the minority. It also created among us, the minorities, a constant state of vigilance and anxiety. In spite of my tender years, I was starting to comprehend that this matter of learning English in a hurry in an attempt to eventually make my move to the United States for further studies was quite real; it was my and my family's salvation and it was hinging on me because I was the oldest youngster in my family.

Haydarpasha

The Kadiköy wharf where my mother and I were constantly taking ferries to cross the Bosphorus was next to a park my mother had often brought us as children to greet my father on his way back from work, after his ferry docked there.

Clearly visible from where the ferries arrived at the Kadiköy pier was the Haydarpasha Harbor and train station. As a young child and later as a teen-ager, I was completely oblivious to the fact that Haydarpasha was known among the elderly Armenian residents of Istanbul for a far more historically tragic reason.

Around the time that World War I started, it was rumored that a blacklist of Armenian intellectuals and community leaders had been compiled by the Ottoman Turkish government. According to Mikayel Shamtanchian, an Armenian scholar who miraculously survived the ordeal, these intellectuals and civic leaders were arrested from their residences throughout the night of April 24, 1915 by the Turkish police and they were systematically taken to the central prison in Sirkedji on the European side of the Bosphorus. The following summarizes the apprehension Mr. Shamtanchian and his colleagues faced at the time:

"There were several among us who were even taken in their nightclothes and slippers. No one understood why we were being arrested and what would become of us... Next, escorted by gendarmes in small groups of twenty, we were guided to a convoy of buses under strict military supervision and taken to a dock. Here they led us to a motorized boat which would take us toward Istanbul's Haydarpasha Harbor. It was midnight by the time we were escorted out of the boat into the Haydarpasha Rail Station... Though we had not been told anything, by now it was clear we were being sent somewhere via railroad. Every security precaution was being taken, the shrill whistle was heard and the train took off." [11]

Shamtanchian survived this ordeal in large part due to his daring escape from Chankiri, located north of the present day capital, Ankara, which was one of the hubs of the death marches. In November 1915, he took refuge in the relative safety of Ushak in the Izmir Province, whose Armenian community had not been deported. He lived in Ushak for three years, where he worked as a teacher. In 1918, during the time of the armistice following World War I, he returned to Istanbul and taught in Kadiköy's Aramyan Ounchiyan School, later to be my elementary school.

Had I been aware of this historical detail during the time I attended this elementary school for six years (1949-1955), I would have been far more forgiving to the imperfections in its curriculum and appreciative of its caring, although authoritarian, Armenian teachers.

Unluckily, during the years 1915-1922, whatever happened to these 250 deported Armenian intellectuals and cultural leaders in Constantinople also happened to Armenian intellectuals all over Turkey. In its cruel and deliberate way the CUP, Committee for Union and Progress, destroyed a vital part of the Armenian cultural infrastructure. At least eighty-two writers are known to have been murdered around this time, in addition to the thousands of teachers and cultural and religious leaders. Poets and writers such as Daniel Varoujan, Siamanto, who was Adam Yarjanian, Krikor Zohrab, Levon Shant and many others, had elevated Armenian poetry, fiction and drama to new heights. Within the Ottoman provinces, Gomidas who was Soghomon Soghomonian, the sensitive and gifted Armenian musicologist with western training, was single-handedly responsible for gathering and saving the Armenian folk music from the many villages in Anatolia. Without his effort, none of it would have survived. Furthermore, the Armenian Church choral music would not have been as rich and authentic today had it not been for his contribution. Even though Gomidas survived the ordeal of 1915, due to his being an extraordinarily sensitive young man, he was so affected by the horror of what he saw and personally experienced on his way to Chankiri that he became psychotic, bringing his compositions and further musical contributions to an abrupt end. Sadly, he had to be institutionalized for the remainder of his life.

Ride to the Elementary in Horse-Drawn Carriage

Diagonally across from our house in Kadiköy and next to the *Soorp Takavor* Armenian Church's tall walls, a couple of covered black horse-drawn carriages were always ready in anticipation of passengers. It was the Greek coachman of one of these horse-drawn carriages, clad in a dark gray cape and a matching cap, at times resorting to his whip, who was responsible for delivering me to the Aramyan Ounchiyan elementary school every morning and back in the afternoons, during the first three years I attended that school. The winters being cold, often with some form of precipitation, I remember wearing sturdy leather shoes with thick rubber soles which regularly required my father's tender loving care. "Function over form" was mostly the rule around our household in those days. As the years progressed, the horse drawn carriage lost its competitive edge and motor cars became the standard means of transportation on the busy streets of Kadiköy.

Aramyan Ounchiyan Elementary School

Going back to the deportation years, Aramyan Ounchiyan Elementary School of Shamtanchian fame was a bilingual institution of learning with the intent of introducing the Armenian culture and language to Armenian youth between the ages of five and twelve, in a country that was mostly trying to suppress it. When I was five, probably because preschool did not exist at the time to make the transition to kindergarten smoother, I did not initially want to attend any school. I remember it took my mother several weeks to finally convince me that my objection, "Why is my sister Arminé declared a carefree individual, but I have to attend this ancient looking school? It is not fair!" was not valid. During the first week, I must have caused quite a scene in the long and narrow dining hall with a cement floor, a high ceiling, worn-out wooden benches and an iron wood-burning stove. For the first few days, I had unnecessarily elevated my anxiety level to the point of getting nauseated and losing my breakfast. The overseer of the dining room, the cute, always smiling little lady wearing a colorful apron with hair neatly combed back and secured in a bun, who warmed up the meals we brought from home, rushed with a mop to clean up my mess and tried to restore normalcy. She already had multiple responsibilities, including helping the Women's Auxiliary in preparing and distributing lunches to needy children. I must have repeated this unsightly behavior several more times within the same week when my kindergarten teacher *Oriort Hnazant* confidently stepped forward towards me, handing me the mop of *Dndes Mayrig*, the overseer, and said in no uncertain terms: "*Dndes Mayrig* is not your personal servant. If this situation reoccurs, from now on it is your responsibility to clean it up." This sounded rather cruel coming from *Oriort Hnazant*, however, it succeeded in giving an end to the havoc I was creating in the Aramyan Ounchiyan dining hall.

Due to government regulations, there was a moratorium on any major repairs. This situation seemed to have gone on for as long as I could remember; therefore this historic elementary school of Old World charm had been neglected and deprived of the necessary maintenance for its proper upkeep. The same could be said of numerous other minority schools and church buildings. My elementary school was a sturdy three-story stone building surrounded by six foot tall stone walls painted in a soft yellow with a hint of orange, marking its periphery. The warm chatter generated by the Armenian-speaking children in the playground greeted me each day, as I stepped inside its gates and made me feel welcome. In spite of my initial unwillingness to attend this school, in less than a week's time I had started to feel quite safe and comfortable being part of it. I felt I was in the company of mostly caring people in a country which did not always generate that feeling.

The school had an old wooden and somewhat crackling staircase leading to its second and third floor classrooms. On the third floor and facing the northwest, was my favorite airy classroom with its very own competent but somewhat hard-of-hearing Armenian literature teacher, the balding *Baron Serabian*. By most standards, he was past his prime. Most of us felt he had the characteristics of an endangered species. This was because no other teacher knew the wealth of the Armenian language, literature and history in as much depth as he did. Youth interested in studying and teaching Armenian literature did not any longer have a chance to get the uncensored material because to comply with government regulations, history and even literature had to be watered down to a state that was harmless, but no longer genuine. I can say from experience that if you hear this version repeated often enough, you start believing it.

Aramyan Ounchiyan certainly had its share of eccentric Armenian teachers who surely would have benefited from being introduced to some basic child psychology. It would have helped them soften some of their harsh methods of punishment. It would also have helped them become friendlier and more complimentary when they observed some improvement in us; their positive feedback might have even encouraged us to try harder. My paternal grandmother Verkin Menee was using her common sense when at times she advised us, saying: "When nothing else works, a sweet, complimentary word will always manage to get the snake out of its hiding place!"

As students, we knew deep down that our teachers, especially the Armenian ones, cared about us and wanted our welfare, as we cared about them. For the lone scholar of Armenian, *Baron Serabian*, when he fell ill, we as a class spent much time and effort in formulating ways whereby we could help him to basically show him how much he had meant to us. I remember gathering a bouquet of flowers from our tiny but resourceful garden in Kadiköy and requesting my mother earnestly and convincingly enough to take me, together with another classmate, to his distant hospital room across the Bosphorus to personally wish him a speedy recovery.

The Turkish teachers were another story. There were a few kind and understanding ones among them such as Sabiha Hanim. She was the short, plump, grandmotherly type I knew I could trust; she wanted to make learning easier, if not fun for us. During my elementary school years, an association between learning and fun had not quite been established yet. It had never crossed the educators' minds that such an association might even facilitate the learning process.

There was an attractive brunette geography teacher, *Mualla Hanim*, who most of the time had a negative disposition, which deteriorated fast once her terrible temper got hold of her. Responding to Melkon's mischief on one ill-fated morning, she kept hitting the little boy's head so hard with her metal-lined wooden ruler that he had to be rushed to the closest hospital to stop the bleeding and tend to his possible head injury.

It could have been my imagination, but as a six year old I thought our principal, *Baron Burmayan* looked more like a chimpanzee than a human being. He was diminutive; his extremities, especially his arms, looked long and out of proportion to his torso. He had an elongated face, round, smallish, dark brown eyes and an intelligent and introspective look on his face, just like a particular chimpanzee I had seen at the zoo few months back.

Other than being the principal, he was also in charge of whatever rudimentary music department our elementary school had. On the negative side, he tended to be judgmental and unwilling to give one a second chance, unless he detected some hidden musical talent in that individual. I was not one of these lucky ones. From day one I was labeled "tone-deaf" and was excluded from most of the elementary school's worthwhile singing exercises. I did not feel good about this; I figured if someone showed me the steps, the knots and bolts, I could practice and could probably be rehabilitated at least to a level that I could start enjoying singing.

Riding to School in Antranig's Taxicab

When I was eight, my transportation to Aramyan Ounchiyan Elementary in the horse-drawn carriage had come to an end. Initially this had made me sad; but I soon realized I was lucky to have an unusually caring taxicab driver, Antranig, who was observant and willing to go out of his way to listen and even offer help. I later realized he had made an effort to guide me in my everyday interactions; he taught me to strive for the loftier choices even if they were not the most popular ones. On one of our morning drives to school, I inadvertently had said something inappropriate; he tactfully corrected me without offending me.

Later in the afternoon after delivering the other students to their houses, when an opportune moment presented itself, he explained to me the reasoning behind his comment. Each time it ended up being a lesson I would not easily forget. This happened once as I was boasting to an economically less privileged friend about an expensive gift I had received for Christmas. Without being sensitive to her family's limited resources, I was thoughtlessly urging her to get a similar type of doll so we could play with them together. I did not expect this type of insightful comment to come from a taxicab driver. But the fact that it did, helped shape my life. "Status" clouded my value system less, because early in life I had the privilege of knowing Antranig.

Walking Home from Kadiköy Harbor

Up to the time I started elementary school, my mother, my sister, and I would visit the Kadiköy waterfront almost every day. To keep us busy while we waited for my father's ferry to anchor, my mother would often take us to a section of the park which had a small playground from where we could still observe the incoming ferries. Around 5 PM the place would usually be bustling with activity. Children would be on swings and on the merry-go-round. Grown-ups would either be keeping an eye on their children or reading their newspaper on the green wooden benches nearby. The tireless *simit* vendor, who sold sesame bagels, would be busy pushing his special three-wheeled see-through cart, dispensing his fresh and heavenly-smelling, warm and irresistible wheel-shaped bagels. By now he had learned to anticipate my sister and me because we had become one of his regular customers. Still others, sitting on benches, would attempt to strike a conversation with whoever happened to be nearby, although they really were trying to keep an eye on the approaching ferry from the European shore. In the midst of this mostly idyllic scene, it was not unusual for a Russian tanker to be blowing its mournful horn from faraway. As everyone finally detected the approaching ferry readying to dock, their attention would instantly shift to it, because it was the reason why most of us were there.

My sister and I were fond of the colorful seasonally planted annuals in the park, especially the marigolds. However for us children the main attraction of the recreational area was its plentiful sand along with water, which was available from a nearby faucet. This meant we could build the sand castles of our imaginary city. We did this with the help of our aluminum sand pails and shovels which my mother always remembered to bring along. Finally, we would embellish the city we had created with tin bottle caps discarded from glass beer and *gazoz* bottles, dried twigs and desiccated marigolds. In the meantime each time we saw a ferry approaching the harbor, we would run to the gate where the passengers exited and would look expectantly to see if we could detect my father among the outbound passengers. What a simple yet wholesome pleasure it was to see him approaching the gate and to greet him with a hug! Both my sister and I would volunteer to help him with one of his smaller packages. Subsequently holding his hand, all four of us would happily walk towards home.

Amidst this otherwise satisfying experience, what made me apprehensive was that on our way home there was an unusually busy intersection where foot traffic and cars each thought they had the right of way! The absence of a traffic light aggravated the already chaotic traffic situation. No one seemed to be concentrating their attention on the policeman wearing oversized white gloves, who was in charge of directing the traffic and seemed to be blowing his whistle almost nonstop. It appeared to me the automobiles were practically pushing the crowd out of their way. I was terrified that one of the oncoming cars was going to hit us. I would cling to my father's hand tightly and murmur the prayers I knew. However, I also realized that if we did not attempt to cross the intersection, we could be waiting there forever. Fast forward some fifteen years, it must have been this same chaotic traffic situation that discouraged my mother from attempting to drive on the streets of Istanbul, after she had successfully completed the difficult written examination.

Chapter I

View from my Bedroom Window

The *Soorp Takavor* Church was located diagonally across the street from where we lived in Kadiköy. It occupied a very important place in our neighborhood both physically and psychologically. Observing the street from my bedroom window on the 4th floor and facing south, I had an almost unobstructed view of its courtyard. This was the church we frequented every Sunday morning and on holidays. My father was a trustee there. A couple of years back, he and an older trustee friend of his, Mr. Noradoungyan, quite possibly a nephew of teacher Serope Noradoungyan martyred in Ankara, had come up with a novel and rather philanthropic idea. The three stores adjacent to the church had just come up for sale. My father and Mr. Noradoungyan thought that if each trustee could loan the church 5,000 liras a piece, or whatever they could afford and not charge interest on it, within a few years the church could end up owning these stores. As rent was collected, the trustees would get their principal back as well as be gratified to have helped maintain the pride and joy of their community, their church, for the years to come. They must have felt compelled to help, even though they themselves were not financially very secure. They wanted it to survive, because they realized it existed in an inhospitable environment. With the number of Armenians dwindling in Istanbul with each passing year, its future looked bleak.

The store adjoining the church was Spiro the Greek's spacious barbershop with its ever enticing colorful beads hanging artistically at its entryway. Other than adding a touch of elegance to his store, they were serving the dual purpose of keeping the flies out while letting the breeze in. Adjacent to it was the Greek florist Lefter with his elegant, well-arranged, multi-colored gladioli, carnations, mimosas, and colorful roses displayed in uniform tall, white plastic containers.

My Brother Kepi

Every time my mother glanced diagonally across the cob-blestone street from our house at the four story stone building in the southwest corner, it must have sent a chill through her bones. It must have traumatized her and reawakened that tender spot in her heart that refused to heal with time. She must have had frequent flashbacks to that late afternoon in November of 1941, when she and my dad had hurriedly taken Kepi, their first born, to the second story of this very same building where Dr. Tahmaz's general medical practice was. My mother would say of Kepi, "He always had an intelligent question to ask. When he heard your answer, he would look into your eyes and analyze your answer, and maybe ask more questions…" Kepi, bright and conscientious well beyond his five years, had already inquired and compared the cost of a visit to the Haydarpasha Hospital versus consulting Dr. Tahmaz. He had convinced his parents that consulting Dr. Tahmaz was the more fiscally reasonable thing to do. These were the times when every bit of money my father owned would soon be drained out of him to pay for the unreasonable Capital Tax of November 12, 1942 the Inönü government had devised to further crush the minorities.

There being no CT scan or ultrasound at the time, a doctor had to base his diagnosis on his medical knowledge, his experience and his common sense. It seems all three of these faculties had failed him terribly in my brother's case, since Dr. Tahmaz had not felt an interventional attempt of rushing him to the Haydarpasha Hospital right away and operating on him was indicated. Throughout the night his condition kept deteriorating. At the crack of dawn the next morning, while still in his pajamas, my parents rushed him to the Haydarpasha Hospital. He was urgently operated on; but it was too late. After examining Kepi post op, the surgeon in charge had plainly told my father, "It looks like your son is not going to make it." Next, he literally yelled at the orderly to get my mother out of the room. She refused. Although he was in a coma, during the remaining hours of his life she chose to stay by Kepi's side, to permanently preserve in her memory how dear his innocent, trusting and intelligent face looked. Five years had been a very short time; but it had been long enough to develop a one of a kind bond between mother and son. She felt the need to cherish it until his very last moment on this earth.

The surgeon later explained to my parents: "Your son's appendix had already ruptured when we opened up his abdomen; with the state of present day medicine, there was nothing we could do to save him." Watching your child die must be a parent's worst nightmare and the loss of a child must be life's most devastating blow to a parent. She kept repeating to my father, "It feels to me as if a part of me died with him…" The weight of the loss must have literally crushed my parents; especially distraught was my mother because she did not have to go to work every day like my father. For a long time she refused to have anyone touch his bedroom. Kepi's shiny boots, his pants with their round metal snaps past his ankles, his navy blue sweater with colorful stars my mother had knit for him, all made her longing for him even more real. She had almost a stubborn refusal to sever these last physical connections. They sat unmoved in her chest of drawers for several years. It seemed she wanted to turn back the calendar and the clock so she could avoid the pain.

At times she had the illusion that Kepi was suddenly going to appear in front of her eyes triumphantly riding his tricycle. She kept wishing their life before his death would somehow magically return. One week passed, a month, a year; she did not miss her son any less. Many a night she would wake up in pain with a longing for him that would not abate. To her it seemed it was the deepest grief imaginable. She said she had no words to express how she felt except that an integral part of her had left her forever. For a long time, she could not bring herself to eat strawberries, his favorite fruit. She blamed herself for feeding him this fruit the night the dreadful chain of events started taking place. She blamed the strawberry seeds for aggravating the inflammation of his appendix. She held his tricycle responsible for bringing about the acute episode. This might have been the reason my parents never bought a tricycle for me and my sister. In retrospect, if they had, it would have caused my mother much grief by constantly reminding her of the last days of her beloved Kepi.

To ease the agony of life after Kepi's death, my parents found some comfort in church and God. In addition, I attribute their survival and recovery to the strength of their will to put things in perspective. Three years later when I was born, my mother would remark to my father, "I will always carry with me my feeling of grief; but now it seems I have an element of joy as well. I never imagined they could exist together!" I could feel my mother's heart trying hard to make room for me, next to Kepi, her precious first born son who would have carried on the family name, something that was quite important for her. I must admit, this thought has been comforting. Even though Kepi's death represents a very sad chapter in our lives, I revisit it at times because it brings to my mind the comforting feeling of my mother's warm and unconditional love, together with her feeling of unspeakable grief.

My mother never quite got over her loss of Kepi. The fact that he was such a curious child with so much enthusiasm, so eager to question and be challenged by his environment to find out about its complexities and exceptions to the rules at the tender age of five, rightfully made him special in her eyes. During the years following his untimely death, my mother would in some way remember him in her happiest as well as saddest moments. It was about four years before we lost my mother at age eighty-six when she mysteriously stopped referring to Kepi. We knew this was not a good sign. Lewy's Bodies Dementia, which had started robbing her mind of those warm and rich experiences of the past, had also robbed her of her most precious memories of her beloved Kepi.

Continuing to Learn English

By the end of the summer of 1955 I had become increasingly appreciative of my mother because of the important role she had been playing in helping me achieve proficiency in English. However I also realized that I should not get my hopes too high, since I was still dealing with a lot of unknowns. Anything could go wrong at any point that could prevent me from achieving my goal. As my comprehension of the English language steadily improved, I realized I quite liked this language and was eager to learn more about its intricacies. I did not want to return to *St. Benoit* in the fall to study more French. However I was sensible enough to realize that I had little control over my future other than diligently listening to Mrs. Alexanian, going over her list of vocabulary words, verb tenses and idiomatic expressions. I also understood that my mother's drilling me on all of the above was a very necessary part of my preparation and I should refrain from complaining about it.

It was two days before the entrance examination during a scheduled class session, when a most enthusiastic Mrs. Alexanian announced, "Now, the person who can answer this question correctly has a very good chance of doing well on the entrance exam: What do you do in the morning when you get up?" As the other two girls were taking their time to think the question over, I hastily volunteered, "I wash myself; I brush myself; I dress myself; I eat my breakfast, and I go to school."

"I have one more question," Mrs. Alexanian continued, pleased that her efforts so far seemed to have made a difference. "Now, the person who can complete this sentence properly will most likely succeed on the entrance exam: The sun rises; the sun …"

"The sun sets!" I shouted, rather boldly for an otherwise shy and reserved little girl. Up to now this was the first indication I had that I was comparing quite favorably with the other two enthusiastic youngsters gathered around the ordinary table in Mrs. Alexanian's 4th floor humble teaching quarters. That moment must have given me the impetus I needed to start thinking, "If I keep up the good work, perhaps I have a thriving chance of being accepted to this school of my dreams."

For an eleven-year-old, I had been living under a great deal of pressure and anxiety. My apprehension had started taking a toll on me, making me more on edge and less able to relax. My mother was quicker in recognizing this than I was. The evening before the all-important exam, she was getting ready to tuck me in when she looked lovingly into my eyes and said, "Alice, I realize you have been trying very hard to have our efforts make a difference. You certainly have come a long ways, considering only three weeks ago you were a complete stranger to this language. Deep down in my heart I feel confident that you will do fine on the exam." She hugged me; tucked me in and whispered, "Sweet dreams" and was gone.

The day of the exam I had a hurried breakfast and left home relatively early to be able to walk leisurely to the tram station in Kadiköy to catch the one for Bağlarbashi. After I got off the tram at my destination, I started crossing the football-sized field, taking the footpath across it which was dotted with colorful weeds in bloom, including the wild yellow mustard flowers. While walking on this path toward the school, for the first time I wondered how different my life would have been had I not been born to someone as caring and motivated as my mother, but instead to someone *laissez-faire*. Realizing how lucky I was, gave me a sudden dose of optimism. I hastened my steps toward the gate of the American Academy for Girls, at least psychologically ready to take the entrance exam in language proficiency.

Our Milkman

During my elementary school days in Kadiköy when the doorbell rang around 7 PM, it had to be Osman, our diminutive milkman, wearing his usual cap to deliver us a liter of fresh milk from his own cows. He had two aluminum milk pails he balanced skillfully on each side of his horse's saddle, as his two pint-sized measuring cups casually dangled down. Looking back, they remind me of today's inscribed pewter trophies. Osman lived in a distant village and chose the evening hours for delivery because he did not have the luxury of refrigerating the milk during transport. In spite of this precaution, there still were those few days during summer when his milk curdled upon boiling. On those instances, due to my mother's resourcefulness and her unwillingness to waste something nutritious, she completed the curdling process further to transform part of the suspension into something simulating cottage cheese. We called it "*lor*," and ate it halfheartedly after sprinkling a generous amount of powdered sugar on it to make it more palatable.

Our milkman was very proud of the quality of his milk and he would often half-jokingly greet me with a jingle, "Your name is *Alis* and my milk is *halis*," meaning unadulterated in Turkish. At times with a mischievous smile in his eyes, he confronted me with what at first seemed to me an odd question, "How would you like to ride my horse and go galloping with me to become a bride to my young son?" Most likely it was an attempt on his part to see what type of response his question would elicit in me. Many years later, I realized Osman might have known something I was not aware at the time. Initially, he had succeeded in having me run back into our house as fast as I could, until I realized he was only kidding. However, years later after I learned more about Armenian history and the Armenian Genocide of 1915, my mind wandered in all sort of directions. Could our milkman have been raised by a mother who was a Turkified Armenian orphan? Was his grandmother perhaps Armenian and this fact had been withheld from him for a significant length of time? Was his unusual topic of conversation with me his way of attempting to get close to me? In the light of the history I had been exposed to in the U.S., these were all possibilities.

The Permanent Farmer's Market

Behind the *Soorp Takavor* Armenian Church and a block from our house, were the mazelike back streets of Kadiköy. At one end of it, one could find the most intriguing open air market imaginable. It resembled a permanent farmer's market with an abundance of fresh vegetables and fruits, which were such an integral and exciting part of the Mediterranean diet. Each time I accompanied my mother there for produce, it would be bustling with activity. Animated vendors would announce their latest arrival, often citing its reasonable price. The Mediterranean diet, which today has more of a claim to fame than it did then, relied heavily on vegetables, fruits, grains and legumes as extenders of meat. Some of the vegetarian dishes prepared with virgin olive oil, to which my mother so expertly had added her finishing touches were: artichokes with sautéed onions, leeks with parsnips, diced carrots, potatoes and celery root perked up with fresh dill weed and lemon juice. Then depending on the season, there were the special legumes including the myriad types of fresh and dried beans, including the northern white beans, the fava beans and at least three types of string beans, including *Ayshé Kadin,* the lady *Ayshé*

French beans, and *Chali,* the climbing kidney beans. Whenever I had a choice of these delicious and imaginative dishes created by my mother from fresh ingredients, in spite of being a carnivore at heart, I would often favor them over their meat-containing counterparts. Occasionally my mother would play tricks even with her meat dishes. She would give them a new twist by unexpectedly introducing an exotic fruit into them such as caramelized quince, using our special quince grater. This could have easily been her creation.

Holiday Celebrations and Flashbacks

Holiday celebrations, such as Christmas, Easter, New Year's Eve and name days such as *Vartevar* were times when the family got together with relatives and when some of the best creations of my mother got sampled. In her unrelenting pursuit of innovation to enhance and add excitement to her already delectable dishes, she was not afraid to experiment. One of my favorites was her stuffed grape leaves, which had just the right contrast of pungency arising from the lemon juice against a backdrop of the sweet plump raisins, sautéed onions, pine nuts and thoroughly-cooked rice, enhanced by an incredible bouquet of spices including but not limited to: cinnamon, allspice, cloves, red and black peppers and plenty of fresh dill. Somehow, the resulting battle on my taste buds as a child would always end in surprising harmony. "To cook with the right combination of spices," my mother had impressed upon me, "is to help the ingredients towards becoming their best selves." When fresh mussels were in season during the winter months, a similar stuffing paired with my mother's inspiration of the moment, would create something magical for this particular shellfish. Stuffed mussels were my mother's specialty; secretly I would prefer this delicacy of hers to just about any dish, dessert included. My maternal grandfather Iskender was rightfully proud of my mother's creativity in the culinary arts. I had heard him address her with a healthy dose of pride in his voice when he complimented her cooking by saying, "The antlers of the deer develop later than the ears, but they surpass the ears!"

Chapter I

Moving forward some twenty years, to my delight my mother had still managed to preserve her creative touch in cooking. To the astonishment of a number of Middle Eastern food experts in our extended family, she proudly lifted a bottle of Soy Sauce one busy afternoon in our kitchen and turned to me and asked, "The other day I discovered this sauce Asians seem to be fond of. It definitely improves our already tasty stuffed grape leaves; so I am going to use a little of it as well. What do you think?"

"Mom, I love your pursuit for perfection; please go ahead. I hope I will inherit your inborn sense of creativity in guessing which condiments complement each other." I hugged her; I thought I detected a hidden smile as well as a contented look on her face because she was being appreciated in spite of being challenged by problems brought on by a certain amount of forgetfulness due to her advancing age. Interestingly, her previously acquired abilities, such as her performance on her Yamaha brand piano of the Chopin Polonaise and Mazurkas still sounded skillful and accurate to our ears, pleasing us as well as managing to lift her spirits.

My mother's inquisitiveness to try the unfamiliar and resolve to continually challenge the status quo in an effort to take an existing flavor to newer heights, continued even to her later years when we expected her to be more conservative. In the late 1970s when her grandchildren were in elementary school and she was our guest on our Hawaiian vacation, during our hiking expeditions through the untamed countryside of Maui, she would always be tempted to try some unfamiliar fruit. I remember her curiosity toward the fermenting passion fruit we encountered on the way. It enticed her so much that we had a difficult time convincing her it was not wise for her to try it. Similarly in Maui, on our way back from the challenging car ride from Hanna, her choice entrée at Mamma's Fish Restaurant had to be the most exotic fish, in a sauce concocted of the most unusual ingredients! My guess is that, other than the desire to challenge her palate, she also wanted to learn something from the experience she could later add to her repertoire.

Fast forward twenty more years, now struggling with dementia, she was hospitalized at the Huntington Memorial Hospital in Pasadena because she was suffering from severe back pain due to spinal stenosis. I waited patiently to detect that same contented look on her face again when I informed her I was going to stay overnight with her and would not leave her alone in the alien environment of the hospital; but it never materialized. Throughout the night that I spent next to her bed in a chair which would at the most recline into an uncomfortable narrow bed, mother kept pleading with me, "My dear daughter, let's have a plan of escaping out of here. We can do it, if you promise to help me!" It was as if our roles had changed and she had become the child. When I said, "Mom, we brought you here so the doctors and nurses can help you get rid of your back pain so you can feel better," just like an impatient child whose latest wish had not been granted and was unable to see the reason why, she felt betrayed and was upset with me. To my dismay, the powerful giant of the time I was eleven, when she was teaching me English at top speed, was now experiencing the ravages of time on her body. She had been reduced to a mere presence, devoid of reasoning. Although I was aware this could happen, I still had difficulty accepting it, when it was happening to my own mother.

Mother Caters the Patriarch's Reception

In the 1950s when my father was a member of the Parish Council of the *Soorp Takavor* Armenian Church in Kadiköy, and Patriarch Karekin Khatchadourian of Istanbul (1951-1961) was visiting our church in the company of other religious dignitaries, both local and from out of town, my father had invited them, as well as the members of the Parish Council to our house after church for a festive Sunday dinner. This was because other convenient dining facilities did not exist nearby; we lived practically across from the church; last but not least, because my mother was an accomplished cook. However, most of the clergy and the members of the parish council were unaware that they had to climb four flights of stairs to reach the delicious dinner waiting for them. As they headed up huffing and puffing to the fifth floor, not one in their group must have thought that this forced exercise could have been good for them!

Everyone eventually ascended to our guest room on the top floor, which for the time being was converted into a huge dining room with a giant makeshift table with extensions of my father's creation, spanning all the way from the French doors of the balcony facing the street, to the French windows of our covered hallway. The unusually long table which accommodated the clergy and the dignitaries was covered with matching hand-embroidered light blue damask tablecloths and matching napkins with uplifting flower patterns on them. These were embroidered by my mother when she was young. They matched perfectly the color and pattern of the watercolor-like sketches of the blue, green and crème-colored petals of the tulle curtains covering our French doors and windows facing the street. They also complemented the rich dark blue medallions of our Oriental rug with a hint of hot pink and azure blue in them.

The night before, my mother was getting ready for the Sunday dinner by preparing a fancy dish with steamed fresh mullet, peas, diced pickles, carrots, potatoes and capers held together with a spicy mayonnaise, called "*Salatrous.*" In those days, one had to fix one's own mayonnaise from fresh eggs, olive oil, lemon juice and mustard. Most likely due to her mounting anxiety as the day of the event approached, my mom's mayonnaise had failed to solidify. I remember our taking it to our crackerjack Greek *Aunt Elenie* in Moda, about a mile away, and then carrying it back home once the mission was accomplished.

The Role of Istanbul in Creating its Special Cuisine

During the 1950s the waters of the Bosphorus and the Sea of Marmara were not polluted. Because there was great variation in both salinity and oxygen content between the Black Sea and the Aegean, the latter of which had free interchange with the waters of the Mediterranean, amazing species of fish were able to thrive where these two waters mingled. For this reason the fish of the Bosphorus and the Sea of Marmara were said to be especially delicious. The red mullet which tasted best simply poached and dressed with dabs of virgin olive oil, fresh lemon juice and pungent red pepper had long been recognized as the most flavorful choice for a spa cuisine menu. However the "all-around winner" distinction effortlessly belonged to a special turbot, *kalkan*, which was at its best when lightly dusted in flour, salt and pepper and fried in olive oil. It boasted curious buttons as if the fish was left from the dinosaur era; it was so succulent that it would almost melt in one's mouth. Among us children, the news of this fish's being on our dinner menu was enough cause for elation. Its taste lingers in my memory to this day. Moving forward some ten years, I also recall a dinner by which time my father's eyesight had deteriorated considerably due to his haphazardly controlled diabetes. On this occasion, he was deceived by a dishonest fisherman who had sold him a female turbot which possessed a disproportionate amount of caviar and only a minute amount of the tasty flesh for us to enjoy.

It was hard to ignore the dairy which sold the freshest butter and cream. We could buy here rolls of dried and encrusted cream or rolls of soft and fresh cream. The dry rolls of cream had their proponents; however, nothing could live up to the taste and aroma of a soft, fresh roll of cream on a dessert having the basic texture of bread, called "*ekmek kadayif*," which was leisurely browned on the brazier. To cook anything on the brazier was labor-intensive and tricky. It initially involved getting the coals red hot; then shifting them around to maintain a delicate balance so they would not be too bright and burn one's masterpiece or be transformed to ashes too rapidly, without generating significant heat to cook it. When the *ekmek kadayif* was finally cooked just right after multiple rotations of the pan and revitalizations of the coal, it was sweetened with syrup made of honey, sugar and lemon juice.

Visit to Grandparents at Historic Berberian School

During my elementary school years, I remember my father dedicating a significant amount of his time to being a devoted church trustee in an effort to make a lasting contribution to the

Soorp Takavor Armenian Church in Kadiköy, which also helped support my elementary school. As part of his responsibilities, he attended the noontime meetings each Sunday, which usually lasted well beyond the time the church let out.

On that particular Sunday in 1950, after having packed a surprise gift for my grandmother on occasion of her name day, *Vartevar*, my mother, sister and I were planning to take an early tram ride to Üsküdar to visit my grandparents. We were determined to walk the half a mile distance from where the tram dropped us off at Bağlarbashi, to the former Berberian School compound, across the street from the *Soorp Khatch* (Holy Cross) Church in Üsküdar. Of course I had no idea at the time and would find out in covert ways much later, that where we were heading to was once a very meaningful institution in the history of Armenian literature. Having lost most of its select student body and teachers, who were celebrated Armenian intellectuals, authors, and poets to the Armenian Genocide of 1915, the school had no choice but to cease to exist. Additionally, the newly passed regulations in Turkey had banned its renovation and repair, let alone the construction of a new one. This gradual disappearance due to the ravages of time and neglect was a planned strategy to rid the country of all elements Turkey considered foreign. During the 1950s, although the wooden buildings of the Berberian compound were past their prime, they were still intact. It was owned by my maternal grandmother's cousins, the Zambakjians, who rented it out as units to a number of Armenian families, one of which happened to be my grandparents.

While my family visited the Zambakjians when I was a child, I would often inspect their living quarters, especially after I had found out that this was once an old historic Armenian school and that it was located next door to where my mother attended school for many years to learn English. The Zambakjians had made the two-story wooden administration building their living quarters. Due to its many windows and well-planned exposure to the outside, I remember it as always being lit up with sunlight. As the years rolled along and I matured, during our visits to the Zambakjian residence, I would often have flashbacks to half a century ago when a lot of activity would be going on in here. I would imagine heated literary discussions amongst notable writers and poets in the making, while they overlooked the school's extensive gardens below and enjoyed lunch in its dining area.

But right now it was the late 1940s and we were kids, no older than four and six, visiting their grandparents. To city dwellers like my sister and me, the Berberian School enclave and its extensive outdoor areas felt as if we had suddenly arrived at a country home. I clearly remember its sunken garden. We would head straight there after descending a wide circular cobblestone stairway. This was where the various families renting their living quarters from the Zambakjians kept their hens, ducks, geese and turkeys.

Higher up and to the west was the terrace where my grandparents and their neighbors gathered to socialize on balmy, crystal clear summer evenings. It was the best way to escape the summer heat and enjoy the pitch dark night sky, where it seemed practically every star in the Milky Way was visible to the naked eye. It was here that they pondered over the day's events, happy and quite often sad, uncertain what the future had yet in store for them. This socialization seemed to achieve something positive for them, because by the time they were ready to retire for the evening, they felt slightly less disheartened having found out they were not alone in their predicament.

On very special occasions, when my grandparents had decided they were ready to part with one of their favorite ducks, their culinary masterpiece might have taught a thing or two to today's advocates of reduction sauce and fusion cuisine. To top it off, there was their smoked turkey breast with its exotic spices. It included a variety of peppers and cumin, which they had come up with many years before cholesterol was in anyone's vocabulary. My grandparents felt proud of these birds because they had raised them from the time they were ducklings.

I am certain my grandparents must have had flashbacks to the past and imagined the Berberian campus in its days of glory. However for us children, the most exciting part of the compound was the garden encircling the administration building. Close to the border of their property to the north, the Berberian School boasted a stately walnut tree. More centrally located and at a lower level were two majestic pine trees that had witnessed amazing changes in the history of the compound and its people within the last fifty years. Of course these gentle giants had no idea yet that within another twenty years, their existence could seriously be threatened! This is because considering that the youngest Zambakjian was in her sixties, they soon would become too old to be able to maintain it. They would donate it to *Soorp Prgitch* (Savior Saint) Hospital. By the time it would be sold in the 1970s, its new owners, equipped with a demolition crew, would waste no time in leveling it to the ground and constructing numerous condominiums on the grounds of what once was a historic jewel to the Armenian community of Constantinople.

Of course on this day in 1950, as children eager to visit their grandmother on her name day, we were completely oblivious as to what the future was to bring about to the Berberian compound, including its two majestic pine trees. These beautiful pines had an unbelievably high yield of pine kernels. My sister and I would race to that part of the garden every chance we got to see which one of us could gather the largest number of pine nuts. First, we would search for pine cones and carefully extract the nuts hidden so perfectly by nature's helping hand. Besides making our hands sticky, all of this activity invariably would leave black marks on our hands, clothing and faces. I can clearly recall my grandmother saying, "Let's make sure these coal miners get to wash up before our special meal." But we did not care. When we were not lucky enough to stumble upon the pine cones, we had to resort to collecting the individual pine nuts. We had to carefully comb the pine needles carpeting the ground immediately under the two stately pine trees, which always imparted such a refreshing fragrance to that section of the garden. Next came the most exciting part of our adventure. It involved finding two rocks that were relatively flat on one side, so we could crack the nuts without smashing the pine kernels hidden inside. Inhaling their heavenly aroma and savoring their exquisite flavor was the huge reward we got for our effort. This incredible experience must have been so indelibly etched in my memory that even today, the fragrance of a special type of pine tree with cones, after the sun's rays have hit it for a while, never fails to bring back some of these sweet memories of long ago.

My most unforgettable memory of the emperor of desserts, the labor intensive *ekmek kadayif* comes to mind from its association with the same trip to my grandmother on occasion of her name day. My father had promised us that he would leave the trustee meeting at *Soorp Takavor* in Kadiköy promptly when it concluded and would take a *dolmush*, a shared taxi, to join us in Üsküdar at my grandparents.

It was no secret that my mother loved genuine jewelry, especially golden rings and bracelets bearing precious stones. It seems they had a psychologically uplifting effect on her. In spite of my father's request that she not wear any precious jewelry that Sunday, she still had managed to slip on her antique golden ring studded with multiple precious stones with a prominent diamond in the center.

My grandparents must have been looking forward to our visit all week. They had gone through a lot of effort sacrificing one of their precious home-grown ducks for the occasion and had jointly cooked it to perfection, having complemented it with a surprise stuffing. The sweet smell of the perfectly browned fowl with an abundance of exotic spices wafting in the air was enough to raise even a six-year-old child's culinary expectations to quite a high level.

I recall every item on my grandparents' table as being delectable; however for me, the impressive color, taste and aroma of the slightly caramelized dessert, *ekmek kadayif*, had to be the winner. It had a generous amount of fresh cream on top, sprinkled with roughly chopped pistachios and some rosewater to complete the ensemble. Its image and aroma seem to be preserved in my memory, a testament to how unforgettable it was.

Mother's Diamond on her Ring is Missing

There was yet another excitement of a slightly disturbing nature that contributed in preserving this day in my memory for many years. After helping my grandmother with the finishing touches of the main course, my mother suddenly felt like all her cheer was suddenly drained out of her when she realized her ring was missing its sizable center diamond. Everyone in the household had suddenly switched their attention from food preparation to attempting to recover mother's precious stone. Having taken a tram and having traveled some of the distance on foot, it could have fallen anywhere…

Just as I was expecting to hear the dreaded confession my mother had to make to my father when he arrived, I suddenly heard my grandmother's excited voice frantically calling for my mother: "Wilhelmina, come and look. What is this thing shining in the sink? You have to see it right now before it goes down the drain!" Lo and behold, the shiny object my grandmother was pointing at, just five minutes before my father's arrival was my mother's shimmering precious stone that must have fallen off her ring. It was detected by my grandmother in spite of her imperfect vision, and was recovered in the nick of time from a most unlikely location. To this, my Grandmother Vartoo Menee's thought provoking remark was, "It must have been purchased with someone's honest sweat!"

Both grown-ups and children had a cheerful day celebrating my grandmother's name day, the pagan religious holiday of *Vartevar.* We had earlier made a resolve not to breathe a word about the loss and the mysterious recovery of my mother's diamond. It is true that after that day mother seemed somewhat more restrained about wearing genuine jewelry; however, not for one moment did she lose her zest for this type of luxury!

Moving ahead some fifty years, she was at the Huntington Memorial Hospital in Pasadena with an IV going into her arm, when late at night her arm swelled up. The nurse had to literally cut her two delicately engraved malleable golden bracelets using ordinary scissors to relieve the pressure and to comfort her! To this day, I have these two precious mementos lying innocently in my jewelry box. My mother is long gone now, but every now and then when I happen to come upon the contents of this precious box, I caress them as they open a Pandora's Box of warm feelings for me of mostly love and gratitude.

Time Again for the Entrance Exam

Now it was September 15, 1955, and thanks to my mother I was given an incredible second chance to gain admission to the American high school by taking their language proficiency test. As I made my way hesitantly to the same study hall which just three months ago had given me such an unsettling feeling, I found the huge room packed with students, just like before. I could not tell if all these students were there to take the same test I was taking or different ones. I told myself this was no time to get anxious about something I had no control over and tried to relax.

As the two sheets of paper with their typewritten questions finally reached me, unlike three months earlier, I took my time to glance over both sheets. This time around, I felt more at ease because at least I was able to understand the questions. Although the girl to my left with whom I was sharing the double desk was making unnecessary noises, I tried to ignore her and concentrated on what was being asked of me.

As the time to turn in my paper approached, I took my time to review my answers and made sure I had answered everything. I did this with a certain amount of trepidation. Even though this time around I felt a greater level of confidence in my answers, I had no idea how I would rank among all these students competing with me for the ten available spots in the Special C class. The bell finally rang announcing the end of the allotted time, and our papers were promptly collected. One of the teachers announced that the results of our tests would be available in one week.

After turning my paper in, I rushed out of the study hall towards the school yard. My eyes danced over its cluster of colorful annuals planted in increasingly larger concentric circles around the trunks of each sycamore tree whose leaves had already started changing color. I admired the arrangement of the annuals, but I felt most relieved when I was able to locate my mother in the schoolyard. She was there just as she had promised, sitting on a bench, carrying on a casual conversation with another applicant's mother. She seemed satisfied when I told her I had understood the questions and we left the matter at that.

By now my mother and I had not seen my sister Arminé and my maternal grandmother for an unprecedented three weeks. Exiting through the lower gate of the American high school, we passed by the old Berberian School where the Zambakjians lived, but we did not stop there as we normally would have. Instead we headed straight toward Fistikağaci, walking along the winding street with uneven cobblestones one side of which was dotted with wildflowers in bloom, mostly bright yellow mustard flowers and dandelions. We had been unable to inform my grandmother and my sister earlier about our visit because residential phones were not common in Fistikağaci at the time. I can still picture the excitement and delight in their eyes as they opened the door for us. It had been a time of adjustment for them as well. My mother was the first one to break the silence:

"Mom, we both missed you. We don't yet know if Alice got in or not, but I know one thing for sure: We could not have done this without your help. Your granddaughter's extended stay with you could not have come at a more convenient time. By the way, please be sure to tell my Dad when he returns from work at night that his decision to send me to the American school some forty years ago was brilliant!"

In practically no time, enticing smells filled the air. Soon all four of us were sitting around the patio table in my grandmother's balcony which overlooked her garden of newly-planted fruit trees. We were enjoying each other's company as if the recent frantic pace of events had never taken place…

The Butcher

Stepan, who had been my mother's trustworthy butcher throughout the thirteen years we lived in Kadiköy, would always be ready to assist his customers in some capacity when they entered his spacious store located at one end of the open air market. I knew him through *Aramyan Ounchiyan* Elementary, where his son Bedros was my classmate. Due to our limited capacity for refrigeration, there were weeks when my mother would frequent Stepan's store practically every day. From the point of view of a young child, his store was a sight I could not easily forget. Three or four sides of recently slaughtered lambs and sheep would be hanging on hooks, waiting to be sold and processed. When we first entered his store, my mother would ask Stepan for his recommendation of the day, before specifying to him the particular cut and the amount she needed in kilograms. He would expertly carve the meat out of the side of the lamb and shape it into lamb chops and stew. Next, he would place the leftover usable scraps of meat on his large wooden block and using two very sharp knives, he would manually chop them up to transform them into ground meat.

Our Pets

Stepan's store would also shelter a number of kittens which he hoped his customers would adopt. They thrived off the scraps of meat from the various orders of the day. I distinctly remember the day my mother brought home our *Fatosh* from Stepan's butcher shop. My sister and I had fun searching for a name for her and had finally decided on that of the cartoon character in our daily paper. She was an exotic and beautiful kitten possessing practically every shade of brown and gold in just the right combinations on her unusually long and soft fur; she was also quite headstrong. The minute she set foot in our house, she thrust herself forward like an arrow and disappeared into our basement, where we kept the coal we burned in our stove during the winter months. In spite of my mother's many efforts, *Fatosh* would not emerge from her hideout for an entire week! It was only after she had exhausted all the available mice in our basement and was famished that my mother finally succeeded in tempting her out of her hideout with a fresh piece of meat, aided by her flashlight. This was how her long-lasting friendship with my mother had initially started.

Fast forward some forty years, when my mother was visiting us in La Cañada, we similarly knew she again had created a remarkable relationship with our then pet dog *Foofoo*, a mixture of cocker spaniel and poodle. *Foofoo* would never leave my mother's side, especially around dinnertime and was delighted to see her open the closet door where her leash was kept, because it meant she could go for a walk in the neighborhood with her. Since pets in the Middle East were often kept for functional reasons as pest-controllers rather than pets, this love and friendship between my mother and *Foofoo* deserves special mention.

Araksi Adu's Remarkable Grocery Store

On Mühürdar Ave., about six houses down the block from us and to the east was Araksi Hubeserian's grocery store. Her long and narrow store had been a respite for women shopping for the following day's menu. However Araksi Adu, as we lovingly called her, had a far loftier mission in life than just supplying the women with their culinary necessities for the following day or week. When the women of our community came into the store of this remarkable woman who never lost her smile, they relaxed and were able to air their ongoing dilemmas in the hope of getting another trusted person's objective input and if that didn't happen, at least her compassion. I would not be surprised if they frequented her store for a few items each day just for a chance to socialize and let off a bit of steam. Additionally, their homes would get restocked during the winter months with all types of grains, legumes and dried vegetables hanging on strings, such as okra and eggplant. I have recollections of her store with warm feelings of nostalgia tinged with a bit of regret. Regret, because as a young child I was guilty once in a while of dipping my hand into her sacks of grain and legume. In doing so, without realizing it I would be introducing alien grains to an adjoining sack of unadulterated rice, wheat, barley or lentil!

The heavenly aroma of the spices she stocked in glass jars such as cinnamon sticks, black peppercorns, cloves, cumin and *salep*, which came from the root of Orchis mascula and was the source of a delicious hot drink during the cold winter months, might have contributed in making her store magical for me. I wanted to visit it often then and now even if it is only in my world of warm memories. I wonder how she even managed to make a living and remembered to charge her customers in the midst of so much psychotherapy and social service; this was even more remarkable, considering a large percentage of the purchases of the day were made by adding them to the customer's existing account Araksi Adu kept in a sizable hard-cover book. When she was in a hurry, amounts owed were sometimes written on loose pieces of paper, therefore standing a fair chance of getting lost before ever being recorded!

Although at the time a significant share of the internal conflict in families resulted from male chauvinism, in the case of Araksi Adu's landlords Sultanik Hanim and Dikranouhi, the overbearing and ill-spirited mother and daughter duo living upstairs, the conventional male and female roles were oddly reversed. Dikranouhi did not want Majak, her soft and submissive brother to marry and move away with this tall, efficient and somewhat domineering young woman. She knew full well the young bride was not going to tolerate their ordering Majak around. We watched this scenario unfold in front of our eyes, because the bride to be was my classmate Onnik's aunt from elementary school. Both Majak and his fiancée were in their forties, so they were well aware of their behavior and its consequences. Tightening their grip on Majak with false accusations and threats, the wicked mother and daughter team succeeded in obstructing this loving couple's union. It was difficult for us to grasp the makeup of such complex and tyrannical personalities tormenting a loved one. Realizing Araksi Adu had to run her grocery store in the presence of such controlling characters, I now appreciate the complexity of her job even more.

Araksi Adu lived in a modest room behind her grocery store. My mother would let her know each week when she lit the boiler in our second story bathroom by burning wood, so that after our entire family had bathed, she could also make use of the remaining hot water to bathe, after she had closed up her grocery store and pulled down her metal shutters. Her visiting our home was a novelty for me and my sister because she was an interesting and worldly personality. Without making it apparent to our parents, we would open her bathroom door, unaware that by doing so we were sending a draft of cold air her way with the childish excuse of finding out how she was doing. I later found out she was my father's first cousin.

Araksi Adu's husband had never recovered from the typhus he had contracted from the lice during the deportations. She had become a tough and self-sufficient woman after having survived the ordeal and had managed as a single mother to raise two daughters, Peruz and Isgouhi. To be able to do this, she had become a small business owner in Kadiköy operating a grocery-store, to eke out a living for the three of them. After Peruz's marriage and immigration to Visilia, California, she had kept in close contact with her younger daughter Isgouhi who by then had married and settled in Istanbul, having two daughters of her own. After witnessing the untimely death of her son-in-law, she courageously stood by Isgouhi's side and helped support her and her two grandchildren. Remarkably, she had managed to do all this in a completely male-dominated business world at the time. It had given Araksi Adu great satisfaction to see each of her granddaughters get educated and become self-sufficient individuals. She was rightfully pleased that at her advanced age in this small niche of hers, she was able to help the people in her community, while making a living doing something she enjoyed.

At one of her more relaxed moments she would confide in my parents, "You know, Ardashes and Wilhelmina, I am looking all around me, seeing all kinds of people with all sorts of problems. I have concluded that I like our pedigree the best!"

Fast forward some sixty years, it felt like I was traveling back in time when I visited her granddaughters Haigouhi and Mariam in 2006 on the island of Kinali on the Sea of Marmara. On the surface everything seemed to be going smoothly for them. Haigouhi and her husband had chosen to remain in Istanbul after the September 6, 7 pogroms of 1955. When we visited her and her husband, Haigouhi's European daughter-in-law and her two young grandchildren were vacationing with them for part of the summer. They were all hoping to get to know each other better, a happy event by most measures. However we could easily detect the frustration the grandchildren and the grandparents were having when they could not understand each other because they did not have a common language to communicate in!

Haigouhi's sister Mariam's situation was even more complicated. Upon her husband's unexpected demise the year before in Switzerland, in spite of her son's and grandchildren's living there, due to her feeling lonely and having health issues, she felt more comfortable going back to Istanbul, the city she knew, to live there with her sister Haigouhi and her husband when they offered her this choice. It seems every Armenian family has an intricate story to tell about the eventual outcome of the deportations and the Genocide of 1915, which dispersed many a close-knit family's members all over the world, often against their wishes.

Hagop the Shoe Repairman

Adjoining our house and to our west was "Hagop's Shoe Repair." Hagop gave complete satisfaction to practically all of his customers' requests and seemed to have a solution to just about any shoe problem imaginable. Fixing broken heels and reheeling boots were some of his specialties. Word of mouth travelled fast in those days in Kadiköy, therefore it was not unusual for us to overhear a satisfied client remark, "When Hagop fixed my shoe and he sent me out of his store, I felt like a thousand bucks."

In the 1950s being a shoe repairman was a well-respected profession in Istanbul. One could easily blame the cobblestone streets and the extensive amount of walking required for eroding the soles of most shoes. In an effort to extend the life of a sturdy but used shoe, competent shoe repairmen like Hagop often reconstructed the worn out component anew. Thus a good quality shoe, as long as it was the right size, could be repaired to last for a very long time.

My mother had taken a genuine interest in Hagop's new bride, Nevart, because she was such a warm person, young and naïve; she also wanted to help her because they were living in cramped quarters in the attic above his rented shoe repair store.

Now and then, as a six year old I would notice a bizarre look Hagop would get in his eyes for no special reason. It was around this time that my mother became aware of signs of physical abuse on Nevart. One day when she stopped by our house to borrow a special broom, my mother noticed Nevart had a black eye and was complaining of nose bleeds. Upon further questioning, she realized Hagop was the culprit. This was hard for her to comprehend because she knew how much he loved Nevart.

Realizing she is dealing with a problem beyond her level of expertise, my mother suggested that they get help and counseling as a husband and wife team. She must have taken quite a chance in suggesting this, as Hagop could easily have been abusive towards my mother as well. When he refused to take further action and the abuse continued, she encouraged Nevart to secretly move away without disclosing her whereabouts. Unintentionally, I had overheard my mother's private conversation with my father, "Part of me wants to encourage Nevart to move away from Hagop; yet I am reluctant knowing how much he loves her. I wonder if Hagop's mental condition can ever be treated so he can lead closer to a normal life." My mother must have secretly hoped that after his recovery, the two of them could get together once again under better circumstances.

I never found out what kind of a turn Nevart and Hagop's life took because right around then we had to leave for our summer vacation to mountainous Yakacik. Upon our return in the fall, I found Hagop's Shoe Repair as well as their cramped living quarters in the attic to be vacant. Sadly our attempts to get in touch with Nevart never materialized because for obvious reasons she had left no forwarding address. Nevart's smiling saintly face with its delicate features, as well as her kind tone of voice have come before my eyes and rung in my ears on more than one occasion, often followed with a feeling of helplessness on my part. Even continents away in this country, when I see a shoe repair store with old-fashioned service, which is getting rarer these days, I think of Hagop and Nevart. I hope that in spite of the odds being stacked high against them, their story somehow managed to have a happy ending.

Time to Find out

Bright and early the morning I would find out if I got accepted at the American school, a loud knock on my bedroom door got me to jump out of bed. When I opened the door, I came face to face with my mother standing right in front of me with a broad smile on her face. As usual, she was overflowing with energy.

"What is up Mom? You are not drilling me anymore and you look happy!"

"You won't believe the dream I saw this morning right before I woke up. You know I am not usually superstitious; but I believe my dream may mean something positive for you."

"Go on Mom, I am listening," I said impatiently.

"All four of us were in a cherry orchard. The branches of the cherry trees were overburdened, almost to the point of breaking with dark red, ripe cherries. I quickly picked up a handful off the branch closest to me and offered them to you."

We hugged each other and waited impatiently for the day's events to unfold. Right after breakfast, my mother took the tram from Kadiköy and headed toward Bağlarbashi to reach the American school.

"It seemed to me the tram I was riding was moving no faster than at a snail's pace," she later confessed, "I almost felt like jumping out of it to give it an extra push! After what appeared to me an eternity-- thirty minutes of tram ride plus fifteen of walking-- I finally arrived at the upper school gate in Bağlarbashi. But by now I was too anxious to find out what the school's decision was going to be. I was even thinking about what we ought to be doing in case you were not accepted. Not paying attention to anything else due to all these thoughts in my mind, I must have walked right past the roster of accepted students affixed to the front gate. I headed straight to the principal's office. Miss Martin was kind to me. Instead of further aggravating my anxiety by asking me to retrace my steps back to the front gate, she made me feel at ease and asked me to sit down."

"She disappeared for a few minutes out of her office. When she returned, she had a copy of the roster of the ten recently accepted students for 1955 in her hand." Showing it to my mother, she said, "Let me be the first one to congratulate you; it looks like your daughter is accepted into the Special C Class of *Üsküdar Amerikan Kiz Lisesi*."

Later when my mother confided in me she said, "At that moment I was so overjoyed and needed to share my happiness with my family so badly that I was sorry not to have brought you and your sister with me."

The next day, Mrs. Alexanian had called my mother to pass on what Miss Martin had told her, "As usual, your efforts have once again paid off. We ended up accepting a large number of your students to the Special C class. By the way, they also happened to be the ones with the best scores. You must be proud of being able to teach the English language so well in less than four months!"

For the time being, as long as I was accepted at the school of my dreams, it was not necessary to explain to Miss Martin that the length of time the language instruction had taken place was not four months but just three weeks. She could not be expected to comprehend the extreme level of enthusiasm I had in learning this language and my mother's burning desire to teach it to me within the unrealistically short time we had. I was the one who had personally witnessed the suffering of the Istanbul's minorities on its main thoroughfare, Istiklal Blvd. in the aftermath of the Sept. 6-7, 1955 incidents less than three weeks ago. It had bothered me a great deal to have seen the efforts of a lifetime of Armenians, Greeks and Jews destroyed in a matter of minutes. How fair was it to repeatedly be willing to pick up the pieces to start anew as if nothing disastrous had ever happened? In the work of preserving civilization, wasn't it important to understand the past, stress its most obvious lessons so we would not repeat the previous mistakes?

My mother's dogged determination to stick to our grueling schedule every day for an entire three weeks, even in the face of unparalleled savagery during the Cyprus Crisis, had made all the difference. The length of time it had taken us to accomplish the task was not as important as the fact that we had accomplished it. These trying times in our lives when we were working together had achieved another unexpected outcome. They had created an extraordinary bond between us that would last a lifetime and beyond. My mother's solid confidence in me was always going to remain a source of strength for me in handling the next difficult task, even after debilitating illness and death would take her away from me. I would always carry this precious memory tucked in a special place in my heart and would retrieve it when I missed her the most or when I simply needed her reassurance.

This event marked a most memorable day in my family's history. As my proficiency in English improved through the years, it would lead my entire family in a new direction. I was proud to be the initiator of this fundamental change. It would take quite a few years and the maturity the years would bring with them for me to comprehend the true significance of those three weeks. At the time I was in such high spirits that I was quite oblivious as to the many obstacles I would be facing along the way.

"I feel as if a bunch of vocabulary words are still waiting for me!" I told my mother after she gave me the good news.

"You need a vacation," was her answer.

"You think my Dad would be agreeable to it?"

"I will see if he can be talked into taking a little time off of work. We just won't call it a vacation," she said as she directed her energy to some other project that for the time being had captured her attention.

My Exploration of Our Attic

I was thirteen when we had to move away from my childhood home in Kadiköy to be closer to my maternal grandmother in Üsküdar. She seemed to need us more after the sudden death of my grandfather. It was as we were preparing to distance ourselves for good from the only home my father had known for almost thirty years that our mysterious closet with its attic access comes to my mind.

A few weeks before our move from Kadiköy, while entertaining a couple of our Armenian female neighbors in our living room, I had overheard my mother explain to them what the consequences of Turkey's enforcing the *Capital Tax Ordinance* had meant for our family. Apparently during this time for a period of several months, my paternal grandmother Verkin Menee had hidden my father and my uncle Dikran in this very same attic in the style of Anne Frank. She had chosen this unconventional and rather illegal way to circumvent the Turkish government from sending them to ice-covered Askale in eastern Anatolia. They were to be sent there as part of a labor battalion during the harsh winter of 1942 because my father and uncle had been unable to come up with the outrageous sum demanded of them by the Turkish government for owning their business. At the time the government was demanding the Wealth Tax funds as a way of fiscally readying the country in case its participation in WWII was deemed necessary.

Further information on this subject from my sister has led me to believe that although avoiding the manual labor in frozen Askale was an important consideration for my grandmother, the cardinal reason she hid her sons in the attic was to prevent their being mobilized as front line fighters in the line of fire with no uniforms, proper weapons or previous training, in case Turkey participated in WWII. If they were to miraculously survive this hellish challenge, they would then be sent to Askale.[12] Thus on a rainy Tuesday in late November, the two brothers disappeared through the hidden entryway of this fifth floor closet into our attic.

In anticipation of our move to Üsküdar, I had noticed my father had placed a convenient ladder in this mysterious closet to facilitate our packing process. Meanwhile a week earlier, my mother had promised to take my sister to visit her best elementary school friend, Takouhi, for perhaps one last time that afternoon before we were to leave Kadiköy for good. I felt this was an ideal opportunity for me to explore the contents of our secret attic because this chance was soon going to disappear forever. I had found out they would be gone for about two hours, which would give me the right length of time to do some detective work.

Just the thought of my upcoming adventure had been enough to get my heart racing. I cannot deny feeling somewhat apprehensive about my plan; because if I slipped and fell, there would be no one to lend me a hand. The fear of the unknown was contributing to my anxiety as well. As far back as I could remember, I had not been aware of any family member ever climbing into this attic and I had no idea what unexpected articles and memorabilia would be greeting me in this "off limits" site.

As soon as I heard the heavy metal door slam shut behind my mother and sister four stories down, I instantly went to work. Since I knew there was a hidden passageway from the ceiling of this closet to the attic, after fetching my father's powerful rectangular flashlight from his bedroom, I started climbing up the ladder. I felt slightly relieved when the square plywood guarding the concealed entryway that measured about 30cm. on each side responded to my gentle push. The most difficult part of my ascent was thrusting my entire body upward so I could land on the attic floor after reaching the highest step on the ladder. This took a number of tries.

Initially I felt triumphant when I stepped into the attic, but soon I realized I had entered a totally different world. I am not sure what I was expecting to find here, perhaps old unseen trunks, however what I witnessed definitely looked disturbing. It reminded me of a scene from a scary mystery novel I had recently read which had elicited nightmares. I knew the sun was bright outside, but not a ray of sunlight was entering the attic; it smelled hot and stuffy. Even for a summer month, the place looked gloomy. It did not matter which direction I pointed my flashlight, everywhere was covered with a thick layer of dust and cobwebs. Noticing that the ceiling was unusually low, I figured my father and uncle could not have comfortably stood up here except within a ten square foot area of the center. Most of the time, they must have had to sit on a chair unable to move. Furthermore, since not much food could reach them with ease, they must have always been hungry. The wood planks covering the floor were lined with thoroughly yellowed, almost disintegrating issues of the *Cumhuriyet* newspaper, dating back some sixteen years. Shining my flashlight on one of the better preserved copies, I could make out the date on it to be November 12, 1942. On the first page of the paper there was a picture of a desolate thoroughfare in Athens with the question typed underneath: "Do we want a repeat performance?" It was depicting the Nazi invasion of Greece of a year and a half earlier.

In the center of the attic were two crates next to each other, simulating a makeshift table for informal dining, playing backgammon, or perhaps reading. As I directed the beam of my flashlight on the crates, I detected two hurricane lamps with dried up wicks resting on another issue of *Cumhuriyet* with an article about Askale.

As I kept exploring the attic further with my flashlight, no more than a few feet to my right, a sturdy and relatively new cardboard box approximately 25X15X3cm. caught my eye. It was labeled "*hatiralar,*" meaning memories in Turkish, and appeared to be a later addition to the contents of the attic. When I opened it and shined my flashlight on it, at the top of the stack of handwritten papers, I thought I read a description of Aksaray, the town my father and paternal grandparents had come from in historic Armenia. It was in Turkish, but it was written with the letters of the Armenian alphabet. Even with the help of my flashlight, I was having difficulty deciphering the first few handwritten pages of what seemed to be quite a lengthy memoir. Besides, by now I was starting to feel the effect of the intense heat of the attic. Soon, objects started looking black and I almost felt like passing out! Right away I sat down to rest for a couple of minutes. By the time my head was clearer, I had already decided I did not have the time to devote my attention to this historical document right there and then.

Initially I was tempted to remove the stack of papers comprising the document from its box to bring them down with me; but I knew I was barely going to manage to get down the ladder from the attic to the closet myself, even if I had my hands free. Furthermore, even if I had managed to get it down and showed it to my father, my secret would be out. To appear a disobedient teen in his eyes would irreparably damage my self-esteem. Deep down I believed my father must have been aware of the location of this piece of history. My intuition told me that in his infinite wisdom, he must have had a good reason for keeping it here. He might be safeguarding it by leaving it in this non-conspicuous location, since he believed some of its content could get us into trouble if it was discovered by the Turkish secret police during one of their rare, nevertheless likely searches. I also recalled that during my

father's cousin, Uncle John's only visit to Istanbul from New
Jersey in 1948, he had announced in Büyükdere to everyone that
he had brought an important piece of history with him pertaining
to our families' past. Part of me wanted to find out what was in this
memoir there and then. However knowing this was not feasible, I
wished with all my heart that before our move from Kadiköy, my
father would remember to retrieve this document from its obscure
location and safely preserve it so one day I could lay my hands on
it and our past would not forever remain shrouded in secrecy for
me. I also pondered if the passage of time would make me more
mature and therefore appreciate its content more.

As I tried to explore the attic further using my flashlight,
in one corner I recognized a worn-out backgammon set complete
with its original chips and dice. Across from it stood a solitary
white enamel chamber pot, both reminders of a time when this
area must have been used as a provisional Spartan dormitory. It
appeared the two brothers had scarcely returned back here since
they had last used it as their hideout during the administration of
Ismet Inönü, the Turkish president responsible for the excessive
Capital Tax Law of 1942. Perhaps their most recent visit to the
attic few years back, had been for the purpose of depositing this
relatively new cardboard box to this remote attic!

Since after November 1942 most of my father's and
uncle's time and efforts had been spent frantically trying to recover
financially from the aftermath of the Capital tax, they must have
tried to obliterate this unpleasant event from their memory so
completely that they had not ever gone back, not even to recover
any articles of value they might have accidentally left there. My
sister remembers my grandmother's final remark on the subject
regarding their bare existence here: "Ardashes and Dikran looked
so pale and malnourished when they first came out of that hell
hole…"

Saddened but somewhat satisfied with my findings, this
adventure had phenomenally increased my respect for my father,
uncle, and grandmother and what they must have endured just
by living in Turkey during these turbulent years. For a long time
afterwards, I wondered how the two brothers had simply closed

the door of their lives and had vanished from Istanbul proper, to settle in this lowly attic for an entire 2-3 months starting with the chilly November of 1942. As I realized the time had come for me to make the transition from the past to the present, I vowed to share my observations of this day with no one.

Now I had to get out of this hot and suffocating prison without passing out and getting hurt. I also had to make sure I would leave every item as I had found it, including the seal of the secret entryway to the attic. Just as finding my way up to the attic had proven to be physically taxing, so was exiting it. I was only able to handle it after I had placed my flashlight in my sizeable skirt pocket which freed my hands to hold onto the attic floor, as I descended the first few steps down the ladder.

Once I was at the 5th floor level, I made sure I placed the ladder facing the same way in the closet I had initially found it, and remembered to return my father's favorite flashlight to his bedside table. I even roughly dusted the closet floor, because some dirt had fallen from the attic as I had opened and closed its secret entryway. I had even tried to think of an appropriate activity to name in case I was interrogated about what I did while my mother and sister were gone for the afternoon.

I had a suspicion my detective activity had not altogether gone undetected because while having dinner in the evening, my father asked me how I had managed to get a cobweb on my hair in the back of my head. I had searched in vain for a simple explanation; but fortunately I was saved since he had not pursued the matter any further. However in retrospect, I just might have reminded him of that relatively new cardboard box with its historic content, since the attic was the only location in the entire house where one could readily get cobwebs on one's hair.

All the trouble I had gone through before our move from my childhood home in Kadiköy had served a purpose. I had seen unequivocal evidence that our attic had functioned as the hiding place of my father and uncle for at least two months starting with November 1942.

The Unfair Capital Tax on Minorities

On the surface, the Capital Tax, *Varlik Vergisi*, also known as the Wealth Tax, imposed on wealthy citizens of Turkey on November 12, 1942, was intended to raise funds for Turkey's defense, in case the country was eventually dragged into World War II. According to the then administrator of financial affairs of Istanbul and the author of *The Tragedy of the Turkish Capital Tax*, Faik Ökte, it was "one of the most embarrassing events in the financial history of the Turkish Republic."[13] Much credit is due to him for having the courage to write this revealing book, which was originally published in Turkish in 1951. It must have taken a great deal of courage on his part to publicly admit complete disregard for justice on the part of the Turkish government. Being a righteous state official who admitted governmental wrongdoing by authoring this revealing book, Faik Ökte suffered serious consequences. Throughout his remaining life, he felt isolated, because many of his associates rejected him as a traitor.

Hardly 27 years had passed since the Armenian Genocide (1915-1922), and there came another impediment, the imposition of the Capital Tax on the minorities. Promises by the Turkish government that minorities would never again be subjected to discrimination, had once again been conveniently ignored. An eagerness to create a homogenous Turkey belonging to Turks alone had once again become a top Turkish priority.

The emergence of the Turkish Capital Tax was due to this type of overly nationalistic sentiment. It was influenced by widespread Nazi ideology, as well as the racist remnants of Union and Progress thinking.[14] The main motivation behind the Capital Tax was to reduce the minority populations' control over the economy. The tax, paid almost exclusively by Turkey's non-Muslim inhabitants, was imposed quite arbitrarily. A commission, formed entirely of Muslim Turkish businessmen, bureaucrats, and politicians was authorized to determine who would pay what amount of tax. The tax was used as a means to eliminate non-Muslim minorities from commerce and industry. Through discriminatory assessments based on religious affiliation, Christian and Jewish citizens of Turkey were to be assessed at least 5-10 times the rate of Muslim citizens.[15]

While it was initially proposed that the tax was to apply only to the wealthy, in fact it was extended to non-Muslim wage earners and small businessmen, such as my father, uncle, maternal grandfather, as well as craftsmen and peddlers. Assessments seemed to be based on guesswork and were excessive. Furthermore there were no provisions for appeal. In certain cases, people were forced to sell all of their possessions at unrealistically low prices to come up with the money demanded of them, as was the case for my father and uncle. Many sources suggest that some of Turkey's richest families acquired their wealth during this very period.

Muslims, including businessmen owning small businesses, peddlers, salaried workers and craftsmen, were exempt from this tax. Further, no Muslim defaulter was assigned into forced labor camps.[16] Even the cost of printing notices of auctions of the seized property, as well as defaulters' cost of food, clothing, and shelter were borne by the deportees.[17]

Those unable to pay the tax within two weeks of the law's enactment were given an additional two weeks before being arrested. Upon arrest, their property was seized and auctioned off. In the middle of a very harsh winter, the men were sent to form labor battalions to Askale in eastern Anatolia where they would have to shovel and clear the roadway of ice and snow. Ninety percent of the deportees were minorities of Istanbul, a city known to have a moderate climate. It is estimated that somewhere between 1,000 and 6,000 people were sent to this camp close to Erzurum, and around 21 of them died there.

While Faik Ökte places the total blame of this "shameful act" which "degraded the dignity of Turkey," on Prime Minister Rustum Saracoglu, he realizes Saracoglu could not have acted without a clear directive from Ismet Inönü, the president. During these times of chaos and panic, many enriched themselves by becoming the protectors of the weak in this notorious scheme of extortion by the state. "The arbitrary nature of this tax enabled the politically connected and powerful to settle old scores of debts by either getting prohibitive assessments imposed on foes or getting them reduced for friends. The effects of this discriminatory looting by the state left the "major Greek, Armenian and Jewish merchant figures shaken and dislocated."[18] Those who could figure out a way and could afford it, left the country. Others had to nurse their wounds and come to terms with life no matter how painful it was.

Grandma Verkin Hides her Sons in the Attic

Unable to come up with the prohibitive wealth tax sums the Turkish government was demanding of them and in an effort to prevent her sons' dangerous recruitment to the front lines, my grandmother Verkin Menee, with the deportations and the genocide of 1915 still fresh in her memory, came upon the idea that if her sons were diagnosed with diabetes, this might be considered a valid medical reason to exempt them from conscription. Thus she fed them jars of jam to help circumvent a misadventure, which she felt could have a catastrophic outcome for them. Sadly, her efforts only hastened the manifestation of the Diabetes Mellitus she did not know her sons were already genetically predisposed to.

However, they found out soon enough that the government's instructions were very clear; there would be no exceptions. Within the next few days, just like everyone else in the Armenian community, my father and uncle received the decree in the mail ordering them to pay the government the exorbitant tax in no later than two weeks. A footnote of the decree in small print stated that in case they were unable to come upon the indicated sum, they should immediately report to the local authorities so their eventual transport via rail to Askale would be arranged.

Having flashbacks to 27 years ago to their deportation years when she and her loved ones had a frightening brush with tragedy, she knew this could not be an option. The death of her husband from typhus in their gloomy mud hut in Remté in the Syrian Desert was still quite fresh in her memory. So, illogical as it might have been, she hid my father and my uncle in their attic in Kadiköy. The two brothers barely managed to survive there in the cold for over two months on scraps of food, some water and almost no sunlight.

However, this gave them time to figure out how they could come up with the prohibitive sum the government was demanding of them. They discovered several so far overlooked items they could sell, albeit at unrealistically low prices. However it also regrettably resulted in my grandmother's arrest and imprisonment for carrying out her unorthodox plan!

The gendarmes were enraged, when in spite of my grandmother's reassurance to the contrary, they discovered the hidden entrance to our attic. However what annoyed them the most was that this undaunted diminutive woman was willing to defend her sons against all odds, and was even willing to lie to the gendarmes about their hiding place, knowing full well that if it was discovered she would be facing dire consequences.

Dr. Tanielyan Saves the Day

After the gendarmes handcuffed my grandmother, they took her to the closest jail. If she was left to her own resources, she could be languishing there for months. In spite of my mother's immeasurable grief due to the untimely death of her five year old son Kepi only ten months earlier, she used sound judgment and sought the help of their neighbor Dr. Tanielyan, a family practitioner and a well-liked member of the community, who in the past had to have his right leg amputated due to gangrene resulting from his own poorly-controlled diabetes. The medical profession had always been treated with a certain degree of leniency since only a handful of doctors existed in the community at the time. Accompanying my mother through the narrow alleys and convoluted streets of Kadiköy, and in spite of his prosthetic leg, Dr. Tanielyan made it to the jail to plead with the authorities.

The gendarmes had stuck my grandmother in a crowded cell for further questioning, confession, and quite possibly some torture. By now she was so overwhelmed and frightened in this alien and unfriendly environment next to real criminals that she was starting to look like someone irrational. That is when Dr. Tanielyan intervened and said to the jail warden:

"This old woman, as you can see, is senile. I, as her medical doctor ought to know, since she has often acted illogically. Staying in jail is going to further confuse and agitate her. Please be so kind as to release her from her cell so she can go home, settle down, and start being more rational. She will be forever indebted to you for your most valuable assistance."

His profession must have given Dr. Tanielyan invaluable practice in dealing with people to get them to follow his advice. Most importantly, the jail warden thought he was credible and was giving sound advice; therefore, he ordered the gendarme to release my frightened grandmother out of the crowded cell.

By the time they had made it home, it was impossible not to notice the happiness on my grandmother's face, because her freedom to return home with people she knew had canceled out all the fear and misery the earlier jail episode had created for her. At this dispirited moment in their lives, it had been such a relief for my mother and grandmother to be reminded that decent people still existed, such as the jail warden and Dr. Tanielyan. The good doctor had not even hesitated in offering his random act of kindness. Upon my mother's request, he had voluntarily left his office for an unspecified length of time, willing to forgo the income he would have generated by seeing patients. Instead, he had chosen to help my mother in her time of need by testifying on my grandmother's behalf.

The Room of Memories at my Grandparents'

In spite of having to go to Askale for hard labor in 1942, my maternal grandfather Iskender still had to pay the unfair Capital Tax imposed upon him, except over a somewhat longer period. During the following twelve years, he had to work tirelessly to recover from its repercussions. By 1954, with impeccable work ethic paired with frugality, he had a two story, stone apartment building constructed for him and my grandmother in Fistikağaci. They lived in the upper unit, while they rented out the one at the street level.

As a child, I often associated the bedroom I had the privilege of sleeping in to a museum full of mementos of extraordinary objects, although for my grandparents it was more a room of family keepsakes and discarded objects from friends and strangers alike. Some of these objects were readily visible, while I had to search for others. I was happy that my grandparents' preserving these mementos had allowed a few remnants of their past to survive. Imparting further charm to my grandfather's walnut desk standing against the wall was an impressive model mahogany sailboat. It was finished with a glossy varnish and had multiple white sails created out of starched white linen. I reasoned that this might have been gifted to my grandfather by a satisfied client, since around the time he had acquired it, he did not have the excess funds to spend on such an art piece.

The contents of my grandfather's old but charming desk with its two drawers had been an unending source of wonder and fascination for me, each time I was an overnight guest sleeping in this room. I had tested its top drawer a number of times to see if I could open it. To my dismay, I had consistently found it locked. However the deeper bottom drawer seemed to always be accessible. It contained knickknacks among which I had identified a powerful pocket magnifier, an assortment of cufflinks of varying sizes and shapes, foreign coins, a brass letter opener and a pocket watch.

I was most curious about the pocket watch because it looked ancient and was silver filigreed; I reasoned that at one time it must have belonged to my grandfather. After gently trying to make it work, I realized this most unique object must have been irreparably broken and could no longer be wound. How I wished I could go back in time to the days when it was in working order! I longed for it to give me an account of some of the extraordinary hours that had elapsed and activities it had witnessed while it was in my grandfather's possession. I pondered if my grandfather had taken it with him to Askale, the Anatolian Siberia. I even wondered if the extreme cold there might have been responsible for its demise. Until now, I simply had not been aware how complicated and precious this room's contents were.

One morning when I woke up earlier than usual in this extraordinary room, I noticed that a key had been inserted into the keyhole of the drawer that seemed to be permanently locked. I had been hoping for this to happen for quite some time… It meant my grandparents' mystery drawer with its wealth of family history would at least for a little while be available for me to inspect. Being careful not to make it obvious, I cautiously opened the drawer and gingerly sifted its contents through my fingers. There were quite a few stamps tucked carefully in wax paper receptacles and marked according to their country of origin. They were mostly Turkish stamps with almost exclusively Atatürk's portrait on them. There were others from France, Greece and England with their respective queens' and kings' portraits. There were even a few from Helvetia, the present day Switzerland. Some were complete series, with the stamp represented in all of its available colors.

At the bottom of the drawer, neatly tucked in an ordinary shallow cardboard box, I came across a letter which I reasoned justified all my efforts. It looked like it was the first letter my grandfather had written to my grandmother from Askale. The faded handwriting in blue ink unquestionably belonged to him. The envelope was addressed to Vartouhi Stepanyan and the letter was written in Armenian. I am sure he must have had a lot of things he wanted to tell her; but the letter was unusually brief. It looked as if he had to be careful about what he said in it, because the letters from Askale were most likely being censored at the time. It started with the all too familiar nickname he used when addressing my grandmother, *Ma Cherie,* My Love in French, then he went on to give her real name, *Vartouhi.* It read:

I want you to know I am well. I am now a cook in Askale. I work indoors. I pray that you, Hovhannes, Vartkes and Wilhelmina are getting along reasonably well. Hang in there just a bit longer. I miss you very much and send you all my love.

Signed, *Mon Cher,* the nickname she gave him, meaning "My Love."

Although I was too young at the time to appreciate every-thing the letter was saying, I could tell that my grandfather had written it when he was going through difficult times. It sounded as if my grandparents had been separated from each other for some time. Most importantly, my grandfather was proud of the fact and wanted my grandmother to know that he was a cook and worked indoors!

For the moment, to locate and manage to read my grand-father's brief letter in secrecy felt as if I had unearthed some buried treasure. My grandparents must have valued this love letter written during their time of forced separation so much that they wanted to keep it under lock and key. At times when they unlocked the desk drawer to reminisce those unreal days, they must have felt so thankful that my grandfather had survived the winter in the Anatolian Siberia, and most importantly that they still had each other...It would take further maturity from me and the passing of years to realize that as human beings, we are nothing more than memories and the sum of our possessions.

Grandpa Iskender Leaves for Askale

A flashback to the early months of 1942 depicts my maternal grandfather as a merchant, importing textiles from Anatolia wholesale, to distribute them among a number of retailers on the European side of the Bosphorus, thereby making a modest income. He was 54 years old when he was suddenly confronted with an unreasonable Capital Tax the Turkish government demanded of him for owning his business. Having only partially recovered from the ruinous effects of the deportations and not fully-established as a textile merchant yet, he knew he could never come up with the kind of money the government was asking for. Not to subject his family to undue risk, in spite of my grandmother's rigorous objections, he agreed to be sent to mountainous Askale in Eastern Anatolia near Erzurum, at least to delay the impact of the exorbitant Capital Tax on his family's finances.

"This way I will prevent my entire family from sinking with me," my grandmother heard him say. "With God's grace I will come back alive and will try to pick up the pieces. Vartouhi, my love, you will always be with me in my thoughts and dreams. Promise me, you will be brave and handle what it takes to run our household using our savings. I will be back the absolute first chance I get!"

Early the next morning, my grandfather was gone. His train left the imposing Haydarpasha station, Istanbul's main terminal built by Germans, which had first opened to the public in 1872. His train looked different from the usual passenger cars because it had iron bars across its windows. He was headed east through Izmit, eventually to Askale in the company of many other unfortunate Armenian heads of household like him. He found out there were a handful of Greeks and Jews in his regiment as well. The common thread among them was that they were forced to leave their jobs and loving family members behind; they were going to an inhospitable climate where they were expected to do hard labor. Last but not least, they had almost no control over their destiny. On the second day of this odyssey, after his train traversed Eskishehir and approached the Ankara train station, as the sun was setting, a crowd of bystanders ridiculed them. It seemed they were not in the least bit appreciative of the sacrifice my grandfather and others in his regiment were making for their country by risking their lives…

On the third day, as my grandfather's train was continually gaining in elevation, climbing the eastern Anatolian mountainous terrain around Askale, the icy air hit his bones for the first time. Being used to the milder winters of Istanbul, the biting chill felt as if he was approaching the North Pole! Even though his limited exposure to the outside from his train window portrayed a perfect winter wonderland covered under a thick blanket of snow, it did not excite him as it previously had; instead, it started worrying him. The bitter cold had already started to penetrate his clothes, making him shiver. He realized the thinner woolen clothing he had brought along with him would never suffice here; he would not be able to function, especially if he had to work outdoors. That is when he thought of wearing multiple layers of woolen clothing under his coat at all times.

It was mid-November when his train arrived in Askale, where he found the ground to be permanently frozen; he was further told that it would remain that way until April. His labor battalion was assigned to the task of digging daily with a pick ax, following it by shoveling the frozen surface layer to clear the roads of this mountainous town of ice and snow. Regrettably, the 1942 temperatures were running a couple of degrees centigrade below normal. The boots and gloves he had brought along were not sufficient to shield him from the bitter cold. It seemed ever since he had started the manual labor outdoors, his hands and feet had become permanently numb. After a few days, he developed a backache from the constant bending and digging which was becoming unbearable. Next, his palms started developing blisters that would shortly break and cause him agony due to the continuous rubbing against the handle of his pick ax and shovel. Now that he had open sores, he realized they were also in danger of getting infected.

In addition to this being my grandfather's first encounter with the unbearable cold, it was also his first encounter with manual labor. He had heard through the grapevine that a number of the previous draftees from Istanbul had lost fingers and toes because of not owning heavy gloves, thick woolen socks, and sturdy, well-insulated boots. He had also heard there had been a few from the previous group who had never made it back to Istanbul… This was what really upset him. He spent many sleepless nights nursing his back, constantly trying to reposition it on the stiff mattress so it would hurt less. During these times, his thoughts would constantly wander far away to his beloved Vartouhi.

Will Grandpa Survive Askale?

Around this time, word had gotten out that the cook of my grandfather's battalion had suddenly fallen seriously ill, prompting his commanding officer to panic. He needed a new cook in a hurry. His practical solution to this unanticipated problem was to ask everyone in his battalion to prepare his version of a rice pilaf. The laborer who came up with the most flavorful, fluffy, and original pilaf would become his next cook and escape hard labor. My grandfather had never tried his hand at cooking before. But, with enthusiasm heightened by a sudden surge of ingenuity, he used the ingredients he was given in the most creative way. The next day when it was time for the commanding officer to announce the lucky winner, he literally could not believe what he was hearing. Iskender had managed to come up with the pilaf that was judged to be the winning entry!

However, now the commander had started having second thoughts about his selection process. In the light of the 1915 Armenian Genocide, the 1922 deliberate burning of the Armenian section of *Smyrna* (Izmir), and now the 1942 Capital Tax law causing the financial ruin of the surviving Armenians of Istanbul, he started doubting the wisdom of assigning the title of "chef" to an Armenian. It must have crossed his mind that an Armenian cook could seek revenge and try to poison the Turkish officers. It was a good thing he judged my grandfather to be trustworthy!

When narrating this event of some years back to us, his grandchildren, I still can hear the excitement in my grandfather's voice as he proudly described the opportunity that had miraculously saved his life:

"It was not too different from my owning the winning number on a lottery ticket," he would say to us with a smile and a spark in his eyes. He would then immediately add, "Now, don't you forget that by becoming the cook of my battalion, I was also escaping the rough manual labor and the miserable cold of the outdoors during the winter, in this town 1900 meters above sea level!"

I remember that as a child, this was perhaps the only story my grandfather was willing to share with us, his grandchildren, regarding his challenging past. Much later, when things once again normalized in my grandparents' household, this incident gave him poetic license to spend considerable time in the kitchen concocting unusual and interesting dishes, sometimes to the displeasure of my grandmother.

Turkey Abolishes its Capital Tax Law

While the Capital Tax law was abolished in 1944, many businessmen never completely recovered from its disastrous consequences. In addition to careers, businesses, and lives ruined, the most precious currency that was lost by this tax in the area of finance was the loss of confidence of the citizens in the state.[19] Minority businesses were bankrupted by the state. Their assets were purchased at auction by their Muslim co-nationalists.[20] This must have happened to my grandfather's business as well. Upon his return from Askale, he must have had to start from square one.

Edward C. Clark in *The Turkish Varlik Vergisi Reconsidered* explains that probably the prime cause for the postwar reluctance of non-Muslims to move from commerce to manufacturing has been due to the aftereffects of the *Varlik Vergisi,* the Capital Tax. It is possible that Muslim as well as non-Muslim entrepreneurs in Turkey accelerated their capital flows to countries outside of Turkey, considerably delaying industrial development in Turkey. While this tax served as a catalyst for many minority citizens of Turkey to immigrate, other perhaps more resourceful businessmen chose to garner closer relationships with the politically powerful in order to protect their investments. This came at a significant cost and was often borne by the consumer.[21] Turkey could have prospered economically at a much faster rate had there not been the gouging Capital Tax on its minorities.

Taking the Tram to Visit my Grandparents

Prior to our elementary school years, my sister and I looked forward to our overnight visits to our grandparents, the fond memories of which would linger in our memory for a long time. We would get started by helping my mother arrange the special overnight bag with our favorite clothing. My mother would try to bring us back to reality by reminding us that we were going there for only a few days. She would also give us subtle hints that what we packed had to be hand-carried to the tram station and from there to our grandparents' house and back.

If the tram happened to be red, it meant it was first class and its soft and comfortable seats were upholstered in soft dark red leather; if it was green, it was second class and its seats felt somewhat stiff because they were made of stained and subsequently shellacked wood without any padding. As I look back at those days, the most exciting part of the trip for me was when a man in uniform known to be the controller suddenly hopped onto our tram at about the halfway point, almost always without the tram coming to a complete stop. He was there to collect the cash as we bought our tickets from him.

I adored my maternal grandmother Vartoo Menee who often went into great lengths to please us. However, once in a while her stingy side would come to the forefront, such as when the controller was about to approach her to purchase our tickets. She would then whisper in my ear: "It is now time to become a midget!" so I would look more like a child in the exempted age group. This theatrical act was a game for the first few times; but after a while I started thinking that the anxiety this was creating in all of us was not worth the few *kurushes* (pennies) it was saving. Additionally I felt we would be cheating the system, which I did not feel good about. A number of years later, after I found out how the excessive Capital Tax imposed on my grandparents had robbed them of their money and prized possessions and had not even prevented my somewhat elderly grandfather from having to travel to frigid eastern Anatolia to do hard labor, I was no longer so critical.

My sister and I treasured these overnight visits to my grandparents. Even at that very young age, we realized that the most exciting part of our visit was the exceptional cuisine lovingly prepared for us by our grandparents. Although at the time we were not old enough to realize it, we were benefiting from being introduced in a most effective way to some of the basic elements of our culture and heritage. These events would persist in our memory for a lifetime, no matter how far we eventually would make our homes from our original homeland. Each time we visited our grandparents--without exception--we would be treated to extraordinary food with imaginative ingredients and spicing, a heavenly experience, even to the unsophisticated palate of a young child.

Chapter I

Adventures with my Grandmother

On Sunday mornings, my grandmother would take me to the historic *Soorp Khatch,* Holy Cross Church, across the street from the Berberian School. After entering the sanctuary, for a long time my eyes would remain affixed on the intricate design and texture of the altar curtains. The church service, parts of which I did not understand, would give me a chance to admire the liturgical garments of the priest, including his impressive crown. It would be years before I would find out more about them. I would then realize: *Going back more than a century, they had been the work of gifted and art-loving Armenian women of the villages of historical Armenia, who longed to donate these beautiful filigreed textiles they had designed and perfected on the loom for their church. They were the unsung heroes who never got the recognition they deserved. Among the 35 churches in Istanbul, Holy Cross was the richest in the total amount of gold and silver contained on its filigreed textiles, chalices and chrismatories (holy oil vessels). At the time, Holy Cross and other Armenian churches were constantly being subjected to confiscation by the Ottoman authorities because of the precious metals their filigreed textiles contained. The Ottoman Empire would issue a decree to melt down the silver and gold they contained to pay for their war expenses.*[22]

Unfortunately at the time, due to my youth and lack of historical knowledge, I did not appreciate the true value of these sacred treasures. However, I was enchanted by the hymns sung by the members of the church choir. There seemed to be a heavenly quality to them as they transported me, at least in my imagination, into a safer, gentler, far away land…

During the day, my grandmother was resourceful in coming up with activities she somehow knew my sister and I would enjoy. What made it so special for us was that our grandma would give us her undivided attention. No matter how boring an activity it must have been for her, she could always be talked into playing the card games *iskambil* or *kapti-kacti*, meaning seized and ran away, which she had taught us. She would also make sure we won few times, just to whet our appetite…

On other occasions when she had found out through the grapevine that a small-scale traveling circus with acrobats and a magician had arrived in town, she would take us to see it in the evening. We would watch with a certain amount of fear and quite a lot of bewilderment their show of the dancing bear shaking his tambourine to the rhythm of popular Turkish folk tunes; we would marvel at how well the bear was able to carry out his master's commands. The acrobats would hurriedly walk on a thick rope that was at least fifteen feet off the ground with no safety net to catch them in case they slipped and fell. At the conclusion of their program, the diminutive gypsy acrobat would make the rounds with his collection tray. By now quite sleepy and tired, but totally satisfied, we would head back to my grandparents' house. Looking back, I marvel at my grandmother's resilience and willingness to generate laughter in her grandchildren after her own life and that of her sons had been touched with so much loss and conflict.

A Visit to Grandmother's Neighbor from Yozgat

There was a visit to my grandmother's Armenian neighbor from Yozgat in central Anatolia, which had left a number of questions unsettled in my mind. To fit the pieces of the puzzle together took me many years. It happened after I had a chance to investigate further the history and geography of historic Armenia. On more than one occasion, my grandmother had taken me with her to visit her friend from Yozgat, Mrs. *Galipsi*. I was surprised she referred to her as *Yozgatli,* meaning hailing from Yozgat, as if bestowing an honorary title to her, instead of using her own name. I had noticed there were certain peculiarities in *Yozgatli*'s behavior, as well as in that of my grandmother's, when the two women met.

I had observed that whenever my grandmother was invited to *Yozgatli*'s home to share a meal with her, she always practiced a certain routine that seemed to have worked well for her in the past. It consisted of taking noticeably small portions of the foods and taking her time in consuming them. *Yozgatli* would always be very persistent about offering my grandmother more food than she could comfortably consume. Then during the course of the meal, if my grandmother gratefully hinted to her that she could not accept any more food because she was full, *Yozgatli* would solemnly respond to her in Turkish: *ölümü gör,* meaning, see me dead. In spite of being a child at the time, I had found this preoccupation with death unusual and even somewhat troubling.

I started realizing why death played such an important role in *Yozgatli*'s world after I read <u>Armenian Golgotha,</u> the memoir of a most courageous, brilliant, yet humble Prelate, Grigoris Balakian, translated and published by his grandnephew, Dr. Peter Balakian in 2009. The prelate was arrested on April 24, 1915 in Constantinople, along with some 250 other intellectuals of Constantinople's Armenian community, who depended on him for guidance in as many areas as he could provide to survive this journey of persecution, starvation, disease, slaughter and exhaustion. The Prelate Grigoris Balakian persevered to help them to narrowly escape death as their caravan passed through the bloodstained roads from Choroum to Yozgat and onto Boğazliyan in eastern Anatolia. Captain Shukri, the 65 year old head of the Yozgat police, explained to him that: Not a single caravan of Armenians had emerged alive from there between July and September of 1915.[23] When asked how he would atone for these sins on judgment day, his reply was that he was carrying his sacred duty before God, the prophet [Muhammad] because the Sunni religious authority appointed by the Ittihad leaders had issued a fatwa to annihilate the Armenians as traitors of the state; the caliph had ratified the fatwa which meant he had ordered its execution.[24]

In this manner Prelate Balakian was dragging out the dark historical account out of the chief of the Yozgat police Captain Shukri, because he was certain the prelate was also soon to be part of history. Contrary to Captain Shukri's expectations, the Prelate survived to record the history that he had personally witnessed.

At the time I was young and unaware of the sinister hand history had dealt my grandmother's Armenian friend from Yozgat and those from the Ankara province; I am now better able to understand her preoccupation with death because it was a miracle that she survived.

More Mementos from the Room of Memories

During one of my overnight visits to my grandparents, as I was casually inspecting the contents of a remote corner of the room I was sleeping in, a different period in their life was revealed to me. Neatly stacked against a wall and somewhat hidden from view, were several catalogs of samples of fabric my grandfather must have brought with him from his many trips to Anatolia. I figured that as part of his business as a merchant, he must have displayed these samples in a number of fabric stores on the European side of the Bosphorus; he later would have imported their selections from his suppliers in Anatolia. I still remember how proud I was of the colorful apron my grandmother had helped me make by stitching together some of my grandfather's discarded samples. Very patiently, she had taught me how I could gently press on the foot pedal of her pride and joy, the Singer sewing machine, which occupied a special place by the window in this room of memories. Under my grandmother's expert guidance, this elegant little machine created the desired finished product every single time!

Fast forward some ten years, while a student at the American high school, and again, with my grandmother's help, this sewing machine made it possible for me to produce a dress of my own design, despite my inborn inaptitude in sewing. This dress was an assigned project in Home-Economics class and a requirement for my high school graduation.

After another decade passed, I remember my mother's last trip to Istanbul from Los Angeles, shortly after my father's passing. She had made the trip to downsize, pack and transport my grandmother's belongings, settle her business affairs essentially to bring her to the States to live with us. In casual conversation, I remember her mentioning Haig, a handsome man in his late fifties. At this difficult time in my mother's and grandmother's lives, he had unselfishly extended a helping hand to my mother. A flashback of some thirty three years would reveal Haig in a completely different role, this time as an unsuccessful aspirant for my mother's hand in marriage. On this final and most challenging trip of my mother's, instead of holding a grudge against her, Haig had helped her finalize the intricate sale of my grandmother's apartment building. During the five years we lived in Üsküdar, I recall his having married a Turkish woman; I remember it well because she was always accompanied by her standard-sized poodle, which was a somewhat unusual occurrence in Turkey at the time.

In gratitude to Haig's act of kindness, in addition to whatever other compensation they must have agreed on, my mother had gifted him and his wife my grandmother's foot-operated workhorse and by now probably antique, elegant Singer sewing machine. As I recall the bittersweet past, I still can hear my mother's voice explaining to me, "Your grandma's eyes welled up as she reluctantly parted from her dependable friend, the Singer sewing machine." It must have awakened myriad memories for my grandmother, as it probably was one of the last objects of significance for her to leave that room of extraordinary memorabilia.

My mother had also related to me another curious event of the past which I cannot easily forget. When she was engaged to be married to my father, Haig's mother was disappointed with my grandparents' rejection of her son as their future son-in-law. She was so curious to find out what the lucky groom to be looked like, that she had a rather unusual request from my grandmother: "Vartouhi, can you sometime invite me over when your future son-in-law to be will be visiting, so I can meet him!"

My grandparents, just like all the rest of the people who have meant so much to me, are gone now. However, it seems no matter how far away I may have traveled from my origins, even if it is continents away, I will always carry with me the precious memories of my past homes and those of my grandparents' snugly tucked in my heart. They will safely stay there for retrieval when my thoughts travel in their direction. Even now, they provide a special type of continuity connecting my present with my past, awakening special feelings of love and longing.

Our Summer in Yakacik

During the summer of 1951 our family vacationed in Yakacik, a small town situated among the hills, to the southeast of Istanbul. We were vacationing there for a few months during the summer, to give my younger sister Arminé a chance to breathe the dry and refreshing mountain air in an effort to treat her lingering whooping cough. However, this little mountain town offered us a wealth of experience we had not anticipated. Due to its topography, it had beautiful red hills which could be reached by just taking a comfortable fifteen minute stroll from the town center. Called *Ayazma*, this out-of-the-way section of Yakacik contained a natural spring and a primitive run-down café with brown oil-cloth-covered tables, which boasted an exceptional view of the surrounding hills. The proprietor seemed to know his regular customers and there was a shy, timid, and overworked serving girl. Even the smell of the wind was special here because the hills surrounding us were covered with wildflowers and herbs such as sage, lavender, and especially a rose-scented geranium called, *itir* in Turkish. To this day, the fragrance of this special herb brings back fleeting memories of long ago. It takes me back to special hikes with my father on certain weekends, under crystal-clear skies. Yakacik's intense sun and dry mountain air performed its own magic in enhancing the fragrance of the many herbs indigenous to this area. Their dainty blossoms, readily recognizable up and down the hills, would be teeming with colorful butterflies and buzzing bees. Regrettably, at the time the trails were not well-maintained and occasionally became challenging, involving brief spurts of clambering down rocks, making us wish we owned better hiking shoes; however, we did not let this inconvenience stop us from exploring the area. On occasion the additional challenge even imparted an element of suspense to our already adventurous hikes. We would take advantage of a fresh spring we happened to come across to rest and refuel by having a snack, so that we could continue the excitement a little while longer.

Yakacik was also where I learned to appreciate birds, especially swallows. On the occasion of my completion of first grade, I was gifted a book in Armenian about a unique type of swallow and her adventures. With limited material available due to censoring, nature was one of the few remaining "harmless" areas teachers could resort to. I had just learned the beautiful Armenian song about "*Dzidzernag, eem karnan siroon trchnag,*" Swallow, my lovely bird of spring. How privileged I must have felt when to my delight I spotted a pair of swallows actually starting to construct a substantial nest of mud they magically transformed into cement, where one of the exterior walls of the house we rented joined the roof. After the tiny eggs finally hatched, I could hear the birds and would watch eagerly as the youngsters greeted their mother and father with sighs of delight as they fetched worms and insects for them and placed them inside their throats. The mother and father birds did this tirelessly numerous times in one day with such exceptional devotion.

During the summer we were vacationing in Yakacik, Pompon, our faithful cat of many years had her final litter of five adorable kittens. My sister and I would spend hours caring for these kittens and were fascinated with the way they interacted with their environment, played and learned. We had named the kitten which was weaker than the rest, *Jimlondos* for no special reason other than the fact that it sounded funny! We also took pity on this kitten with longer hind legs than usual, because her birth defect was making locomotion challenging for her, impeding her ability to compete for a nipple. In spite of our efforts to augment her diet with store-bought milk delivered with a medicine dropper, one morning we found her unresponsive. We were very sad; however, this also made us realize there were certain problems we did not have solutions for.

After confirming with my mother that *Jimlondos* was no longer living, we embarked upon preparing an appropriate burial site for her. We thought it had to be complete with a marker, a cross and flowers. Although we realized she was only our pet, we wanted closure since we had seen death treated in this manner before. Had we realized how disapproving our Turkish landlord Tevfika

Hanim would be of our plan, we would surely have come up with a more acceptable alternative. In no uncertain terms she told us: "I will not allow the burial of any creature other than myself on my property!" She promptly unearthed our dead kitten, which we had laid to rest in a small shoebox. She scattered her marker, the wooden cross and her beautiful wildflowers we had spent so much time and effort gathering, as if they were all worthless.

Teary-eyed, we realized we had no choice but to comply with her wishes. However later on that day she must have realized that she was only dealing with five and seven-year-old children and that she had overreacted. She later allowed us to bury *Jimlondos* in a remote corner of her backyard with no marker and no cross. This had been a sad but worthwhile learning experience for both of us. We realized that even though memories were very precious, no one wanted constantly to be reminded of death. Even more significant was our realization that since our landlord was a Muslim and we were presently citizens of a Muslim country, we must have overstepped Tevfika Hanim's level of tolerance for our religion.

Yakacik had its own special cuisine, and our local butcher was eager to familiarize us with it. I clearly remember his offer to us one Saturday morning: "If you purchase the tomatoes, several types of green pepper including the thin, hot variety and green onions from the grocer next door and bring them to me, I will do the rest and see to it that you get an unforgettable dinner." To the shish kebab-sized chunks of fresh lamb and fresh vegetables, he added generous amounts of fresh herbs which grew wild in the neighboring hills such as thyme, rosemary, oregano. Then he expertly wrapped all of this securely first in parchment, and then packaged it one more time in a thick, pink, fire-resistant paper, making sure the entire package was leak and oven-proof and indestructible. He then labeled it with our name and instructed us to hand carry it to the town baker to place it in his huge oven, alongside his breads and his trays of thin bagels in the shape of wheels covered with sesame seeds, called *simit*. When it was time to pick up our dinner, it smelled so heavenly that our entire family could not wait to taste this most unique dish of the mountains, called *kağit kebabi,* paper kebab.

Life in Yakacik was such a departure from the city life I experienced in Istanbul with pedestrians, trams, taxis, and cars swarming the streets. Everything was at a slower pace here, with plenty of time for people to socialize in outdoor cafés. I often saw people playing backgammon as well as card games, while they sipped on Turkish coffee served in demitasses, and dark tea served in tulip-shaped, see-through, miniature glasses. The one additional hour of travel each way on the bus between Yakacik and Kadiköy, in addition to the boat ride from Karaköy by way of the Galata Bridge to reach his workplace in Eminönü, meant my father had to travel a total of two additional hours each day in a bus, often on rough roads for his daughter's welfare, to help clear the vestiges of her lingering whooping cough.

On one of his trips to Yakacik that summer, my father had brought along his older brother Dikran as a houseguest to our modest summer rental. After many years, Uncle Dikran had finally been able to satisfy his wife's yearning to see her sister Verjin by arranging a trip for her, accompanied with their daughter Sona to Lyon, France by way of Marseille.

Aunt Verjin's Story

It was during our visit to Istanbul in 2006 that for the first time I found out about the doomed love story of my aunt's sister which was set against the backdrop of the Armenian genocide, nearly a hundred years ago. Having just returned from Historic Armenia, I was describing our paternal grandparents' house in Aksaray to my cousin Sona, when after having kept silent all these years, it must have functioned as that loose thread in an ancient tapestry whose tightly woven threads could tell quite a tale if we only knew how to unravel them. The story of her stunningly beautiful Aunt Verjin, her maternal aunt whose family lived in Kastamonu by the Black Sea, gushed out of her pursed lips:

The young Turkish mayor of nearby Inebolu[i], Ulvi Alacakaptan, had fallen in love with my Aunt Verjin and wanted to marry her. It was 1915, the year of the cruel deportations and massacres premeditated for the demise of the Armenian people.

With the excuse of being in the war zone, the entire Armenian population was being targeted and deported, even from the neutral province of Kastamonu, which did not have a significant Armenian population. Furthermore, it was far removed from both the northern and southern war zones.

Verjin Balian helped her father in his humble clothing store in Kastamonu's covered bazaar. It was here that the young mayor of Inebolu[i], Ulvi Alacakaptan, first met her while he was trying on a number of shirts. She was helpful, caring and in his eyes "simply beautiful." Her angelic voice and beautiful green eyes had created a distinctive impression on him. Deep down in his heart, he was convinced: "It was love at first sight" for him. Although he wanted to ask for her hand in marriage from her parents in the conventional way, he knew he would not stand a chance because he was a Turk and a Muslim.

Right around this time, the political environment in and around Kastamonu had deteriorated markedly by the arrival of Atif Bey as governor. Mayor Ulvi was quite aware that the new governor was inciting animosity in the region towards Armenians. Due to information available to him by virtue of his governmental post, he knew the lives of the Armenians in the region would soon be endangered because of the imminent deportation and massacres that were being planned for them. They would soon be uprooted and sent to march from the Black Sea region, all the way south to the Syrian Desert. Ulvi knew the majority of the deportees would not survive the trip, especially the less resilient among them, namely: the children, the sick, the elderly, and the postpartum. In addition to being harassed along the way, they would soon run out of money and provisions; they would become fatigued and ill.

By now, the triumvirate of Talat, Enver and Jemal Pashas had taken over the Ottoman government and their agent Governor Atif Bey had already ordered the Armenian males of Kastamonu to be separated from the female population with the intention of forming a labor battalion. From what my grandmother had told my sister in bits and pieces, my Grandfather Iskender had already been called upon to become part of this battalion. Soon afterwards, a gendarme ringing my grandmother's doorbell had ordered her

---

i   Inebolu is the port of Kastamonu on the Black Sea.

to leave her home to congregate in the courthouse with the rest of the Armenian females in the Kastamonu province. At that critical moment, she had the insight to trust the care of her six-month old infant, my mother, to her Turkish neighbor, instead of dragging her along and making her miserable. Miraculously, within the next few days the paths of my grandmother and grandfather happened to cross, at which time she was able to inform her husband of the whereabouts of their infant daughter, whom he promptly picked up. [25]

Going back to the Mayor of Inebolu, Ulvi Alacakaptan, he believed that during these pressing times he could help Verjin's family in an effort to win them over. In all probability, he could procure an official document for them, with a governmental stamp, stating:

"The thirty members of the Balian family should be allowed safe passage to Constantinople."

He was further willing to assign two official guards on horseback to accompany their caravan to ensure their safe arrival in Constantinople. He figured this might be the only way he could convince the Balians to change their mind and approve of his marrying their daughter. Deep down, he knew it would also be one of the few ways he could save the lives of Verjin's family members and relatives. However, no one at the time could guess it would also spur a sibling of hers to pursue a dangerous and unexpected mission in the years to come.

When Verjin's parents Hagop and Yester asked her opinion of the mayor, her response was: "Mayor Ulvi seems to be a decent person. My entire family's safe passage to Constantinople matters a lot to me. No matter where I live, I will always remain your loving daughter and will always keep in touch."

After thinking it over, the Balians realized they had a distinct advantage in Ulvi's proposal, compared to the rest of their Armenian neighbors in Kastamonu. After receiving an affirmative response from Verjin, they decided on a scaled down informal wedding which would take place in the mayor's residence in Inebolu. Attendance from her side of the family would be limited to immediate family members only.

Right after the wedding ceremony presided by the imam, the very same evening the Balians joined the rest of their Armenian neighbors in the painful, yet unavoidable task of going over their possessions to make the critical decisions of what to keep and what to sell or simply give away. The next few days were spent displaying their household items for sale so that the Turkish inhabitants of Kastamonu could come by and offer cash for their goods at unusually depressed prices. The cash the Balians hoped to raise in this fashion would be invaluable to them during their long trip to Constantinople, as well as for their survival afterwards, until they had formed a clearer picture in their mind of where they would be settling and how they would be making their living.

The head of each family in the Balian caravan, which consisted of their extended family and totaled thirty in all, bargained for a horse-drawn carriage with a covered top, complete with a coachman for the one way trip to Constantinople. They took with them quilts and pillows, which were especially necessary for the elderly and the children among them. Mayor Ulvi's two trustworthy gendarmes accompanied their caravan on horseback and ensured their safety, a very important service considering the lawlessness of the times. The women took along a number of ready-made foods with them for sustenance, such as the dried soup "tarhana" made of dried curd and flour, which they could easily reconstitute by simply adding hot water, as well as cheese, olives, bread, dried fruits, nuts, and water.

I was pleasantly surprised when Sona mentioned that my mother, who was only six-months old at the time, was also a passenger in one of these carriages and was resting snugly against my grandmother's chest while she was being breast-fed, as the Balian caravan headed west toward Constantinople. This was because Verjin's father Hagop and my maternal grandfather Iskender were first cousins. Before 2006, I had not realized how important a role Aunt Verjin had played in my own family's survival. Without Verjin's sacrifice and Ulvi's help, my then six-month old mother had almost no chance of surviving the deportations and the Armenian Genocide of 1915-1922.

The trip took them five long days. Along the way they made several stops in towns such as today's Bolu, Düzce, Adapazari, Izmit, and Gebze. Some of these were overnight stops in khans, which were traditional resting points for travelers and their horses.

When Verjin's young brother Sarkis was a ten year old boy in Kastamonu, he used to take care of their Turkish neighbor's several sheep, their border collie, rooster, and few chickens, in return for a couple of pennies a week. He did this long enough to realize that only getting an education was going to liberate him and put him in charge of his own destiny. With this in mind, after his family settled in Scutari (Üsküdar) on the Asian shores of Constantinople and he completed Armenian elementary school there, he enrolled in the Armenian Lycee Getronagan, located across the Bosphorus on the European side of the city. It was a famous High School established by Patriarch Nersess Varjabedian, of Constantinople, having opened its doors for the first time for instruction in 1896.

To arrive at Getronagan on time, he had to get up before 6AM each morning; after a rushed breakfast, he had to walk the considerable distance to catch the tram which would deliver him to the Scutari wharf. Here he would get in line to buy his ticket and jump on the ferry to take him across the Bosphorus to Karaköy, where he would have to walk the entire length of the Galata Bridge. At this hour of the morning, he would see peddlers selling "pideh," a type of thin bread baked with a cheese or spicy beef filling. It was not that he did not wish to buy one, since he had at least another 15 minutes of fast-paced walk remaining to reach his destination, but he knew he could not afford it. He then had to walk the lengths of eight additional streets running in the northeast direction, until he reached Getronagan. He was awarded a scholarship at this Armenian Lycee, as long as he maintained a healthy grade point average.

During the summers, Sarkis worked at odd jobs to help raise money for his transportation expenses. He was quite disciplined and conscientious about it all. Ever since he had started attending Getronagan, he had made a habit of setting aside a respectable portion of the modest allowance he received from his father for a cause close to his heart, he called, "Rescue Mission." He had been quite secretive about the purpose of this fund.

Throughout the eight years that his sister Verjin had been living in Inebolu with Ulvi, she had been corresponding regularly with her parents in Scutari. It was through his mother that Sarkis received news of Verjin and of his now seven-year-old niece, Eminé. As a teenager passionate about his heritage, he felt strongly that his sister and her offspring should preserve their Armenian roots.

During the course of casual conversation with his mother, Sarkis found out that within the last week in June of 1924, a mayors' convention was planned in Ankara, to which all the mayors of little towns in the different provinces were expected to attend. His mother had also informed him that Verjin and his niece Eminé were planning to stay behind in Inebolu during this convention, since they had decided Eminé was still too young to travel.

Lately, Sarkis's thoughts had been drifting in the direction of his sister Verjin and his seven year old niece Eminé. He had been single-handedly planning the elaborate details of how he would abduct them to bring them to Constantinople, because he felt that by doing so he would be "rescuing" them. His school year at Getronagan would be completed by the end of the third week in June. What better time to carry out this sensitive and tricky operation than during the mayors' convention in Ankara, when Ulvi would be away from Inebolu for a while!

When his targeted date arrived, Sarkis started on the first leg of his trip. He bought a second-class ticket from the Haydarpasha train station, where he couldn't help but notice its impressive grand clock. As he jumped on the train headed east to Adapazari, nearly a hundred miles away, he was relying exclusively on his "Rescue Mission" funds. The relatively long train ride had given him time for some introspection. He realized that a number of things could go wrong in the execution of his complicated plan at any point during this trip, leaving him wide open to face grave consequences. This thought sent a chill through his body; but by now, he had so much time and money invested in his plan. To turn back at this point would only prove he was a coward; it would damage his pride and confidence in himself irreparably.

Chapter I

Sarkis's trip from Haydarpasha to Adapazari was relatively eventless. When he got off the train at Adapazari as an
inexperienced seventeen-year-old, he realized he had to bargain
with one of the idle carriage drivers in the field that flanked the
train station, something he had never done before. Up until then,
he had never given it much thought to the qualifications he should
be looking for in a trustworthy coachman, either. Luck was on his
side when he took a chance and hired Ali, who reassured him he
knew the way to Inebolu. It took them three six-hour days on bumpy
roads and two nights in khans to reach the hilly and forested Black
Sea coast, which would lead them to Inebolu. His anxiety level
was also pretty high along the way, because he realized he had
to allocate adequate funds for their return trip home, when his
expenditures for shelter and transportation could even run higher.
He had to keep track of all his expenses and make his "Rescue
Mission" money last until they had reached their final destination,
Scutari.

Early on the third day, as Ali led their carriage to the
summit of a thickly-forested hill, Sarkis caught a glimpse of the
dark waters of the Black Sea in the distance and knew they were
approaching Inebolu. He felt a knot in his stomach as he realized
he might also be on the verge of disaster. He could feel his heart
beating faster, as he thought of the next set of difficulties he was
about to face. Following his instructions, Hagop and Yester had
kept Verjin completely oblivious to Sarkis's special trip to Inebolu,
especially involving its underlying purpose.

When Verjin first detected Sarkis from her upstairs bedroom
balcony, after she heard the untimely loud knock at her front door
with a familiar voice calling her name, it took her a minute to
overcome the initial shock before she could make it downstairs
to open it for him. Brother and sister, who had been living apart
for nearly eight years, hugged each other with tears in their eyes.
Sarkis was a ten-year-old little boy when Verjin had last seen
him in Kastamonu; now he was a tall and handsome young lad.
Hearing the excitement downstairs by the front door, Eminé soon
joined them. As Verjin introduced Eminé to Sarkis, he could detect
a look of astonishment in her eyes as a gamut of feelings ranging
from fear and suspense to sadness went through Verjin's.

Eight years ago her parents had tried to keep it a secret from Verjin, but she had overheard Sarkis's heated objections to her marrying Ulvi. She could easily guess why her young brother had gone through this lengthy and complicated trip to arrive in Inebolu at her doorstep, while Ulvi was out of town. As the coachman Ali was taking his time feeding and watering his horse and grabbing a bite himself, Sarkis had the difficult task of explaining to an emotional Verjin what his plans for her and Eminé were. Verjin's happiness of being reunited with her brother after a long separation had now suddenly given way to despair... It was clear to her that she was not going to have much of a say in the matter. Sarkis kept repeating to Verjin in a solemn voice why his taking her and Eminé with him to Istanbul and away from Inebolu would be in the best interest of their entire family. At one point when Verjin showed signs of rebellion, Sarkis raised his voice and said:

"Verjin, I expect you to cooperate, because I do not want to hurt you by doing something extreme."

Now the time had come for him to turn his attention to his cute seven-year-old niece. He realized he did not have a lot of time to win her over. Bending down to her eye level, he whispered in her ear in Turkish the question:

"Emine, benimle saklambac oynar misin?"meaning, how would you like to play hide and seek with me?"

For the next ten minutes Eminé's happy sighs of surprise could be heard throughout the house. After the game ended and she left for her bedroom to play with her dolls, Verjin finally had the courage to pour her heart out to Sarkis. With tears in her eyes, she told him that Ulvi had been a good man and that both she and Eminé would miss him terribly. She ended her conversation with two thought-provoking questions:

"Isn't it enough that Ulvi saved our entire extended family of thirty from a certain death and helped transport them safely to Constantinople? How can I now turn around and betray him?"

It was not going to be easy to convince Verjin. However, witnessing Sarkis's personal and financial sacrifice for this monumental undertaking as a teen-ager, and additionally noting his serious, almost threatening tone of voice, she could tell he meant business and that he would not hesitate to go to unpleasant extremes if he did not have his way...

For the rest of the morning, brother and sister carefully avoided any serious interaction, especially when Sarkis realized he needed to display an air of civility rather than one of confrontation, while he and Verjin were accompanied by Eminé. With Verjin's help, they packed the bare necessities of clothing for both of them, as well as a large comforter. Sarkis placed Eminé's worn out security blanket she had named "Felek," meaning Destiny in Turkish, and two pillows in a large sturdy bag. In all this hurry, Verjin made sure she had grabbed a recent family photograph depicting the three of them during happier and less complicated times. They packed some food for everyone, especially for Eminé, to last throughout their trip until their arrival in Scutari. This included the "chöreg", the sweet leavened bread with eggs, Eminé adored.

When they were finally ready to leave picturesque Inebolu on the shores of the Black Sea, the only town seven-year-old Eminé had known until then, she started crying and kept asking Verjin the question:

"Is my "Baba" (father) going to join us at the end of our trip?" This and similar penetrating questions further intensified the misery of an already emotionally drained Verjin. It was a good thing she managed to hide most of her emotional turmoil from Eminé. At the end, the rag doll Grandma Yester had sewn for her and sent along with Sarkis from Scutari seemed to do the trick. She was temporarily preoccupied with it and quite excited about the idea of riding in a horse-drawn carriage, right next to her mother.

With impeccable planning and organization in squirreling away his allowance, quite rare for a seventeen year old, and blessed by good fortune, Sarkis had succeeded in abducting his sister Verjin and his seven-year-old niece Eminé from their home in Inebolu. After a long and complicated journey, which involved two overnight stops in khans on the way, Sarkis compensated the coachman Ali for his services and bought their return train tickets at the Adapazari station. The scenic journey on the train from Adapazari to Haydarpasha proved to be the most exciting part of their trip for Eminé, since it was the first time she was experiencing a train ride. As long as her mother was by her side and her rag doll was resting on her lap, she did not complain. By the time they disembarked the train at the Haydarpasha Central Station, Sarkis had become aware that most of his "Rescue Mission" money had been exhausted, although they had not yet reached Scutari. He had to talk his sister and Eminé into covering the distance from the Haydarpasha train station to the Kadiköy tram station on foot and had to help his niece at times by giving her a ride on his shoulders, so that they would have enough tram money left to make it to Scutari. No one looked especially happy as they got off the tram at Scutari, although young Sarkis had somehow managed to accomplish the impossible.

As could be expected, throughout the trip Verjin looked withdrawn, revealing her inner desperation and did not communicate much except with Eminé. Once she arrived in Scutari and was reunited with her parents, she hugged them with longing and tears in her eyes. For a very long time, she seemed to be barely holding on. She continued to have mixed feelings about the abduction, because it had suddenly and permanently separated her and Eminé from Ulvi. Just thinking about him would often bring tears to her eyes, although she would do everything within her power to hide them from Eminé. The separation had further made her realize how much she loved Ulvi and that there might never be anyone else she would want to share her life with in the future...

Because they had left Inebolu in such a hurry, there had not been time to even write a short note to Ulvi, expressing how she felt towards him, to thank him, bid him farewell and hope that one day he could find the compassion in his heart to forgive her. In fact Sarkis had plainly cautioned her against doing any of that. He had said that Ulvi could easily have them traced through the law enforcement authorities, sending him straight to jail, and place their parents in a state of endless mourning. He added that in their old age that was not what they needed. "It would be a tragedy for our entire family," was how he expressed it.

For a very long time, Verjin harbored guilt feelings every time her thoughts went Ulvi's way. It was a lot of change and adjustment for Eminé, as well. After arriving in Scutari in late June of 1924 and experiencing a rather shocking change in her immediate environment, Eminé started attending the American Academy for Girls that fall as one of the first youngsters enrolled in their newly-established kindergarten class.

To my surprise, Sona said they had used my mother's birth certificate to register Eminé at the American school in Scutari. This American school was the same one my mother would be attending and the same one I would later attend.

Consistent with his meticulous attention to detail, Sarkis had exercised the last bit of precaution by instructing Verjin not to give the school Eminé's legal last name. Furthermore, the Balians had changed her first name from the Turkish Eminé to a far more Armenian sounding Yevkiné, in an effort to also avoid difficult explanations she would be faced with at school among her circle of friends and their parents...

Ulvi must have been a true gentleman not to retaliate, since he was the rightful husband of Verjin and the genuine father of seven-year-old Eminé. It must have broken his heart when on his return from his Mayors' Convention in Ankara, Verjin and Eminé were nowhere to be found.

The story might have ended there, but it didn't. One year later in 1925, when Sarkis graduated from the Armenian high school Getronagan and earned his first 500 liras, he considered it a top priority to make the necessary arrangements to transport Verjin and his niece Yevkiné out of Istanbul to Saint Etienne, France, 40 miles southwest of Lyon. Just as Sarkis had planned, his abduction of Verjin and Eminé had safeguarded their Armenian ethnicity. However Verjin never stopped missing Ulvi. It seems he had eternally conquered her heart while they had lived together in harmony in the picturesque little seaport of Kastamonu, by the name of Inebolu, for over eight years.

As Verjin started living in Istanbul, she became increasingly aware that within the Armenian community her reputation was ruined, even though she had legitimately married Ulvi, so she could save the lives of her relatives. Unfortunately, a happy future was not to be in the cards for strikingly beautiful Verjin. She chose to remain single, preferring to live with her memories of Ulvi, rather than marrying someone she did not care for.

As the years progressed, Verjin gradually started to feel contented that Yevkiné was getting the love and caring of her grandparents, while also becoming familiar with the Armenian language and customs, making her transition to the Armenian community in France smoother for her. Sarkis was hoping that all of this would later help Yevkiné secure a safe and comfortable future by facilitating her meeting and marrying an Armenian New Yorker in Lyon, France. Sadly, this would also mean that her contact with her mother Verjin would remain minimal. Travel between continents was lengthy, difficult, and also costly, because on each occasion Verjin had to take more than a month off of work. Even though Yevkiné had offered to help her mother financially, by the time Verjin returned home to the competitive marketplace of Saint Etienne, she realized other merchants would often have taken over her territory. Furthermore, Yevkiné's time would soon be occupied with the demands of her own husband and children. Therefore, Verjin mostly relied on painfully slow correspondence across the Atlantic for news from Yevkiné and she could not always convey in her letters everything she wanted to express to her.

Verjin's communication with her older sister, my Aunt Arousiag in Istanbul, was not as frequent as she would have liked, either. In 1950 she had written to Arousiag alluding to medical problems, but she had not once mentioned cancer. Sadly, it was when the two sisters finally managed to get together in 1951 in Saint Etienne, that my Aunt Arousiag discovered Verjin was suffering from an aggressive form of breast cancer with metastasis.

My cousin Sona, who had accompanied her mother to Saint Etienne in 1951, had the following to say about her encounter with her Aunt Verjin:

"It is too painful for me to think back about our trip to France with my mother to visit Aunt Verjin. I almost could not recognize the beautiful face I always remembered from her previous photographs. She was only skin and bones... Nevertheless her mind was clear and she wanted my mother to remember the days they had spent together in Kastamonu."

Both sisters' thoughts wandered back to a time when they were in their teens and living in the plains south of the Black Sea, when a nice brisk walk would take them to the most distinctive feature of Kastamonu, the historic fort located on one of its highest hills. Arousiag now took the initiative to remind Verjin of their very own secret pathway with its diverse vistas they so enjoyed taking on their way to and from the fort. She also reminded Verjin of the pine-clad rugged mountain ranges which were visible to the north and which extended all the way to the Black Sea.

In spite of the discomfort she was in, Verjin nodded approvingly, not once taking her eyes off of her sister. A slight smile seemed to materialize on her face. Amid tears, the two sisters hugged each other with thankfulness in their hearts to be able to have had this time together, realizing that it was probably going to be their last...

I only wish that Aunt Arousiag had the foresight then to take Verjin's misfortune as a premonition to get a thorough medical checkup herself. Fast forward eleven years, one day while kicking his soccer ball, her five year old grandson Ara had accidentally bruised her right breast with his ball. The painful hematoma had not disappeared in the expected length of time. A medical examination, soon confirmed by x-rays, would prove it to be an adenocarcinoma with metastasis. Unluckily, in another year it would be my mother who would be in Aunt Arousiag's previous role, this time helping her sister in law. Sitting next to her hospital bed, she would reminisce a time sixty years ago when my mother must have been a six-month old baby in her mother's arms, when Aunt Arousiag's beautiful sister Verjin had saved her and their entire family's lives by marrying Mayor Ulvi Alacakaptan of Inebolu...

(Endnotes)

1   Pamuk, Orhan, I*stanbul*. New York: Random House, 2004(translated by Maureen Freely), p.173.

2   Vryonis Jr., Speros, *The Mechanism of Catastrophe*. New York: Greekworks.com, 2005, p.108.

3   Personal Communication, Bedrosian, Aida, 2008.

4   Vryonis Jr., Speros, *The Mechanism of Catastrophe*. New York: Greekworks.com, 2005, p. 95.

5   Personal Communication, Dalian, Arpie, 2009.

6   Personal Communication, Dalian, Arpie, 2009.

7   Personal Communication, Dalian, Arpie, 2009.

8   Akcam, Taner (Armenian Genocide Studies, Clark University) 'Researching Turkish History books online', Armenian *Weekly online,* Dec.4, 2014.

9   Hovannisian, Richard, *Armenian Sebastia /Sivas and Lesser Armenia*. Costa Mesa: Mazda, 2004, p.446.

10   Linder, Fay, *The History of Üsküdar American Academy 1876-1996*.Istanbul: SEV Printing Publishing, 2000, p.33.

11   Shamtanchian, Mikayel, *Genocide Library Volume 2 The Fatal Night*. Studio City: H&K Publications, 2007, pp.1-17.

12   Personal Communication, Garboushian, Arminé, 2016.

13   Ökte, Faik, *The Tragedy of the Turkish Capital Tax*. London: Croom Helm Publishers, 1987 (translated by Geoffrey Cox) p. xvii.

14   Nigogosian, Aram, 'The Tragedy of the Turkish Capital Tax,' *Armenian Review* 40 (Winter 1987): 142.

15   Ökte, Faik, *The Tragedy of the Turkish Capital Tax*. London: Croom Helm Publishers, 1987 (translated by Geoffey Cox) p.35.

16   Ibid p.70

17   Ibid p.76

18   Ibid p.91

19   Ibid p.93

20   Ibid p.94

21   Clark, Edward C., 'The Turkish Varlik Vergisi Reconsidered,' *Middle Eastern Studies*, 8 May1972:213.

22   Marchese, Ronald, "*Splendor and Pageantry: Textile*

Treasures from the Armenian Orthodox Churches of Istanbul," Cal State University, Northridge Lecture @ Ararat Eskijian Museum, Jan 31, 2015.

23   Balakian, Grigoris, *Armenian Golgotha*. New York: Alfred A. Knopf, 2009, (translated by Peter Balakian & Aris Sevag), p.135.

24   Ibid p.146

25   Personal Communication, Garboushian, Arminé, 2016.

Life in ISTANBUL

CHAPTER II
LIFE IN ISTANBUL

My Father's Unwillingness to Plan Vacations

Summers seemed to last forever when I was attending *Aramyan Ounchiyan* Armenian elementary school in Kadiköy. There were long stretches with no special activities planned. I realize now that most Armenian parents in Istanbul faced enormous pressures and anxieties, and planning interesting, child-pleasing activities was not their top priority. To us children, oblivious to history and politics unless they grew turbulent, life seemed to be all about fun and games, with special holidays scattered in between.

As I grew older and wiser, I realized that one lasting legacy of the deportation years on my father had been to steer him clear of making plans for his family's non-essential activities such as vacations. He was most concerned with providing for his children, ensuring their safety, and making sure they received a first rate education.

My father was also reluctant to take us on vacations because the unwarranted Capital Tax of 1942 must have completely depleted our financial reserves. I must have been halfway through elementary school, by the time my parents could finally restart setting aside some money for their children's education and our family's future. I have to admit that at the time I was attending the American Academy for Girls in Üsküdar, I could not comprehend why my parents would have more important concerns in the back of their minds than traveling to scenic and historic sites in Turkey, like many of my affluent Turkish classmates often did.

As I matured and became more aware of the political unrest in Turkey, I recognized that staying within our means was more prudent. Once I observed firsthand how helpless minorities such as Armenians were during the country's periods of upheaval, I realized why my parents would avoid visibility at any cost.

My Father's Extraordinary Caution

Looking back, I also realize that my father was a truly honest man and, in his profession, "a helper of the little guy." "The get rich quick" philosophy was never in his DNA. It gave him a sense of satisfaction to assist his fellow Armenians as they approached him for help before they left Turkey for safer havens. He earned a small commission for this work, but shouldered a disproportionate amount of the risk with each one of their moves.

Throughout the seventeen years I lived and observed my father in Istanbul, I concluded that he was a person of perennial vigilance. This characteristic served as a valuable trait for him while we lived in Turkey. It must have been a legacy left from the deportation years when he guided his family's oxcart as its fourteen-year-old driver up and down the treacherous roads in the Taurus Mountains, crossing the Bozanti pass to Adana, close to the Mediterranean Coast. His adventurous nature, as well as his exemption from the draft, because he was not quite fifteen, had made him perhaps prematurely the right candidate among the extended family members for this demanding task. Throughout this ordeal, my uncle Dikran who was seven years older, hid in an inconspicuous corner of the oxcart under some blankets and sheets. I had often heard my grandmother tell me that my father Ardashes loved adventure from the time he was very young. It seems, out of sheer necessity, he had to learn to deal with stress very early in life without caving in…

His own father was a casualty of the Syrian Desert and died from the typhus he had contracted from the lice in the filthy freight train that had earlier hauled the sick soldiers from Damascus to Aleppo, before transporting his extended family to Katma, the center of the exiled population in early 1917. It was located six hours north of the city of Aleppo in the southern Syrian Desert, as specified by the Triumvirate of Talat, Enver and Jemal Pashas. My grandparents had no choice but to settle in mud huts in the lowly village of Remté, which met the government's guidelines for Armenian deportees because it was at least two hours away from the nearest railroad station located in Daraa. However, the inhabitants of Remté and environs had extremely low sanitary standards. Having no organized way of disposing of their bodily wastes, they were rendering the drinking water unsafe for the inhabitants of the entire village. Although my father and his extended family escaped the killing fields and were not massacred, as deportees traveling east to Deir-el Zor were, they lost one third of their immediate and extended family members to typhus fever and dysentery epidemics. By this time their family's savings had been exhausted, and my father had no choice but to become the family's breadwinner. Despite his lack of any formal education beyond first grade in a one classroom schoolhouse in central Anatolia, he quickly learned how to read, write, and figure out the arithmetic necessary for the business he embarked on: *money-changing.*

After their lengthy and painful saga in the Syrian Desert, some of the surviving members of my father's side of the family settled in Constantinople (Istanbul) because it was a cosmopolitan city and therefore considered relatively safe. My father also thought this city would offer educational opportunities for the future generation, which he himself had been deprived of in Aksaray. He would also be able to make a living there without struggling to learn a new language.

Over the years, my father became progressively more knowledgeable in his profession of money-changing. However, the anxiety of the deportation years never quite left him. Until he finally retired and left Turkey for the United States in 1967, he could never escape from being under its burden.

During the years we lived in Turkey, my father felt it was his responsibility to safeguard his family from the consequences of unexpected political mishaps such as the "*Capital Tax.*" These dreaded decrees by the Turkish government must have produced the same aftereffect on him, as well as on other heads of Armenian families, as a "post-traumatic stress disorder." Just thinking on this subject, I can recall his calm and collected voice, responding to my and my sister's request to plan a sight-seeing vacation, with the statement: "Let's see if we will wake up alive and well tomorrow morning!" The only difference is that it makes perfect sense to me now, whereas it did not then…

Swimming in Fenerbahché

Left to her own resources, my mother tried to introduce excitement into our summer days in the best way she could. *Fenerbahché* was a beach on the Sea of Marmara southeast of Kadiköy where she would take us on certain warm and sunny summer mornings when she felt especially energetic. After hopping on the tram near the Kadiköy ferry station, it would take us 45 minutes to arrive there.

Once we reached the beach resort with its many cabanas, my mother would buy a ticket to enter the complex and was given the key to a specific cubicle. We were not poor; however, because my father's refrain: "We do not know what tomorrow might bring," dominated our lives, our cubicle would be past the prettier section of the beach with its spacious cabanas. We would instead head towards the section of the beach where the cubicles formed a large wooden square measuring forty feet on each side, and stood above water which was at least three feet deep. We would descend the wooden stairs to get into the water, and head from the circumference of the rectangular area either toward the Sea of Marmara or the sandy beach. I had considerable anxiety descending this staircase, and would cling tight to the banisters until my mother was ready to accompany me. She had frequently demonstrated the motions I had to implement to be able to swim, but I was too scared to do it on my own.

Struggling Not to Drown

On one of these swimming excursions, I remember having had quite a scare. After that incident, which haunted me for a number of years, it took me a while to regain my confidence and be willing to learn to swim again. As usual, my mother with her infinite enthusiasm would want to introduce my sister and me to all sorts of new experiences. But this time she had overestimated my ability to learn to swim from just a few simple demonstrations. Self-consciousness on my part did not help either. The rectangular area in *Fenerbahché*, which resembled a large swimming pool, was crowded with my peers. Although I did not know any of them, I still strived to look respectable in their eyes. As I look back at our trips to *Fenerbahché*, I still have flashbacks to that particular day, when I struggled simply to breathe and stand up in the three feet deep water. In my attempts, I kept seeing what appeared to me the giant feet of others in the water, none of which I could reach to ask for their assistance so I could resume an upright position. When I finally managed to stand up on my two feet and was able to make it to one of the wooden staircases, I took a deep breath. The next thing I remember is my mother's voice; "It seems you are starting to learn to swim!" In response, I thought it was best for me to just keep quiet… However, at least for some time, I was no longer enthusiastic about going to *Fenerbahché*.

Swimming pools in the 1950s were very rare in Istanbul because of the freezing temperatures during the winter months and the huge expense their maintenance required. The next time I would attempt swimming again was at least six years later in a summer camp in *Caddebostan*, two miles southeast of *Fenerbahché*. There was a raft at some distance from the camp where many of my fellow campers were swimming to; they were resting there and then swimming back to the shore with a sense of accomplishment on their faces. It looked as if they were having so much fun. I had to overcome my fear of swimming by putting to work what my mother had been demonstrating for me all along. Lo and behold, it worked! I did not have the best form, but I had managed to reach the raft in the distance. I rested there for a while and soon was able to swim back to the camp, demonstrating a far greater level of confidence than ever before.

Unexpected Visitors at Camp

I was thirteen when my mother had signed me up for the American girls' camp in *Caddebostan*. It was my first experience away from home for an entire week. I was not convinced everything about my camping experience was worthwhile; however, it made me realize I had taken for granted many things in life, such as the love and caring of my parents. Other than encouraging me to swim, camp helped me become more independent. I still remember a few of the campfire songs I learned there, which always prompted me to visualize that charming city, Istanbul, which I had called home for my first seventeen years.

In all honesty, my most vivid memory of the *Caddebostan* camp was the Sunday afternoon when I inadvertently detected my parents by the chain linked-fence separating our camp from the summer villa next door, which exuded plenty of old world charm. The academic year that had just ended had been an unhappy one for me because throughout the year my unfair geometry teacher Nuriye Hanim had downgraded me on virtually every exam.

In spite of the dismal grade Nuriye Hanim thought I deserved in geometry, I must have managed to do well in everything else. My parents must have been aware of my gradually eroding self-confidence in math. They had received my report card at home and they could not wait to give me the good news, although they were fully aware that visiting the camp while it was in session was strictly forbidden.

I had realized early on that my father's occupation as a money-changer demanded a high level of confidentiality. I did not know in what context my father had gotten to know the inhabitants of the stately seaside villa adjoining our camp in *Caddebostan*. Neither did I know what random act of kindness on his part had prompted the owners of the villa to allow my father, accompanied by my mother to enter their spacious grounds, which seemed to have ample frontage to the Sea of Marmara. Nevertheless, my father's sly smile that afternoon had spoken volumes to me. Somehow quite unexpectedly, both my parents and I had emerged enriched and contented for different reasons from this otherwise "forbidden" experience on that summer day on the northeastern shores of the Sea of Marmara.

My First Year at Üsküdar American Academy for Girls

It was in 1955 when my academic career started at *Üsküdar Amerikan Kız Lisesi*. I know that no other school could have so thoroughly taught a new language to an eleven-year-old, while also making it engaging and fun.

It had been about five months into the school year when Miss Lillian Brown, an elderly retired teacher, approached me at school and asked if she could accompany me on my return trip from school to visit my home the next day. Her intent may have been to discover how life was progressing for a minority Christian family in the aftermath of the Cyprus Crisis of 6-7 September of 1955, since I was one of the very few new Christian students attending the school that year. "I am sure it would be fine with my mother and we would be happy to have you; but you would need to walk some distance and be willing to ride the tram with me from Bağlarbashi to Kadiköy. I also have to warn you that you will have to climb four flights of stairs once we get to my house," I informed her.

My warning did not change her mind. Miss Lillian Brown was quite enthusiastic and energetic for her age. She took the walk and the four flights of stairs in our neat but quite ordinary house as a welcome challenge. Other than the tea accompanied with pastries, feta, and *kasher*, a hard cheese of the Balkans, my mother, true to her character, had taken the occasion to try something she had just learned to prepare on Miss Brown. It was mini open faced goat cheese and pistachio sandwiches, a delicacy I later found out the mighty Ritz Carlton had a habit of offering its well-heeled guests at teatime. Unfortunately it did not pass muster with Miss Brown, who might have had her own sanitary concerns in its preparation.

My mother and Miss Brown discussed political and religious topics in general terms, but neither party seemed willing to tackle any core issues. Before dark, I walked Miss Brown back to where she could pick up her tram in Kadiköy. This was the first and last time any event of this nature took place during my career as a student at the American Academy for Girls in Üsküdar.

Throughout the year, I enthusiastically attended my classes. For the first year, I had a classroom in a secluded corner of the campus. It was akin to running into a quaint but hidden guesthouse in a lush, secret garden by pure chance, except that it had enough capacity for twenty-five students! I was also privileged to have some of the same excellent faculty who taught the rest of the school. I felt that arriving at this secret garden on the school's campus every day for an entire year, to study a language which would be instrumental for my progress, was a pleasure and never a chore.

My Encounter with Saadet Timur

During my first year at the American school, Saadet Timur was my Turkish literature teacher. To my dismay, she would at times make fun of my last name *"Lafciyan"* saying, "Someone among your ancestors must have never stopped talking!" This was because *"lafci"* in Turkish meant "person of words." I knew the real reason why, two generations ago an ancestor of mine was given this family name and, what's more, I was proud of it; but I did not dare confront my Turkish teacher with this viewpoint. My paternal great-great grandfather Abraham had always been very precise in his selection of words. His neighbors in Talas, in central Anatolia, had recognized his skill and enjoyed his company because his few words always carried a lot of weight. They would often be thought-provoking and entertaining at the same time. It was said that someone amongst the townsfolk would often propose, "Let's go visit *Lafci*; we will have a worthwhile conversation and a good time with him." In other words, my ancestor possessed the exact opposite trait Saadet Timur accused him of. But I was an Armenian, a Christian minority living in Turkey, a Muslim country; contradicting my teacher could cost me. She had to come to the realization out of her own accord, if she chose to do so.

It would be four years later when I was in 9th grade, when my Turkish literature teacher Saadet Timur would reevaluate her previous hasty judgment of my great-great grandfather Abraham. I had worked hard during the previous semester and had managed to get good grades in all my classes with the exception of her Turkish Literature class. While traversing the hallway which connected the old administration building to the newer classrooms, she must have been surprised to see my name among the students who had made it to the honor roll; therefore, as soon as she entered our classroom, she asked me to step forward for a recitation. We had been studying the old Turkish literature called *"Divan Edebiyati,"* which incorporated extensive vocabulary from the Arabic and Persian languages. It was poetic and verbose. However, to interpret it, one had to find its hidden meaning by translating its metaphors and similes. I had previously looked them up and penciled them in my book. I had not yet had a chance to erase them because few days back she had asked me to recite on a different subject. I had not anticipated to be called upon again so soon. Before I had a chance to ask her to exchange my book with her unmarked copy, I found myself in the process of answering her questions to her satisfaction. I did not wish to break the positive rapport I had established with her for a change. From that day on, Saadet Timur treated me with more respect.

We had to write essays in her class on certain classical plays we had studied and later seen performed on stage. I knew I had a few classmates whose parents were university professors. This type of an assignment was a breeze for them because their parents would help them by suggesting original ideas and later embellish their scripts until they looked polished.

I did not know at the time, but the truth was that my father was denied formal schooling because a locust outbreak had forced his grandparents to move west to Aksaray from more cultured Talas, where further educational facilities were available. However, when I looked back and compared my situation with my Armenian classmates who had graduated with me from *Aramyan Ounchian* elementary school, I knew lady luck had smiled upon me. I had somehow managed to enroll in this select American school, which I owed in large part to my mother. In addition to knowing English, she also happened to have a practical approach to math, as she had studied through the 10th grade at the same American school I was now attending. She had taught me the concept of proportions at a relatively young age and in such a way that I could figure out the right answer to the problem no matter how sneaky the presentation was. Still, Turkish Literature was not her area of expertise. Therefore, in this area I was basically on my own. Even so, as unwanted minorities in a frequently intolerant country, my parents had learned a few valuable lessons. They had learned never to give up! I grew up observing them practice this principle. Both of my parents always encouraged me and my sister to try, in spite of any shortcomings we might have had. During one of these discouraging episodes, after I had a heart-to-heart conversation with my father, I felt emboldened. I started thinking that I could probably do it on my own; I should go ahead and try, and never give up. I have to admit I did not like the fact that help was unavailable to me in these specialized areas. Although I often had to try hard without a great deal of immediate success, these academic challenges ultimately helped me persevere. In the years that followed, they helped me become a more confident and self-sufficient person.

Graduating Class Pictures in the Hallway

During my first two years at *Üsküdar Amerikan Kiz Lisesi,* I especially enjoyed traversing the long and narrow corridor which faced the school's extensive gardens and connected its older administration headquarters with its more recently constructed classrooms. This timeworn corridor had a special allure for me because as I walked along it, a compacted history of the school from its earliest days would unfold in front of my eyes, depicted by the class graduation pictures hanging on its walls. These were arranged in perfect chronological order starting with the late 1920s all the way to the early 1950s. The young graduates all looked beautiful, and enthusiastic, wearing elegant long gowns of their choosing, enhanced with hairstyles reflective of the times. A flashback to the graduating class pictures makes me realize that almost all of the young ladies looked oblivious to the complications life would shortly have in store for them. This type of class picture, where one could detect the essence and the fashion of the times, came to an end in 1952 when an abrupt transition was made to class pictures depicting the graduates in caps and gowns.

During my first two years at the school when these graduation pictures were still being displayed, I would create all sorts of excuses so I could pass through this special hallway. I had already identified my cousin Sona who had continued to live in

Istanbul and her cousin Arshaluys, who had moved to Marseille, France in the 1930s, and had married a French Armenian there.

Commemorating Atatürk

Semiha Hanim was my geography teacher in 6th grade. She had graduated in 1926 from the senior-high section of the very same school. After completing her education further, in 1943 she had qualified to be a geography teacher at her alma mater. Three years later, the school Principal Miss Martin had elevated her to the position of vice-principal.

Every year on November 10th, we had a custom of honoring the anniversary of the passing of Mustafa Kemal Atatürk, Turkey's greatest hero, by gathering in our spacious auditorium where representatives of grades six through eleven would recite poetry, read essays, and put on short plays depicting his life and times. Although I was able to recite poetry with genuine emotion, I thought I had a number of Turkish classmates in 6th grade that could do a far better job in reciting a poem dedicated to him. After all, Atatürk was their greatest idol. Being part of an Armenian minority did not usually favor me for sought after positions; however, Semiha Hanim's firm conviction that I should be the one to recite this poem in remembrance of Atatürk, had initially surprised and later raised a number of questions in my mind. So far the only history I had studied had been biased and it had been in Turkish. Based on it, Armenians were not even part of world history during the Atatürk years, since there was no mention of them in any of my Turkish history books.

There were times when I could not help but wonder if all of Mustafa Kemal Atatürk's decisions and moves during times of war and peace were as fair and honorable as I had been led to believe. Now I had to recite in Turkish the poem which included the lines:

It was the 10th of November;
The year was 1938.
As the sun was rising
In the horizon,

Early, on this special Thursday morning,
Our savior had approached the end of his mortal journey.
It was the destiny of our redeemer
On this day
To travel the road that was to lead him to our Lord.
In times of war
And in times of peace,
His accomplishments were
Nothing short of spectacular,
The hills would come alive
With a special sound of music
When he exclaimed:
"How lucky I am to be a Turk!"
Every human being ought to shed tears
And mourn the death of Atatürk.

Initially I was proud to be the one reciting this poem in front of a student body in excess of 500 students, accompanied by quite a few teachers. I was sure most of my Turkish classmates in 6th grade would have given anything to be in my shoes. Right as I was getting ready to recite it, suddenly all sorts of thoughts kept racing through my head. I could not help but wonder if this "honor" bestowed upon me was in reality a double-edged sword. I had started questioning whether all the praise for Mustafa Kemal Atatürk was well-deserved. I also wondered if what I would be reciting about the mighty leader was "nothing but the truth." Was he really as honorable a human being as all of Turkey claimed him to be?

Past History Comes to Life for Me on this Day

I had heard from my mother, a former student of the same American high school, that my teacher Semiha Malatyalioğlu was one of the first Turkish graduates of the same school at a time when the student body was predominantly Armenian. She had hailed from Malatya, which I later found out was a city that served as a center for transit for Armenian deportees arriving from Sivas. Their final destination was the arid Syrian Desert. The Armenians who had remained in Malatya after 1915 were threatened in several ways. Arshag Alboyaciyan refers to these attacks in his book *Badmutiwn Malatio Hayots* (Stories of Malatya Armenians):

In 1924 Armenians were leaving Malatya in massive numbers since a band of brigands made up of 15 individuals would engage in marauding activity every night to a different Armenian's house demanding gold, silver, and cash from the residents, beating them almost to death until they complied. This organization terrorizing them and ruining the tranquility of their neighborhood was: *Ateshoğlu Yildirim.* The first house they trampled was that of J. Keole-Tavitians. After they had beaten Master Garabed, they pocketed 50 Ottoman gold pieces and left. They carried on in this manner for an entire month. During one of these raids they affixed a declaration on the main gate of their mother church ordering them to clear the area in five days, saying: "Your leaving this area will be a good thing; otherwise *Ateshoğlu Yildirim* will burn you all."[1]

Armenians understood that the organization's aim was to intimidate them into leaving Malatya so Turks could take over their properties. Under these dreadful circumstances, guided by the leadership of their priest, D. Sdepan, on November 9, 1923 [right after Mustafa Kemal had established the Turkish Republic], the 35 Armenians representing the Malatya Armenians met and decided to forward a telegram to Mustafa Kemal, asking for his assistance and for some reassurance for their security and for the right to live in their houses. They stated that if their citizenship was not recognized and they were required to leave, that they should be informed officially and not by the raiding of their homes.[2] Their request remained unanswered; the signatories as well as Father D. Sdepan were asked to leave the country and the 35 families had to follow suit. Over the following months, Armenians continued to leave Malatya either for Syria or for Constantinople.

Semiha Malatyalioğlu must have been living in Malatya with her parents when the above somber events were taking place. I wondered what her personal feelings were on this matter. I questioned whether attending the American Academy for Girls in Scutari at the time with so many Armenian students and being taught by so many devoted Armenian teachers had perhaps predisposed her to empathize with them. On many occasions she must have observed their pain and disappointments and on a few rare occasions, their joy. Did she perhaps feel there was a bond between her and me, as a minority, although many years separated our experiences? Or did she want me to recite the poem, knowing full well what pain, misery, and irreparable loss of lives the Atatürk years had brought to the few Armenians who had somehow miraculously survived the Armenian Genocide of 1915-1922?

Prior to this occasion, I could not recall a time when I had so much difficulty in memorizing a poem as on that day of November 10, 1956, when I was simply unable to commit to memory this relatively simple poem Semiha Hanim had assigned to me to recite. I finally had to read it, although I tried hard not to make it obvious.

The souls of my ancestors who had been attacked and murdered by Turkish guerillas in the town of Marash late in January of 1920, many of whom had been burned alive while seeking refuge in their schools and churches elsewhere in Anatolia, others who had perished through exposure in the area's snowbound mountains while trying to escape,[3] were mysteriously guiding me. They were insisting that I read the impartial history. Another mysterious voice was asking me to question the tragic fire of Smyrna (Izmir). How could it have been pure chance that it had started in the heart of the Armenian quarter?[4] However, what was even more inexcusable and about which I would find out some fifty years later, was that in 1936 Atatürk had given orders to his adopted daughter, Sabiha Gökcen, an orphan of Armenian heritage, who had been trained as the first female airplane pilot of Turkey, to bomb Dersim (Tunceli). This mountainous region of eastern Anatolia west of Erzincan was the only province in Turkey with an Alevi majority. Armenians in this area had established good relations with the Alevi Kurds who had helped them avoid the deportation, enabling them to survive the Armenian Genocide of 1915. Ironically, Atatürk's ordering the bombing of Dersim and blowing into pieces its Kurdish population, many of whom were of Armenian ancestry, by his adopted daughter of Armenian heritage, demonstrated his ultimate lack of empathy for one's roots.

It is no wonder that in a most covert manner, just before I was to get on stage to recite the poem in Atatürk's honor, my ancestors were reminding me to pause and question the historical facts to discover the real truth.

A Two-faced Mustafa Kemal

Looking back to around 1920, it was apparent that a "two faced" approach was evident in policies Atatürk had implemented towards Armenia: High on his list of priorities was to please the world powers by touting he was concerned for the security of Turkey's neighboring nations, including Armenia. However, at the same time he was secretly instructing the Commander of the Eastern Army, Kazim Karabekir Pasha "[to] *do his utmost to both politically and physically eliminate Armenia.*"[5]

The National movement led by Atatürk had many members who reaped great financial profit from the Armenian Genocide and even directly participated in it. Mustafa Kemal had pardoned and rewarded these criminals of 1915. One such person, Topal Osman had later become "Commander of Kemal's Bodyguard Regiment"; another one, Ali Cenani, a former Unionist deported to Malta by the British, under Atatürk's administration later served as Turkey's "Minister of Trade and Commerce."[6]

Aware of the gravity of accusations of genocide, Atatürk approached the issue with a great deal of caution and sensitivity, especially when he met with representatives of western states.[7] Therefore, even though Atatürk rightfully called the Armenian Genocide "*A Shameful Act,*" he failed to bring to justice the perpetrators of this crime, and instead often rewarded them by assigning them to higher posts and by allocating pensions for the families of those sentenced to death.

Atatürk assumed the same "two-faced" attitude in his personal life, towards his wife Latife Hanim, to whom he was married for a total of two years (1923-1925). He used a double standard, depending on what was most convenient for him at the time. Latife Hanim was a cultured woman who was educated in Europe. Besides being multilingual, she had studied literature and music; she was familiar with political science and the law, having completed several years of law school. Her opinions were doubtless influenced by her exposure to western culture. She was a firm believer in women's rights.[8] It appears Mustafa Kemal appreciated her and benefited from her opinions; he took advantage of her exceptional intellectual, linguistic, leadership, organizational and secretarial skills.[9] He received indispensable assistance from Latife Hanim as he was struggling to create the Turkish Republic. However, after about a year into the marriage, despite his advocacy of women's rights, his male chauvinism started dictating his moves. Throughout his married life to Latife Hanim, and after their divorce was finalized when he was still the president of the Turkish Republic, he failed to assign her a single significant position in any of the capacities she excelled in, where her various skills would have helped the country as well as her self-esteem. Furthermore, even though Mustafa Kemal was an advocate of European law and women's rights, when he decided he wanted a divorce, he still went about it the old-fashioned Ottoman way on August 11, 1925, by announcing the annulment as a brief official proclamation coming from him, the husband.[10]

In practically identical fashion, Mustafa Kemal subjected Halide Edib, another competent female Turkish scholar with whom he had worked closely, to the same oppressive treatment. Halide was a brilliant novelist, philosopher, lecturer, feminist, politician, and orator who, during Mustafa Kemal's years of struggle for Turkey's independence, had functioned in many capacities, but most importantly as his head intelligence officer. This type of unfair treatment infinitely frustrated and disappointed Halide to the degree that she referred to conceiving two completely dissimilar Mustafa Kemals in her head. One was someone she had admiration for. The other generated anger in her.[11] Even though Halide had great confidence in Mustafa Kemal's ability as a competent and persistent commander capable of saving the country, she disliked his dictatorial style. He had made this authoritarian style obvious to Halide when he had told her in no uncertain terms, "I am not interested in any criticism or idea. I simply want my own way. I am solely interested in my orders' being carried out." [12]

What Halide had concluded in her evaluation of Atatürk's character was that he was not a commander of unusual courage, but he had boundless ambition and extraordinary endurance. She had observed that he lacked empathy, because he did not feel any pain for those facing death on the war front. She readily accepted his leadership, but had problem with his style of implementation because she found it too dictatorial.

When the national struggle came to an end, Halide and her husband Adnan were greeted with much fanfare as heroes by the citizens of their own country. But now this very important woman was left without a significant job, such as an ambassadorship to the United States. She was left unemployed and cast aside, in her words, "morally lynched." As the war ended, Mustafa Kemal and the nationalists thought their need for Halide's special talents had ended as well.[13]

Halide wanted to tackle women's rights and human rights issues in Turkey to make the country more democratic, whereas Atatürk and his followers wanted to continue with autocracy. From 1923 until 1929 Turkey lived through a number of non-democratic years. During this interval, the newspapers were under heavy censorship. After his success, Atatürk had started eliminating his enemies. Even commanders, representatives in the parliament, and generals with opposing viewpoints were imprisoned. Many innocent people were being punished unnecessarily and being murdered.

During the summer of 1925, to save her life as well as that of her husband Adnan's, Halide decided it would be in their best interest to leave Turkey. In spite of her ventures in the lecture circuit, the couple often found themselves short on funds in cities such as Paris and London. They did not have the necessary financial means to live in London. The truth was that when Turkey truly needed talented, informed, and hardworking citizens such as Halide and Adnan, Atatürk robbed the country of this precious resource by making them unavailable. A life of exile was forced upon Halide and Adnan because of Atatürk's intolerance of Halide's views. The progress so far Turkey had made in the area of civil rights had been extraordinarily slow, meanwhile it had become another one of the fashionable dictatorships evolving around the world which functioned at times on the principle of discouraging the opposition through fear.[14]

Due to all the above inconsistencies in Atatürk's character, I now comprehend--better than I did on November 10, 1956--the real reason why I had so much difficulty memorizing the simple poem honoring him on the 18th anniversary of his passing: The poem I was to recite elevated him to an extraordinary stature he did not deserve. My ancestors, who had endured immeasurable hardships and discrimination during the Atatürk years, could no longer remain silent. They let me know, in mysterious ways, that I had to learn more about what had really transpired during the Atatürk years--beyond the sanitized history in my Turkish textbooks.

My Commute to Üsküdar American Academy

To solve the problem of the long commute to the American Academy for Girls in Üsküdar, my mother had located a carpool I could join for my first year at the school. Inci (pronounced Eenjee), one of the girls in my carpool, was in eighth grade and lived only two doors down from us on Mühürdar Blvd. She was an attractive blond with long wavy hair. From her mature appearance, I thought she was at least two years farther along at school. I later found out she had to repeat some of the grades; regrettably, the following year she would drop out of the school altogether. The other two girls in our carpool were twins who were seniors. They seemed intelligent enough; however, they were bored of school and were only interested in having a good time. On more than one occasion during the spring months, instead of going to school, the remaining members of my carpool had arranged for our elderly driver Mehmet to drop them off somewhere in the hills where beautiful wildflowers and butterflies abounded. Mehmet would later pick them up slightly before 4PM at a prearranged location, before picking me up from school. Spring fever must have gotten to them! I represented the opposite extreme, because I finally had the privilege to attend the school I had been dreaming of for so long. I always wanted to arrive on time for my first class. More than a couple of times, due to either Mehmet's old car's mechanical problems or due to the rest of the carpool's wanting to do something other than going to school, I had been tardy. Before the school year was over, I had decided that I would go along with my carpool for the balance of the year; however, for the following year when I was a 6ᵗʰ grader, I did not want to participate any longer, as I did not fit in.

Taking the Tram to School during the Cold Spell

Managing on my own to get to the American school in Üsküdar had its own set of challenges. For the following two years I would walk to the tram station in Kadiköy to catch the one that would drop me off at Bağlarbashi on its way to Kisikli. After getting off the tram, I would have to traverse a sizable field before I could reach the school. During the unusual cold spell of the winter of 1957, the Danube River emptying to the Black Sea had frozen, dumping substantial chunks of ice to the Black Sea. The mini icebergs had managed to travel through the Bosphorus, all the way to the Sea of Marmara. They had remained intact for a number of days due to the extreme cold and had presented an unusual hazard to the captains of the ferries who had to navigate around them. In fact, on foggy mornings, this exercise had become quite a challenge for them.

The first day of my commute to school during this cold spell, I was lucky that the rate at which the snowflakes were descending from the sky had eased somewhat by the time my tram had dropped me off at Bağlarbashi. The football-sized field I always walked across was almost unrecognizable because it was completely covered with a thick blanket of fresh snow. The scenery made me feel as if I was in a gallery appreciating beautiful paintings depicting winter scenes, each one capturing the winter wonderland from a different perspective. The bare branches of the trees in the distance were completely outlined in white. With each step I took to cross the field, it felt as if my boots were sinking deeper into the soft snow. When I finally decided to glance back, I realized I could trace my footsteps all the way back to the covered little shack where the tram had initially dropped me off. I realized this was perhaps the closest I would get to an arctic adventure on my way to school! After enjoying the solitude of this winter paradise and feeling the soft, fresh snow through my woolen gloves, I was finally able to make it to school.

Except for fewer students, it was business as usual during my first period. At the end of my second period, a representative of the administration came to announce the cancelation of our classes for an entire week due to the cold spell. This certainly put everybody who had been able to make it to school in a festive mood, freeing us from our responsibilities. I remember one more unexpected vacation of this sort the following year during the Asian flu epidemic. However the novelty would soon wear off, and it would not take long for us to realize what an integral part of our life school was.

The Ethics Committee

It was now the beginning of my second year at the American high school, and by now I had had an entire year to make the transition from my Armenian elementary school. I had found out that most of my classmates had definite strengths and were quite competent in a number of disciplines.

I do not recall what particular incident had necessitated the formation of an Ethics Committee, other than the fact that a brand new principal, Miss Morgan, had arrived at the school. She had thought the school would be better off if students had more say in the administration. To help achieve this end and to be able to handle more objectively any disciplinary problems that might arise in the future, she thought the school would benefit from having an ethics committee (*Adalet Divani*) with a student representative from each class, elected by that class.

I was not a particularly outgoing student, mostly due to my nature but also due to the fact that I was the only Armenian student in my class. Since I was representing Armenians, a minority, I knew that being vocal and shining among my Turkish classmates could never be in my best interest. After all the ballots were counted, to my surprise I found that in spite of my being Armenian and having made absolutely no attempt to get their votes, my Turkish classmates had chosen me to represent them in this committee. At the time, this had given me a deep satisfaction because it showed they trusted me. In fact I had felt more contentment on this occasion than when several years later in 11th grade I was elected to be the "May Princess" from my class.

My Classmate Refika

With a few exceptions, most of my teachers at junior high seemed reasonable and must have had sufficient background in psychology to realize that they should not subject a student to unnecessary stress, especially if she seemed to show vulnerability. Naturally there were exceptions. Refika, a classmate of mine in 6th grade, was both diligent and bright. She was among the few who had managed to be on the honor roll throughout the preparatory grade, when the main emphasis was on teaching the English language to the newly-arriving students. However as we started 6th grade, her performance had suffered inexplicably. I had heard through the grapevine that she had a demanding mother with a tyrannical personality, who had unrealistic expectations of her. Refika had been able to satisfy her demands while she was in preparatory grade, but it had taken its toll on her. Confronting 6th grade, which came with a number of additional courses while we still had to build on our proficiency of the English language, had put a lot of pressure on us all.

That same year we had an accomplished, albeit eccentric, Turkish music teacher, Piraye Hanim, who seemed to take pride in making us anxious. In preparation for her class the night before, I recall asking my mother to play the tunes of C and G majors several times on our seldom-used piano downstairs, so that I could vocalize the right pitch. We must have looked comical while we practiced indoors with our coats on, in the freezing room two stories below our living room, where my mother's piano stood. After repeating this exercise several times in the chilly room without making appreciable progress, we decided I was as ready as I was ever going to be for Piraye Hanim's dreaded class. After a good night's rest, the following day when it was my turn to recite, I realized I had quite inexplicably become hoarse; no sound would come out of my vocal chords no matter how hard I tried. Piraye Hanim was not amused; she readily communicated to me her obvious displeasure, as she assigned me an incomplete grade. I was thankful she had not gone further than that.

As soon as it was my classmate Refika's turn, my usually serious classmate had suddenly started giggling uncontrollably. She was unable to perform any of what Piraye Hanim was asking her to do, while her unrestrained laughter kept irritating the music teacher. Lacking the insight that Refika was not ridiculing her, Piraye Hanim became progressively more confrontational. After this experience, Refika, the most scholastically gifted student of preparatory grade, became dysfunctional. She was unable to keep up with her studies; her grades suffered and her behavior often became inappropriate. Sadly, in another semester, she was no longer enrolled at our school.

A Visit to the American Aircraft Carrier Forestall

Another flashback to 6th grade brings back recollections of a certain Saturday morning when, by sheer luck, I happened to be the student chosen from my class to tour the renowned American aircraft carrier Forestall, which was docked on the Bosphorus for a few days in 1957. I was the lucky one because my homeroom teacher had arbitrarily picked my name out of a hat. This event is clearly etched in my memory because for the first time I was going to be on a massive ship from whose flight deck aircraft could take off and where they could land. As we approached the aircraft carrier from the harbor, my first impression was that it was unlike any other kind of sailing vessel I had seen before because it was so massive. It was literally a world unto itself. However the occasion also stayed in my memory for another and totally unrelated reason.

After I found out I would be touring this floating city, I was very excited and did not really know what to expect. Esin, the student leader who guided us to the ship, was a senior. She was a tall, slim, and attractive blond. For the occasion, she had chosen to wear high heels and a tight blue suit. Although her outfit looked attractive, it seemed somewhat inappropriate and rather unsafe, considering we had to ascend and descend the narrow stairways of the ship. The midshipman from Forestall, who was our tour guide, immediately took a liking to her. He started directing his explanations exclusively to her. This gave the rest of us in the tour group the impression that we did not exist. Meanwhile, Esin seemed to be relishing every bit of this special attention because at some point she even separated herself somewhat from us. Other than touring the state of the art aircraft carrier and its sensitive machinery practically on our own, the tour had turned out to be an unexpected exercise in observing the methods an overly interested young sailor utilized to charm a beautiful young woman! At the conclusion of the tour, I even overheard the sailor ask Esin if she would be interested in meeting him the following day when the aircraft carrier would be docked on the Bosphorus for an additional day! I never found out what her response was. The entire experience had ended up being an eye opener for me, considering the sheltered life I had been leading.

An Unexpected Knock at my Grandmother's Door

I had been attending seventh grade for no more than three months when, on a chilly January morning, an unexpected loud knock at my grandmother's front door would change life forever for her and us. A policeman in uniform was knocking on her apartment door to break the sad news to her about my grandfather. My maternal grandmother, Vartoo Menee, thought it was all a mistake and had a hard time believing him until he presented her a sealed envelope containing my grandfather's pocketbook, keychain, and watch. The policeman explained to her that my grandfather had instantly died of a massive heart attack after hurrying to catch the ferry about to leave the Üsküdar wharf. My already emotionally fragile grandmother realized she had lost her dearest companion. It did not help that at times she had been unnecessarily critical of him. Many a time she had taken him for granted, neglecting to tell him how much he meant to her. My parents realized they needed to step in and help my grandmother in her time of need. Therefore, we spent most of the following several months making arrangements to move out of the only house I had known all my life in Kadiköy, to the lower story of my grandmother's well-constructed light pink stone apartment building in Fistikağaci. My father also had the additional responsibility of settling my grandfather's accounts with his suppliers in Anatolia, as well as with the retailers he delivered his merchandise to across the Bosphorus.

From where we lived, it now took me and my sister fifteen minutes to walk the winding country road lined with uneven cobblestones, and an almost continuous field of weeds and wildflowers on one side, and gated residences with extensive front and backyards on the other, to reach the lower gate of the American high school in Üsküdar. It was on this country road that, to my surprise, I was on occasion greeted by a domineering rooster who thought he owned the road and at other times by a shepherd with a staff guiding his flock of sheep. We eventually managed to reach the lower gate of the school. Fast forward forty-four years, on my trip to Turkey in 2006, I made a point of visiting this special school that had meant so much to me. I found that its lower gate, which had made my everyday commute from Fistikağaci possible, had been permanently blocked for a number of years after the last doorkeeper had retired. My husband and I had to walk to Bağlarbashi to reach the school through its upper gate. To my surprise, my alma mater was now coeducational! I could only recognize two of its several buildings. There was no longer any evidence of the open field I had to traverse once I had gotten off the tram to reach the upper gate of the school, because several multiple story buildings were standing on the land where it used to be. I could see that the passing of time had indelibly changed my alma mater, as well as its immediate neighborhood.

Chapter II

The Open-Air Movie Theater in Bağlarbashi and Two Wells

It was a balmy summer evening in 1960 when my sister and I had convinced my mother to take us to the open air movie theater in Bağlarbashi. This humble outdoor theater had made it possible for us to enjoy a number of worthwhile American films which on occasion depicted history. They also gave us an opportunity to hear English spoken with the proper inflections. During the films, my sister and I often tried to comprehend what was being said in English, before the translated Turkish subtitles would appear underneath.

On that particular evening, the disorderly state of the outdoor theater had left a lot to be desired. Most importantly, the theater's periphery was not properly illuminated, and for unknown reasons there were dug up areas close to the entrance which had not been properly barricaded.

While my mother was waiting in line to purchase our tickets for the evening's feature film, all of a sudden I felt that I was no longer on firm ground and that my feet were no longer supporting me. I must have been in a state of free fall for a second or two and tumbled down a distance of almost ten feet. When I finally had my rude awakening, I was in pain because my rear end had hit the hard cement floor in what seemed like a pitch dark dungeon! In reality, I had landed at the bottom of a dry well. During my descent, a thick iron rod had dug into my left quadriceps muscle, making it bleed. When I realized what had happened, the first thing I did was to try to stand up. I wanted to make sure that my legs could still support my body and that I could move my arms. However, the most traumatic part of my experience was when I tried to yell so people, especially my sister, could hear me. To my surprise and dismay, initially no sound would come out of my vocal cords no matter how hard I tried. Furthermore, when I was at the bottom of the dark, dry well, I had a sudden flashback to my mother's scary experience when she was seven. Sometime back, she had told me about the time when they were living in Scutari (Üsküdar) when she had fallen into a real well, the lid of which had snapped shut on top of her!

A Greek neighbor, Kaliope had come to visit the family one afternoon; my mother had wanted to be helpful by getting up on a chair to fetch cookies for her from the cookie jar high on the shelf above the well. Unable to grasp the jar, she had lost her balance and fallen on the lid of the well; the lid had unexpectedly opened, trapping her inside and had instantly snapped shut above her, leaving no clue for anyone as to her whereabouts. During her fall, she somehow had managed to grab onto a protruding rock in the interior wall of the well, but she was tiring fast. Fortunately, in contrast to my misadventure, she was able to yell. However, her shrieks were hardly audible because they were coming from deep down, with the lid of the well tightly sealed. Thank goodness Kaliope noticed my mother's absence and inquired, "Where is Wilhelmina?"

By then everyone had started searching for my mother. It was again Kaliope who thought she had heard a faint sound coming from far away and had an inkling of an idea that Wilhelmina could be trapped in the well. When she opened the lid, everyone thought it was a miracle when they detected the cute seven-year-old hanging tight onto the wall of the well, still sporting her neatly-ironed, pink ribbon placed centrally on top of her shiny blond hair. Being the least panicked one among them, Kaliope had already thought of a way of getting my mother out of the well. This was crucial because she was exhausted and her fingers were hurting from hanging tightly onto the coarse, protuberant rock. Kaliope quickly grabbed the nearby pail which had a thick rope securely attached to it. My grandparents had been using it to lower their perishables down the cool well to prevent spoilage. At once Kaliope lowered the pail to Wilhelmina, telling her to catch and hold it tight with both hands and not let go. They both could hear the echoing of her instructions, which under more normal circumstances would have sounded amusing. As a woman of impressive physical strength, Kaliope single-handedly managed to pull my mother up the well. Once Wilhelmina was extracted from the well, there was much laughter, rejoicing, and celebration, extending into the late hours of the night.

Unlike my mother, I was removed from the dry well amid angry grumbles of bystanders who complained about an irresponsible government that had failed to barricade a source of obvious danger in a public area, namely the entryway to a poorly illuminated theater. Whenever I glance at the thin foot-long scar on my left quadriceps, my thoughts go back to that balmy evening in the summer of 1960. I feel grateful that I survived what could have been a serious accident with just the cleansing and sterilizing of the cut the iron rod had inflicted on my left quadriceps muscle, without even receiving the necessary series of tetanus shots!

Life with My Sister

My sister Arminé was two years younger but three grades behind me in school. This was because right after starting elementary school, at a time when mumps, measles pertussis (whooping cough), and rubella vaccines were not discovered yet, I had contracted the whooping cough virus and promptly passed it onto my sister. My recovery had been relatively eventless; however, the virus hit my sister brutally, her alarming cough lasting a long time and worrying my parents. My mother had taken her to a number of physicians, including one who had suggested an extreme but unverified mode of treatment. Dr. Karakashoğlu's unorthodox recommendation was to place Arminé in a special chamber in her office, followed by my parents accompanying her in an airplane to Uludağ, the tallest mountain in the area. Her reasoning was that the cumulative effect of these two procedures implemented in succession, would dry up the mucus in Arminé's windpipe, which was causing her irritating cough. We were fortunate that my parents were independent thinkers and would not jump into conclusions without concrete evidence. Our family physician, Dr. Missirlian had also cautioned my mother that Dr. Karakashoğlu had recently acquired the specialized chamber and that the last child who underwent the procedure had not come out of the contraption alive.

After a summer vacation in the Yakacik highlands, my sister gradually recovered from her persistent whooping cough, without my parents' having to resort to additional extreme measures.

However, our family practitioner Dr. Missirlian recommended holding Arminé back for another year before enrolling her in kindergarten.

Sister's Attempt to Gain Admission to the American School

I must have been in seventh grade when it was my sister's turn to try her luck at the dreaded entrance examination in American Academy for Girls in Üsküdar. In spite of being quite young at the time, we were well aware of the importance of being proficient in English. Acceptance at this school would immeasurably simplify life for my sister and our family in the years to come, especially if her future plans included continuing her studies in the United States. History had repeated itself far too often for us to believe in the wisdom of remaining in Turkey as an Armenian minority.

Just like me, my sister was unable to compete equitably in the entrance examination, because she had been taught the math and science courses in Armenian rather than in Turkish in elementary school. Although I tried to minimize the significance of the outcome in both her and my parents' eyes, the idea of my sister having to attend an ordinary Turkish high school, while I was attending a better-quality institution where my English would constantly improve, had saddened me. I must have expressed my feelings to my mother, because she visited my school twice during that summer to talk to the assistant principal. She inquired if there was any way Arminé could take a language proficiency test as I had done, to improve her prospects of acceptance.

Miss Morgan, the principal, had been on leave during that particular summer to visit her mother in the United States. Her representative, Miss Millet had a certain sternness and assertiveness about her that you did not dare challenge. As far as empathy was concerned, she certainly did not measure up to the two previous principals we had gotten to know. After initially being willing to talk to my mother when we had first received the letter of rejection, she abruptly changed her tune. When she noticed my mother in front of her office door a second time, without even finding out what had brought her there, she tactlessly raised her voice to the level of a reprimand, complaining, "How can I make this woman understand that we cannot grant admission to her daughter!" Her statement must have hurt my mother deeply, because that unwelcome reception from Miss Millet had marked her last visit to my school for the summer.

It was a good thing my mother did not have to face further disappointments after her last and less than satisfactory encounter with Miss Millett, because a month later our family once again had a strike of good fortune. For reasons we never fully comprehended, an anonymous complaint was lodged, which essentially stated: "In spite of the fact that this American high school was initially founded by American missionaries for the purpose of teaching English to Armenian Christian students in Turkey, not a single Armenian is listed among those admitted to the incoming preparatory class of 1958." After that, events suddenly took an unexpected turn. It was speculated that at that point the Prime Minister of Turkey, Adnan Menderes, had taken the matter into his own hands and declared an unprecedented government directive, applying to that year only. It required foreign high schools, especially those teaching English, to accept additional applicants, among which would be a healthy number of Armenians. This must have created a nightmare for school administrators; however, it certainly helped my sister! Arminé remembers that four Armenians, including Yerchanig, Marminé, Arshaluys and herself, were among the additional students accepted in 1958 as a direct outcome of this directive.[15] The families of the students affected by this initiative were kept in the dark until everything was finalized. A week before Arminé was to reluctantly start her classes at the Turkish Lycee across the street from us, where my mother had already paid her tuition for the fall semester, a letter addressed to my sister and her parents mysteriously appeared in the mail from my American high school. In this letter, Principal Miss Morgan was stating the school's decision to accept Arminé to their preparatory class for the fall semester of 1958. She was welcoming her and asking that her parents promptly stop by at the administration building during their hours of operation to register her, unless their plans had changed, in which case they needed to hear from them as soon as possible.

Two miracles for two kids in a period of three years... As far as our family was concerned, this was better than winning the most highly-prized lottery ticket! We were ecstatic. At the American Academy for Girls in Üsküdar, Arminé soon proved herself worthy of the vote of confidence bestowed upon her, easily living up to the school's expectations.

With this latest development, from my grandmother's house in Fistikağaci, it took us twenty minutes to leisurely walk to the lower gate of our school each morning. We were often accompanied by classmates and other students from the school living in our neighborhood and would engage in lively conversation with them about the week's events. We had a fulfilling but simple life revolving around the school and its serious academic core--the English language, science, and mathematics-- all of which were taught in English. Literature was taught both in English and Turkish, while history, geography, and the social sciences were all taught in Turkish. Classes started at 8:10 AM and lasted until 4:10 PM with an hour and a half break at noon to give us time for lunch, play volleyball, and to visit with friends. Volleyball was the most popular sport. Due to my Turkish friend Ayda's encouragement and lots of practice, I learned to enjoy this sport and improved in it enough to be on my class team by the time I was in 8th grade and on my school team by the time I was a senior. It was a challenging sport and added a new dimension to the highly academic nature of my school life.

An Unfair Accusation

One day, as we were returning home from school on the winding road lined with irregular cobblestones, I noticed that my sister Arminé had been unusually quiet. As I took a closer look at her, I noticed her eyes were red and realized she had been crying. As I gently asked a few questions, her responses were interspersed with sobs. What I finally gathered was that Nuriye Erben, a Turkish math teacher, had substituted that day for her regular math teacher, Miss Morgan. Nuriye Hanim had given the class a test previously prepared by Miss Morgan. At some point during the test she had accused Arminé of cheating, claiming she had glanced at the paper of the student sitting next to her. My sister and I had been close and would usually discuss the day's events with each other. By then I was familiar enough with her honest nature to realize that if the devil had gotten into her on this particular occasion and had forced her to do something improper, she would be the first one to let us know.

Nuriye Erben happened to be my algebra teacher for that year; furthermore, she was to be my geometry teacher for the following year in 8th grade. I reasoned that any action I would take to defend my sister could be interpreted by her as a threat deserving a reprisal. Miss Morgan must have held Nuriye Hanim in high regard, since she had been the one to welcome her as her guest in her home for the summer months in Izmir, as well as the one to teach her Turkish when she had first arrived in Turkey with the intention of replacing our retiring principal, Miss Martin. One part of me was telling me not to get involved. However, my sister's sad face, as she sobbed, "I swear I did not do it," pulled me in a different direction.

By the time we made it home, Arminé's dissatisfaction and quest for justice had intensified to such a level that I felt compelled to take the 15 minute winding road back to school to talk to the principal, Miss Morgan, even though I knew it would be dark by the time I made my way back home. In spite of it being after hours, Miss Morgan was willing to hear me out in her office. Her suggestion was: "The only way to settle this issue would be to give your sister a completely different test on the same subject tomorrow and see how well she does on it."

After school the next day, Arminé completed the new test Miss Morgan had formulated for her with flying colors, essentially proving Nuriye Hanim's accusation to be unfounded. However, to my disappointment, Miss Morgan must have discussed the previous day's events with her, including my 5:00 PM visit. I wish she had not! It was after this event that I realized how valuable it would be for foreign teachers who are new to a country to be given a crash course in the objective history and politics of the respective country, including how they have dealt with their minorities in the past. Studying and being spoon-fed the sanitized version, as it existed in their history textbooks, often failed to present the true picture. It could even produce unintended and undesirable results as it did in my case, with ramifications often extending well into the future.

Retaliation

From that day onward, throughout the two years that she was my math teacher, Nuriye Erben persistently punished me for having questioned her judgment and for having helped my sister. Whenever I took a test in algebra or geometry during this period, she retaliated by reducing my score with an entire grade, and sometimes even by two. There came a time when I dreaded receiving my corrected math paper back because I could count on a disappointment each time, in spite of having solved the majority of the problems correctly. After a while, the repeated disillusionments started having a negative impact on my self-confidence. Each time I would patiently confront her, showing my work with the correct answer she had overlooked; she would make an incremental change in my grade which would not amount to anything significant. I finally came to the realization that since I was part of a minority living in Turkey, I had no choice but try to coexist peacefully with the Turks, wearing on my face what the famed director of film and theater of the 1950s, Elia Kazan, had rightfully described as *"the Anatolian smile."*[16]

However, the deleterious effect of Nuriye Erben's mistreatment would not be limited to my 7th and 8th grade mathematics classes and did not finally disappear when these classes ended. In a most inconspicuous way, it would remain dormant like a virus in my psyche, suddenly springing back to life years later, when it would find me susceptible once again.

Hümeyra Hanim in Yessayan High School

It had been forty years since the incident with Nuriye Erben, when I found myself once again discussing the issue of prejudice, this time with a younger distant cousin similarly educated in Istanbul in *Yesayan*, an Armenian high school for girls. I realized that the way my math teacher punished me was not an isolated incident. Hilda's history teacher Hümeyra Hanim in *Yesayan* had intimidated her in a similar fashion when Hilda had mustered the courage to ask her the question that had been in the back of her mind for a long time: "Why is it that in all our history books there is never any mention of Armenia as a country, in spite of its having existed at the time?" Her question had obviously made Hümeyra Hanim feel uncomfortable. She had responded to Hilda by saying that she would have an answer for her the following day after consulting with her colleagues. Her devious response to Hilda the following day was: "The answer to your question is: *It is of no consequence!*" Then she had similarly started deducting from Hilda's grades, producing the same ill-feeling Nuriye Erben's behavior had produced in me.

Anna Agoshian's Story

I must have realized that I suffered a significant setback to my self-esteem in Nuriye Erben's math classes, because at some point I had started having doubts and questioning myself regarding my aptitude in math, and at times could not help but wonder if it was slowly deteriorating. However, the person who had been disadvantaged the most from her prejudice and unfair treatment-- unfortunately also instigated by her mother's insensitivity--was a dear Armenian friend I had during Junior High, Anna Agoshian. She had been a member of our team of three students in Mrs. Alexanian's master class of English during the summer of 1955, and had started studying with that legendary teacher six weeks earlier than I had. Both of us had been lucky enough to be accepted to the preparatory grade of the American high school the very same year. She was a boarder, since her family lived on the more affluent European side of the Bosphorus, from where a commute to Üsküdar every day was more time-consuming. I liked Anna because she was friendly, cheery, and honest; however, she had a status-conscious mother in a country where Armenians had to avoid visibility at any cost. In my friend's case, the combination of being Armenian as well as visible, proved to be a fatal flaw and did not bode well with Nuriye Erben.

At the end of the school day each Friday, Mrs. Agoshian used to pick Anna up from the American school in her expensive car, which made a conspicuous statement with mostly negative repercussions among the Turkish students and their parents, the majority of whom were not so lucky. It reflected her mother's insensitivity and was a source of envy among many students and faculty alike. Mostly with the intention of being helpful on rainy weekends, but also with the desire to maintain good relations with the teachers, Mrs. Agoshian would give rides to our Turkish Literature teacher by transporting her in her car, which would cross the Bosphorus on a steamer. Her good intentions worked well for Saadet Timur; but they backfired when it came to Nuriye Erben. In addition to rejecting Mrs. Agoshian's offer on that particular rainy day, our math teacher was enraged with her forwardness. Because Anna was an average student in math, Nuriye Erben had failed her in 7th grade algebra. Too proud to repeat the same grade with younger students and with the same unfriendly math teacher, Anna's family had instead chosen to pull her out of the American high school where she was getting an excellent education at a modest price. Rumor had it that Anna's affluent parents had enrolled her in an expensive school in Switzerland. After that incident, I never heard again from my once enthusiastic and cheerful classmate.

The Rambler Father Almost Bought for my Mother

Anna Agoshian's mother's courageous driving record in the busy streets of Istanbul brings to my mind how five years later, in the fall of 1962, with encouragement from my father, my mother had almost consented to boldly place herself behind the wheel as Anna Agoshian's mother had done. That same year, which happened to be the year I graduated from the American high school and left Istanbul to study abroad, the American Motors Co. Chief in the U.S. was George W. Romney. Since my sister was now accepted at the American Girls' College in Arnavutköy, which was on the European side of the Bosphorus, and my grandmother by now had once again become self-sufficient, my father thought our moving to Nisantasi on the European side of the Bosphorus would simplify both of our two necessary commutes: to his office in Eminönü and to my sister's College in Arnavutköy.

Upon my father's suggestion, my mother agreed to assist with the transportation of both family members around town. She studied day and night to successfully pass a written test on the mechanics of the automobile. This was called for because at the time getting a driver's license required her to have a basic understanding of how the essential parts of an automobile functioned since she was expected to know what to do in case her car broke down. Of course she also studied the traffic rules and regulations before attempting to take the actual driving test on the crowded streets of Istanbul.

I should not neglect to mention that the whole thing started when we first saw the color-coordinated, boxy, shocking-pink-roofed two-tone Rambler of American Motors with its matching light pink body in the brochure my father had picked up from the car dealer sometime in January of 1962. He was hoping to purchase the car for my mother so she could drive it, since his eyesight had been deteriorating due to his poorly-controlled diabetes. Of course he had no way of knowing that American Motors was not a well-respected car company at the time and that its Rambler brand was a reject, with its 1962 model having one of the worst track records among the American manufactured cars to date. This was because people who owned Ramblers complained about their noisiness and non-responsive steering mechanism. It was said that on the road the car often generated a blue cloud of smoke and when it was kept indoors, it dirtied the floor of the garage because it both burned and dripped oil. Many Rambler owners noted that the car would often not start unless two able-bodied people pushed it or unless they rolled it down a hill! Where my parents would soon be living in Nisantasi, none of these dangerous-sounding requirements would have been realized, because Nisantasi was essentially flat and it was heavily populated.

One might ask: "But why were my parents almost getting ready to buy this pink car with shocking pink accents that could be spotted anywhere?" The answer was that my mother had successfully completed the almost impossible to pass written section of the department of motor vehicles test. She was such a disciplined and determined person that if she put something in her mind, nothing would stop her until she had accomplished it. The Ramblers, under the direction of American Motor Company Chief George W. Romney, were being shipped at the time to countries like Turkey because, due to their poor design and construction, they were not selling in the United States where they faced stiff competition from formerly tested car models.

I am not sure what single event caused my parents to finally lose interest and decide against purchasing the pink American Motors Company's Rambler they had their eyes on, except that I am glad something did! Most likely, they realized they might not be living in Istanbul for more than two to three years at the most, because they were eventually planning to join me and my sister in the United States. Another reason could have been the rapid deterioration of my father's eyesight, because for practical purposes he needed that faculty in addition to sound judgment to be a decent guide to my mother, the driver. Last but not least, the chaotic flow of traffic and pedestrians through the irregular streets of Istanbul which did not have marked lanes, might have scared my mother. In any case, it seems their skipping the purchase of the Rambler of American Motors was a wise decision which prevented many further problems from arising. For my mother, the entire exercise might have served the purpose of restoring her confidence in herself, because against all odds and to everyone's surprise, she had somehow managed to pass the mechanical portion of the motor vehicle test with flying colors!

Preparing to Leave Istanbul

In August of 1962, besides funding my college education in the United States, my parents were generous enough to offer me something they themselves never had: a sightseeing and cultural tour of Europe. It was to take place on my way to Los Angeles, my final destination. However, as more of the tour's details unraveled, this unique adventure, planned by four people with clearly different priorities, ages, and backgrounds seemed to take a life of its own.

My parents knew the Berberians socially, whose son Jack had graduated from Robert College in Istanbul. He had already managed to secure himself a job in engineering in Northern California after having completed graduate work in engineering at Purdue University in Indiana. He was helping his sister Marlene in her search for a job in chemistry. His mother Angie, quite energetic both mentally and physically for her age, was the go-getter of our group. Her plan was for her husband to eventually join them in Northern California, thereby completing the emigration of their entire family from Istanbul.

The travelers in our non-homogeneous group had varying interests and agendas in mind. Angie had a not-so-secret plan of my meeting and perhaps marrying her son Jack in California. I felt adjusting to college life in Southern California after arriving there from Turkey, in addition to having Uncle Jacob, my father's genius but non-communicative cousin for my academic advisor, were already considerable challenges for me to deal with; I did not need additional ones!

Our European travel group also included Angie's niece Astrid and nephew Gary. Astrid was a short, friendly woman in her late thirties with noticeable kyphosis. Gary was her younger brother, a handsome, tall, carefree bachelor who did not seem to have a single worry in the world. On the positive side, he was an accomplished ping pong player, a passion I also happened to share with him at the time. It kept us entertained as our ship hopped from one Mediterranean port to another; in addition, it gave us a fair amount of exercise on the ship where other forms of exercise were not readily available in those days. As it turned out, Gary did not have any background or interest in art, the main reason why we were taking this tour in the first place! Our plan was such that as our ship arrived at select European ports, we would take the train to reach European centers of art and culture, provided they were within easy reach.

Before leaving on this unconventional trip, the four of us, along with other acquaintances of the Berberians, met on a balmy starlit summer evening in Kadiköy, at an informal dinner party in Mr. and Mrs. Berberian's backyard, underneath the pine trees. I distinctly remember the romantic Turkish record that kept playing throughout the evening, *"Hatirla ey peri o mesut geceyi. Camlarin altinda caldigin buseyi. Beni mecnun ettin, sen de olaydin. Askimi inkar edersen Allahdan bulaydin"* meaning, "Remember dear fairy that blissful evening when you kissed me under the pine trees. You captured my heart and made me fall madly in love with you. I hope the feeling is mutual. May God punish you if you deny and fail to reciprocate my love!" In the privacy of my bedroom that evening before falling asleep, I wondered if there ever would be a time for such a romantic moment in my future…

Facing So Many Challenges

After being a student at the American Academy for Girls for a number of years where practically all of my classmates were Turkish, I had sensed that I should not ask my parents too many questions about the history and politics of Turkey because as they would try to answer them accurately, I would unnecessarily be placing them in a position of risk. Therefore as frustrating as it was for me and my sister, during the time that we lived in Turkey, many of our parents' and grandparents' prior years in that country remained shrouded in secrecy for us.

I was thankful that my parents had ensured my proficiency in English. Now, as I was graduating from the American Academy for Girls in Üsküdar, I realized that it was going to be quite a challenge for me to adjust to the new life waiting for me, since I had led quite a sheltered life in the past. Suddenly, at age seventeen, I would be completely on my own in a totally different country halfway around the world. However, I also realized this was probably the most opportune time for my parents and me to initiate this bold move to an impartial country, such as the United States, with the purpose of continuing my education. For quite some time, I had been hearing my paternal grandmother's proverb echoing in my ears, "Good fortune may not knock on your door twice!"

I was excited about the many opportunities the United States could offer me. While I was a student in Turkey, on a number of occasions I was disillusioned at being slighted for my performance, just because I was Armenian. By now I was aware that prejudice created a lasting unsettling feeling which lingered on and stood in the way of progress. Besides, I did not want to constantly think twice about the consequences of each word I uttered and worry that it could be misinterpreted and come back to haunt me and my family.

On the other hand, through the years I had grown to love Istanbul, that magical city I was so privileged to be born in. Many of my precious, deep-rooted childhood memories belonged to this one-of-a-kind city. Its history and its unique geographic location--surrounded by alluring seas, the aquamarine waters of the Bosphorus joining Europe and Asia--could be found nowhere else in the world. Equally unique were its *yalis,* the waterside residences on the Bosphorus, and its mansions perched up high on its four islands on the Sea of Marmara overlooking its azure waters. Their images, be it in the sunshine in vivid colors of green and blue or muted at night and visible only through their reflections in the dark-colored waters of the sea, further romanticized the city in my mind's eye. Deep down I did not really want to leave this place. Neither did I want to abandon my two precious grandmothers, my aunt, my cousins, and the many warm memories I had with them in this amazing city. Besides, quite a few of them were elderly. I did not know how much longer I would have the satisfaction of having them by my side to cherish. If only I had had the foresight and courage to ask them questions about their past experiences and had recorded them for posterity… I would then have preserved this last chapter in their lives intact with their genuine thoughts and responses. They would have offered me inspiration, strength and wisdom to face the difficult transitional years of my life that were quickly approaching.

Summer Vacation in Suadiye

Before leaving for the United States, I wanted to do everything in my power so my fast-approaching academic career in the United States would be a success. I was even willing to undertake some labor-intensive tasks which varied from the plausible all the way to the bizarre. I did not complain; instead I was happily energized because I was working towards a goal I valued.

During June 1962 my Aunt Arousiag had made plans to spend her summer vacation with her daughter Sona and family at an upscale resort hotel on the waterfront off the southeastern coast of the Sea of Marmara in *Suadiye*. As a graduation present for me before leaving for the United States, she had invited me to share her room at this classy summer resort with her for an entire month. I had very special feelings for this aunt; I would have gone with her without hesitation no matter where she chose to take me. As destiny had it, in less than two years I would lose her suddenly to an aggressive form of breast cancer without ever being able to see her again after our memorable month together on the scenic southern coast of the Sea of Marmara.

The resort my Aunt Arousiag had chosen ended up being quite an unexpected treat for me; it was luxury I had never experienced before. A variety of delicious dishes I could choose from were supervised by the chef and served to us by stylishly uniformed waiters on tables clad with white linen tablecloths and napkins where a small vase of fresh flowers always greeted us. Adding to the lavishness of the setting was the element of surprise, with different food choices presented at each meal. As though this were not enough, live musicians performed in the evenings, playing familiar eastern and western melodies for our dining pleasure. Later in the evening, as the music got livelier, they would play popular tunes for the hotel guests' dancing and listening pleasure. In this environment, I often felt that I was only imagining the idea of going to California, thousands of miles away; it all seemed quite unreal.

When I woke up in the mornings, I was more in touch with reality. I would spend most of my time on a terrace shaded by neatly trimmed bushes of jasmine, honey-suckle, and trellises of apricot and pink-colored bougainvillea. The bright blossoms of the bougainvillea and the perfume of the honey-suckle and jasmine in the morning air made the place a true paradise. The terrace overlooked the calm Sea of Marmara and the sandy beach stretched in either direction as far as my eyes could take me. Every once in a while I would lose myself and fantasize. After the morning fog lifted, I would swim in the calm, refreshing waters where the waves were gentle and the water invigorating. I had the once-in-a-lifetime luxury of having the entire day to myself to read and do as I pleased. Although I read some, I mostly enjoyed Istanbul's natural beauty from the perspective of this extraordinary terrace. As the time to leave the country approached, more often than not I wished my circumstances were different and that I did not have to detach myself from Istanbul, this jewel of a city, in search of an unknown future.

Future Plans and Bidding Farewell

True to my character, to facilitate my plans to attend college in the United States, I had also chosen a very ambitious project for myself. I had reasoned that the excitement of the setting in *Suadiye* was capable of taking the dullness of most chores away. Besides, this way I would not feel guilty for all the luxury bestowed upon me. My project was to slowly but surely expand my vocabulary, working at it each morning for an hour or more by studying the Thorndike dictionary. I had started with the letter "A" and by the end of my stay in *Suadiye*, I had managed to reach the letter "E." I would select words from the dictionary I judged I ought to know to have a good command of the English language. The dictionary showed me how these words were used in everyday practice and how they fit into the sentence structure; their repetition helped me register them into my long-term memory. In this exercise I also got a secondary benefit I least expected; I became fascinated with the derivation of words and started guessing what their meanings might be. This exercise could have been a boring one for most people; however it proved to be a challenging one for me. Because the words which started with the letter "A" got repeated the most, even to this day I have a better understanding and recall of the definitions of words that start with the letter "A"!

No more than a few weeks after leaving *Suadiye*, I was hugging and kissing my family and loved ones. I was waving them goodbye minutes before our ship started blowing its deafening horn and spewing its grayish smoke. Now I suddenly found myself shrouded in a feeling of unanticipated sadness. I realized that as our ship gradually moved farther and farther away from the dock, so was I moving forever away from my loved ones and my sheltered life. From now on I would have to make my own decisions, hopefully intelligent ones.

My father had thoughtfully arranged for my immediate and extended family members to be there to bid me farewell. I was now solemnly becoming aware of the fact that I was distancing myself perhaps forever from these special people who had helped shape my life so profoundly during my formative years. These were the years when love and caring really mattered. They had not gone about this guiding process forcefully, but one step at a time by just being themselves and by being there for me whenever I needed them. It was just as much how they had said things as what they had said. It was just as much what they had cooked, knit, and sewn for me as the special fairy-tales they had concocted on my sick days so my misery would leave me a minute sooner. They had comforted me when I was down; they had shared my moments of accomplishment with me; they had given me prudent advice expecting absolutely nothing in return. It was also about how they had allowed me to experience and appreciate our unique Armenian culture, with its sad elements somehow always outnumbering the happy ones. I also realized that, since we lived in Turkey, they had to do most of this teaching covertly.

Until this moment, it had never occurred to me that this might be my last goodbye to my paternal grandmother Verkin Menee, who at times could not recall the day before yesterday, but the distant past was as fresh in her memory as could be. One day when I was two and was caressing and marveling at the creases on her face, I had asked her, "Why do you have these, Menee?" She would tell me. "You see, these lines are where I keep all my memories..." She had kept crocheting decorative borders for our pillow cases, mostly from memory when her eyesight had become less than perfect. She would be the one to gently spread a shawl over me when I unexpectedly fell asleep on the sofa after an exhausting day at school. In one of her fairy tales, the heroine would often repeat a refrain in Turkish: "*Ne idik; ne olduk; daha ne olacağiz,*" meaning, "What we were; what we are; and what is yet to become of us!" She conversed in Turkish because during her youth, Armenian was declared a forbidden language in central Turkey where they lived. I had often wondered as a child, what my grandmother's heroine's words might really be referring to. Now as our ship was distancing itself further from the dock, the true meaning of her concise sentence was unraveling before me, regarding both our family and our entire nation.

My favorite Aunt Arousiag was also at the dock. She had loved me practically as much as she had loved her own daughter Sona. Fast forward some 44 years, on our 2006 trip to Istanbul, my cousin Sona recalled with melancholy the time when I was four. I must have been traveling on the tram in Kadiköy with her mother, my aunt Arousiag. A Turkish female passenger sitting across from us had remarked, "Madam, there is such a striking resemblance between the little girl on your lap and you; yet you seem too old to be her mother. Will you solve this conundrum and satisfy my curiosity? Can you kindly tell me what your relationship to the little girl sitting on your lap is?"

Earlier I had promised not to be too emotional during our goodbyes. However as the ship was blowing its horn repeatedly and distancing itself from the dock, it was getting increasingly difficult for me to identify my loved ones waving at me. Now I could feel my heart beating faster and my eyes welling up. For the time being I tried hard not to think about my immediate past, that very important chapter in my life, and instead tried to concentrate on my once in a lifetime vacation in Europe that was almost here;

it was not easy. It was too bad I had to come so close to losing what was so precious to me to appreciate its true value... However, I could not deny that there was something on the bright side as well, because I was also leaving behind a world of fear and a life filled with everyday prohibitions.

As the ship distanced itself farther from the dock, it never occurred to me that it could be as long as forty-four years before I could return to see this special city again and that when I did, it would look so dramatically different. Therefore, I better internalize and register to memory all the sites of this extraordinary city which spoke to my heart's strings. Unfortunately, at the time I lacked the maturity and intuition to realize this. On my trip to Istanbul in 2006, I made a point of seeing my old hometown of Kadiköy. When I did, it felt as if I was stepping into another time and place. I felt as if it had changed unacceptably. The skinny five story house that shared so many of my family's most intimate memories was, to my disappointment, now an "Endoscopy Center!" Familiar faces were no longer present in the church that anchored my childhood. Time had raced on and changed things for better and for worse. All my grandparents, all my aunts and uncles were gone. Time had even changed me. However, on the positive side, I realized that no matter how far away I had moved from these rich memories, I was still able to carry them with me in a special place tucked close to my heart, together with the warm people who had made them so very special for me.

My European Vacation

Before leaving Istanbul we had informed friends and relatives at quite a few ports, so we could communicate with them and benefit from their knowledge of that particular country and language. Our first stop was Athens, Greece, where our ship stopped overnight. I bonded with my father's cousins, the Stambolians; I had seen them once before when I was four, on the occasion of my father's cousin Uncle John's arrival from New Jersey for a family reunion. They helped us find our way around Athens and showed us the Acropolis.

It had never crossed my mind then that sometime within the coming years I would develop a close relationship with these cousins from Greece, who a number of years later would immigrate to Los Angeles. We would mutually try to interpret what my father's genius, albeit uncommunicative cousin Jacob, who was their maternal uncle, was trying to accomplish and how we could soften the blow of his next intricate plan.

I feel good about having kept in touch with Susan who later would become my shopping buddy at Ohrbachs, a department store in West Los Angeles which has been defunct for some time now. Some years later Susan would become my precious bridesmaid. Fast forward another twenty years, I also remember with melancholy Susan's visit to my husband Greg's internal medicine office in Pasadena in 1990 with an ampoule in her hand, that she was led to believe contained the chemical formula believed to be the cure for her breast cancer, which by then had metastasized to her bones. Susan was convinced this chemical was going to save her life. After determining it to be harmless, although knowing full well it could not live up to its therapeutic claim, Greg was the only physician who was willing to inject her with the contents of this ampoule, thus significantly improving her depression at least for a little while longer. When she was living in the valley and struggling to fight the metastasis of the cancer to her lung, it was again Greg who answered her questions with patience and empathy and gave her the trust and compassion she needed.

Witnessing this special relationship which had blossomed between us and Susan was her younger sister Meliné. When she too was diagnosed with a deadly form of pancreatic cancer, Greg could not change the course of her destiny either; nevertheless he again patiently and knowledgeably answered her questions with compassion. When we lost her as well, I felt like I had lost one of my last connections to our family's past, as well as to Greece.

Seeing More of Europe

The next stop on our itinerary was Nice and Cannes in France, where my maternal Uncle Vartkes accommodated us in his modest villa and showed us the typical tourist attractions. It was here that for the first time I met my French cousins and got reacquainted with my Aunt Juliette who had previously visited us in Istanbul accompanied by my uncle. It was also here where I got my first hint that even though I had not yet traveled very far from my home base, that close relationship among my family members I had been so lucky to have, was missing. I realized how precious that bond was and I wanted it to survive throughout my parents' lifetime and beyond.

Next, the ship took us to Naples where it would anchor for three days, enabling us to take the train to Rome. We did extensive sightseeing in this city and marveled at the sculptures of Michelangelo and the masterpieces of Leonardo da Vinci which I had recently studied about in my History of Art class. We took a scenic boat ride to the Isle of Capri, which looked like a jewel in the Mediterranean. Closer to the summit, where we had a panoramic view of the emerald isle surrounded by the intense blue of the Mediterranean, there were specialty stores selling apparel. I clearly remember making one of the few purchases of my entire trip from this location. It was a silk skirt with avocado green and yellow patches against a background of brown with modern black lines and white accents, whose fibers had a soft porcupine like texture. To this day I still have a special affection for this special silk skirt, even though I cannot recall when I wore it last. I do not wish to part from it because it connects me in some magical way to my past and all the unforgettable people, places and events associated with it of some fifty years ago. If it will only take such a little garment hanging in a remote corner of my closet to remind me of so much, I feel it has earned its keep. I have to admit it must have been of good quality, because nearly fifty years later, its colors and luster are just the way they were on the day it was purchased.

Our intention of visiting the historic sites and museums of Italy and France as a group was in theory a good one. It gave us a certain confidence one gets with larger numbers, and additionally made the trip more affordable for us. However, it also presented some unanticipated problems, because our group was not homogeneous.

On several occasions satisfying each person became an impossible task. When we arrived in Rome, to everyone's astonishment, Gary wanted to visit the zoo! We separated from him to see the Vatican, including the Sistine Chapel, the museums and the spectacular churches housing the many masterpieces and the priceless statues of Michelangelo.

Taking a train from Rome, which did not have enough seats for us all, we arrived in Paris. Mrs. Berberian's relatives helped us there with our accommodations. I had never seen a museum like the Louvre before. However, the time we had allotted to see its spectacular collection was way too short; it was not even enough to whet our appetite. Once we had seen a few of the masterpieces, it seemed even more difficult for us to be willing to leave the place, knowing such exquisite artwork existed and that there was so much more of it for us to see. However, I still felt privileged to be able to view at least a few of its masterpieces.

Starting to Feel Anxious

Having been on my own for the first time in my life, in the back of my mind I was already beginning to have certain anxieties about college life in the United States. As the date for me to take the Air France flight from Paris's Orly airport to New York approached, other questions started popping up in my mind: "What was my father's cousin Uncle Jacob really like? Would his expectations of me be realistic? Would I be able to satisfy them? Was what I was getting into a double edged sword?"

Less than a month ago when I was vacationing in *Suadiye* with my Aunt Arousiag and cousin Sona's family, Sona had warned me about Uncle Jacob with her curious comment:

"Be careful about Uncle Jacob's love of science. He thinks it is very easy and that anyone can handle it effortlessly. The fact of the matter is his mind is wired differently and it is easy only for him!" With a flashback into memory lane of some twenty years ago, she had hesitated for a moment as if even remembering it was inflicting a certain amount of pain for her, and then she had proceeded to explain:

"By 1937 the Turkish Ministry of Education had required that graduates of the American Academy for Girls in Üsküdar pass a matriculation exam successfully in Turkish, if they were to attend the university. Provided that they had satisfactorily completed this exam in science or literature, they would then be allowed to apply to their department of choice." Exhibiting the same pained look on her face, Sona had gone on to give me the rest of the details: "All of my friends were planning to take the exam in literature, since our school had prepared us more thoroughly in that field. Furthermore, if there were areas in literature that I was deficient in, I could easily make up for them on my own. Upon my father's suggestion to consult Jacob, when I posed the question to him about making the choice between science and literature, his response was unequivocal":

"You should take it in the sciences. It will involve a lot less work; in addition, you will have acquired all this scientific knowledge. I will help you in areas where you may need further help."

Sona went on to explain, "Soon after I started studying for the exam in science, I realized I had not been exposed to these types of scientific and mathematical concepts and problems until then; but it was too late. In spite of Jacob's help and my hard work, I still failed the exam. In the end, I had to study literature as my friends had done and had to retake the matriculation exam in that discipline." She went on, "He thinks everyone is like him; he is a genius in the fields of mathematics and physics and we are not."

Uncle Jacob's Education and his Interaction with Kepi

A flashback to the early 1920s would find my father's and his Cousin Jacob's family reaching Constantinople and eventually settling in Kadiköy. Jacob started attending the Sultanian elementary school, following it with an American high school education. He later graduated from the Technical University of Istanbul with a degree in engineering. Being the nerdy type, he would not say much in class, not even to exchange ideas with his peers. However he was brilliant in theoretical thinking, especially as it applied to mathematics and physics. He had an intense desire to achieve perfection in these fields and was quite willing to help people around him to achieve this goal, especially if he thought they were capable and motivated enough to do it. This was why he had allocated time three times a week for teaching sessions to my then five-year-old brother Kepi. The young boy would gather his books and head toward Uncle Jacob's study upstairs for a brisk session in reading and arithmetic, far surpassing the seriousness and devotion expected of a typical five year old.

Both of them must have been getting something special out of these sessions, because Kepi surprisingly prepared for them with the maturity of an elementary school student and kept asking his mother if it was time for his lesson yet. For Uncle Jacob, the interaction was most therapeutic because it was a way he could communicate with another human being, an area in which he needed much help and practice. Kepi must have succeeded in introducing the human element and humor into Uncle Jacob's life, without being obtrusive. To his surprise, he liked it. It had been difficult, if not impossible, for him to achieve this in his everyday life. It also made him realize how much he loved children, especially this exceptionally motivated and charming five-year-old son of his cousin. Unfortunately, the warm relationship they had cultivated was abruptly terminated six months from this date by Kepi's sudden demise because of a ruptured appendix which had gone misdiagnosed.

Uncle Jacob's Ancestry

The circumstances under which baby Jacob was brought up in Aksaray, in central Turkey, his survival during his family's deportation years in the Syrian Desert, his family's arrival in Constantinople, his schooling there and finally his teaching engineering at the Technical University of Istanbul until his departure in 1941 for graduate work at the University of Illinois at Urbana-Champaign, may shed some light into how his past may have had a role in shaping his character.

As far back as I can remember, Uncle Jacob was perhaps the most brilliant of my father's cousins and the family hero we all looked up to. In his academic as well as intellectual pursuits, he had reached a level of excellence no one in the family before him had attained. After some investigation into our family history with the help of a recently discovered memoir of my Great-uncle Abraham, I came across some intriguing information about his father, my Great-uncle Parsegh, who had been a valuable resource to the Ottoman government in the area of civil law during the 1890s up to the deportation years, especially in the eyes of Jemal Pasha, who was somewhat more innocuous among the three *CUP* (Committee of Union and Progress) government leaders.

Earlier during the period of the *Young Turks,* the movement responsible for steering the Ottoman government to perpetrate the Armenian Genocide of 1915, when significant numbers of gifted Armenians were not being utilized for the good of the country, Jemal Pasha wanted to amend the situation to some degree. He wanted the Ottoman government to benefit from the talent of people such as Great-uncle Parsegh in civil law, and utilized it well. Great-uncle Parsegh's versatility was in the areas of law, government, and languages; he had one of the best legal minds of the time in central Turkey. What is equally noteworthy is that for the most part, he was self-educated. He had an acute sense of justice and the desire to uphold the rights of the weak, although socially, according to my mother who was the new bride in the extended Lafdjian family, he was not always the easiest person to get along with. He was quite familiar with the *sharia*, the sacred Muslim law derived from the *Qur'an,* which essentially denied rights to Christians; however, he had also familiarized himself with western law which was far more democratic and equitable to Christians.

His colleagues respected him for the way he was able to dissect complex matters into more manageable components. Due to his ability to repeatedly come up with ingenious, yet simple solutions to difficult problems his colleagues often overlooked, and due to his willingness to implement justice without allowing socioeconomic status to be a determinant, he had the trust of higher officials as well as that of the ordinary townsfolk. Therefore, many government authorities as well as the general public tolerated and often welcomed his making the transition from the *sharia law* to the Western law as the need arose. He made this transition with regularity, because few legal authorities at the time knew how to navigate their way through the two essentially contradictory sets of laws and regulations. Once his talent was recognized and publicized by word of mouth, Parsegh traveled extensively among the many provinces of the Ottoman Empire, especially through the central part of present-day Turkey to routinely settle legal matters as an arbitrator. For this reason, during his very early years, young Jacob grew up having only minimal contact with his father.

Reunion of Cousins in Büyükdere

It was a summer weekend in June of 1948 when my father was informed of a telegram that had unexpectedly arrived in Büyükdere, the summer home of the Hatunoglus on the eastern shores of the Bosphorus, from his Cousin John, Great-uncle Abraham's son in New Jersey. He was informing his cousins that he would shortly be arriving in Istanbul and was hoping to see them all and get to know their families, sometime during the 2nd week in August. This was exciting news since no one in the family had seen Uncle John for the last 25 years.

My intuition tells me that his visit may have had a dual purpose. After Great-Uncle Abraham's demise, his memoir had been passed onto him and he wanted to share its precious content with his cousins. He must have been aware that in its existing handwritten form in Turkish, using the Armenian alphabet, access to it by future generations would remain quite limited at best.

The real celebrants of this reunion were the cousins, who had miraculously lived through the Armenian Genocide of 1915-1922. Their fathers, who were the three brothers, namely my Grandfather Kerovpé, Great-uncle Abraham, and Great-uncle Parsegh, had either not survived it or had long passed on. The cousins who were now living in Istanbul and Athens agreed that since Uncle John had been willing to travel the long distance to reconnect with them, they should also consider the occasion a perfect opportunity to remember the past and honor the memory of their fathers and uncles. They wanted to thank them for the important role they played in the survival of their generation.

For this family reunion, all the surviving cousins able to get away for the weekend, as well as their families, would get together with Uncle John in Büyükdere on the Hatunoglu property, where he would be staying, and where Monam and Arsha had been living for the past several years. The Hatunoglus, Monam and Arsha had graciously volunteered to provide the visiting relatives modest overnight accommodations for that weekend.

By the time the anticipated date arrived, everyone was in a celebratory mood. The visiting relatives could not take their eyes off of the shimmering Bosphorus as they directed their gaze in its direction from the Hatunoglu's patio. They spent considerable time there, socializing with each other amid the lush vegetation which included the red and yellow hibiscus, trimmed and perfectly cared for by Mr. Onnik Hatunoglu. To top it off, the weather in August was mild in Büyükdere with only an occasional breeze, and the arrival and departure of the ferries at the quay, which was partially visible from their patio situated on a gentle hill, kept the children occupied.

Aunt Elise, one of Aunt Arsha's and Uncle Jacob's older sisters, had married Sarkis Stambolian in the late-1920s, few years after my father's family had arrived in Constantinople. The newlyweds had decided that after the dust had settled, Athens, Greece would be a safer place to get established to raise a family than Constantinople. In making this decision, they were fully aware, although not totally enthusiastic about having to learn Greek, to be able to conduct a reasonably thriving business in that country. It was a good thing that initially Sarkis Stambolian's boss in Athens had happened to be an Armenian from Turkey, who knew Greek and with whom he could converse in Turkish. For this historic reunion, the Stambolians had brought along their two daughters Susan and Meliné who were in their teens at the time. The evenings became a special time when the two sisters entertained everyone by reciting poems of Siamanto and Taniel Varoujan and brought to life the folk music of Gomidas. This rich culture, which they shared with their relatives, was the work of Armenian intellectuals who had perished during the Armenian Genocide of 1915.

My uncle Dikran, Aunt Arousiag, my cousin Sona as well as my family including my parents, my two-year-old sister Arminé and myself, four-years-old at the time, were the relatives from Istanbul who completed this remarkable reunion. They personally had been survivors of the first genocide of the 20th century by the Young Turks.

Unfortunately at the end of the deportations and genocide, my father and uncle did not have many choices for a place they could settle in, except for cosmopolitan Constantinople. Other alternatives would have involved separating family members from each other for significant lengths of time. The special bond my father had cultivated and enjoyed throughout the deportation years with his mother, after losing his father to the typhus epidemic in the Syrian Desert, had precluded this choice and had favored his remaining with members of his family in Constantinople.

The conspicuously missing relatives in this reunion included their cousin Jacob, who at the time was studying at the California Institute of Technology in Pasadena. Aunt Rose was another sister of Uncle Jacob, who was with them in Istanbul in the 1930s but had later left for Lyon, France to get married to an Armenian there.

Repatriation of my Maternal Uncle Hovhannes and Family

What happened to those who had miraculously survived the Armenian Genocide of 1915 was that after they were driven out of Turkey and were dispersed around the world, many among them longed to go to Armenia, the homeland of their dreams. However, instead of being able to establish there and prosper, they were either exiled to uninhabited regions of Russia such as Siberia, or faced unsurmountable difficulties including starvation due to the policies of the ruthless Russian dictator, Josef Stalin. These were the courageous Armenians, totaling around 90,000 who were involved in the Great Repatriation of 1946-1948.[17] Among them were my oldest, most handsome and educated maternal Uncle

Hovhannes, his wife Arpiné, and their seven-year-old son Armen. Even though they escaped being exiled to Siberia, they suffered an equally terrible fate.

Having lost some 300,000 of its inhabitants during WWII, in 1945-1946 the population of Armenia was around 950,000. However to have representation in the Supreme Soviet Politburo, a republic needed a population of at least one million. It seems the repatriation program was created so Armenia could be a self-governing republic.[18] It was also thought that money and resources would flow to the country more readily once it became such a republic.

To encourage repatriation, delegates from Armenia and the Soviet Union traveled to many countries, including France, where my Uncle Hovhannes was living with his family at the time. However, neither local nor central government agencies in either Armenia or the Soviet Union had accurately evaluated Armenia's resources and ability to accommodate and settle these repatriates.[19] Instead, they presented an unrealistically rosy picture of what immigrants would find once they and their families arrived in the country, which could not have been farther from the truth. Additionally, after winning WWII many candidates for repatriation had started to believe the Soviet Union could finally be transformed into a normal country where they could settle.

Because Uncle Hovhanness was patriotic and trusted the statements of the delegates, he liquidated his successful grocery business in Marseille, France. He used part of the proceeds to pack seven huge, sturdy cardboard boxes with the contents of their rooms in Marseille. He made sure he included his wife's beloved piano in one of them. The remainder of their proceeds went into the buying and packing of supplies with which he would construct a house in Yerevan for his family.

Unfortunately in February of 1947, when they finally reached the port of Batumi in Georgia, accompanied by their cargo on the ship Pobeda, the constant rain of the area would not cease for an entire month while they waited for a train to take them to Yerevan. The living accommodations they were offered in Batumi were less than desirable; however, the state of their cartons containing their furniture, piano, clothing and belongings fared even worse, because everything was soaked and damaged due to the significant precipitation and the unavailability of proper storage. Meanwhile, the first order of business upon arrival in Batumi of the distrustful Stalinist government had been to give each repatriate a bath, to ensure the new arrivals would be free of germs.

In spite of the less than welcoming reception they had so far received, when they first arrived in Yerevan, my uncle, who had been an amateur photographer, used his camera to take a picture of his motherland so he could mail it to his brother in France. He had no idea that the paranoid political system that existed in the Soviet Union at the time, would view everyone as a potential traitor suitable for exile or execution. Due to his attempt to photograph his motherland, my uncle was apprehended, and his camera confiscated, because as far as the Stalinist regime was concerned, he was a spy and therefore an enemy of the people.[20]

Those who came from abroad were placed under strict surveillance in Armenia due to pervasive distrust and suspicion, but also to prevent the spread of dissatisfaction and disappointment, which could theoretically lead to a public rebellion. It was the rule to imprison everyone who aired views against the government, or worse yet, to banish them to Siberia. Therefore, because Uncle Hovhanness had initially publicly blamed the Soviet government for unfairness and incompetence, he had started harboring fears that he could soon be facing the same dark destiny. Every time he saw KGB policemen arriving in their neighborhood and arresting people, he was afraid that next time it would be his turn.[21] In its inhumanity, Stalin's repression reminded Uncle Hovhanness of the horrors of the 1915 genocide his people had endured in the hands of the Young Turks. It manifested itself in the form of poor living conditions, starvation, and inhumane methods of interrogation, called "continuous probing." These interrogations were carried out under blinding lights and often lasted for days or even weeks in a society where coerced confessions were standard and accusations alone were as good as death sentences.[22]

Meanwhile, in the freezing cold of the winter, officers took my Aunt Arpiné and her seven-year-old son Armen to an uninsulated building at a high elevation. Aside from having to contend with the crowded, substandard living-quarters, unemployment and the scarcity of food, the Stalinists demanded that they constantly sell their belongings, so they would generate cash to buy whatever little was available to eat, so they would not starve to death. The Stalinists also demanded possession of my Aunt Arpiné's piano. Upon hearing this, my habitually agreeable aunt made a big fuss because she realized that the piano and English lessons she could offer, would be her only way of making a living. In the end, the piano remained the only significant possession their family was allowed to keep.

On our visit to Yerevan in 2014, my husband and I actually had the good fortune of seeing this piano, which had suffered water damage on its wooden veneer and was replaced by my cousin Armen.

A cousin of my mother's, Silva Ghazarian, who was eleven years old at the time, whose father and my maternal grandfather were brothers, described their family's first living accommodations in Yerevan of some 68 years ago thus: "The government agents took us to the 1st story of an uninsulated house on a mountaintop, where my family consisting of my two sisters, my parents and I were to live, while Cousin Hovhanness, his wife Arpiné and their son Armen occupied the floor above us. Also assigned to our living quarters consisting of two bedrooms and a single bathroom, were two 17 year old young Armenian male repatriates from Europe. It is difficult to have a good sense of what life was really like in the Soviet Union during the Stalin days." Then Silva continued to explain further the more serious problems they faced: "What scared us the most was that we would wake up certain mornings to discover that the family living next door to us had mysteriously disappeared in the middle of the night, having been ordered to board a train to Siberia."[23]

Uncle Hovhanness grew increasingly frightened by the looming threat of government reprisals. He became disillusioned by the loss of his dreamed-of homeland, felt guilty for having subjected his family, as well as a number of other families, to huge hardships, executions, and substandard living conditions in the middle of a cold winter, including having to subsist on small amounts of bread and onion if they were lucky enough to procure them. All of this became too difficult for my sensitive uncle to bear. His attempt to escape from the powerful pressure and self-loathing, and to lift his feelings of oppression by the state gradually brought about his disassociation from reality, his neurosis. In 1956, as his mental health deteriorated further, he had to be moved away from his loved ones. He was transferred to a mental health asylum all the way in Dilijan, a three hour bus ride from Yerevan, where he spent the last five years of his life.

His cousin Silva Ghazarian recalled in a melancholy tone the last encounter she and her mother had with him in Dilijan. She said: "My most handsome of all cousins, Hovhanness appeared unkempt with an extremely long peppered beard, which extended all the way to his lower extremities, as he announced to us: 'Now I will be going to the garden to gather some vegetables so I can fix us a meal.'" Sadly, few years later in 1961, he committed suicide. What an unfortunate end to the life of an intelligent, ambitious, and dedicated man who had tried so hard to be helpful to his country, but instead was denounced as a "traitor to his native land" and was humiliated…

Aunt Rose and her husband, who likewise had attempted to make the courageous move from France to Armenia during the Stalin era, had also faced extreme hardships. They came close to being exiled to Siberia, but somehow had been spared. Life in Armenia improved somewhat after Stalin's death on March 5, 1953.

Problems Facing Uncle John

The person who had traveled the farthest for the reunion in Büyükdere--and the reason it was happening in the first place--was Great-uncle Abraham's son, Uncle John. He had come all the way from the United States, from New Jersey. Naturally, his cousins wanted to hear everything he could tell them about his experiences, since the last time they had seen him was 25 years ago when he was attending the university in Beirut.

In late May of 1923, he had graduated from the Syrian Protestant College--today's American University of Beirut--where he had majored in business. After graduation, he was hired as an assistant travel agent to accompany those few lucky Armenians who had miraculously survived the genocide, so they could reach Marseille, France, on a steamship. From that city, he helped them through the intricacies of the French rail system so they could arrive in Cherbourg, the port city from which large steamships would leave to cross the Atlantic to arrive in New York Harbor.

After repeating this trip a number of times, he was emboldened and decided he wanted to immigrate as well. He was the first young man in his extended family to undertake this courageous journey across the Atlantic, to land alone in an unfamiliar country where he knew no one. The experience must have left an unforgettable mark in his memory, because he related it to his cousins in Büyükdere as if it had taken place yesterday:

"Before I could board the steamship at Southampton, England, they had me answer numerous questions on a manifest list. There were a few of these that had caught me by surprise, such as 'if I had ever been a polygamist or anarchist and if I was carrying at least $25 on me.'" At this point, being his own boss, he thought it would be a good idea to choose to be a steerage passenger so he could save his money for a future business venture once he arrived in the States. Of course, he had no idea it meant he would descend down steep stairways into the enclosed lower decks, which felt as if he was imprisoned for the entire length of his ocean journey in a dark, crowded place that smelled of sweat. It also meant an entire week of sea-sickness and deplorable living conditions which included: overcrowding, inadequate washrooms, non-existent ventilation, and the stench of unclean bodies. Next, Uncle John went on to describe what it was like as their ship approached New York Harbor:

"When that week of misery finally ended, all of us immigrants in steerage were in a state of shock, physically, mentally and emotionally. As our ship moved north through the Narrows into New York Harbor and we could see the tip of Manhattan, the first object we saw was the Statue of Liberty with its torch, standing proud and tall. It seemed to symbolize hope for all of us new arrivals."

My father also remembers his cousin saying, "After our ship docked in Manhattan, while cabin passengers were being released to New York, we the steerage passengers were transferred across the pier to a waiting area. Each one of us wore a name tag and had a manifest number. We were then assembled into groups according to our manifest numbers and were packed on the top deck of barges, while our baggage was piled on the lower decks." Interpreters directed them up a steep stairway to the Registry Room. A doctor stood at the top of the stairs watching them for signs of health problems for which they would be denied admittance. As each immigrant passed by a doctor, he would examine their face, hair, neck and hands and with a piece of chalk in his hand, he would scrawl a large white letter on their clothing. This letter would indicate if they passed or would be detained for further medical inspection. Some of Uncle John's remarks would reverberate in my father's ears: "The great hall teeming with people reminded me of the Tower of Babel, where one could hear so many different languages being spoken. At Ellis Island, I witnessed endless lines of refugees. So many fates were hanging in the balance. If I made it, I knew that at the end there was a promise of opportunity. As I gathered my suitcase and the rest of my belongings to get in line to wait for my turn to come, I worried about the dull cough I had developed during my last two days on the ship. I wondered if it would complicate matters for me." He had reason to worry, because the final words of the doctor examining him were:

"I cannot issue a clearance for you to enter the U.S. before we find out more about your cough." Then he put in an order for his transfer to the hospital ward of Ellis Island for observation. When he reached the hospital ward where non-qualifiers at first try were taken, my father clearly recalls his cousin's sadness: "I felt isolated and frankly quite discouraged. There were rows of beds, some with patients in them. It would have been difficult for me to survive there for long. Then as fate had it, on the second day of my stay, the nurse in charge of my unit happened to be Florence. She had been the only person so far who had shown me some compassion." Within the next few days, his cough improved. Finally with an admittance card and box lunch in his hand, his journey through Ellis Island had concluded.

He was ferried on a barge to the train terminal in Jersey City and was allowed to enter the U.S. He remembered walking along quite a few city streets that day which looked grim, noisy, crowded and dangerous. The electric trolleys still ruled the streets at the time alongside the automobile, which was starting to gain in popularity. There still were a fair number of horse-drawn carriages around with horses' droppings everywhere. The couple of factories in the vicinity were belching black smoke. My father remembers his cousin commenting, "I have to admit, it was not the most pleasant introduction to the U.S.!"

When Uncle John arrived in 1923, there was a tuberculosis epidemic in New York due to overcrowding and also because antibiotics had not been discovered yet. In spite of his being a steerage passenger, the tab for his trip all the way from Beirut and across the Atlantic still had made a dent in his finances. Since during the deportations, his twenty year old brother had been among the innocent victims of the typhus epidemic, his father had given him the lion's share of whatever was left.

"Meanwhile, because I had to immediately start spending a portion of the money since I had to rent a room at a tenement house, the amount I had initially set aside to start a grocery store business was constantly dwindling. As I further cut corners in my daily expenses, the quality of my diet started to suffer. It had been some time that I was not getting enough rest and sleep, because I was on a constant search mode to investigate different locations where I could start my business venture. Being all alone in a foreign country, it was so difficult to know who to trust and where to open that grocery store."

He soon met a young man in his tenement house that appeared to have similar goals and offered to be his business partner. "I should have been more discriminating, but I was getting quite impatient with every passing day," he admitted to his cousins. The two partners were just getting their business venture off the ground, working long hours when he started noticing a significant lack of energy and a deep cough which would wake him up at nights. After explaining the situation to his partner, he took the trolley and headed to the closest hospital so a physician could check him. After taking his temperature and listening to his chest, the doctor recommended hospitalization, because he suspected he could have pneumonia. The hospital ward did not look too different to him from that on Ellis Island, except that here sheets were hung from the ceiling to separate the beds on the ward from each other. Uncle John's recovery was painfully slow.

When his partner finally visited him in the hospital, from the account he gave, Uncle John realized he had not been punctual in meeting deadlines for the payment of the goods delivered to their store. "I realized I had made a poor choice for a business partner. But I was not yet strong enough to be on my feet at this crucial time in the life of our business. Of course all of this frustrated and depressed me. However not everything was gloomy about my hospitalization. One week into my hospital stay, a new nurse was assigned to my ward; I could not believe my eyes when I realized it was Florence, the same kind nurse who had cared for me on Ellis Island. She recognized me too and made every effort to make my stay comfortable and my recovery smooth."

Due to this unusual coincidence, as well as due to his feeling all alone in an unfamiliar land, Uncle John started feeling close to Florence, since by now she had helped him more than once during a particularly difficult and vulnerable time in his life. "When it was time for my discharge, we exchanged phone numbers. I gave her the phone number in the hallway of my tenement house. Two days later, she called me to find out how I was doing and in this way we started seeing each other." Once his business started running more smoothly, their relationship slowly evolved into a romantic one and ultimately culminated with his asking for her hand in marriage. At this point, every one of his cousins in the spacious backyard in Büyükdere cheered and empathized with him.

In time, Uncle John's life story took an unexpected turn. Although Florence had been the perfect nurse during his two hospitalizations, as the years progressed, her character went through a major transformation. Many years later when I again met Uncle John in person in New Jersey in 1962, from what he described, I gathered she had become a controlling, jealous, and paranoid wife.

During the reunion of the cousins in 1948, in addition to refusing to accompany Uncle John on this trip to Istanbul to explore the city and meet her husband's cousins after a separation of twenty-five years, Florence had made it clear that this was the only trip she would allow John to take to see his side of the family. The reunion was further saddened when Uncle John felt responsible to announce another unpleasant detail: "I am so happy to be here today with so many of my relatives--especially my cousins; however, if you were to come to New Jersey, I could never be able to reciprocate this wonderful favor, because my wife Florence would not be as accommodating as you!"

Fast forward to nineteen years later to the winter of 1967, when my husband Greg was stationed in Edgewood Arsenal in Maryland, we made a special effort to visit Uncle John in Paramus, New Jersey, for what would be a last time, when we were on our way to New York to see the newly-released musical of that year, *Cabaret*. It was virtually impossible to communicate with him on the phone to arrange a meeting for any significant length of time. In the end, the way we managed to meet with him was by having Greg's cousin's wife Alidz, play the role of a long-distance telephone operator. Good thing there was no "Caller ID" at the time! Perfect in her role as a telephone company operator, Alidz managed to get Uncle John on the phone for a person to person call to talk to me. Even then, he agreed to meet Greg and me only briefly at a soda fountain for no more than fifteen minutes. The few minutes that we spent together on that day created an indelible mark in my memory as I became quite aware of the pressures he was under. "Any more than this brief meeting will make Florence very suspicious," he confessed.

"Don't worry Uncle John; I can easily go back in my memory to 1962 when I had first arrived in the U.S. in New York City. We had a good time together then, and you had taken me to

Radio City Music Hall to see the Rockettes perform some amazing toe-tapping numbers," I reminded him, mostly to cheer him up.

When it was time for us to part, he made sure to hug both Greg and me. I noticed he had become teary-eyed and his voice had become halting at times. I could not help but have a flashback to forty years ago when he was an enthusiastic young business school graduate from the American University of Beirut setting foot on Ellis Island, along with other immigrants with high hopes and plenty of dreams. His courageous effort to be the first one from his family in the aftermath of the Armenian Genocide of 1915 to leave the Middle East, to make a fresh start in the New World had solved certain problems, but it had also created a slew of others...

Life in Büyükdere for Monam and Arsha

In 1941, a short while after Uncle Jacob had left Turkey for the United States, his mother Arshaluys, whom we lovingly called Monam, and his sister Arsha had moved to the summer resort of the Hatunoglus in Büyükdere, on the Asian shores of the Bosphorus. They rented their spacious two-story guesthouse year round, while they kept a watchful eye on their extensive property. Monam and Arsha seemed quite pleased with this arrangement, although at the time they probably did not realize that they were perhaps living the happiest years of their lives. By now mother and stepdaughter, who were not that far apart in age, had become the best of friends. When I was lucky enough to be their guest as a child in Büyükdere, I often had the impression that they were on a perpetual vacation on the Bosphorus against the stunning backdrop of nature. Their few recurring, as well as extraordinary expenses were being taken care of by Uncle Jacob and my father. For a change, they were accountable to virtually no one. They felt responsible biweekly to compose a joint letter to Jacob, in which they would carefully include all their activities he would approve of, giving special attention to their choice of words. They wanted to make sure their actions would please and not upset him. After multiple revisions, each one of these letters would eventually pass muster and be mailed to him.

During the summer months, Monam and Arsha were always overjoyed by the arrival of their landlords, the Hatunoglus. Their property in Büyükdere was quite unique, with the main residence situated on top of a hill overlooking the vegetation of the lush green valley below and the gorgeous Bosphorus in the distance. Another reason Monam and Arsha enjoyed the company of the Hatunoglus during the summers in Büyükdere was because it encouraged them to engage in plenty of daydreaming and pleasant anticipation. In the back of their minds was the great expectation that once they were united with their beloved Hagop (Jacob) in the United States, life for them would be far more fulfilling.

Unlike other small parcels with insignificant backyards, the Hatunoglu's was an extensive estate on multiple levels with several unusual fruit bearing trees, vines and vegetables and salad greens lovingly cared for by Mr. Onnik, as everyone called him, the retired tailor who had married into riches. To this day, his curly brown hair, tanned, red, and overheated face, often dripping wet with perspiration and his entire body totally exhausted from gardening most of the day, readily comes before my eyes. After nursing his various types of berries, fruit trees, and salad greens with devotion, by early afternoon he was ready to return to his residence, carrying an armful of greens and an overflowing basket of his latest produce. It was in his garden that as an eleven-year-old I had my first introduction to arugula, which had surprised me by creating a tickling sensation in the taste buds at the tip of my tongue. Once when I had accidentally paired this salad green with one of Mr. Onnik's freshly picked heirloom tomatoes he had offered me, I had thought it was the most perfect salad green I had ever tasted!

Mr. Onnik's wife, Madame Nini could have easily been a character from a novel. She was a vivacious woman who had a carefree outlook towards life. Even as a child, I could tell that she was taking too many things nonchalantly. From the two-story guesthouse where Monam and Arsha lived, which was on a hill ten feet above their landlord's, I could often hear her high-pitched laugh often punctuated with phrases in French, a language she was fluent in. She either did not wish to be bothered by the existing problems of the world or she just wanted to give us that impression. She entertained herself most of the time by either leisurely sipping on Turkish coffee, knitting, or by conversing with her sister Therese. In sharp contrast to Madame Nini, her older sister, whom we all called *Tante Therese,* was a woman with a flat affect. I had overheard that she had always wanted to be a nun. Her family had tried to talk her out of it and had eventually succeeded. However, being forced to make this decision against her will had saddened her and most likely was the reason for her sarcasm.

Madame Nini's brother, whom everyone called *Oncle Joseph*, was a retired surgeon, a confirmed bachelor, and a regular visitor at Büyükdere during the summer months. He was a chubby, short fellow with a similar disposition to that of Madame Nini. I often had difficulty imagining him functioning as a surgeon in real life. The third guest in their household was Mr. Onnik's longtime friend, Mr. Kevork.

The Hatunoglu's past was shrouded in a certain amount of mystery. Some years before I knew them, Mr. Hatunoglu's tall and handsome business associate Kevork, who was quite a Casanova, apparently frequented the Hatunoglu residence with regularity. There was even a rumor that the good-looking and sociable housewife Nini might have had a dark secret involving Kevork and that he may have fathered the Hatunoglu's only daughter Lillie. It is entirely possible that people entertained these thoughts about her due to her relaxed nature and easy sociability. The striking resemblance in facial features and mannerism between Mr. Hatunoglu and Lillie had left no doubt in my mind that what I was hearing was pure gossip.

Madame Nini often tried to decipher everyone's fortunes from the coffee grinds which settled at the bottom of their demitasses after they had taken their time to leisurely sip on the thick Turkish coffee until they had exhausted it to the last drop; they would then turn the demitasses upside down on their saucers and would allow plenty of time for the coffee grinds to drain and settle down in their graceful cannikins. Finally when it was time, since the circumstance made her an "informal master of ceremonies," Madame Nini would live up to the occasion with puns and concoct stories about romantic events waiting to happen to the owners of these demitasses, thus generating what seemed like unending laughter. In the absence of television, this proved to be a significant source of entertainment for everyone. At other times, one would find her playing card games, reading novels or simply having a good time. Thus the Hatunoglus were the best neighbors and landlords that Monam and Arsha could have ever desired for socializing and relaxing and daydreaming during the summer months, while they were waiting impatiently for correspondence from Uncle Jacob to inform them that they could finally immigrate to the United States to join him. This wait would take approximately nineteen years. J. Edgar Hoover, the notorious FBI director who had made it his life's mission to watch over Uncle Jacob and others like him, and the Armenophobic second president of Turkey, Ismet Inönü, must have played significant roles at least during the initial part of this delay.

In an effort to make the long and lonely winter months more bearable, Monam and Arsha had cultivated a thriving friendship with the energetic young Armenian couple, the Markarians who lived down the hill from them, not too far from the front gate of the Hatunoglu property. As fate would have it, fast forward some thirty years, this couple would immigrate to the United States, becoming my husband Greg's patients from Orange County.

My Decision to Study in the States

By the time I started my senior year at the American High School in Istanbul, I had unequivocally decided to study in the United States, believing it to be the land of opportunity. I thought it would be where I could advance in my chosen field, provided I worked at it hard enough. My father did not stand in my way because he trusted me, as well as his academically-oriented cousin Jacob in Southern California, and thought his guidance in academics would be invaluable to me. Additionally, being ahead of his time, he did not discriminate; he felt a daughter had just as much a right to a fine education that led to a career as a son did. The way he had so eloquently expressed it to me and my sister was: "Education is a golden bracelet which will set you free."

I was so thankful my parents were willing to trust me to venture alone to study thousands of miles away from home. I was coming from a tightly knit Middle Eastern background where conventionally things were not done this way. However, having observed many political crises in Turkey throughout their lives where the outcome for the Armenian minority had without exception been detrimental and at times deadly, they realized we had to take advantage of opportunity when it presented itself. When this window of opportunity disappeared, it was likely to vanish for an entire generation or more. My entire family realized this and thought I better join the race before it passed me by.

During the summer of 1968 when my parents were planning to leave the country permanently, my mother had mentioned that right up to the evening of their departure, Armenian families rich and poor would come to my father's office in Eminönü, trusting him with their life's savings and hoping that he would take on the responsibility of transferring their funds overseas, charging them a modest commission for his services. It had taken my father years to develop this unique friendship and trust among his business associates, clients and friends. My sister recalls a particular summer evening around this time, when all three of them were packed and preparing to leave Turkey for good. An elderly Armenian gentleman had requested to meet with my father in our apartment in Nisantasi to drop off a substantial sum of money he wanted my father to transfer abroad for him. She clearly remembers there being only two chairs in an otherwise bare room, when my father asked his client:

"You know Mr. Ekshian I will be leaving the country tomorrow; how can you trust me with so much money, knowing that you will not be able to contact me once I leave the country?" The elderly man thought for a moment and answered him with absolute calmness in his voice:

"You have been honest throughout the years with our people here with their life's savings, Mr. Lafdjian; that is the reason I trust you."

In the light of this trust, when my parents emigrated out of Turkey, I now realize that the loss of identity as well as self-worth must have been quite a serious matter for them. It was going to be much harder for my aging parents to adjust to the customs and language of a new country and culture than it was going to be for me. At the beginning, there would be long stretches when they would not have any friends or social network.

Burglary before Leaving Istanbul

Around the time that my parents were preparing to leave Istanbul for good, Ahmed the doorkeeper of their apartment in Nisantasi, must have gotten a whiff of an idea that their days in Turkey were numbered. Therefore he had seized the opportunity to steal my mother's priceless *Longines* watch with its solid gold, thick, interwoven band, as well as my father's automatic *Omega* watch with its sizable digits he had somehow trained his eyes to decipher, in spite of his progressively-failing eyesight. They had purchased both of these precious items the previous year when they had briefly stopped by in Geneva, Switzerland on their way to the United States. They probably had such special memories attached to them that they would not have been willing to part with them at any price. My father had been the companion with the photographic memory who could come up with the accurate calculations, managing them all in his head to make up for his failing eyesight. My mother had been the faithful wife and brave communicator with her imperfect French, augmented with her grammatically perfect English, attempting to finalize their trades. Now in Nisantasi, at one of these opportune moments when their door must have been left ajar, the doorkeeper of their apartment complex had sneaked in and stolen these precious articles from them.

This being Turkey, they could not have the doorkeeper indicted, even though they were convinced almost beyond the shadow of a doubt that he was the culprit. If they turned him in to the authorities and the doorkeeper chose to testify against my parents, announcing that they were leaving the country for good, it would have opened a Pandora's Box for them. They would have been detained for an unspecified length of time, subjected to lengthy interrogations, and most likely would have missed their scheduled flight. Then there was the fear my father's profession as a money-changer always exposed him to. The doorkeeper could have easily created havoc for him with a single unfounded accusation...

(Endnotes)

1   Alboyadjian, Arshag, *Batmutiwn Malatio Hayots* , Beirut: Sevan Press,1961, p.966.
2   Ibid p.967.
3   Dobkin, Marjorie Housepian, *Smyrna*, 1922.NewYork: Newmark Press, 1988, p.88.
4   Ibid p.9
5   Akcam, Taner, *A Shameful Act*, New York: Henry Holt & Co.2007, p.326.
6   Ibid p.342
7   Ibid p.345
8   Calislar, Ipek, *Latife Hanim*, Istanbul: Dogan Kitapcilik AS, 2006, p.203.
9   Ibid p.272
10   Ibid p.326
11   Ibid p.224
12   Ibid p.223
13   Ibid p.284
14   Ibid p.338
15   Garboushian, Arminé, personal communication, 2007.
16   Schickel, Richard, *Elia Kazan*, New York: Harper Collins, 2005, p.2.
17   Carabetian Koundakjian, Armine, *The Repression of Armenian \ Repatriates during the Stalin Era*, Yerevan: Self-publication, 2012, p.51.
18   Ibid p.38
19   Ibid p.37
20   Ghazarian, Silva, Telephone communication with France, Nov, 2014.
21   Stepanyan, Armen, e-mail communication via son Hovik, Sept. 2015.
22   Carabetian Koundakjian, Armine, *The Repression of Armenian Repatriates during the Stalin Era*, Yerevan: Self-publication, 2012, p.55.
23   Ghazarian, Silva, Telephone communication with France, Nov, 2014.

Life in ISTANBUL

CHAPTER III
AMERICA

Leaving for the United States

I had become quite reflective the year I was getting ready to leave Turkey to pursue my college education in the United States. Perhaps it was a sign of maturity on my part to look back and evaluate the basic components of my high school education. This exercise helped me realize that my parents had given me an excellent start by exposing me to seven years of expertly taught, grammatically correct English. However, so much was about to change for me so abruptly within the next few years. Suddenly at age seventeen, I was going to be completely on my own, in a totally different country halfway around the world. Although I realized it was probably the best thing my parents could have done for me, I also felt anxious because I had no idea what I would encounter along the way and how successful I would be in the end.

By now and mostly through unspoken words, I had sensed that in spite of having made many positive contributions throughout history, my people had constantly been subjected to political turmoil and persecution while they lived in Turkey. Although the situation seemed to be calm for the moment, things could change radically quite suddenly, depending on which way the political winds were blowing.

Unable to Go Back for Many Years

Forty-four years later, now as a naturalized citizen viewing the state of affairs in my adopted country, many a time I still have the sense of being neither here nor there and yet in both places at once. There were times when I was confronted with what it meant to be "the other" to those who lived next door to me. There were those who were intrigued with that slight accent and would want to find out more. Then there were those few whose prejudice prevented us from having a meaningful association. Due to family obligations and job constraints, it took me some forty-four years to go back to see Turkey again. Although Istanbul had changed beyond recognition with its population multiplied tenfold, it still stirred up memories from the past as I felt a close connection to this charming city of my past. I also felt a special bond to my hometown of Kadiköy, with its quaint little Armenian Church, *Soorp Takavor*. As I lit a candle, prayed, and proceeded toward the altar to take a seat at a second row pew, for a moment I had a flashback to the days when I was actually living on Mühürdar Ave #44, almost across from this church. I remembered how my sister and I could not wait for it to be Sunday morning, especially during Christmas or Easter so we could go into this sanctuary. The heavenly chants of the church's choir, which we often joined as part of the congregation, had a way of captivating me and taking me to a gentler and more melodic world I now can only dream about. I cannot easily forget the yearly funeral procession for Jesus Christ which took place on the Saturday before Easter. The fragrance of the colorful spring flowers decorating Christ's burial chamber would impart a lasting light perfume throughout the entire church compound. It would also gently remind my mother to take my sister and me on a tram ride the following Monday to visit the cemetery where our dear departed relatives lay for their final rest. Our parish priest Father Kalenderian would offer a special prayer for their souls, while the smell of burned incense radiating out of his censer made our connection to the past more complete. Upon our return home from the cemetery, we would have lunch with our relatives and reminisce the treasured times we had shared with these loving family members who were no longer in our midst.

On my 2006 visit to Istanbul, the extraordinary lunch my cousin Sona had prepared for us duplicated the tastiest seafood, vegetables, and pastry my mother always managed to create during her younger and more energetic years. I felt I belonged in this place because in so many ways it felt like home to me; but I also knew I could not necessarily stay there.

Our Visit to Family's Ancestral Home in Aksaray

As part of the same trip to Turkey, when we traveled towards Historic Armenia and followed the diligently recorded descriptions of Great-uncle Abraham in his memoir, to our surprise we found that some 91 years later, my grandparents' sturdy residence in Aksaray, located 60 miles west of Gesaria (Kayseri), as well as the *Pasha Hamam* (public bath) had managed to withstand the test of time. Both buildings were still operational. We were greeted by an elderly refugee from Kazakhstan and her grandson living on the first floor of their residence. The moment we walked into the roomy and cool kitchen of my grandmother, the ghosts from her days in this once busy kitchen were suddenly brought back to life for me. I could picture her cooking up a storm on the cast iron stove by the thick stone walls. I again felt a special connection to the land and to my ancestors who had lived here until their forced deportation in 1915. My father must have had so many memories of this ancestral home with its nearby brook eventually reaching the Euphrates, its grape vines and fruit trees, its state of the art *Pasha Hamam* across the street from it, which my Great-uncle Abraham was instrumental in constructing within its predetermined budget. Mgrdich was the master architect behind the project. The Pasha Hamam had definitely improved the quality of life in Aksaray. Its building materials, including the marble for the floors, the entry hall and the hot and cool rooms for men and women had arrived from different parts of the country.

Throughout history, the *Turkish Hamam*, a descendent of the baths of ancient Rome and Byzantium, was the site of the world's great bathing rituals. It was a place not just to get clean but also to recharge and relax. Women would take food there, such as olives, *sarmas* (stuffed grape leaves), and baklava, which they would be served with Turkish coffee, after they were clean and refreshed.

I can imagine how my father and grandparents and great-uncles must have felt, when on just a week's notice few years after the grand opening of the *Pasha Hamam* to the public in Aksaray, they were ordered to leave everything behind and move on south towards the hostile Syrian Desert. Sometimes I wonder how they could have been so oblivious of the risk hovering over them one year from the outbreak of WWI. But then, this was where their homes and businesses were. They did not have better alternatives. A number of my father's relatives who survived would eventually settle in Constantinople (Istanbul), which at the time was an unfamiliar city for them. It was large, cosmopolitan, and visible; therefore it could provide them with an additional element of safety, although this too was fleeting. The dislocation from their homeland must have created havoc for my people for generations. My relatives were dispersed throughout the world, never to know each other intimately again. As a result, our language, literature, and culture suffered irreparably.

To this day, in the United States there are times when I am torn between hanging on to the old ways of family and tradition, versus adopting a lifestyle in the image of modern immigrants. In my new homeland I enjoy the solace that tradition offers me; yet I have to be prepared to bear the hidden burden that may come with it. I have to think of my children's and grandchildren's future and what all this will mean to them. I could strictly stick to the traditions of my homeland, but in doing this I may alienate the new generation.

Aksaray

In November 1918, the Lafdjians had managed to reach Beirut from the desert village of Remté and had settled there for about a year. At the time, due to the victory of the Allied forces against the Ottoman Turks, Cilicia was promised to the Armenians by the French. Therefore the Lafdjians found the political situation in Anatolia favorable for them once again and on May 1919 they headed back towards Mersin on the Mediterranean coast of Turkey. They were hoping to resettle in their homeland of Aksaray. They wished to return back there because they had too much invested in that town, including their well-constructed two-story residence, the *Pasha Hamam*, farmland and income properties in and around the town of Aksaray. Most importantly, in spite of the Armenian Genocide of 1915, they had continued to maintain a mutual trust in the local people of Aksaray with whom they had conducted their business.

Irreconcilable Differences among Allies and Outcome of WWI

Looking back to 1920, because the Allies were taking an unreasonably long time in reaching consensus to partition what was left of the Ottoman Empire, on August 20, Armenians took matters into their own hands and declared their independence in Adana in historic Cilicia. This declaration was immediately rejected by France. Postwar disagreements and the desire to claim ownership of the newly-discovered oil in the Middle East were now creating serious problems among the Allies. Exhausted by its large number of WWI casualties from Germany and overextended in its postwar commitments, France was now unwilling to commit additional troops and resources to Anatolia. Under these conditions, the solemn promises of protection and autonomy made by the Allies to the Armenians during the war were quietly but firmly disregarded.

Constantinople

Right around this time, the political environment radically changed as a result of the many military victories of Mustafa Kemal Atatürk, including the fall of Marash to Turkish Nationalists on February 1920, the covert Allied help offered to Mustafa Kemal, and the withdrawal of the French military from Cilicia. Consequently, Armenians were once again at the mercy of Turkish fanaticism. By midsummer 1919, while the British forces in the Ottoman territories were melting away, the Turks were preparing to fight as they had not fought before.[1]

It became obvious to the Lafdjians that Anatolia was once again becoming an unfriendly environment for Armenians, making any type of a resettlement plan there virtually impossible. The only alternative they now had was to leave the past behind, including their extensive properties in Aksaray, take the first ship available from Mersin, and move their entire family to Constantinople, still by far the most cosmopolitan city in Turkey. Thus they gathered whatever remaining diminished resources they had after living practically as nomads for the past four years, to push forward for a fresh start in yet another unfamiliar city: Constantinople.

Uncle Jacob

When the deportations first started, my father's cousin, my "Uncle Jacob" was a three year old passenger traveling in the ox cart my fourteen-year-old father was driving from Aksaray. He was less than communicative, but grew up to be an extremely bright student in mathematics and physics. After arriving in Constantinople, he graduated from the engineering department of the Technical University in Istanbul with B.S. and M.S. degrees in 1933 and 1937 respectively. Subsequently, he applied and was accepted for a teaching position at his alma mater because he had been the highest ranking student in his engineering class and had been recognized by the faculty as an exceptional student in that field with plenty of promise for the future.

To his surprise, in 1941 he won the most coveted scholarship the Turkish government offered: an all-expenses paid education in the United States towards an advanced degree.

In the United States he received his graduate degree in Electrical Engineering from Caltech in Pasadena in 1951. In his personal life, Jacob was a habitual loner and had difficulty relating to others. He often avoided situations where he needed to communicate with people, be it family, relatives, or colleagues. Although by today's standards he might have been considered a near-autistic introvert, his behavior may also have been influenced by prolonged separations from his father early in his life and during his teenage years, depriving him of a role model. It could also be the reason why he had never updated his personal information in the Caltech alumni records, since his name frequently appeared on the university's "lost alumni" list.

It was some thirteen years after Jacob's graduation from Caltech, during my parents' first visit to the United States during the summer of 1964, when I finally learned about Jacob's earlier years in Turkey. The following is what my father had to say regarding his cousin:

"The origin of Hagop's difficulties in the U.S. when he first arrived there as a university student had all started with his stormy relationship back home with Ömer Inönü, the older son of the Turkish president, Ismet Inönü. Ömer was an engineering student when Hagop was a lecturer at the Technical University of Istanbul. As smart and inquisitive a student as Inönü's younger son Erdal was, Ömer had no interest in engineering; he wanted to ride on the coat-tails of his father to advance.

"Ironically, Ömer found himself in the class of a bright young Armenian lecturer with an abundance of moral fiber, albeit sorely deficient in diplomacy. Earlier in the week, while supervising the final exam in engineering at the university, Hagop had caught Ömer cheating. He had warned him to refrain from such unacceptable behavior and threatened to report him to the university authorities if it ever recurred. However, Ömer assumed his family connections would still protect him, and he continued to ignore Hagop's warning and proceeded to cheat. So, at the conclusion of the exam, what does my cousin do? Without giving it a second thought, he reports Ömer to the university authorities."

Clearly, recounting these experiences deeply troubled my father. I detected his powerful tone of disapproval as he spoke on the subject—one that he recognized as deeply taboo for an Armenian to mention in Turkey. He continued:

"Hagop was a genius in electrical engineering; but he was not practical. He did not see how reporting Ömer would provoke his father, Ismet Inönü. After all, Ismet Inönü was the President of Turkey. He had all sorts of power to thwart Hagop's progress. He should have realized by then that since he was an Armenian, he should never have tried to teach a lesson to an Inönü in Turkey.

"By the time President Inönü became aware that an Armenian lecturer had reported his son's academic dishonesty, Jacob had already left Turkey for the United States to study at the

University of Illinois in Urbana-Champaign on his prestigious scholarship. The only way Inönü could get back at him now was to warn the United States Government of Hagop's "alleged communist activities." Of course, he did not hesitate to do exactly that."

Those familiar with US history no doubt know that Inönü's timing in the United States coincided perfectly with Red-hunting government committees and the forever suspicious FBI Director J. Edgar Hoover. This was a time when any threat of communist activity could result in tapping phones, sifting through garbage, opening mail, and shadowing every footstep.

In retrospect, if Uncle Jacob had not been in such a hurry and had consulted his peers about the appropriate action to take regarding the president's son, he could have pursued a less extreme course of action. Perhaps, in addition to explaining to Ömer that he would need a "working knowledge" of engineering concepts for a viable future in the field, Uncle Jacob could have aided Ömer with some of the concepts he had missed and assigned him additional problems. However, to do so would involve social interaction, something Jacob always tried to avoid.

At the time, Uncle Jacob may not have been aware that he was playing Russian roulette by reporting the misconduct of the son of the highest-ranking official in Turkey. He was also ignoring lessons he should have learned long ago from history on how undeniably prejudiced Ismet Inönü had been in the past towards Armenians. His hasty disciplinary action, although warranted, ended up having far-reaching consequences for him.

Life at University of Illinois at Urbana-Champaign

World War II had already thrust its ugly head when Uncle Jacob had become a graduate student at the University of Illinois in Urbana-Champaign in September 1941. Jacob had taken on a job as a lab assistant to cover his incidental expenses. Being conscientious, he hoped to forward his mother and sister a modest sum every few months to cover any unforeseen expenses they might have had.

Adjusting to university life in a new country halfway around the world did not prove to be an easy task for Jacob. To perplex him further, around this time something completely unexpected and unpleasant started happening: Upon his return to his room at the end of a long day, he found his books, correspondence, and student lab experiments in a state of complete disarray. It even occurred to him that someone was tapping his phone and sifting through his garbage.

These disturbing events kept recurring and began making life quite miserable for Jacob. Initially, he had no clue why he was being singled out for this persecution. He started becoming increasingly suspicious. Soon he started to dread the end of day, when he had to return to his room, his only domain where he was entitled to some privacy.

Caught up in his pride and fearing the stigma of seeking professional help, he decided to personally tackle the problem. In spite of the monetary and physical hardships involved, he even moved to a new address, hoping his life could somehow revert back to normal. Nothing helped. Instead, becoming increasingly paranoid, he kept coming closer to the verge of a nervous breakdown. When he could no longer function in the capacity expected of him at the university, one afternoon he headed in the direction of the Medical and Mental Health Services. He waited for his turn and after a while he was able to talk to a health care professional. All of this was counter to his style, but under the circumstances even he thought he had no other alternative.

He was finally referred to a psychologist who started helping him by fitting the pieces of the puzzle together. To take a complete history from Jacob took several sessions. Finally the psychologist had to confront him with his finding: Jacob was having schizoid episodes. After first reassuring Jacob, he then tried to trace its origin.

A number of additional sessions with the psychologist led them to trace Jacob's difficulties back to the Turkish president, his son, the cheating incident, and ultimately, to J. Edgar Hoover. Some years later J. Edgar Hoover's name would be tarnished by his systemized abuse of power; however, until that point, Hoover ruthlessly sought to destroy his enemies--real and imagined--with no thought to the rights of law-abiding citizens. Jacob must have been reported to the FBI as a dangerous foreigner and suspected Soviet agent. That would explain why the FBI had been monitoring his mail and his phone conversations ever since he had arrived in the U.S. from Turkey!

According to my sister Arminé, my father at some point recalled how two Turkish secret police officers paid an unannounced visit to his office in Eminönü during the winter of 1942 to question him about his cousin Hagop Lafdjian, now living in Illinois. Because the FBI had repeatedly come out empty-handed in its investigation of Jacob on the Urbana-Champaign campus, and also because my father succeeded in reassuring the Istanbul secret police of Jacob's impeccable character and nonexistence of communist ties, the FBI finally ended its witch hunt.

Consequently, the disruptive activities which had been driving Jacob to the edge of paranoia for almost a year suddenly stopped as mysteriously as they had begun. However, the damage was done. Jacob's schizoid episodes continued ever since his arrival at the University. He kept having auditory and visual hallucinations which impeded him from progressing at the university and leading a normal life.

Other than for its universal academic reputation in engineering, Jacob had selected the Urbana-Champaign campus of the University of Illinois because of its close proximity to his cousin Nver, Great-uncle Abraham's daughter who now lived in Chicago. He had reasoned that perhaps an occasional visit to see her and her family on certain weekends could help him get over his homesickness. There was also Nver's daughter, Berjouhi, for whom he had special feelings. However, since he lacked the necessary social skills, he failed to approach her tactfully.

"He had designs on me; I could not stand him," was the way Berjouhi expressed her feelings towards Jacob many years later, when she had taken a vacation to visit Southern California. Since she was not a social person herself and somewhat lacking in empathy, she must have made Jacob feel snubbed. Thus, instead of finding himself in a warm and welcoming environment, he must have felt depressed and isolated in an unfamiliar country thousands of miles away from his home base.

Move to Caltech in Pasadena

After almost six years at the University of Illinois at Urbana-Champaign, Jacob had not realized any significant academic achievements, due to his recurring but slowly diminishing schizoid episodes. Jacob recognized the time had come to remove himself from his present environment, which was only reminding him of his days of distress. Therefore, in the spring of 1947, he finally gathered the courage to apply to the Engineering Department of California Institute of Technology in Pasadena. He was accepted and started attending this university on September 26, 1947 until June 8, 1951, when he received his M.S. in Electrical Engineering with a minor in Physics. He worked in Caltech under the tutelage of physicist Dr. Sophus Epstein on the Electromagnetic Theory. His work can still be viewed in the engineering department of Caltech in Box 28, folder 26, labeled, "Lafdjian's Problem."

Uncle Jacob's years at Caltech in Pasadena were happier and more productive than his years at the University of Illinois at Urbana-Champaign. Great-uncle Abraham's brother-in-law, Dikran Kazanjian, who was now an antique dealer in Pasadena, had been spared from the initial deadly wave of deportations from Aksaray and had moved to Konya. In 1923 when Atatürk came to power, Dikran Kazanjian and his daughter had first headed to Constantinople, and then emigrated to the U.S. shortly thereafter, settling in Pasadena.

When Uncle Jacob first came to know Dikran Kazanjian in 1947, Kazanjian was living with his widowed daughter, Eve Melkonian and granddaughter Rose. When they found out that a relative of theirs was studying at nearby Caltech, they gladly welcomed him to their home and into their lives on numerous occasions. Kazanjian's spacious antique store was located on the northeastern corner of Raymond and Green streets in Pasadena.

As Uncle Jacob would soon find out, their living quarters on Allen Ave. was unlike anywhere he had been so far. Their acquaintances from church, as well as other social circles, would often stop by to socialize. It was here that for the first time Uncle Jacob felt at ease enough with Eve's daughter Rose, to mention the disruptive searches of his living quarters in the past and the nightmares he still had about them. Meanwhile Rose had a difficult time believing him, because what he described sounded so unreal and more like a chapter from a mystery novel to her. Indeed, some fifty years later Rose acknowledged to me that at the time she believed it was all a figment of his imagination.[2]

Uncle Jacob stopped by at Aunt Eve's residence on Allen Ave., which was within walking distance from Caltech, whenever he felt lonely or when he missed the authentic Armenian delicacies his mother used to prepare for him in Istanbul. In stark contrast to Jacob's personality, Aunt Eve was very outgoing. In spite of being a diabetic and of modest means, she would stock her house with delectable food items she was ready to dish out for her guests at a moment's notice. Additionally, her hospitality, her antique furniture, her European-themed paintings, her demitasses, and statuettes made of genuine English porcelain, all from Uncle Dikran's antique store, must have given him the impression that he was entering an almost regal, yet friendly and welcoming, environment.

When it was time to have a bite, both the content and the presentation of Aunt Eve's elegant table with its many Armenian delicacies, including the *pastirma,* the cured beef, the *beorek*, the pastry with melted cheese in the center, the fine porcelain dishes loaded with string and feta cheeses, the Kalamata and the green olives all presented on an exquisitely embroidered tablecloth, could easily have been the envy of a Ritz Carleton's afternoon tea. It was even more surprising and impressive knowing that the creator of it all, Aunt Eve, was not even able to walk with ease due to her congenitally displaced hip joints.

To his pleasant surprise, Uncle Jacob realized that while visiting them, he was able to leave his paranoia behind; he could relax and even take a break from his theoretical thinking, especially when he was lucky enough to be their only guest.

Uncle Kazanjian's Antique Store

Dikran Kazanjian's spacious and unique antique store in downtown Pasadena was a respite for Jacob where he could take a breather from his engineering dilemmas. He never quite knew what he might encounter each time he stopped by at this unusual store. The way business was conducted here contrasted strikingly with the uncompromising accuracy his engineering problems required. He could roughly search through stacks of paintings and heaps of articles, many of dubious value, every once in a while to come across a diamond in the rough!

Through Kazanjian's antique store, Jacob was acquiring another interest and perhaps an unexpected expertise. He was learning to evaluate art by conducting his own research on paintings he believed could be worthwhile. In fact, sometime within the next fifteen years he had become the proud owner of a Smithsonian-registered landscape by Thomas Moran. Looking into the future, it makes me wonder and worry what might have become of it after his demise. I knew he did not believe in wills. His heirs would not be sophisticated enough to conduct any research on the artwork they inherited as he would have done. While watching "Antique Showcase" on PBS on Monday evenings, I cannot help but wonder that his Thomas Moran landscape could possibly land there one day for appraisal, after having been purchased at a garage sale for an inconsequential sum!

Uncle Jacob's Future

Although he possessed the intellect of a genius, Jacob had considerable difficulty relaxing when he first met someone with whom he was expected to socialize. This was why he was at a loss for words when a friend of the family had arranged a date for him to meet a female Armenian scientist who could be a potential friend or perhaps a life companion. In spite of remaining in the same room for nearly an hour, he did not have the slightest idea how he should go about creating a conversation with her to break the ice.

It was 1960 and Uncle Jacob was nearing fifty, when upon the suggestion of a family acquaintance from Istanbul, he was introduced to Aida Achekian of Beirut, Lebanon. Although they had corresponded for a while, the circumstances under which Jacob had met Aida and married her were not essentially too different from having met her as a picture bride. The two met face to face for the first time in Aida's twin brother's house in Montreal, Canada. Uncle Jacob had traveled there from Los Angeles and Aida had flown the long distance from Beirut, Lebanon.

It must not have taken them long to realize that if they were considering marriage at all, this would perhaps be the last chance they each would get. For this reason, things started happening at a faster pace. Within two days of their first meeting, Jacob asked Aida out for dinner and took her to a French restaurant in town, which he had carefully selected.

When they arrived there, he asked the *maître d* for a somewhat remote and quiet table. After a memorable seafood dinner of salmon with a delectable French mushroom sauce, it was time for *crème brûlée.* This is when he unexpectedly dropped to one knee next to Aida, turned to her, and blurted out, "Will you marry me," as he produced an engagement ring from his pocket. She accepted, and he planted a kiss on her lips. This was perhaps the happiest day in their lives; he, for finding the courage to propose; she, for the chance to dream about a future together.

They planned a modest but formal church wedding in the Armenian Apostolic Church in Montreal. It was bittersweet in that no members of his side of the family could be present. However, copies of their wedding photograph depicting them in each other's arms reflecting their bliss, with Aida wearing an elegant ivory-colored two-piece, taffeta suit with a matching pillbox hat were mailed to Monam and Arsha as well as to us in Istanbul. Even though Aida's hat was part of the ensemble and was definitely called for on this occasion, during the ensuing years I remember her as someone with a special fondness for hats. She would often wear a hat, even if the occasion did not necessarily call for one. I would later realize it might have been for the purpose of obscuring her thinning hair on the top part of her scalp.

The scaled-down reception and dinner that followed the church ceremony, was prearranged by Jacob with assistance from Aida's brother and family. It was held in a restaurant with a talented pianist who played appropriate romantic selections for the newly-wed couple's dancing pleasure. They seemed to be truly happy, as Uncle Jacob's rarely beaming face and Aida's contented expression reflecting an inner bliss were depicted in the photograph I had first seen when I was still a high-school student living in Istanbul. The guests, which consisted of Aida's parents, her brother's family, and a few additional relatives, raised their goblets to celebrate the occasion and wished the newly-wed couple much happiness.

The pleasantly cool weather during the summer in Canada was a welcome change for them. For the evening, Jacob had made reservations at an elegant, centrally-located hotel in Montreal, so they could explore the city together a while longer. Early the following morning, they started their journey west towards Lake Erie in his rented car. To create an element of mystery and to surprise Aida, he had not disclosed to her their final honeymoon destination. However, she was able to guess, as she caught a glimpse of Lake Ontario in the distance; it was going to be Niagara Falls.

Niagara Falls, Ontario was even then considered a booming tourist city with high rise hotels. Checking into one on the Canadian side of the falls, they witnessed the ongoing sound and fury of the Horseshoe Falls, which stretched between Canada and the US. To their amazement, the water was cascading down some 185 feet to Lake Ontario. Because of his scientifically-oriented mind, it must have especially fascinated Jacob that the 45 million gallons of water they were witnessing dashing down, had first started flowing some 12,000 years ago and had eventually carved the present enormous gorge.

The Niagara Falls' natural and spiritual beauty inspired them both. They wanted to explore the area behind the Horseshoe Falls in an effort to get closer to the cataracts. After putting on their raincoats, headgear and water-resistant footwear, they carefully started descending the stairs. On their way down, they observed smaller branches of the waterfall cascading over moss-covered coves. They had descended more than a third of the way, when they realized that in spite of the precautions they were taking, they were not going to escape being drenched behind the curtain of famous water. There was something both fearful and attractive about surging waters where you could stand next to the roaring rapids to see and feel the charging waters up close. As they made their way by white-tipped cataracts, they wondered how many cities in the world existed in the proximity of nature this raw. They stood there for a few minutes taking in the grandeur, breathing the mist. Suddenly Aida excitedly pointed to the rainbow arched above the gradually darkening sky, directing Jacob's attention to it the minute she detected it. To them it looked like magic and due to their festive mood, Aida considered it a sign of good luck.

But they were getting somewhat cold now because they had gotten wet. They hurried up the stairs to seek the comfort of their hotel room and its warm shower. They must have both relaxed and fallen asleep, because it was totally dark when they woke up. After having a late dinner, they decided to return to see the falls under moonlight, to experience what that would feel like. Although there appeared to be too many lights for them to easily locate the moon and the stars, the constant flowing of the Niagara Falls became a source of power and romance for them. These exciting three days would linger in their memory for some time to come. Although Niagara's popularity as a tourist destination may have warred with their desire for privacy, it still was a magical time for both of them.

Aida was the initiator of their conversations; but it did not matter, because it led the way to further conversation that helped them to get to know each other better. They were slowly starting to adapt to one another in the presence of this amazing force of nature. On the third day of their honeymoon at Niagara Falls, after a wholesome breakfast of blueberry pancakes with maple syrup, sausage, and fresh raspberries, they drove to the nearby Toronto airport to return his rental car and to take the next plane to LAX. By now they were ready to settle down in the two bedroom apartment Jacob had earlier rented for them in Santa Ana, in Orange County.

Orange County

After receiving his engineering degree from Caltech and being hired by Hughes Aircraft in Orange County, Jacob had found it convenient to settle there. At some point he must have wondered how the county had first gotten its name. In 1871, when the area was first named, only a few orange trees existed there. The abundant crops at the time were corn and grapes, and neither one possessed the comparable charm to attract new residents. But when railroads expanded through the area and blight wiped out the grape industry, oranges gradually became the main cash-producing crop. According to county records, by 1947 there were more than 65,000 acres of oranges of the Valencia variety in Orange County. By 1951, when Jacob was just starting to work for Hughes Aircraft, their value had soared to above $40 million. Ironically, the fruit's success also brought about its downfall. The population started to skyrocket. So did property taxes, land values, and the cost of water.

Unfortunately, this also happened to be a time in Orange County when the profitability of citrus groves was rapidly changing. By 1961, when Jacob had settled in this area for some time, picking oranges would soon cost growers more than what they could sell them for! Radical changes were already taking place in the landscape of Orange County, as real estate development had started taking over the land where the orange groves had long existed.

Uncle Jacob had deliberately chosen the location of the new apartment he rented with his mother in mind, because it was in a complex only a few yards from an orange grove. In about a year's time, when his mother would finally arrive in the States, he wanted her to be able to take a leisurely walk along the rows of orange trees to appreciate how the branches above bloomed with white stars. Most importantly, he wanted her to smell the magical scent of their blossoms.

A full year after the newlyweds had first settled in Orange County, Uncle Jacob's mother Arshaluys whom we had nicknamed

"Monam" and sister Arshagouhie whom we called "Arsha," would join them in their two bedroom apartment. Soon after their marriage, Aida, who was already a pharmacist in Lebanon, would enroll in the School of Pharmacy at USC to complete the few courses she needed to get her California license as a pharmacist. Meanwhile, the fragrant orange orchard across from their apartment, where Monam would take her relaxing strolls, while inhaling the sweet scent of the orange blossoms overpowering the air, would vanish in another two years' time, replaced by yet more apartments.

I Arrive in Los Angeles

I arrived in the United States one year later, in 1962, as a naïve seventeen-year-old to attend college. My trip to the Los Angeles International Airport from Paris via New York had been long and tiring, involving a considerable time change. After getting through customs without a major setback, I met Uncle Jacob for the first time in LAX, where he was accompanied by Monam and Arsha. Hugging them after a year of separation, as we were trying to locate Uncle Jacob's car in the multilevel parking lot of LAX, before asking me about how my trip had been or how my parents were, he informed me that the following day would be the day for me to see Disneyland with his pharmacist wife Aida, since that happened to be her day off.

I believe that because Uncle Jacob was an engineer, Disneyland, besides being a fantasy world built around sentimental characters, must have held an additional mechanical appeal for him. By then it had already been in operation for the past seven years and had been enormously popular. Even though in size and innovation it was only a fraction of its present self, it still was a place of creativity where imagination ruled. I appreciated that he and Aida were willing to offer this opportunity to me as an act of kindness; however, it also became my first clue that in the future Uncle Jacob might not give me many choices.

It is practically impossible for me to forget my first night in their inadequately-insulated apartment complex in Santa Ana. We had arrived late at night from the airport and I had just fallen asleep in Monam and Arsha's room on a mattress they had placed on the wooden floor for me, when all of us were rudely awakened by a woman's screams coming from the apartment unit directly above us. Already apprehensive due to a change in time and environment, I initially was scared because I did not know what to think. Monam and Arsha soon reassured me, explaining that it was the upstairs couple's ritual of squabble before they made love! I could not help but think that although I had been in the United States for less than a day, things had already taken a turn to the bizarre...

The Magic Kingdom

The following morning after I was introduced to Uncle Jacob's wife Aida and we had breakfast together, we left for Disneyland as previously planned. We were in a good mood, anticipating a day full of fun and surprises. Just a preliminary glance as we entered the park had sufficed to reassure me that it would easily surpass my expectations. Actually, having just arrived from Turkey, I had difficulty even imagining such a place could exist.

The first amazing sensation for me after entering Disneyland was our ride in the monorail. I soon found out it was the first one to operate in the Western Hemisphere since June 1959, four years after the park had first opened its doors to the public. We had been inside the park for no more than two hours, when around 11 AM Aida informed me that we had to locate her car in the Disneyland parking lot. When I politely asked her why we were doing this when it was not yet time for us to leave the park and there was so much more for us to see, to my surprise, she responded with: "Our sandwiches are sitting in my car and we need to pick them up."

This would not have been a problem under normal circumstances; however, Aida had not remembered or recorded where she had parked her car. As for me, mostly due to culture shock, I had not paid attention to where we had left her very ordinary-looking white car in the vast sea of vehicles in a parking lot which I later found out could hold as many as 12,175. A time zone change of ten hours had considerably dulled my brain. It seemed to me even with the standards of fifty years ago, trying to locate Aida's car in the Disneyland parking lot would have been an impossible task.

Although I realized we eventually had to locate her car to make it back home, our loss of all this precious time just to have our sandwiches did not make any sense! I thought part of the fun of going to the Magic Kingdom was to take a break from running around to enjoy a special meal in an unusual setting. When I found out what the sandwiches we were searching for were, I was even more disappointed, although I tried hard not to show it. The night before, Monam had remarked in Turkish, "I could not figure out what type of chicken it was; I have already cooked it for three hours and it is still too tough to chew!" Few years later, after familiarizing myself with the different types of chicken being sold in the supermarkets at the time, I realized that Aida must have bought "stewing" instead of "frying" chicken, but had neglected to inform Monam about it.

A full two hours later, after almost taking an inventory of all the cars in the Disneyland parking lot and after getting overheated and exhausted, we finally located Aida's car and the chicken sandwiches! Now our goal was to enjoy a few more of the attractions of the magic kingdom during the remaining time.

In *America the Beautiful,* with its enchanting tune *From Sea to Shining Sea,* we stood in the center of a windowless circular room and viewed the most awe-inspiring sites of the national parks of the United States as they unfolded panoramically before our eyes. I would treasure the beauty of nature in our national parks throughout the years, but I had first been introduced to them in *America the Beautiful* with Aida in Disneyland. It may be that my extraordinary desire to visit our country's national parks goes back to this first encounter.

Next, we went to the Opera House on Main Street where we saw the *Great Moments with Mr. Lincoln* show. I cannot do justice to it if I tried to express the wonder and fascination I experienced with the rest of the audience as a mechanical Mr. Lincoln, who was already my hero of American history, rose from his chair to deliver his famous *Gettysburg Address* in his rural Kentucky dialect. For the first time in history, he was challenging the existing prejudice by granting former slaves political and civil rights. I thought it was an eloquent enough piece of literature that could have come from a distinguished writer, not just a politician. It has persisted in my memory and has echoed in my ears ever since that day.

Having just arrived in the United States from Turkey, the true meaning of "government of the people by the people for the people" had an even more profound significance for me. Having heard Mr. Lincoln deliver his Gettysburg Address was more than enough to compensate for our exhausting and unpleasant search for Aida's car earlier in the Disneyland parking lot! It must have created a long-lasting impression on me, because the following year, for a speech class in La Verne College, when I was asked to select a speech to critique, without giving it a second thought I decided on *The Gettysburg Address.* In delivering it, I tried to take the class through Lincoln's masterpiece, to explore its motivation and meaning, to have my fellow classmates feel the grief and passion this melancholy genius was experiencing. In spite of the awkward fashion in which our Disneyland trip had started, I still appreciated Aida's willingness to spend her precious time to share the many wonders of the Magic Kingdom with me.

After living in close quarters in their Santa Ana apartment for a couple more days, in spite of my initial unwillingness to rush to Disneyland the very next day after arriving in the United States, I tended to agree with Uncle Jacob that time spent in the Magic Kingdom was by far a better alternative to time spent in their modest apartment, which only provided us with the bare necessities. With my arrival, the number of its residents had increased by one--at least until La Verne College opened its doors for the fall semester to its incoming students. Even though I had barely arrived in their household, I could sense that the close quarters put pressure on relationships that were barely strong enough to handle a straight gaze and an honest conversation.

In time, being rushed to Disneyland after arriving in the United States became a recurring and almost haunting memory. It is said that history often repeats itself. Two years later, after being away from my parents for what seemed an eternity, we were reunited in late August of 1964 in Los Angeles. Words could not express my happiness. The plane they were traveling in from Switzerland would initially land in San Francisco where they would get a chance to renew their acquaintance with their long-standing friends, the Berberians, who by then had settled permanently in Northern California in Palo Alto, in close proximity to their son. It was two days prior to my parents' scheduled arrival in Los Angeles for our long-awaited reunion, when they got a very urgent call in Palo Alto from Uncle Jacob, saying: "It is absolutely essential that you change the date of your arrival in Los Angeles so you can be here one day earlier than scheduled."

"But Hagop," my father sensibly responded, "what is the reason for this urgent change? We already have bought our plane tickets to arrive in L.A. in two days; besides, for the next two days the Berberians have made plans for us to see the San Francisco area." However, when he detected the urgency in Uncle Jacob's tone, he felt compelled to make the change in their schedule. It must have reminded him of the days he had lived in Istanbul as a money changer, when an element of fear always accompanied him. This type of ultimatum made him uncomfortable. When my parents finally arrived in LAX, after having had to pay a hefty penalty for the last minute schedule change, and after having placed their hosts up north in an awkward situation, they soon found out the reason for the urgent change in plans was none other than a trip to Disneyland, dictated by his wife Aida's schedule.

The Corvair and the Trip to Coronado Island

With the progression of years, Uncle Jacob had developed an unusual preference and an almost unrealistic fondness for the Corvair brand of General Motors car. This model was first unveiled in 1959 by Chevrolet General Manager Ed Cole, who had been influenced by the European cars like the Volkswagen. The Corvair was unlike any Chevy ever produced because it was rear-engined, air-cooled, and came with a four-wheel independent suspension.[3] Of course Uncle Jacob could not have been expected to predict that within the coming few years General Motors would be forced to discontinue this model because of a number of fatal accidents, as well as Ralph Nader's 1965 *Unsafe at any Speed* campaign against it. It is interesting that a government study later would conclude the Corvair to be just as safe as any other contemporary car. I have to give credit to Uncle Jacob for his thorough understanding of engineering and Physics principles as they applied to this car, because he made this determination many years before the scientific community.

The Corvair figures into another strange and amusing tale about Uncle Jacob and his family. With the passing of years, Uncle Jacob had developed a definite business interest in real estate and had acquired a very desirable condominium on Coronado Island, south of San Diego with a superlative view. Just like previously when he had bought houses everywhere, but had hardly been able to live in any of them, with his usual eccentricity he had neither leased the Coronado Island property, nor taken advantage of it by vacationing there alone or with relatives. At this time, the now married daughter of Monam and Arsha's previous landlord in Büyükdere, Lillie Hatunoglu had decided to take a lengthy, once-in-a-lifetime vacation to visit Monam and Arsha in Southern California, accompanied by her husband and young daughter Lorie. On this special occasion with the Hatunoglus', Jacob decided to take them to Coronado Island in his own unconventional way in his non-air-conditioned Corvair, accompanied by his mother and sister on a blisteringly hot day. Two weeks after their well-intentioned, but less than pleasurable trip, the Hatunoglus visited us in La Cañada when Lillie confided in us:

"We were grateful that Mr. Lafdjian was willing to go out of his way for us; however, there were six of us in a car which could comfortably and safely only accommodate five. As if that were not enough, we were carrying our sheets and towels on our laps because the condominium was not stocked with any of these necessities. Don't forget that Corvairs do not have any trunk space," she added, her voice reflecting the discomfort the experience must have subjected them to. "I will never forget how comical, yet miserable, each one of us looked in the packed car in the scorching heat. During the entire two-hour long trip, droplets of perspiration were trickling down our foreheads as we were holding onto the towels and sheets on our laps, constantly resisting the urge to use them for a more immediate purpose!"

Uncle Jacob's Expectations

My problems in La Verne College did not result from the difficulty of the courses, but the tough guidelines and unrealistic expectations imposed on me by Uncle Jacob. He wanted to hurry me along in Calculus by having me hop and skip certain familiar and at times less familiar concepts as he must have easily done. Because of his familiarity and expertise in the physical sciences, especially in mathematics, and because well-paying jobs were more readily available in these fields, he seemed to spontaneously guide me in this path. He should have realized that it would very likely be an idea I could welcome, but he and I should at least have had a conversation on this subject. Besides, I should have been allowed to advance in mathematics at my own pace, since my high school in Turkey had not adequately prepared me in this discipline. Although secretly it pleased me that Uncle Jacob had confidence in me, it was also generating a fair amount of unnecessary anxiety, which later could prove detrimental to my progress in this discipline. I often pondered, "Uncle Jacob thinks he is the student and not I."

It was then that I had a flashback to the time I was about to leave Istanbul when my cousin Sona had emphatically warned me: "Do not forget that Jacob is a genius in the field of mathematics and physics and we are not." However, I felt a genuine responsibility to do my best to please him, while I also tried to make some academic progress. On occasion, when the pace became too fast and frustrating, I would reassure myself with the thought, "He is doing all this for your own good. He has nothing to gain from it."

Dr. Armand Covell

It was upon the second week of my arrival in America, in August of 1962 that I met Dr. Armand Covell. This general practitioner was introduced to me by Monam and Arsha as, "your Uncle Jacob's friend from Istanbul." They had also mentioned that on more than one occasion he had offered them the use of his villa in Palm Springs. With genuine sincerity, he had expressed willingness to give Uncle Jacob the key whenever he thought it was an opportune time for him and his family to go there, so they could spend some tranquil time in the desert. The recent infringement upon the newlywed couple's privacy with my arrival in the apartment might have played a role in Uncle Jacob's concluding that this was as good a time as any to take the good doctor up on his offer. Uncle Jacob would drive Monam, Arsha, and me to Palm Springs; he would return back to Santa Ana to be with Aida, while the three of us would stay behind and spend the last week in August in Dr. Covell's air-conditioned villa in the vicinity of Ocotillo Lodge, bonding with each other and swimming in its pool.

We knew that with August came record high temperatures in Palm Springs; no one in their right mind would willingly visit the desert then. However, the villa was likely to be more spacious than Uncle Jacob's Spartan living quarters in Santa Ana, and unlike some of his far-fetched ideas, this seemed to be a practical one for the three of us.

I was not completely sure how Uncle Jacob had gotten to know Dr. Armand Covell. From the show of enthusiasm by Monam and Arsha each time the doctor's name was mentioned, I presumed the friendship went all the way back to the time when they were both students at the Technical University in Istanbul. Arsha had mentioned that the doctor had often expressed his gratitude to her brother by saying, "If I had not had Hagop's help in math, I probably would not have made it to medical school."

After learning English, Armand had crossed the Atlantic in steerage class in an ocean liner, eventually making it to New York. Owing to his medical training in Turkey, he had first worked as a medical technician while studying for the FMGE (Foreign Medical Graduate Exam). Once he passed the exam, he secured an internship in general practice at the Los Angeles County Medical Center, where at the time both USC and Loma Linda Medical Schools jointly participated in a physician training program.

Apparently at the end of WWII the United States had a physician shortage because many doctors had been shipped to the Japanese front, more specifically to Burma (Myanmar), in the South Pacific. Armand's determination and hard work had paid off for him. After legally changing his complicated-sounding last name to the more fashionable Covell, in time he had been able to afford his present lavish lifestyle, which included a vacation home in the desert, in addition to a main residence in Monterey Park with a commanding view of the mountains during the day and the lights of downtown Los Angeles at night.

From the time I had first met Dr. Covell during the summer of 1962, I remembered him as a short, affable fellow in his late forties. After becoming a general practitioner and settling in the Monterey Park area, he had fallen in love and married Patty, a young, pretty blond at least fifteen years his junior. They had two adorable children, who were elementary school age. The family seemed well-adjusted and happy, according to Monam, who was a close acquaintance of Dr. Covell's mother Anjel, their friendship going all the way back to their days in Istanbul.

In 1961 when Monam and Arsha had immigrated to Southern California from Istanbul, Uncle Jacob had taken them to Monterey Park to visit the Covells on a day when Anjel was expected to be there. The visit had turned out to be bittersweet, because as soon as Uncle Jacob had disappeared into the study to have a private conversation with Armand, Anjel solemnly proceeded to pour out her heart to Monam and Arsha:

"*Digin* (Mrs.) Arshaluys, you don't know what an un-expected misfortune has befallen upon us! My son Armand had volunteered to sponsor his nephew from Istanbul so he could attend college in America. To be able to help him on a regular basis, he thought the college ought to be close to where they lived.

"Having experienced first-hand what it was like to be a disliked minority in Turkey, through hard work, my Armand became a successful physician and soon after that, a U.S. citizen. He wanted to give back something to his people. He wanted at least someone else from his extended family to benefit from his good fortune. He knew that without his help, his young nephew Haig would continue to be under the yoke of the Turkish government and would be subjected to the next unfavorable law applying to minorities. Therefore, with much monetary sacrifice on his part, he sponsored Haig so he could attend Whittier College."

Anjel continued relating to Monam and Arsha her son's entire story. Her voice was breaking at times because the emotional content was becoming too painful for her to bear. "Haig spent many weekends with Patty and the children, while my son was busy seeing patients in the hospital and in convalescent homes in and around the San Gabriel Valley. Haig was a few years younger than Patty, tall and handsome, and before long, a romantic relationship must have developed between them. They were able to keep it a secret until one afternoon Armand happened to arrive home early and found them making love. This was a chilling moment for him. All this time he had been working long hours thinking he was doing his best for everyone."

Now Anjel was unable to control her tears, although she was determined to relate to her friend everything she knew, "Now, *Digin* Arshaluys, I no longer know what the future will bring for them. I promised my son I would help him with my grandchildren any way I could." Getting all this off her chest to her longtime friend seemed to have had a therapeutic effect on Anjel.

Dr. Covell's exhausting schedule and long absences from home had played a role in nurturing a romantic relationship between an attention-starved young woman and a homesick teenager. At the time, Haig was not mature enough to realize the deep wound he was inflicting on a helping hand. The progression of events had suddenly taken an unexpected and unfortunate turn; nevertheless it was yet another one of the sad immigrant experiences…

Our paths did not cross again with Dr. Covell for another thirty three years. Then, I recognized him in the chapel in Laguna Hills at Uncle Jacob's funeral, although he did not seem to remember me. He had come to pay his last respects to his friend Hagop. By then he was being assisted in a wheel chair by an unassuming, gracious, and tastefully-dressed woman in her late sixties with strikingly expressive, large brown eyes and neatly combed dark brown hair, often attributed to women of Armenian heritage. What spoke the truth was this woman's silence in the presence of her all-embracing love and care for him. Watching them from a safe distance, I was convinced this was well beyond what was expected of just an ordinary caretaker.

La Verne College

As for me, life in La Verne College as a freshman was exciting; however I could not help but be apprehensive at times, because for the first time in my life I was living thousands of miles away from the protected family environment I had taken for granted for so many years. In spite of the friendliness of the students and the faculty, I initially went through a period of "mini grief" similar to the yearning that sets in after the death of a loved one and even lost some weight. I found the names of certain foods in the cafeteria to be misleading: What they called "salad" in La Verne was mostly sweet, consisting either of grated carrots and raisins with a sweet dressing on top, or made up of medicinal-tasting lime Jell-O blended with canned pineapple and cottage cheese. By Middle Eastern standards, especially those of my mother, these were not salads but at best lowly desserts!

In desperation to mimic the mainstay salad with fresh tomatoes and cucumbers my mother so effortlessly prepared several times a week in Istanbul, I rushed to the nearby Alpha Beta supermarket after my last class one afternoon, to purchase the necessary ingredients and utensils. I have to admit that after having recently arrived from Istanbul, the convenience of finding everything I needed under one roof was a welcome change for me; however, I soon realized I was being overly optimistic in expecting to recreate even the simple salad of my childhood from the ingredients I had managed to buy. The cucumbers were huge with gigantic seeds; their skins were sealed with wax to increase their shelf life; most importantly, they lacked the flavor I normally associated with them. The tomatoes were not ripened on the vine but had gotten pink during transport, and thus lacked the real aroma and taste of my mother's freshly-purchased tomatoes from the open air market in Kadiköy. Alas, my effort had not helped get over my homesickness but instead had exacerbated it!

The casseroles in the La Verne cafeteria were all new to me and required my taste buds to make some basic adjustments, none of which came very readily. During my first week at the college, I was getting out of the cafeteria basically hungry. It must have been one of my pangs of hunger right before bedtime, heightened by the sweet smell of slowly browning meat and onion that finally led me to the *Spot* one evening. After that, subsequent to completing most of my studies in the library until around 9 PM, I would next pay a visit to this almost hidden fast food place in the basement of Miller Hall for my real dinner; it would be one of hamburger and French fries with plenty of ketchup. Unfortunately I did not seem to have difficulty in adjusting to this almost addictive fast food!

After a few months of this regimen, paired by very little exercise, I noticed I was not easily fitting into many of the outfits I had brought along with me, because I was gradually learning to tolerate a number of the main courses in the La Verne cafeteria as well. I was essentially having two dinners! Eventually with some reluctance, I gave an end to my 9 PM *hamburger and fries escapades.* I think the reality of my isolation from my family in Istanbul had sunk into my consciousness and I had changed, not at first but gradually, until I had learned to accept the cuisine in the cafeteria as the norm.

Life in Miller Hall

It seemed friendly students were plentiful in Miller Hall, which was my dormitory in La Verne College, with the regrettable exception of my roommate, Cara Smith, a local girl from Ontario. She was an only child and a Type I diabetic, which had left her with a number of issues she had not so far managed to come to terms with. I wish when the Director of Admissions, Mr. Kempmeier was about to assign me a roommate, that he had a more in depth knowledge of Type I Diabetes as well as of her being an only child.

Having enrolled in a few of the least challenging courses, she was there not so much to acquire knowledge but to pass the time, hoping that by osmosis she might pick up a few concepts by the time her boyfriend graduated from the Naval Academy in Annapolis and married her. She simply had no empathy or interest in finding out what living abroad thousands of miles away from one's home for the first time might feel like. Every two days and always around bedtime, she would reapply her nail polish in our room, which without exception would induce an allergic cough spell in me. It had made no sense to me that the only reason Mr. Kempmeier had teamed me up with Cara was because she lived close by in Ontario and could take me to her home some weekends, so I would feel less homesick. I never even found out where Cara Smith lived! However I did have a number of memorable experiences with other friends I got to know from Miller Hall.

My first holiday in the United States, Thanksgiving, will live in my memory as long as I live. We used to celebrate plenty of national holidays in Turkey, such as Independence Day. There were several Armenian religious holidays my family observed such as *Vartevar,* a holiday left from Armenia's pagan days, at which time if you were caught outdoors, you could be doused with water! Then, in August was *Asdvazazin* in honor of the Virgin Mary, mother of Christ, when the blessing of the grapes took place. Although each holiday was unique and had its own special significance, because we were kids, we looked forward mostly to the feasts that followed them. Having my mother's delicious culinary masterpieces in mind, I had a feeling quite a few of the grown-ups might have agreed with me.

To be asked to join my friend Laura Shelby and her family in the San Bernardino Mountains for the entire Thanksgiving weekend, was the greatest treat I could have asked for. Coming from a city background where apartments, office buildings and stores were the norm, the tranquility of open fields with plenty of fragrant wild flowers teeming with buzzing bees was such a welcome change. As to the Shelby family's many fruit trees, they were enjoyed by plenty of song birds conducting their own informal concerts in the wild, while they also occasionally got a chance to peck on the ripe fruit in their mini orchard. Laura said that their entire family enjoyed the tart and crisp Granny Smith apples throughout the fall season and that her mother liked canning their pears so they could enjoy them throughout the year. An assortment of neatly arranged glass jars with their special lids was ready and waiting for her, for this very purpose. Everything looked very organized, and yet quite laid-back.

My first Thanksgiving Dinner with them was a very pleasant turkey feast complete with trimmings, including chestnut stuffing, cranberries, and yams, all of which were novelties for me at the time. Additionally, there were extra sweet peas cooked to perfection and home-made apple pie served with fresh cream for dessert. Of course the apples were the tart Granny Smiths from their very own orchard; Mrs. Shelby had devised a way of using another labor of love of theirs, fresh honey from their beehives, in preparing her delicious apple pie. All of this was new to me and I associated the entire experience with being a pilgrim who was treated to a special feast and was so very thankful for it. Yet I couldn't help but be taken aback at the uncanny similarities that existed with my own tight-knit family in Istanbul: lots of affection, a healthy attitude toward spirituality, and an appreciation for communication and education.

Everyone at the formally set dinner table made me feel at home. Also invited to the Thanksgiving celebration was Laura's aunt, whom I could tell my friend was very proud of, because she had the special title of being "Actor Cary Grant's Secretary." This distinction had impressed Laura. "I really want to do something in life that could make a difference for people and would also make me famous; but I do not know what that might be," was her comment to me.

I had tried to tell her, "I like your idea of making a difference; but I would not emphasize the being famous part; if it happens, welcome it; but do not go through life as if that is your first priority." She had given me a questioning look and smiled, as if I had been missing something important. Probably, among all the students I had met in La Verne College, I felt she was the most genuine. I will never forget her caring expression and her gracious smile, when I needed it the most as a homesick teenager far from her home base.

After Cara Smith complained that my cough was causing havoc with her diabetic control, she was promptly given permission to move into a different room with an assortment of roommates to her liking. This turned out to be a blessing in disguise for me, because I had absolutely nothing in common with her. Although I was alone in my room for a number of weeks, I did not feel lonely because most of the students living on my floor were friendly and caring; they would often drop by my room first, before they went to the cafeteria for breakfast or dinner. Besides, thanks to Uncle Jacob's ideas about what my schedule should be and due to my eagerness to follow his suggestions, my challenging courses were keeping me very busy. It felt as if I was constantly trying to make up for the prerequisites of courses I was supposed to have had before.

Marie S. was my next roommate. She was pleasant and a breath of fresh air after Cara; however, from the very beginning, she gave me the impression that she was unrealistically optimistic and easygoing about her studies. I never saw her study any subject; instead, the night before an exam she would listen to morale boosting tapes which repeated at great length how capable she was and how she had everything going for her to be a top achiever. I did not want to be critical of her, especially after my previous unpleasant experience with Cara, but deep in my heart I did not think this was the proper way to prepare for an examination, especially for the type of courses I was enrolled in.

There were several evenings during winter when things seemed somewhat odd to me, and when she would not make it back to Miller Hall. The next day she would tell me that she had gone to the home of a prominent client of her father's, who was a television personality and lived in La Verne. She would later explain that the reason she went was because it would have been too cold and lonely to sleep alone in her bed in Miller Hall! I was realizing that thousands of miles from my home in Istanbul, people had different priorities and lifestyles. There were times when I wondered if I was in the right place.

Uncle Jacob's Guidance

Trying to survive my first year in college in the U.S. had not been easy. I was trying to adjust to college life in a totally different country, while I was also trying to constantly live up to Uncle Jacob's high and at times unrealistic academic expectations. Before I had left Istanbul, my philosophy professor Mr. Webster, who had recommended La Verne College to me, had said nothing about its strengths being in the areas of education and religion, and I had been too naïve at the time to ask. In spite of my academically demanding schedule, I wasn't just burying myself in books, but was striving to be a relatively normal and social student, interacting as much as possible with a healthy cross-section of the student body. I felt compelled to do this because I was single-handedly representing Turkey, Armenians, and the Middle East. This difficult task of wearing so many hats often prompted a number of students to ask me questions, which called for explanations and clarifications on my part.

I had noticed that many of the students in my chemistry and math classes in La Verne College lacked the inquisitiveness to question the outcome of a chemical reaction or wonder if alternate solutions existed for the same calculus problem. I felt confident that for the time being I could handle these courses; however, could I in the future be able to make the leap to a more reputable center of learning in the sciences and still survive?

There also was my awkward relationship with Uncle Jacob's wife, Aida. Although it certainly was not my intention, I must have been somewhat of a threat and competition in her eyes for Uncle Jacob's time and attention. On one of my weekend visits to their house, in the evening after I had cleared a concept in Calculus with Uncle Jacob, as I was trying to get my homework completed, she mysteriously turned off the lights. I interpreted this as a signal to me indicating: "She had had enough. It was time for me to go to bed now!" Upon further deliberation over this subject, I realized that, other than at Christmastime when I was their house guest, I had rarely seen the newly-wed couple share moments of real affection.

I later discovered that their happiness--especially that of Uncle Jacob--depended on Aida's ability to bear a child in spite of her newly-diagnosed infertility issue. This problem was further complicated by a lack of empathy from Uncle Jacob. Growing up without a useful role model for a husband and father during his childhood and teen-age years, Jacob was clumsy in his approach to marriage. Realizing this, I became more sympathetic towards Aida. However, I simultaneously had a flashback to twenty-five years back, to the mutually enjoyable arithmetic lessons that an enthusiastic Uncle Jacob gave to my then five year old brother Kepi in Kadiköy, just before he was getting ready to leave for the United States. I have to admit I sympathized with him as well!

Experiences with Uncle Jacob

During the few weekends when I visited Uncle Jacob and his family after my classes at La Verne College had started, he was extremely helpful to me in mathematics, especially in Calculus. It used to fascinate me that with no outside resources to help him, he somehow knew the derivation of every equation. Due to my limited experience in that field, I couldn't help but marvel at his expertise.

Occasionally, when Aida was at work as a pharmacist, Uncle Jacob would try to familiarize me with their neighboring towns as he was also trying to take care of some of his everyday chores. I remember at least two occasions when he took me to a nearby beach town called Newport Beach to buy fresh bonito. A local fisherman had caught plenty of this fish in the early morning hours and was selling it off his boat which rested on the sand, as if it had run aground. He weighed the fish using an old-fashioned scale consisting of a beam supported in the center, with a pan on each side, the first to hold the fish and the second, his brass weights to neutralize the weight of the fish. I would not in my wildest dreams have expected this sleepy town of Newport Beach, in less than fifty years to become the lavish and sought after beach resort it is today where there are more upscale homes, multistory condominiums and hotels visible than sandy beach.

Another pleasant and unexpected weekend experience I shared with Uncle Jacob and his extended family was our trip to the town of Idyllwild in the San Jacinto Mountains. Having been a city dweller all my life, their cabin in the woods, for which we had to fetch firewood from the nearby forest to keep us warm, left an indelible mark in my memory. While in the woods, I could hear and on occasion spot some of the most colorful birds with complex tunes. I remember an especially brightly colored one buzzing backwards, upwards, downwards, then forwards, then jerking into a new position on the air. To me it seemed to be having fun. Next, I would catch sight of a chipmunk for the first time and smell the invigorating scent of pine needles in the refreshing mountain air. In spite of the academically uncertain situation I was in at the time and the resilience it required of me, I realized I was still very lucky to be given this chance to distance myself from the city and from my studies for a little while to be able to appreciate the beauty and solitude of the woods and its hidden treasures.

By the time Christmas vacation 1963 came around, I could sense that life in Uncle Jacob's household was becoming more problematic. During the fall enrolment period, I had found out that one of the requirements to graduate from La Verne College I had overlooked was the completion of an upper division religion course. To use my time most effectively, I had decided to read the two prerequisite textbooks of the undergraduate religion course on my own, and had gone ahead and enrolled in the *Teachings of Jesus*, the upper division course. I was in the process of typing up my term paper for this course during Christmas break in their new house in Tustin, when an agitated Uncle Jacob suddenly materialized in the room, ordering me to stop. I suspect some unpleasant memory from his past having to do with the staccato sound the typewriter keys made, were the culprit. I instantly stopped my activity and upon my return to the college, I had to quickly locate and pay someone from the English department to type the paper for me, barely meeting the deadline.

An Effort to Graduate Early

La Verne was a small liberal arts college located thirty miles northeast of Los Angeles. It had a caring faculty and student body. Where else would Dr. Myers, a busy historian teaching the freshman requirement, *History of Civilizations*, be willing to delve into a completely unrelated field and offer to teach a foreign student like me trigonometry? In spite of his good intentions, after I had my first session with him, I realized how unnecessarily difficult I was making life for him. I heartily thanked him and took the task upon myself, because by then I had started to realize that in some instances in life I would have to travel alone.

La Verne's strength lay in its *Department of Education*. It also had a worthwhile history department. However I felt that with the exception of physics, the sciences and math courses were not being taught by faculty who had the enthusiasm and the depth of knowledge these disciplines required. I was majoring in Chemistry. It did not take long for me to realize that the department I had declared my major in, happened to be the least well-equipped one in the entire college. To steadily progress in chemistry with the eventual goal of venturing into biochemistry, as our plan was with Uncle Jacob, a lot of the burden was going to fall on my own shoulders. Besides, I wanted to do especially well in all my courses to show both my parents and Uncle Jacob that I was serious in my pursuit.

I have to admit that both the faculty and the administration of the college had been unduly generous to me by giving me college credit for courses I had essentially taken at the high school level. I attribute this to two factors which I believe played a role: The first was that La Verne College had judged my high school courses to be at a higher academic level than they really were because the European *Lycee* system was unfamiliar to them. The second was that during my initial enrolment for the fall semester of 1962, the school had already decided that the credit units they would award me for my previous work would be based on how well I performed academically during my first year at the college.

These two decisions naturally moved me in the direction of doing my very best so I could be granted the most credit units. I had reasoned that after I had satisfied most of my graduation requirements for La Verne College, I could next transfer to a university with a highly-regarded chemistry department; I would enroll in their Physical Chemistry course and ask for my transcripts to be transferred to La Verne College to satisfy my graduation requirement. With this plan in mind, when I found out that no 1st semester Organic Chemistry course was being offered in La Verne College for the fall semester of 1963, I made plans to enroll in a reputable Organic Chemistry course at a large university during the summer months.

My Summer Classes at USC

I managed to locate such a course at USC. Initially I had a great deal of difficulty because I was trying to acquire the knowledge of an entire semester of Organic Chemistry in one month, while at times I was also making up for what I might have previously missed in general chemistry in La Verne College. Then there was the difficulty of keeping up with lab. To my surprise, I realized that although the accelerated course was exhausting all of my time and energy, I was actually enjoying the challenge! However, I also realized that if I were to get the utmost from this rather expensive and intensive course in the company of plenty of premed students, I should drop its lab and concentrate solely on the Organic Chemistry course, because I simply did not have the time to do both.

I was learning so much in the course that I enthusiastically enrolled in its 2nd semester sequel, which to my delight was taught by even a more capable chemistry professor than the first one. I was so motivated in doing well to establish a good foundation in Chemistry that I managed to get a B+ in the final, in spite of not having taken the course for credit, since I was not simultaneously enrolled in its lab. What this course really accomplished for me, other than making me realize I enjoyed Organic Chemistry, was to increase my confidence in myself.

Initially, my roommate at USC was quite surprised and could not understand why I was working so hard. During those eight weeks, my only time away from Organic Chemistry consisted of an early, leisurely Sunday dinner with my roommate at a nearby steak house, which was reasonably-priced and would always culminate with a personally-created chocolate sundae with vanilla ice-cream, chocolate sauce and chopped peanuts with a maraschino cherry on top. Considering the minimal exercise I was getting at the time, this Sunday dinner was probably not calorically the best choice for me; but it would without exception make me feel good, because I felt I was rewarding myself at the end of each week for another concentrated period of hard work. After our dinner, if we had time to spare, we would take a brisk stroll from the eatery to the Rose Garden in front of what was then *The Museum of Science and Industry*, where showy and colorful roses greeted us.

I was lucky to have Anita for a roommate during that summer because even though she did not seem to be a very serious student, she had empathy. She had even surprised me on my birthday with a well-functioning travel alarm clock, since she had realized mine had not always been reliable. She was there primarily to familiarize herself with USC, because she was contemplating becoming a student there, and secondarily to get a perfect tan so she would attract many boyfriends. At the end of summer when we parted, she had not yet made up her mind about the former, but there was no question in my mind that she had accomplished the latter.

Visiting Beth in Sacramento

My friend Beth, whom I had come to know in La Verne College, lived in Sacramento. Less than a week before the start of the 1963 fall semester, I had received a call from her in Santa Ana asking me if I would be interested in visiting her in Sacramento for a few days until our residence halls were ready to accept students again for the upcoming fall semester. She had suggested that if I flew to Sacramento and stayed with her for a few days, she could drive both of us back to La Verne right before the start of the fall semester. I had just completed two fast-paced summer courses in

Organic Chemistry at USC, competing with premed students; I could definitely use a break. Besides, it would give me a chance to get to know the country, the culture and its people better. I would also be easing the congestion for everyone in Uncle Jacob's overcrowded apartment where I was already noticing the first signs of tension and frustration among its residents.

As soon as I arrived in Sacramento, Beth met me at the airport with her younger sister to drive me to their home. When we arrived there, her mother told me she had a surprise for me. "I think it might make you feel at home," she said. I did not realize at the time that the surprise was also coming with a tall order! Mrs. Bates lost no time in promptly producing for me a recipe for a *beureg*, a type of Middle Eastern pastry she had cut out of her local paper.

According to the recipe, I had to come up with the dough from scratch by using certain proportions of flour, water, melted butter and egg by first blending these ingredients and then kneading them. When I judged the dough to have gotten to the right consistency, I had to use a rolling pin to create several relatively thin layers to fit into a circular metal pan, making sure I brushed each layer with melted butter to prevent it from sticking to the layer above it. I first prepared the spicy ground meat filling so I could place it in the pan halfway between the first and second bunch of layers of dough. The preparation of the meat filling, which consisted of sautéing the ground beef and adding chopped onions, parsley and spicing, consisting of red and black peppers, salt and allspice went without an incident; but the preparation of the thin layers of dough was another story!

I was not sure if the recipe Mrs. Bates had cut out of her local paper was flawed because it had the wrong proportions or if it was my lack of experience, but in spite of diligently following the directions, I was simply unable to get the dough into a consistency I could work with. After a number of failed attempts, which were fast ruining my confidence and making me look incompetent in the eyes of my friend, I was reluctantly ready to give up. Then it dawned on me that Beth's family was planning to have my *beureg* as their main dish for our dinner! In my desperation, the idea of gradually adding a teaspoonful of water at a time to the dough while I kept kneading it came to my mind. At this point I was willing to try anything!

My gamble must have paid off because the addition of two teaspoons of water converted my so far unruly dough, into one that was now manageable. Using my rolling pin, I was for a change able to create three relatively thin circular layers on top of which I could spread my spicy meat filling. To complete the rest, I rolled out three additional layers which I placed one after another on top of the meat filling. I finished off the top layer after brushing it with a thin layer of clarified butter. When the beautiful, lightly browned and delicious-smelling finished product finally came out of the 400 degree oven at dinnertime, no one in my hungry host family could tell they had come extremely close to not having the dinner they had set their hearts on!

By the end of summer, with my knowledge in Organic Chemistry now resting on a solid foundation, and having demonstrated a respectable academic performance during my 1st year at the college, I reasoned that if I played my cards right, I could complete all of my requirements and be able to graduate from La Verne College at the conclusion of my 2nd year there; then I could transfer to a more highly regarded institution in the sciences for Graduate School. I must admit that although my Chemistry professor Dr. Eikenberry had left a lot to be desired as a college chemistry professor, as a counselor he was priceless in helping me realize this almost impossible dream. When I realized I needed two additional upper division history courses to be able to graduate, he knew exactly what those two courses could be.

History is an area I benefited from in La Verne College, because it was the first opportunity I had where this subject was taught objectively. Following Atatürk's directives, the history and maps in my Turkish textbooks did not even mention the names of certain countries such as Armenia, which at one time had conflicts with Turkey.

Two Exceptional History Courses

I was ecstatic when I discovered that, solely for that summer, two exciting upper division courses were being offered by the history department of La Verne College, namely: *Colonial America* and *Westward Movement.* Consisting of informal lectures led by my former American History professor Dr. Davis, those enrolled would explore the entire United States as well as parts of Canada for six weeks, in a comfortable, air-conditioned Greyhound tour bus, visiting the different locations where the various historical events had taken place. The idea also appealed to me because studying history in this manner would add some visual insight to the historical perspective that would both be valuable and unforgettable in the years to come.

After we had encircled the entire country by bus, what impressed me the most was that by the end of the colonial years, as America's founding fathers gathered in Philadelphia in 1776, other brave souls from non-colonial America had begun their journey west from Santa Fe, N.M., hoping to find a way to the Pacific Coast. Negotiating with Native Americans and struggling over harsh terrain, they may not have had any idea at the time that the thirteen colonies were declaring their independence from Britain, asserting their right to life, liberty and the pursuit of happiness and that all of this would create a country that would one day comprise much of Northern America. Stories of the exploration of the western frontier during the latter part of the 18th century and into the early 19th often involved encounters with Native Americans, who lost territory, autonomy, culture, language and much of their population.

I could not have asked for any more inspiring and enriching history courses; however, before the year was over, I had to submit two comprehensive term papers to the history department of La Verne College. To do so, I not only had to read history texts but also had to observe the topography of the land where the first colonies were established, where their battles were fought, as well as the vast expanses of land the western settlers had to traverse in primitive carriages, and sometimes on foot, against all sorts of odds. All of this made history come alive for me and made it infinitely more meaningful. Dr. Davis and his staff had diligently reserved our overnight accommodations ahead of time in over thirty towns and cities throughout the U.S. and Canada, and the experience left an indelible mark in my memory.

Although our tour group consisted mainly of a homogeneous group of students from La Verne College taking these two courses for upper division history credit, there also were a few older women in the group who were enrolled in the classes for enrichment purposes only. Among this latter group were two women whose interest was not on this unique way of learning, but elsewhere. Since Dr. Davis's wife was absent from our tour group, these women seemed to have an unusual amount of personal interest in the professor. However, because of his professional conduct throughout the tour, their efforts failed to lead to what they might have had in mind.

At the conclusion of our tour, as I tried to substantiate my observations with statements from Dr. Davis's lectures and from publications I had purchased from some of the museums and historical sites, I felt that for a novice like me these unconventional history classes were a somewhat expensive, but nonetheless invaluable introduction to US history.

An Additional Bonus of the Tour

Being part of this unique history tour would give me an additional advantage I was not counting on. It gave me the opportunity to taste the distinctive cuisines of the different geographic regions of the country. The French-influenced Creole cuisine of Louisiana, the Southern cuisine of Maryland and Virginia with their perfectly fried chicken served with honey, were so different from what I was familiar with. By now I had become tolerant, even somewhat adventurous, having long abandoned my initial insular way of judging food of two years ago when I had first arrived in California. Dr. Davis consistently made good choices of eateries, representative of the regional cuisines, and his protruding abdomen was a reliable witness to this fact! However he helped enrich my entire experience, as well as that of my taste buds, introducing me to cuisines and their dishes I may not otherwise have had the courage to try. Among the several delicious regional foods I experienced, the shrimp creole of New Orleans in Louisiana would long remain a favorite and end up being the dish I would take the time to learn to prepare and serve to my family within the coming years.

Being somewhat compulsive by nature and already apprehensive about my soon-approaching first semester at the university, I had decided that while I was on the tour, I would devote some time each day to organize my thoughts about the day's experiences and would write them down. Having done this, I could easily focus and expand on certain areas of interest to me and by the 40th day of the tour, I would have a detailed outline of the important topics that were covered. I felt this record would in turn help me with the two papers that were expected of me.

The Kosches

As I started the fall semester of my second and final year at La Verne College, I was surprised to find a new but somewhat familiar-sounding name among the faculty. The previous year's Calculus course was now being taught by a Mr. Kosch, who I was told was more of an expert in music than in math. His name, as well as his unusual set of credentials in both disciplines, reminded me of a teacher who had taught upper division math about eight years ago in my high school in Üsküdar, as well as across the Bosphorus at Arnavutköy College. I realized I was familiar with the name because his wife had been my favorite English teacher when I was in the preparatory grade at the American high school, around the same time.

In 1963, a philanthropist from the Church of the Brethren had stepped forward to fund my previous Calculus professor Mr. Herbst's education towards a PhD in mathematics at a Midwestern university. My instincts led me to believe that the new teacher substituting for him for that year's Calculus classes, might be the same Mr. Kosch I knew from my American high school in Üsküdar.

Two weeks later the issue resolved itself when I accidentally ran into Mr. Kosch on campus. I instantly recognized him as the advanced math teacher and the music expert who I had thought had somewhat prominent ears and was married to my capable English teacher back in Istanbul. He seemed to be quite moved by the discovery as well, because it gave him a reason to look back longingly at the years he and his wife had spent overseas as teachers in Istanbul. During our conversation, he happened to casually state, "Last year my wife had to undergo open heart surgery in Los Angeles. Talking about charges... Do you know what the thoracic surgeon charged per hour for her open heart surgery?"

"I have no idea."

"It was an outrageous $500 per hour."

"Wow! I am sorry about that. A teacher's salary must be peanuts compared to that type of charge."

"I am commuting three days a week from Redlands to teach the Calculus course in La Verne College for this year. I will talk to my wife and perhaps on my way back from La Verne on a Friday afternoon you can have a ride with me and visit Audra and me leisurely over dinner in Redlands. We just may surprise you with an authentic Middle Eastern dish!"

"That is very thoughtful of you, Mr. Kosch. By the way, I hope Mrs. Kosch's health is much improved," I added with a healthy dose of wishful thinking.

"She is capable of improving; however, most importantly, she has to want to do it," was his answer I was not expecting to hear.

Although I was happy we had made a pleasant and somewhat unexpected connection to our mutual past in Istanbul, I did not know what to make of his last remark. Instead of asking further questions about what seemed like a painful subject for him, I decided to wait until I heard from him again.

It was two weeks later on a Friday afternoon that Mr. Kosch and I embarked on a trip to Redlands in his car. Less than ten minutes into the ride, he said:

"Granted it will delay us a bit, but it would be helpful if we first headed in the direction of the Fedco store in San Bernardino so I can pick up a couple of items before heading home. By the way, if you need anything, you will find both their prices and the assortment they carry to your liking. You can take about ten minutes to buy what you need, while I complete my shopping; then you can locate me at one of the checkout counters where we will be paying for our purchases."

"Are you sure I will not be inconveniencing you if I pick up an item?"

"Absolutely not," he reassured me. I took advantage of his offer by selecting a simple light nightgown for myself, because the sleepwear I had brought with me from Istanbul was not purchased with Southern California's warm weather in mind. When I located him at one of the checkout counters and was getting ready to pay for the item, I thought it was somewhat inappropriate on his part to comment:

"Nowadays young women are no longer wearing night-gowns; they are not even wearing underwear when they go to bed."

When we finally reached their home in Redlands, it warmed my heart to see Mrs. Kosch again after so many years of living worlds apart. I remembered her clearly as my English teacher of the Preparatory Class, who had assigned me the role of Hansel in the play *Hansel & Gretel*, the only play in which I was given a significant part during my entire school career. Her facial features clearly revealed that she had once been a beautiful woman; however, her heart ailment must have negatively impacted her appearance. I had difficulty recognizing her as the same beautiful and energetic lady I had gotten to know eight years ago with dark blue eyes, a light complexion, and long, wavy, soft blond hair loosely gathered in the back with a thin, black velvet ribbon, always eager to introduce us to a new word or expression.

"Welcome to our home. How do I look since you last saw me in Istanbul?" Mrs. Kosch inquired, before I had a chance to completely get a hold of myself.

"Good, but different," I responded compassionately. Perhaps she was expecting to hear a more complimentary response from me. Being truthful by nature, that was the best I had been able to manage for the moment.

Husband and wife had gone through the trouble of preparing a shish kebob dinner which Mr. Kosch proceeded to cook on their small brazier. The execution of all this must have taken quite a toll on them both. We had a satisfying and highly emotional evening as we each recalled our memories of Istanbul and the American high school, of which they had both been such an integral part. I was saddened by seeing Mrs. Kosch age so prematurely. Additionally, the fact that Mr. Kosch was placing a significant portion of the blame of his wife's incomplete recovery solely on her attitude had bothered me.

It was later in the evening, as Mr. Kosch was driving me back to La Verne College that the subject of our conversation somehow unexpectedly diverted to photography:

"On and off, for the past few years I have been photographing a number of exceptional, although not necessarily the most popular sites in nature," he commented.

"Do you have any particular goal in mind or are you doing it just for fun?" I asked. He gave me a sly smile and then went on to say:

"There is a remote chance that National Geographic could reward me monetarily for the project, if the magazine chooses my work to appear in one of its future issues."

"Wow, really?"

"Here is what you could do, if you are interested. You could be an incidental spectator in the background in some of my photographs. I know for a fact that the magazine oftentimes likes to have a bystander in the background in its depictions of nature." I was speechless at first. Then I barely managed to say:

"But Mr. Kosch, I have neither had hiking nor camping experience. Wouldn't these be requirements to reach these extraordinary sites?" His answer was:

"Mostly yes," to my relief,

"Sorry Mr. Kosch, although what you are describing definitely sounds exciting, I would not know the first thing about hiking long distances and camping there. Besides I don't even own hiking gear."

Since by now I definitely had become more cautious, especially after hearing his earlier remark regarding young women no longer needing nightwear at bedtime, I was desperately searching for a legitimate excuse to get me out of a situation where I would be in close quarters with him. The absolute certainty with which I had countered his offer must have done the trick.

Nearly three years had gone by before Mr. Kosch's name came up again. I had promised to drive Semiramis, a former classmate of mine from the American Academy for Girls in Üsküdar, who was now completing her graduate studies in UCLA, to Pilgrim's Place in Claremont, to visit our retired high school principal Miss Martin, who had been a resident there for the past six years. During our conversation she happened to ask me, "Have you met anyone else from the American Academy for Girls in the United States, other than your classmate Semiramis?" When she found out my response consisted of my naming Mr. Kosch, instead of being pleased, her expression became one of displeasure. The remainder of her conversation with me carried the undertones of a reprimand, as if I had a sinister role in contributing to the current apparently wider chasm between the Kosches.

Uncle Jacob's Social Relations

Following his graduation from Caltech in Pasadena, Uncle Jacob had been hired by Hughes Aircraft, based in Orange County as an aeronautical engineer. He was employed there starting in 1951 all the way until August 1962, which roughly corresponded to my date of arrival in the United States. He must have left his job around this time to venture into a completely different area, namely real estate. His move could have been instigated by an internal reorganization at Hughes Aircraft, which was in the process of relocating its headquarters to West Los Angeles around that time. It is also quite possible that during the company's restructuring, in spite of his superior intellect, Uncle Jacob may not have been favored by the higher ups in the company due to his extremely reserved nature and his noticeable awkwardness in social situations.

Most marketing executives would agree that their greatest challenge is to find people who understand their business and who have the quantitative and technical skills to create the appropriate model for them. However, they would also agree that the successful candidate would additionally need to possess a certain level of communication whereby he can persuade others that his insights are worthwhile to pursue. This probably was not the case for Uncle Jacob. "As extraordinarily capable as your uncle is in the field of engineering, he somehow no longer seems to have his job," was the way his sister Arsha had expressed her concern to me during one of my visits early on, when we were alone.

As the years rolled along, they gave me further time to reflect on Uncle Jacob; I have come to the conclusion that I now tend to favor an alternate explanation. I feel that less lofty factors might have complicated his decision, such as the prospect of money. Prior to my arrival in Southern California from Istanbul, my father had forwarded a respectable sum of money to Uncle Jacob. To be able to make a living, in addition to be able to save some, had often meant putting himself in harm's way for my father, whereas at the time it might have simply meant "seed money in easy reach" for Uncle Jacob. Before this money had arrived at his bank, my father had written to his cousin instructing him to place these funds in a joint account under his and my names to be earmarked for my and my sister's education and for our family's future financial needs.

Uncle Jacob's longing for a real estate business of his own, in which he would be accountable to no one and would not need to communicate much, especially at a time when he was unemployed and when the Orange County landscape was readily changing, must have seriously tempted him. If he could have only communicated with my father regarding what he was planning to invest his money in and for how long, they could have easily reached a mutually satisfactory agreement. However, Jacob did not go about it in a transparent way. Instead, never mentioning to my father where he had invested his funds, he instead subjected him to unnecessary anxiety and suffering when he and my mother, accompanied by my sister, had made the trip to Southern California during the summer of 1964 to visit me. Uncle Jacob repeated the same callous behavior the following year in 1965 when my parents had once again made the trip to California, on the occasion of a second family reunion.

My Father's Health Problems

A few months before leaving Turkey in 1964, my father's eyesight had suddenly deteriorated considerably, due to retinal bleeding brought on by his poorly controlled diabetes. Two months prior to their departure, my mother had written to me, lamenting:

"After seeing the world in pink for two entire days, presently your father cannot see much, with the exception of bright lights. What is worse, his ophthalmologist does not think much can be done at this point to save his vision."

At the time my mother's letter had created a chilling effect on me, but I had realized there was not a whole lot I could do other than to try to do my best in my studies. We would have to wait until he arrived in the United States to find out what ophthalmologists here would have to say. However when my parents arrived in California during the summer of 1964, Uncle Jacob was viewing my father's disability in a totally different light and telling me:

"Your father is blackmailing me to make me feel sorry for him, so I will yield to his wishes and return him the funds."

Although my long-awaited reunion with my parents and a wonderful educational opportunity had become a reality for me and would in turn be for my sister, it was also turning out to be a bittersweet experience for my parents. Ironically, my father, who had helped everyone else until then by transferring their funds to the countries they had emigrated to, now needed help himself. When he wanted to know from his cousin what had happened to the funds he had thus far forwarded, a hostile attitude would always take possession of Uncle Jacob.

"I already told you; they are safely invested," he would reply to him.

"Can they be sold then?" my father would hesitantly inquire. To this question, Uncle Jacob's firm and unflinching response would consistently be:

"They cannot be sold," with no further explanation as to the reason why.

Each attempt at communication on my father's part, which would involve his finding a driver to take him from Eagle Rock in Los Angeles to reach his cousin's residence in Tustin in Orange County, would predictably end in an impasse. For my father, who had taken great pride in being caring and helpful to everyone, including his aunt and cousin Arsha, Jacob's present callous attitude toward him simply puzzled him and became a constant source of frustration for him. It caused his blood sugar control to deteriorate, not to mention the not so obvious deleterious effects it must have had on his cardiovascular system.

Monam and Arsha's Prior Life in Kadiköy

In contrast to the mysteriously hostile and callous attitude that had taken over Uncle Jacob starting in the summer of 1964, during their days in Istanbul in the 1950s, my father had consistently been a caring and nurturing nephew to his Aunt Arshaluys and cousin Arsha. They had lived for many years on the Bosphorus in Büyükdere, in their rented guesthouse with its extensive gardens belonging to the Hatunoglus. When living there alone during the winter months became increasingly unsafe for the two elderly women because of the growing political turmoil in Turkey and the area's sparse population at the time, my father had offered them living quarters, free of charge, in our centrally located five-story rented house in Kadiköy. In time, he had become the person they would consult before making any significant decision, while they were waiting for the legal paperwork for their U.S. residency to materialize. To us kids, who were always enriched with their presence, this wait seemed to have taken forever.

Around 1955, it was not unusual for us to visit Monam and Arsha a couple of times during the summer months in the spacious guesthouse they were renting from the Hatunoglus. In fact, Büyükdere had been the destination for our celebration, after we had found out I was accepted as a student in the preparatory class of the American Academy for Girls in 1955.

Approximately three months later on a cold winter weekend in November 1955, my father had wanted us to make an urgent trip to Büyükdere to check on Monam and Arsha. Had it been during the summer months, this would have been an extremely enjoyable trip, since on its way the ferry frequented several quaint little towns on the eastern shores of the Bosphorus, which had managed to preserve their old-world charm. However, it was winter now and the weather was chilly, with some precipitation.

My father's real mission was to check on his aunt and cousin, whom he had been unable to reach by phone. He had last heard from their landlords, the Hatunoglus, who spent their winter months in Kadiköy that Monam had been ill and was finally recovering from a prolonged flu. We had been isolated from them due to the distance, the cold, and our unforgiving schedules.

A drizzling rain started as we hurried into the ferry from Kadiköy. A bitter cold wind followed us everywhere, making the leafless trees on our way tremble, as we finally boarded the special ferry to take us along the eastern arm of the Sea of Marmara. We could not help but seek its lower protected quarters from where we could still follow the sudden meteorological changes and their effect on the landscape.

Within the space of a few hours, rain had turned into snow and had accumulated noticeably along the Bosphorus. The seafront was empty on the European side and appeared paralyzed. Through the window across the aisle from us, I could see that a light fog had descended, prompting our ferry to blast its foghorn. A barely visible light ray through the fog, created a nostalgic view of the snowcapped hilltops above the Asian shores.

Following a long and bumpy ride, we finally got off the ferry at Büyükdere, after the quay staff had attached a gangway to our ferry. Good thing we were wearing waterproof boots and had our coats on, because we certainly needed them since we were only partially protected by the quay. For a little while, my sister and I admiringly watched the sizable snowflakes descending nonstop from the sky, as our boots sank into a soft blanket of pure white and fluffy snow. For us kids, this was the greatest bliss and adventure…

Fortunately, my father was able to talk an idle taxi driver into giving us a ride up the Hatunoglu's hill to their guesthouse. Because we had no way of informing them earlier via telephone, Monam and Arsha were truly surprised and overjoyed to see us. The pleasant reunion had especially relieved my father's worries and satisfied him, because he finally had his long-awaited peace of mind that his aunt was out of harm's way.

We did not stay with them long because the next day was a working day for my father and a school day for me and my sister. Monam's soothing homemade chicken rice soup was simmering on their wood-burning iron stove downstairs, and it totally hit the spot. She followed the tasty and comforting soup with several servings of her rich signature cookies, *shekerlokmasi,* which simply melted in our mouths. After we helped ourselves to generous portions of Arsha's candied fruit, we knew what they had offered us would keep us satisfied until we would reach Kadiköy again, late at night.

As soon as the snowfall eased and gave us a window of opportunity, the four of us gathered our energy to negotiate their hill. For a change we were walking downhill, being careful, and taking our time not to slip and fall, as we were heading back towards the Büyükdere quay to catch the next available ferry. We felt the need to rush back, because at the time of our arrival when we had inquired at the quay, we were told that due to the unpredictable weather, the ferries could be canceled at any time without prior notice. We did not wish to risk being stranded in Büyükdere any longer than that weekend.

On our way back to the quay, we saw a few people in black coats and jackets rushing home through the darkening streets. Just before nightfall, the scenery became even more magical. Since it was considerably colder now, we noticed large icicles hanging from the trees in the gardens we were passing by, especially in those with a northern exposure.

The boat ride on our way back from Büyükdere was considerably shakier and less pleasurable, because the weather once again had gotten colder and windier. Fewer lights on the Asian shore were visible now. The fog horns were at work full blast, creating an eerie feeling and leaving a great deal to our imagination.

After transferring to a different ferry which would take us to Kadiköy, we finally made it home late at night, quite sleepy, tired and cold, but satisfied for the time being that all was well with Monam and Arsha.

An Unexpected Knock at the Door

Every now and then I remember an evening in March of 1964, in my rather Spartan dormitory room in Miller Hall in La Verne College, when my routine was unexpectedly interrupted by a loud knock at the door. When I opened it, I heard a friendly female voice on the other side say:

"Hurry, someone on the public phone is asking for you."

As I rushed to the phone, which was centrally located in a cubicle next to housemother Zook's living quarters, I heard Uncle Jacob's voice on the other end. For a change, his usually monotonous voice had an element of excitement in it!

"You have an appointment with the UCLA's Dean of Letters and Sciences tomorrow. Make sure to bring a copy of your transcripts with you, including the most recent ones and I will meet you in front of Miller Hall around 1:00 PM," he said.

It must have taken a lot out of Uncle Jacob to make this appointment for me, because I knew how he dreaded to communicate with people. The ordeal he had to endure the following day for my interview was going to be anything but simple for him. He would first have to drive north from Tustin in Orange County to La Verne to pick me up; then he would have another drive of similar length heading west to reach Westwood. I was thankful he had taken this initiative, which involved a certain amount of risk, to get my transfer to UCLA started. The transfer was going to be difficult for a number of reasons: First and foremost, I was hoping to eventually become a graduate student at UCLA, second, I did not have a strong foundation in the field I was hoping to go into and third, I seemed to be in a hurry. Dressed somewhat formally, I was ready and waiting for Uncle Jacob long before his expected 1:00 PM arrival time. As I entered his car, I told him how grateful I was for arranging this interview for me and for taking me to UCLA. Beyond that, most of our trip transpired in silence, except for those rare instances when I helped navigate him by following our route on his folding map.

As we entered Westwood, the neighborhood looked quaint, but once we made our way to the campus, it looked larger and more intimidating than any I had seen so far. By the time Uncle Jacob parked his car in the designated parking lot and we located the building and room to meet the Dean of Letters and Sciences, we both felt as if we had already accomplished a complicated task and we had not even started.

The dean was friendlier than I had anticipated; he was approachable and greeted Uncle Jacob and me in a rather warm manner. After looking over my transcripts, he seemed somewhat pleased and said:

"I can tell you have kept yourself busy with all sorts of classes since you have been in this country."

Although I did not realize it at the time, he must also have been aware that as a foreign student, I would be bringing a new perspective into their classrooms and dormitories. Besides, I would be paying full tuition; therefore I would not be a financial burden on the state. The timing might have been just right, since by then cultural diversity was starting to become a desirable quality to have for universities throughout the United States. The dean's next comment was more realistic and practical:

"We at UCLA are unable to give you college credit for courses you have essentially taken at a high school level in Turkey; however, I can see that you have made considerable progress in a short time. We probably can accept you as a student under Limited Status," I heard him say.

"What is Limited Status?" I inquired.

"It basically means you can take any number of courses to complete your requirements for the department you are applying to in graduate school, provided you maintain a "B" average," was his simple explanation.

I was so excited to hear him say there would actually be a way I could attend UCLA that I did not even think of asking him any further questions, particularly if there would be a counselor who could help guide me in my selection of courses towards a certain department. It may have been a habit of mine left from my student days in Istanbul, where the *modus operandi* for a minority student was to refrain from asking too many questions.

"When you have successfully completed just about all of the undergraduate requirements for the department you are interested in, you can then apply to be admitted as a graduate student to the university," he said.

Those were the Dean's last words before he shook our hands and wished us well. He asked his secretary to see to it that I had received all of the necessary paperwork to complete to mail back to his office, so I could be admitted as a *Limited Status Student* for the fall semester of 1964.

Prior to our meeting, I had wondered if there was any possibility that Uncle Jacob and the Dean might have known each other earlier from Caltech. It must not have been the case, because we promptly thanked him and left his office without Uncle Jacob having contributed a word to the conversation.

Attending UCLA as a Limited Status Student

What had transpired between us and the UCLA dean would have been considered a definite success under normal circumstances. However, since I would not receive any academic counseling except from Uncle Jacob, this *Limited Status* would become an albatross around my neck. Of course, I would not be aware of its full significance until it was time for me to attend the various math and chemistry classes I was enrolled in. As my advisor, Uncle Jacob would simply forget that I was not as gifted in mathematics as he was and that I had never gone through a logical progression of courses in that discipline, but had proceeded in a hit-and-miss fashion.

Compounding my anxiety, at least initially, was the sheer size of UCLA and the fact that I did not know a single soul there. At the time, in spite of its desire for diversity, the university was not where it needed to be with regard to integrating international students by responding to their needs, especially one with the handicaps I had. Before the fall semester had officially started, I was informed by the university that I would need to be tested on my knowledge of the English language, which would also include writing an essay on an arbitrarily chosen subject. The good news was that I had scored in the 98th percentile, in spite of not having taken a single course from an English department since graduating from the American Academy for Girls in Üsküdar. I was indebted for this to my mother, to Mrs. Alexanian, and to my American high school.

Looking back, I would have been so much better off had I enrolled in a less advanced math course initially for acclimatization and perhaps in an introductory literature class to expand my horizons, in addition to the Organic Chemistry I was planning to take. I now realize that even if my eventual goal at the time was to become a biochemist, when it was time to hire, even pharmaceutical companies would prefer creative and well-rounded applicants able to deal with complexity and who could think for themselves. Similarly, nothing is akin to a literature student spending hours reading a good book and living with its author. Instead, I signed up for Organic Chemistry and 4th semester Calculus, a prerequisite for the Physical Chemistry course at UCLA which I needed to complete to graduate from La Verne College.

"You should take the 3rd and 4th semesters of Calculus simultaneously, because you would get an A in the 3rd semester Calculus and it would raise your grade point average," was Uncle Jacob's advice to me. It did not make a great deal of sense, but I had a lot of respect for him and had no one else I could count on for direction; therefore, I went along with his plan. In retrospect, I now realize that no matter what type of status I had at UCLA, I still should have requested them to offer me some guidance, since I was a foreign student attending the university for the very first time.

Ever since I had enrolled in these two upper division Calculus courses concurrently and had started attending them, the earlier welcoming words of the Dean had long lost their reassuring effect on me. Instead, the necessity of maintaining a B average appeared increasingly intimidating in my eyes. Pushing me to the brink, it was as if my capacity to endure was being tested. I feared that if I failed to perform according to the university's expectations in these courses, I could be deported back to Turkey, because I was on a student visa.

Nightmarish flashbacks to the time I was in 7th and 8th grades and subjected to Nuriye Hanim's prejudice were stirred up and started to haunt me all over again. A decade ago her unethically depreciating my grades in algebra and geometry rippled through my mind. Despite evidence to the contrary, I had a relapse and started doubting my ability in math. These destructive thoughts were chipping away whatever little confidence I had left in me. It was then that I realized how difficult it must be for someone to overcome the lifelong effects of psychological trauma and for the unpleasant effects to heal. But I kept telling myself: "You have to try. Not trying to succeed is worse than failing."

Fast forward to the present, on every occasion that I have ventured to that general area of the UCLA campus where my Calculus 4 classroom once stood, I can feel my heart beating faster and being shrouded with a feeling of despair. I attribute this to a mild form of PTSD debilitating me and reminding me of the enormous stress I must have been under in the fall of 1964.

During the fall semester in 1964 as a brand new student at UCLA, unlike the time in La Verne College, I was no longer able to get Uncle Jacob's help. There were a number of reasons for this. Public transportation by bus from Westwood to Tustin was complicated and time-consuming. However, weighing in even more in my mind was the fact that during casual conversation the previous month, Uncle Jacob had accused my father of blackmailing him when my father had mentioned to him that he had been essentially blind for almost a year. This lack of empathy towards my father on Uncle Jacob's part had deeply wounded me, making me determined not to ask for any further help from him. I knew my father's blindness had been due to his poorly controlled diabetes. From what I had observed, when he dealt with clients he always upheld the virtues of honesty and trustworthiness, strength and courage, even in the face of adversity.

To complicate matters even further, as time passed and Uncle Jacob's wife Aida was unable to conceive a child, despite her extensive fertility treatments which included cutting a wedge in her ovary to facilitate the release of an egg, their marriage had started to show signs of unraveling. I could imagine what an enormous disappointment Uncle Jacob must have suffered after finding out that his wife would be unable to bear his child, since he had constructed his existence and happiness on this premise ever since he had married Aida four years ago. Unquestionably, he had seen his share of trouble when he had first arrived in this country. At this point in his life he wanted nothing more than to come out on the other side with a family and a child of his own.

Although Monam and Arsha had been a big help in food preparation and housework, they had also been in the way of the couple's achieving their much needed privacy. Under these circumstances, I did not want to aggravate their problems further and thought it best if I distanced myself from them for a while. Therefore, in spite of my desperately needing that extra assistance in math, I was left out there on my own to face the music.

Science in a Competitive Atmosphere

Although initially I was somewhat bitter that Uncle Jacob pushed me towards the physical sciences for which I had inadequate preparation, in time I realized that this path may have been a blessing in disguise. I only wish he had not hurried me so much, but had let me progress at my own pace.

To be able to study Chemistry in UCLA in the 1960s was quite a privilege. It gave me an opportunity to familiarize myself with the most recent breakthroughs in the field. The 1953 discovery of DNA's double helix was one of modern science's watershed moments. Taking these advances in molecular genetics to the next level, it would pave the way for extraordinary advances in medicine. It had only been ten years since Watson and Crick had discovered the model for DNA and here I was studying it in my Organic Chemistry class from a text authored by Crick himself. Later on, although my genetics class would become challenging for me at times, it also offered me a personal glimpse to the direction in which molecular genetics was headed. It was a pleasure to be taught these basic science courses by real authorities who were truly excited about their fields of expertise. Some fifty years later, as genome-sequencing technologies and immunotherapy became available; researchers would be experimenting and making use of the ingenious idea that they could help patients use their bodies' natural defenses to fight certain forms of cancer.

It did not take me long to realize that all my classes, except for Calculus, were teeming with capable but also extremely competitive premed students. I also had to adjust to the undecipherable accents of professors who had come from all over the United States as well as the world, even from countries as far away as Sweden. They often dished out new scientific concepts at an unprecedented pace which at times were difficult for me to follow.

Nellie, my roommate in Sproul Hall, was the first African American young woman I had gotten to know. She was enrolled in the same Physical Chemistry class for which the 4th semester Calculus was a prerequisite, but she was having a very difficult time. I clearly remember her telling me, "Nobody in the class seems to be getting a passing grade." Three weeks into the course, Nellie surprised me even more when she announced that she was going to get married and would be withdrawing from UCLA for the current semester. I congratulated her, but was saddened by the fact that at least for the time being, she was giving up her studies. As I contemplated how things would turn out for me, my confidence was obviously shaken by my roommate's comments and path of action. Obviously it was less than reassuring to find out that the only other person I had so far gotten to know in this huge university would soon be leaving. Consequently, this was a time when my homesickness again became quite overwhelming. Since I now was alone more at UCLA, I had more time to dwell on what I was missing back home in Istanbul.

Life in ISTANBUL

Most mornings, after I rushed through breakfast and picked up my sack lunch from the Sproul Hall cafeteria, I enjoyed my long walk downhill and along the athletic field, then uphill to the main campus by the library and Royce Hall. By the time I reached this part of the campus, I usually felt more relaxed; perhaps because I realized that, in spite of everything, I was still pretty lucky to be a student here.

My long walk would finally lead me to the historic buildings where some of my classes were held. I liked my Organic Chemistry lectures, despite the fact that the professor had to lecture in a large auditorium. I did not even mind the lab accompanying the course, which was far more manageable in size compared to the huge class. Unlike the experience I previously had during my summer Organic Chemistry lab at USC, I could now keep up with the class. However my 3rd and 4th semester Calculus courses were a different story. My last calculus class had been the 2nd semester Calculus class I had taken in La Verne College over a year ago. It frustrated me when I could not remember if a concept was altogether new to me or if I had been exposed to it before, but not in enough depth. More than once, the thought crossed my mind that if I was having difficulty handling the prerequisite for Physical Chemistry, how was I ever going to deal with Physical Chemistry itself?

Uncle Jacob had suggested that I pay for the services of a tutor for a few sessions, to help me with my Calculus classes. Even though I was not convinced this was the best solution, I still gave his suggestion a try. I soon discovered that my choice of tutor had been a poor one. He did not have as thorough a knowledge of Calculus as Uncle Jacob did. I was simply not benefiting from his help; additionally, I was wasting precious time and money.

Once again, the prospect of success started looking daunting in my eyes. There were a number of times when, after becoming discouraged in my Calculus classes, I would try to release my frustrations in a diary I had brought along with me from Istanbul. This helped me heal at least partially from my thorny experiences and the dislocation I was experiencing by getting the poison out of my system. I soon realized I would have to make a quick and rather serious decision about at least one of my Calculus classes, since my previous exposure to this field had not been a comprehensive one.

Gregory Ketabgian

.When the entire Lafdjian family lived in Aksaray, 60 miles west of Gesaria in central Anatolia, Dikran Kazanjian was Great-uncle Abraham's brother in law. As I have earlier described, Dikran immigrated to California in 1923 from Constantinople, was living with his widowed daughter Eve Melkonian, and operated an antique store in downtown Pasadena. Aunt Eve, as I affectionately called her, was a very warm individual who always strived to make people around her feel happy and satisfied, without ever expecting something in return. When she heard that my parents were visiting from Istanbul during the latter part of the summer of 1964, she invited my entire family over to socialize and have dinner, as well as meet another relative of hers through marriage who was from Gesaria, Artin Kitabjian. With a sly smile in her eyes she said to me:

"I want you to meet their son, Dr. Gregory Ketabgian, who is completing his residency in Internal Medicine at the LA County Hospital."

Already apprehensive about my being categorized as a "limited status student" at UCLA, I was certainly not interested in adding any more complications to an already demanding schedule. Therefore, I must have been somewhat indifferent. I later found out that Greg had been on call for the last thirty-six hours straight during the previous day and night, having admitted some forty patients with serious medical problems at the LACUSC Medical Center. With the help of his two interns, he had ordered the pertinent lab tests and X-rays to diagnose their medical problems and in many cases had taken the preliminary steps in their treatment. Thus, when his mother asked him to drive his father and her from Eagle Rock to Aunt Eve's residence in Pasadena that evening for dinner to meet "these people from Istanbul," he was also reluctant.

It was a good thing that a thorough soak in the bathtub had relaxed his muscles and helped improve his disposition. No wonder he had initially looked pale and rather lethargic to me that evening! I do not recall having a particularly interesting conversation with Greg that evening; however, our fathers, as well as Mr. Kazanjian, looked contented and seemed energized for the entire duration of our visit. I could see it in their eyes and hear it in their voices spilling with enthusiasm, what being Armenian meant to them, as they reminisced with pride and nostalgia all sorts of detail involving their family life, summers, church and community activities in Aksaray of nearly fifty years ago. I had not realized until then how much they had in common and how their pride in their ethnic heritage had such an important role in making survivors out of them.

Greg called me a week after I had moved into Sproul Hall in UCLA and asked if I would be interested in going out on a date with him. It was the Saturday before the fall semester officially started, when I agreed to go to an ice skating show with him at the Sports Arena. I had no idea at the time that where he was taking me was a pretty costly place for a first date! Our time together ended up being more relaxing and fun for me than for him, because he suddenly had to face two unanticipated and rather challenging problems. The first was his realization that he had accidentally locked his keys in his car after he had parked it in the Sproul Hall parking lot before picking me up. At the time this must have been somewhat easy for him to handle, considering the simple way the locking mechanism for cars was designed during the 1960s. His second and more difficult challenge was to back up his car virtually the entire length of a street, to escape a traffic jam created by a USC football game at the Coliseum.

If Greg had not risen to the occasion, our ice skating show would have been over by the time we made it there. His quick thinking and resourcefulness had saved the evening for us. He had found a wire clothes hanger to unlock his car, and taking things at stride, he had been willing to back up his car for quite a distance. I could sense he was an intelligent, hard-working, yet level-headed person--all qualities I held in high regard.

In spite of the pleasant time we had together, my precarious situation at UCLA prevented me from pursuing what might in the future develop into a romantic relationship. I was afraid it could further complicate my academic situation. Thus, for the following two weeks I made a number of serious and rather unforgivable mistakes. The first one was when I called him to turn down his invitation to see Shakespeare's *Hamlet*, after I had initially accepted it, and after he had already purchased the costly tickets from Royce Hall. When I explained that I had to study further for my 4th semester Calculus test, Greg passed the tickets on to his intern at the hospital, so at least he and his wife could enjoy the play.

As if failing to keep one promise was not bad enough, a week later for a Sunday evening, Greg had asked me to accompany him to attend an Armenian Choral Group Concert at the Wilshire-Ebell Theater on Wilshire Blvd. For a second time in a row, my anxiety about my studies prompted me to call him the day of the event to decline his invitation, in spite of his already having purchased the tickets. Anyone else's patience would have been exhausted by then and would have said, "Good bye and good riddance!" but Greg was a gentleman.

He had ended up going to the concert alone. During intermission, who does he come face to face with in the crowd? Of course, Aunt Eve; she was limping along energetically as usual, depending on the extra support she always got from her cane. She must have looked concerned when she saw Greg alone. Her first remark to him, in the form of a question was:

"Where is Alice?"

"She said she cannot go out for now because she has to study," was Greg's response.

"I will call her tomorrow and talk to her," Aunt Eve had responded, making it obvious that she was annoyed with my behavior.

Since I had seemed uninterested on repeated occasions, Greg's Medical School classmate from USC, Bill Lenzer who was from Fresno, had approached him in the hospital cafeteria sometime during the previous week and said:

"My wife tells me we must have purchased tickets to the same Choral Concert at the Wilshire-Ebell for Sunday. We'll see you there." Then after some hesitation, he had added: "By the way, you know my wife is Armenian. Her sister is a member of the choral group that will be performing there. If you are interested, I could introduce her to you." Greg had agreed and had gotten to socialize with the Lenzers during intermission, at which time they had managed to introduce Bill's sister-in-law to him.

It was the following day in the evening that I got a rather harsh message on my phone from Aunt Eve warning me, which sounded as if it could have come from my own mother:

"Alice, you better think twice. You are making a big mistake."

In spite of the overwhelming academic hardships I was facing in UCLA at the time as a Limited Status student, I listened to Aunt Eve and contacted Greg. We picked up our relationship from where we had left, even though I had come dangerously close to losing him.

Greg's Helpful Suggestions

Other than his sympathy for the extreme academic pressures I faced, Greg had ideas about alternate ways of tackling my obstacles. He verbalized it to me in the form of a question: "Why do you insist on going into Biochemistry where so much Mathematics is required? Can't you perhaps go into Human Physiology where you would be studying more about structure and function, but where a background in chemistry would still be helpful?"

Greg was looking at my situation in a new light that I had never even considered before. He helped me realize there could be a new path where I could turn failure into opportunity. In essence, he was showing me how to navigate my way through one of life's storms.

Greg was right that Human Physiology was a related field to Biochemistry, and that it also dealt with the body at the molecular level but required far less mathematics. The lectures would not be any simpler, or the competition any less--actuality it was more-- however, it did mean that I would be rewarded in equal proportion to the effort I put into my studies and would not be disadvantaged for my gaps in mathematical knowledge. Yet the huge classes, the quick pace of the lectures, the lack of an academic support system, the stiff competition from premed students, and last, but certainly not least, the albatross around my neck of "limited status" kept making life difficult for me.

On the morning of April 24, 1965, right when I was in the midst of this difficult adjustment period and on my way to one of my classes, I inadvertently noticed a poster attached to a mature tree trunk in bright red letters that read: "Honor the Memory of 1.5 million Armenians who perished 50 years ago. Join us at 12:00 noon at Kirchhoff Hall #25 at a meeting of the Armenian Students' Association to honor their memory." Even though my precarious academic situation at the moment was directing me in a different direction, the poster prompted me to head towards this gathering. Sadly, this remembrance to honor the memory of my ancestors had become the first opportunity for me to find out what had really happened to my father and grandparents 50 years ago during the Armenian Genocide of 1915. The knowledge I gathered through the documentary they showed angered me, because for all these years Turkey had unfairly managed to conceal this history from me. As the U.S. was opening a new world of opportunity for me, although my path was by no means straightforward, I also realized that adversities to my progress were no longer going to be the rule here.

After giving it some thought, I had to swallow my pride and drop my 3rd semester Calculus class, which I was expected to excel in, if Uncle Jacob's prediction were to materialize. Luckily, I was able to get out of the course just in time without causing any permanent damage to my academic record. For reasons I could only speculate, I had to fight more of an uphill battle in the less advanced Calculus 3 class than in Calculus 4. It is quite possible that my two previous Calculus courses in La Verne College may not have covered all of the concepts I was expected to know.

I marveled at how effortlessly the student sitting two rows in front of me was able to arrive at the solutions in my 4th semester Calculus class, while I was struggling and was only able to manage a C+. Now I somehow had to get an A in one of my classes so I could continue as a "limited status student" with a fair chance of being accepted as a graduate student at UCLA in the Department of Physiology after I had completed all my prerequisites.

I was lucky to be able to do this in Dr. Crescitelli's Cellular Physiology class, which dealt with the eye. I had put a lot of effort into my independent project for this class and it seemed my work had pleased the professor. It was when I received this good news in the mail that I realized I needed to share my happiness with someone, in just the same way I needed a dialogue with another sympathetic soul to ease the pain of an unpleasant outcome. I must have made too much noise jumping up and down with joy in my dormitory room because next thing I heard was my phone ring. It was the girl downstairs in the room directly below mine, asking me to stop the racket!

During my semester break, when I contacted La Verne College's Chemistry department regarding the Physical Chemistry course I had to complete to receive my B.A. from that school, they agreed to substitute it with the Physical Chemistry course offered for botanists at UCLA, which did not require Differential Equations. I learned a great deal in this class. It was here that for the very first time I benefited from a support system. Ann was an enthusiastic graduate student from the Philippines who was taking the class with me. Missionaries from her church back home were sponsoring her graduate work, so that in time she would return to her country and be able to teach this discipline.

As I grew more comfortable in my relationship with Greg and looked forward to our next meeting, my initial daunting and impersonal image of UCLA was also slowly fading away. By now I had started to know a few people in each of my classes, thus the university was slowly becoming a friendlier academic environment for me. I wish I could say that my classes were getting easier as well, but they weren't. It was not unusual for the mean score on some of my Organic Chemistry and especially Biochemistry tests to be no higher than 50/100, but I was happy that for a change I was truly learning.

With every passing day, I was appreciating the amazing body of knowledge I encountered in each of my courses. Some of my classes, such as Vertebrate Zoology, included exciting field-trips to places like Marineland in Palos Verdes, which was similar to Sea World but on a smaller scale and is unfortunately defunct at the present, as well as to Malibu Creek, which was an estuary where the ocean tide met the creek emptying into it and created a natural habitat for a large variety of birds and marine life. Many of my courses required research papers, which encouraged a different and more independent type of learning. I was thankful that although I had started attending UCLA in an unconventional way, in less than two years' time I had become a graduate student in the department of Human Physiology, which was part of the School of Medicine, and was already benefitting from the university's vast resources.

Because of his typically inexpressive nature, I never found out how Uncle Jacob had approached the Dean of Letters and Sciences at UCLA to get that appointment for me, but I was certainly grateful that he had, because it had paid mightily by making attending this great university possible for me. Of course I was also most thankful to Greg, whose experience, ideas, and resourcefulness had vastly expanded my options. Best of all, unlike the time I was enrolled in Calculus 3 & 4 simultaneously, with my self-confidence at an all-time low, I was now slowly but surely gaining it back.

In spite of Uncle Jacob's conflicting opinion regarding my field of concentration, I was happy to have selected Human Physiology. Several years later, when I was ready to join the work force, having chosen this area for specialization would be a blessing. It would improve my qualifications by providing precious insight into the functioning of the human body at both the gross anatomical and molecular levels. In a practical setting such as a medical office, I would thus be quicker to recognize the danger signs in a patient as they came up, when the chain of events did not proceed in the expected fashion.

A Visit to Uncle Jacobs

It was late in December of 1964 when Uncle Jacob and Aida invited Greg and me to their home in Tustin so that they, as well as Monam and Arsha, could meet Greg. As a couple, Uncle Jacob and

Aida did not have much of an interest in investing in any new or used durable furniture on their recently-purchased house. During our visit, I was surprised to notice that this principle applied to even their kitchen cabinets. Some of the cabinet doors had been missing all the way from the time they had first purchased the house. After waiting for a year and a half, Monam and Arsha must have decided to resolve the problem themselves, even though they knew theirs would only be a temporary fix. They had ingeniously fashioned curtains from floral textiles they had come across in the cupboards of their new house. They had used an existing sewing machine to sew and hang them, to protect the china and hide their pots and pans from being in plain view. It must have been an activity that kept them challenged and busy.

What Uncle Jacob and Aida owned as furniture in their living room could best be described as old-fashioned rattan armchairs with foam rubber cushions, encased in avocado green and orange denim, which appeared long past their prime in preserving their original color and elasticity. They did not own a sofa, although their living-room was large enough to accommodate one. When we arrived at their home and Greg tried to sit in one of their rattan chairs to carry on a conversation with Aida, the mesh under the cushion suddenly gave way and in the midst of our astonished gazes, he suddenly found himself sitting on their living-room floor!

I was of the opinion that Aida was displeased to live in a house that was not altogether hers. Since she had to share this one with a mother and sister-in-law, she did not feel motivated to furnish it, although she certainly was making enough money as a pharmacist to make it happen. As for Uncle Jacob, he did not seem to care one way or the other on this particular subject. Lately upon further contemplation, I have been viewing the few surviving pieces of the muted pink and gray German porcelain china set, outlined by a silver edging--their wedding gift for Greg and me--with far greater reverence than I had before. After all, the two of them had made a rare purchase with us in mind, whereas they had not done it for themselves during the previous five years.

Courtship

By early spring of 1965, in spite of the physical distance separating us, Greg had become an important part of my life. An outing to Santa Monica Beach on a weekday morning, when both of us happened to be free, led to a leisurely, romantic walk on the beach, followed by a seafood salad lunch in a restaurant with a sweeping view of the Pacific Ocean. I must have enjoyed our outing so much that I did not even complain about the disagreeable dressing on my salad, since my knowledge of salads was still "a work in progress" at the time. The time we spent together that morning had been magical, including the walk hand in hand on the firm sand by the water's edge. We had made a game of narrowly escaping getting soaked by the incoming tide and the approaching waves, as we mimicked the sandpipers and relished the serene Santa Monica Beach on that special weekday morning, so unlike its congested state on weekends.

In another month, when Greg had one of his rare vacations as a first year Internal Medicine resident, and had asked me if I would join him for the weekend in San Diego, my response to him had been positive. It felt as if we each needed a respite from our rigorous schedules to pause and enjoy some rare carefree time life was for a change offering us.

Polynesian restaurants, whose claim to fame was their imaginative landscaping and décor, rather than their gourmet cuisine, were the popular eateries of the day. I can still picture our enchanted eatery of that evening with its entryway through a miniature bridge, under which ran what looked like an actual brook. It meandered through the restaurant and the serene sound of the running water complemented the soft Polynesian music in the background. After some waiting, we were lucky to be seated at one of the tables by a cove next to the leisurely-running brook, with shiny black pebbles on its banks, and dimly lit tropical vegetation in the distance. After our Polynesian drinks arrived with their colorful tiny umbrellas, and we took a few sips, I felt paradise probably could not be too different from this. It was in this magical setting that Greg proposed to me and I accepted.

It was a Sunday evening and Greg's vacation extended into the following week, but Monday at UCLA, with its overabundance of premed students, would be hectic as usual. Neither one of us wanted to face reality so soon. Therefore, when Greg offered that we stay overnight in San Diego and return the following morning, although it was atypical of me, I did not object. By then I was also feeling more confident about my ability to handle the classes I was enrolled in, which no longer included Calculus 3 and 4.

Wedding Plans

When the news of our engagement reached Greg's parents and sisters, according to the Armenian tradition, they wanted to plan a formal engagement party for us at Greg's parents' house in Eagle Rock. They invited quite a few of their close relatives on Greg's maternal side of the family, as well as their family priest, Father Yeretzian. To live up to the occasion, for the first time in my life I remember going shopping in Westwood to a number of specialty clothing stores on my own, to select an appropriate outfit. In the end, I was pretty happy with the simple and elegant light blue sleeveless dress I had purchased with an interesting texture resulting from minute folds in its fabric as the sole contributor to its originality.

Also invited for the occasion, and representing my side of the family, were my sister Arminé, Aunt Eve, Uncle Kazanjian, Uncle Jacob, Aida, Monam, and Arsha. My parents were happy for me and Greg, but they had to celebrate the event in spirit only, thousands of miles away in Istanbul. However, they promised they would be with us for our upcoming wedding that summer.

When my parents arrived from Istanbul in early July of 1965, they rented an apartment within walking distance to Greg's parents' residence in Eagle Rock; this was to simplify the preparations for our wedding, as well as to facilitate communication between both sets of parents, in a country mostly alien to them.

During this period, I also recall driving my sister each morning to Cal State LA and back for four weeks, to help her satisfy a requirement in U.S. History. This activity also helped me build much-needed confidence in driving, which I would soon need for my everyday commute to UCLA.

Uncle Jacob's Marriage

As Greg and I looked forward to joining our lives, sadly, Uncle Jacob and Aida seemed to be moving in the opposite direction. Some fourteen years after their marriage, the undesirable aspects of Uncle Jacob's character--namely his inability to communicate, his controlling nature, and his lack of empathy--would take a toll on their marriage. After their unique wedding in Montreal, their relationship regrettably would disintegrate ending in divorce.

Although Uncle Jacob would never mention it in conversation, it was no secret that one of his most important priorities in life had been to have a child, especially a son. He must have often had flashbacks to some thirty years ago when he lovingly had tutored my enthusiastic five-year-old brother Kepi. Unfortunately, in spite of his extreme yearning, Uncle Jacob would never again experience such a warm relationship with a receptive child, especially in the role of a father; this was because by 1964, reproductive specialists had ruled out Aida's being able to conceive a child due to her polycystic ovaries.

This finding must have become an unending source of frustration and unhappiness for them throughout the remaining years of their marriage. At the time, medical advances in treating infertility were limited, and adopting a child was out of the question for Jacob. It must have eventually become untenable for Aida to tolerate Jacob with all his idiosyncrasies, while also having to continually live with his mother and sister.

The desire to have a child of his own must have haunted Uncle Jacob all the way into old age, because when he was hospitalized for bowel obstruction at age eighty, my sister remembers him specifically instructing the radiology technician to shield his testicles during radiologic imaging. After the tumor obstructing his bowel was surgically removed, the specialist had recommended radiation therapy to safeguard him from future recurrences, since there was no evidence of metastases to any other organ at the time.

Even then and all the way into his mid-eighties, Jacob's desire to father a child influenced him to refuse this life-saving treatment.

My Parents' Difficulties in the States

When I first arrived in the United States at age seventeen, I remember how difficult it had been for me to make the myriad adjustments, whether cultural, social, or purely academic. At the time I had not even given much thought to what such changes in their immediate environment would mean for my parents, who were considerably older and more set in their ways. Yet, their survival instinct, coupled with their resilience of spirit, and combined with their unconditional love for their children, would embolden them and lead them on to face life in an unfamiliar country. So far life had taught them how fragile and yet precious each moment was. Now, four years after I had first arrived in the United States, they were relocating once again at a relatively advanced age and venturing into uncharted territory. It almost required a different sort of martyrdom on their part, prompted by the desire to give top priority to the welfare of the next generation.

While sharing an apartment in West Los Angeles with my sister, my mother's efforts once again concentrated on her all-time favorite--cooking. It had been the lens through which she experienced life and at this critical point in her life; it also had the additional benefit of pleasing my father and sister. Therefore, when my father found out that my sister was going to be late in arriving home from her UCLA class, while my mother had already started the preparation of a favorite dish in which she was missing a key ingredient--parsley--my father would not allow his blindness to hold him back. Instead, he would navigate alone towards the nearby supermarket; then via smells and "a kind of batlike echolocation" and resorting to the rudimentary English words he had managed to pick up, his sense of smell being his most dependable guide, among the different greens he somehow would manage to locate the parsley my mother needed. As he returned back to their apartment triumphantly with the parsley bunches in his hand, he did not once complain about his blindness or about the physical and mental obstacles he had to overcome to first find his way to the supermarket, relying on the special markers only obvious to him. Then, on his way back, he would have to remember to retrace his steps to safely make it home without getting lost. It almost seemed the traumatic event of blindness was slowly making my father stronger and his life more meaningful by encouraging him to explore and find a new way of living.

Somehow my parents had learned to accept and adapt to the hardships along the way as part of life. After having no other educational opportunities available to him other than a one-room schoolhouse in Aksaray in central Turkey for less than two years, my father wanted me to take advantage of the best education money could buy. He offered me this choice in spite of a very unfavorable exchange rate for the Turkish *Lira* against the US dollar at the time of seventeen to one, which was further deteriorating with every passing day. He did not think gender should be a determining factor in the education of one's children. This was the case in spite of the fact that most Middle Eastern men used a different yardstick for their daughters than they did for their sons.

Edgewood, Maryland

During my father's last trip to the United States during the summer of 1968, Greg and I lived in Edgewood Arsenal in Maryland, an hour's distance to Baltimore in the northerly direction. It was the Vietnam era and we felt fortunate he was drafted somewhere within the continental U.S. as a Medical Officer to see patients in the dispensary, instead of being sent to the war zone.

By the time Greg was drafted, I had completed most of my requirements for an M.S. degree in UCLA in the department of Human Physiology in the School of Medicine, with the exception of two additional quarters of coursework and a comprehensive exam. Continuing my studies in Baltimore at Johns Hopkins or at the University of Maryland was not an option, because neither university had a master's degree program in my field. Since Greg had been most receptive to all the hardships I had to persevere through to get to this point, he was agreeable to my returning to Los Angeles to share an apartment with my sister during the fall and spring quarters to complete my remaining requirements. During what would have been the winter quarter at UCLA, I was happy to return back to Edgewood Arsenal to join him.

In spite of the limitations of our military base, these two-and-a-half-months marked a blissful time in our lives which we will always remember and cherish. Snow had transformed the entire arsenal into a winter wonderland. The subzero temperatures of that winter had even made it possible for us to skate on a nearby pond on our military base.

I also remember these two and a half months as an adventurous time in cooking. Having been a novice in this field until then, for a change I now had time in my hands to try all sorts of dishes, especially Armenian and Middle Eastern ones. Using recipes from a cookbook gifted to me by my sister-in-law Shaké Balekjian, and buying some of the ingredients from a quaint Greek store in Baltimore, I actually made many of the ethnic dishes come to life with varying degrees of success. I even got my two enthusiastic American neighbors Elaine and Mimi, whose physician husbands had similarly been drafted, and were looking for an exciting indoor activity during the unseasonably cold winter, to join me in this endeavor. Taking place in our modest apartment, our cooking sessions would often produce ethnic Armenian dishes which we would share with our spouses at dinnertime.

My Graduation and my Parents' Arrival

When Greg took time off from the dispensary in Edgewood to attend my graduation during the first week of June in 1968, we were also celebrating the happy news that in four more months we would be the lucky parents of our first child, Ani.

It was the last week in June when we picked up my parents from the lobby of a hotel in New York, after they had arrived there from Istanbul, and took them to the Tavern on the Green. It was Greg's idea, and a good one at that. My mother and I had not been able to restrain our giggles when we saw Greg in a white jacket borrowed from the eatery, with the purpose of passing muster to join us for lunch on the green.

Subsequently driving south on the New Jersey Turnpike, it was past dinnertime by the time we made it to our adequate, but bare-bones, two-bedroom apartment on the military base in Edgewood. We were happy that we would be able to accommodate my parents for a couple of weeks. At nighttime, our living room with its sofa converted into a comfortable queen-sized bed and cooled by the window air conditioning unit, became their makeshift bedroom. However, the arrangement proved to be somewhat noisy at nights. This was because the cooling system had to work constantly to keep up with the high temperature and humidity of the Maryland summers. After Greg and I showed them the special sites in and around Edgewood, including the private little forest that led us to the Chesapeake Bay, we took them sailing on the Susquehanna River and had them explore the charming, expertly manicured Longwood Gardens in nearby Delaware.

Previously Greg and I had made special plans to celebrate my parents' last week with us, since after a number of trial runs within the last four years, my 68 year old father with my mother on his side, had finally arrived in this country to stay. We were all in a festive mood as Greg drove us leisurely in the southern direction towards Virginia Beach and onto Ocean City in Maryland. We wanted to explore these beach cities with them, while we also wanted them to be in more comfortable and quiet sleeping quarters for at least some of the evenings, before it was time for them to leave for Los Angeles.

It was after my visually disabled father had enjoyed a celebratory dinner in a unique and relaxed environment with the cool ocean breeze and the informal spiced steamed crab served at the Phillips Seafood Restaurant in Ocean City, that he extended Greg and me a spur of the moment invitation:

"After you get to your room and relax for a while, I would like you two to join us on our balcony to watch the sun set on the Atlantic Ocean. You never know; you may at the time also be the recipient of a rather unexpected document." With this remark, my father had succeeded in introducing an element of intrigue into a day that had already turned out quite pleasant for everyone.

My Father's Unexpected Surprise for Us

When Greg and I leisurely approached their room and were guided to their balcony, I instantly recognized the box my mother was holding gingerly in her hands. I recalled having seen it for the first time some ten years ago in the attic of our Kadiköy house, during my "secret mission" when we were ready to move away from that house. It contained my Great-uncle Abraham's account of their earlier lives in Talas and later in Aksaray, including their odyssey starting July 1915, as it related to my father's side of the family. It was the saga of their journey towards the south Syrian Desert after they were deported by the Ottoman Turks from their hometown of Aksaray in central Turkey.

Just as I had trusted that he would, my father had remembered to pick up that special box from our attic before our move to Üsküdar. In spite of the risk that carrying this document subjected him and my mother to, in case it was detected by a customs' officer in Istanbul, my father had made sure it traveled with them on the plane to the United States. He must have realized that life was too short and that he did not have all the time in the world to get this precious document to us. I clearly remember him saying to me:

"At some point when the pace of life gets slower for you, I want you to translate it into English, so our family's trying days during the 1915 Deportations and the Armenian Genocide, the epidemics that took the lives of a third of our extended family members, including that of your grandfather and great grandfather, will not be forgotten." I think he must have thought the risk of sneaking this document into their luggage was well worth taking, because it would be precious in the future not only for me and my sister, but also for our children and our children's children. With it, he was making sure that an important part of our family's past history would survive. It was probably the most valuable and sacred treasure my parents could have brought with them from the old country on what was meant to be my father's last trip out of Istanbul.

We Lose Monam

One evening in 1985 my sister called to give me the sad news about Uncle Jacob's mother, Monam. She had suffered a massive stroke and was hospitalized at the Desert Regional Medical Center in Palm Springs. By now it had been several years since Uncle Jacob and Aida had gone their separate ways. Since I was planning to accompany my husband Greg for a medical convention to the same general area in the desert that week, I decided to visit Monam and Uncle Jacob at the hospital, to show them that I cared. I also wanted to thank them for all the sacrifices they had made for me when I first arrived in the States.

After I located Monam's room at the hospital, it broke my heart to find her unresponsive. However, throughout my hour-long visit, her gaze would always settle in my direction. I could tell Uncle Jacob was pleased to see me and interpreted the focusing of his mother's eyes on me as a positive sign. The way he was interpreting it, one would think she had regained some level of consciousness and was not completely at the mercy of her reflexes. In fact, he derived so much satisfaction from this peculiar behavior of his mother's, that throughout our visit he kept documenting it by taking several Polaroid pictures of her, some of which included me at her bedside. I covertly questioned his mental and emotional state and was worried that he was not always in touch with reality because his mother's movements were involuntary and not necessarily due to brain function, since she was comatose and unresponsive.

However, it might be possible to come up with a different and perhaps more positive explanation to clarify Uncle Jacob's behavior. In the face of the pending devastating loss of his mother, he might have been paralyzed with fear and thus was trying to grab onto any positive glimmer of hope. He might also have tried to find solace and redemption in hanging on to connections with others from the past. Since he did not have a significant number of these connections left, my presence by his slowly dying mother was still a crutch for him. He wanted to preserve all possible evidence that his mother was still showing signs of life and survival. If I eased his pain a little by being there, I am happy and thankful for that.

We lost Monam shortly after this last encounter in Palm Springs.

Every once in a while as I rummage through old photos, I come across the Polaroid prints Uncle Jacob had wanted me to keep. Yet, instead of feeling good about the comfort I may have provided him at the time, I feel shrouded with a sense of profound sadness. This is because I think of how Uncle Jacob--as a brilliant scientist--had been able to achieve only a small fraction of his full potential in life. His near-autistic introversion, his lack of empathy, and paranoid character had left him unfulfilled in his professional as well as personal life.

Uncle Jacob's Real Estate Ventures

After being employed as an aeronautical engineer for about ten years at Hughes Aircraft, Uncle Jacob's interest had completely shifted to Real Estate. He would keep himself busy acquiring properties in Orange County with the intention of renting or leasing them. Because of his difficulty in communicating, his unwillingness to trust managers, and the vestiges of his paranoia, delegating responsibility had become increasingly difficult, if not impossible for him. He must have been aware of this fact early on, after he had acquired his first apartment complex in Santa Ana, where most of his tenants were Spanish–speaking. His solution at the time had been to teach himself Spanish in order to personally handle the necessary tasks, thus circumventing outside help.

After his divorce from Aida and after relinquishing half of his properties to her, he still was in possession of a significant number of them. Some of these properties were quite valuable, including the condominium on Coronado Island with a panoramic view of San Diego as well as his latest acquisition, a newly-built modern house in Yorba Linda. There were others in locations as far away from each other as Palm Springs and Santa Ana. It must have never crossed his mind that as he got on in years, traveling the long distances between his properties was going to become increasingly challenging for him. He must have never internalized the idea: "Time is fluid and we are here for a little while only."

Eventually some of Uncle Jacob's real estate holdings would deteriorate due to neglect, whereas the potential of others would not be realized because he was unwilling to trust anyone else to rent or lease them for him. Meanwhile, he kept filing his income tax returns meticulously, doing it all by himself, providing all the information the IRS required of him on each of the properties.

My Last Encounter with Uncle Jacob

Unlike the time I first arrived in the States, I had started to have conflicting feelings about Uncle Jacob ever since I noticed his callousness towards my father in 1964. He had been unwilling to give him even a partial accounting of the money he had earlier forwarded to him that was to be earmarked for our family's future financial and educational needs. My father had no idea what a percentage of these funds remained, and when he could once again claim ownership to them. Worrying about his finances in an unfamiliar land had negatively impacted his health, deteriorating the control of his diabetes.

On the other hand, Uncle Jacob was the reason why my parents had allowed me to make that first critical move away from Turkey as a college student and first-generation survivor of the 1915 Armenian Genocide. With him as my counselor, the first two years of college had not been easy. However, his help in Calculus, as well as his aid with my eventual transfer to UCLA, had made it possible for me to complete a graduate degree in a sought-after field at an internationally respected university. Looking some ten years into the future, this degree would give me a sound background in the physical and health sciences, making it possible for me to function knowledgeably in an Internal Medicine office for many years. I had to emphasize the positive and forgive Uncle Jacob for his lack of empathy.

It was January of 1989 when Greg and I invited Uncle Jacob and his sister Arsha to join us for a memorial in my father's memory at St. Gregory Armenian Church in Pasadena. It was to be followed by an elaborate dinner at our home in La Cañada, on the occasion of the 20th anniversary of his passing. Both of our older daughters were attending college on the east coast by then; therefore, they could not be with us. After the church services, our youngest daughter Lena accompanied Uncle Jacob in his car to help him with directions, so both he and Arsha could reach the commemoration dinner at our house with ease. As usual, he did not want to say much. By then, his difficulty in communication had become even more pronounced. He did not initiate any of the conversation, even though it was his first visit to our recently-constructed house. In spite of my proximity to him at the dinner table, I was essentially unable to reach him.

After Uncle Jacob had dessert and was relaxing in an armchair, it was Greg who brought up the subject of his health and medical care. He expressed his genuine concern as a medical professional by asking him:

"We heard you had certain medical issues having to do with your bowels. How is everything now?"

Uncle Jacob responded with, "Oh, it was all a mistake on the part of the doctors. It all had happened because I had eaten quite a few persimmons the prior week and they had blocked my bowels. Everything is better now." It was obvious he did not want us to delve any deeper into his health issues.

"From a medical point of view, it might be worthwhile for you to routinely follow up with your physician, just to be on the safe side," Greg suggested to him; but his words fell on deaf ears.

As scientific and accomplished as Uncle Jacob was in engineering, physics, and mathematics, he often became amateurish and obstinate when the subject turned to medicine and his own health. In these areas, he was in a constant state of denial and took no precautions. He should have recognized that since his father had succumbed to metastatic colon cancer, and since he himself had a tumor removed a few years earlier, he could theoretically have inherited a familial gene for colon cancer.

Six years later, in April of 1995, my sister learned from Uncle Jacob's niece Meliné that, while driving to his Yorba Linda property, Jacob had barely managed to pull to the side of the freeway before passing out. An ambulance had eventually arrived and paramedics had taken him to the emergency room at St Jude's

Hospital in Fullerton. Examination and blood tests revealed an end stage metastatic colon cancer, with the malignancy having spread to his liver. After his hospitalization there, my sister was in daily contact with Greg, so he could guide her in her communications with his medical team. Greg made sure they offered him palliative care only, to avoid unnecessary treatments which would prolong his suffering. We lost Uncle Jacob on April 7, 1995.

I Write His Eulogy

On the morning of Jacob's funeral, his niece Meliné called me and asked me if I would write his eulogy. She requested that I include his life's memorable events and achievements, so she could pass it onto the officiating clergy. I willingly accepted the responsibility. Some years back, I may not have been able to forgive him for the callous way he had treated my father in his time of need. His guidance in math was also inconsiderate. In spite of my sketchy background and my lack of confidence, he wanted me to hop and skip the concepts as he would have been able to do. But I had forgiven him for all of the above. I knew that if it weren't for him, I might still be living in Turkey, suffering from the many political upheavals that would take place with unpredictable regularity, as they always had in the past.

I would forgive him and make sure that the modest number of people gathered in the chapel in Newport Beach would remember him for his sharp scientific mind, his pursuit of perfection, and his willingness to help his relatives in this country, although it all had to be handled in his own way and on his own terms.

(Endnotes)

1   Dobkin, Marjorie Housepian, *Smyrna1922*. New York: Newmark Press, 1971, p.57.

2   Jemelian, Rose, Personal Communication, La Canada, CA. 2005.

3   Wenzlick, Dave, as told by A.J. Baime,"Corvair Fascination That Grandma Started," *The Wall Street Journal,* Aug 20, 2014, Part C.

CHAPTER IV
GREAT-UNCLE ABRAHAM'S MEMOIR

My Father's Boldness

The special box I first laid my eyes on in the attic of our Kadiköy house in the summer of 1957 contained the meticulously recorded memoir of my Great-uncle Abraham, his family's life in Talas and later in Aksaray, and the adversities he and his extended family encountered during the deportations and the Armenian Genocide of 1915-22. His words, "You can't imagine these things unless you have gone through them," had left a lasting impression in my psyche. I felt a genuine responsibility to recount this saga, which my father had managed to save in the nick of time from the attic of my childhood home in Kadiköy.

The process of remembering and recording the events of those almost "unreal" years must have been a mixed blessing for great-Uncle Abraham, mostly painful, yet in some ways strangely restorative. Being among the few literate survivors of the genocide from his town, his labor of love might have helped him psychologically by getting the poison off his chest by placing him in the role of the family historian attempting to save this history, which otherwise would have remained buried. In his memoir, Great-uncle Abraham brings wisdom and wistful humor and the bite of the thinker against the pretenses of the world. He worries about the legacy his generation is leaving for posterity. Writing in despair at the collapse of his country and personal fortune, he at times philosophizes, because he is thinking beyond who has won the immediate battle.

Discovering this history has been invaluable to me, and will continue to shed light on the history of scores of Armenian deportees who perished under the scorching sun of the Syrian Desert and the few that miraculously survived against great odds. Great-uncle Abraham does not neglect to mention the kind Turks like Batdal Pasha and the ethical imam of Aksaray, Sherif Efendi. In the years to come, his work will be of interest to our children and our children's children. The original, written in Turkish using the Armenian alphabet, and presented to my husband Greg and me by my father in the balcony of our Ocean City hotel against the gentle breeze of the Atlantic Ocean on that summer evening, is my translation and interpretation of these documents.

I will always appreciate my father's willingness to emigrate late in life from Istanbul to the U.S., by which time he was blind, knowing that he was arriving in a country where the language and culture would be altogether foreign to him. His other admirable decision was to secretly resurrect this memoir, after safekeeping it in our Kadiköy house's attic for ten years, transporting it first to Üsküdar and later to Nisantasi, most importantly having the courage to bring it along with him in his suitcase on his final plane trip to New York City with my mother in June of 1968. If customs officers in Istanbul had gotten an inkling of the content of this ordinary-looking beige cardboard box, they could have easily arrested him and canceled his trip as well as that of my mother's.

As secretive and silent as my father was about our past history while we lived in Turkey, once he and my mother arrived in the United States, he wanted his two daughters and his future grandchildren to find out about our family's past in the Ottoman Empire. He wanted them to be informed about their life before and during the rule of the Young Turks, as well as how his family was affected by the deportations and the Armenian Genocide of 1915-1922. Furthermore, he wanted to pay tribute to his uncle, Great-uncle Abraham for recording this history for us because in doing it, he was also giving a voice to the suffering and the dead, interpreting their mutilated dreams and visions so they would not be lost and forgotten.

I loved the idea that my father still possessed the mental alertness and sense of humor to want to surprise us by suddenly and unexpectedly producing this memoir in Armeno-Turkish, in its easily-recognizable box, in the unlikely setting of their hotel balcony in Ocean City, Maryland. The setting did not quite match the panorama of the Sea of Marmara from our fifth floor balcony in

Kadiköy, but it was close. It left an indelible mark in my memory since it also represented the first as well as the last true vacation I recall taking with my father, before he would pass away six months later and become part of history himself. He must have realized that this memoir, about which he had been so secretive while we lived in Turkey, contained much of what he wanted us to know about our family's past in that country, but had been unable to express. What follows is my translation and interpretation of Great-uncle Abraham's memoir, hidden in that mysterious box for so many years.

Life in Talas

During Great-uncle Abraham's days in the 1880s, the head of an Armenian family in Anatolia would without exception be a male. To support his family, he often had to travel alone to a number of major cities on business; they often included Constantinople (Istanbul), Smyrna (Izmir), and Adana. He would negotiate with merchants in these cities, so he could ship his crops to them and import from them goods which his town needed. Generally speaking, his travels required not days, but weeks and often months. Most of the time, he would be gone for a period of two to eight years. Upon his return, he would spend a blissful period of six months to a year with his family. This rather unconventional way of life was called, *Bantukhtutiun* in Armenian.

During this period, the construction of the rail line connecting central Anatolia to Constantinople had not yet been completed. Therefore, businessmen most often traveled from the interior of Anatolia on horseback and sometimes on mules and donkeys. They often passed through cities such as Ankara and Eskishehir. In those days, even a one-way travel to one of these cities would take the better part of an entire month.

Upon his return, our Great-grandfather Ghazar would spend up to twelve contented months with his wife and children in Talas. He was a cotton merchant, who had made a living traveling in this manner for some fifty-one years. Each trip on horseback netted him 20,000-25,000 piasters (*Bahegan*), the equivalent of 200-250

Turkish Liras of the day, which for the time was a significant sum. His travels mostly took place during the winter months because the hot summers of Adana often exposed the travelers, as well as its residents, to disease.

Talas, located at a higher elevation than *Gesaria* (Kayseri), was its upscale summer resort, and was only an hour's distance from it on horseback. Talas had about 4,500 residences. Of these, 1,800 belonged to Turks, 1,700 to Greeks and the remaining 1,000 to Armenians.

The History of Armenians in Gesaria

According to Great-uncle Abraham, it was assumed that the Armenians of this area were expatriated from Armenia to Persia by Shah Abbas, some 450-500 years ago. They later emigrated from Persia to the area around Gesaria, Talas, Everek, Fenesé, Chomakli, and Tomarza about 350-400 years ago. These six towns would subsequently become heavily populated areas where prominent Armenians lived. Great-uncle Abraham relates: "During my childhood years of 1870-1880, Armenians lived happily and comfortably in these towns and villages. Our town of Talas was even more exceptional."

Upon their return from *bantukhdutiun,* most heads of families brought home horses. On special occasions, upon riding their horses, they would engage in a special sport with sticks and spears.

Weddings were often held in the evenings, with most of the town folk in attendance. Singing and recitations of epic poems passed on from one generation to the next; feasts and merriment would never be in short supply. Residents of the town would dance their folk dances to the melancholy tunes of the *düdük*, a wind instrument similar to the flute, and the *dümbek,* the drum. They would often repeat their unique steps while they held hands and danced in concentric circles, having been completely captured by the melody. Following the rhythm, they would dance as if they were in a trance, like the dervishes. At times they would join each other and at other times they would part from one another. They would sing harmonious tunes, enhancing the magical dance even further with their beautiful voices. They would wear pearls and golden coins strung on their hair and around their necks. Great-uncle Abraham's nostalgia for these days is quite apparent as he remarks, "I am sad that those special days are gone forever. Why did they have to disappear?"

His Neighbor

Great-uncle Abraham also makes several complimentary remarks about the town of Talas: "A number of noteworthy Armenians hailed from this town. The multimillionaire philanthropist Calouste Gulbenkian's parents, uncles, grandparents, and great-uncles all hailed from Talas. Throughout the years, the Gulbenkians had been very supportive of the Armenians of our town. They were instrumental in the sustenance of its Armenian boys' and girls' schools; they supported some 100-200 needy Armenian families living in the vicinity of Talas. They were also the benefactors responsible for the construction of the beautiful bell tower of the Soorp Asdvazazin Armenian Church in Talas. Because of their willingness to extend a helping hand to the needy and to others in town that needed the extra little push, the good Lord blessed the Gulbenkian children and their wealth doubled."

Great-uncle Abraham remembers well one of the Gulbenkian Great-uncles, Avedik, who used to live across the street from them in Talas, and explains the exponential rise of the family's wealth in the following manner:

"Looking forward to 1875-1885, the Gulbenkian family, after the demise of their fathers Kerovpé and Sarkis, left Talas for Constantinople. Few years later, Badrig, Calouste, and their offspring immigrated to New York, Paris, and London, permanently leaving Ottoman Turkey. This was a smart move or perhaps a stroke of luck, because had they continued to live in Ottoman Turkey, most of their family members' as well as their own wealth would have disappeared in no time, as had been the case for all Armenians who remained in that country. In this sense, their emigration to Europe and the United States at the time had been nothing short of miraculous. It gave a chance for their wealth to multiply by a factor of five to ten. They also escaped the racial and religious hatred and persecution the Armenians remaining in Ottoman Turkey had to endure."

Shady Politics in the Ottoman Empire

Great-uncle Abraham continues: "We practically lived across the street from the Armenian Church in Talas. When I was very young [in the 1860s], early one evening the church bells tolled sooner than their customary time. We rushed to the courtyard of the church to find out what was happening. They were announcing that there had been a change of the sultans and that at this point in time, Sultan Murad had become the new Emperor of the Ottoman Empire.

"Later on that day, through the grapevine, we heard that Hamid, the wicked nephew of the sultan, had his uncle Sultan Aziz murdered by undercover agents. These criminals had severed the main artery in his arm and had him literally bleed to death. This was why we were hearing the announcement that Sultan Murad was now the sultan. The reign of Sultan Murad lasted for less than three months. One evening, the church bells tolled a second time, two hours past the traditional hour. This time, it was for the purpose of announcing that since Sultan Murad was judged to be mentally unstable, Sultan Hamid II had now been declared the sultan. We later found out all of these to be the evil formulations of Sultan Hamid. It seemed to us as if they had raised Sultan Hamid to the throne to generate hatred toward us, Armenians. The year was 1872 and we had already seen the ousting of two sultans and the elevation of the lowly Abdul Hamid II to the throne as the Sultan of the Ottoman Empire. Now, going forward twenty six years to the year 1908, everyone in the empire is dreaming of freedom, justice, law and order. Who would think that the evil Committee of Union and Progress that emerged with Talat and Enver at its helm would make us look back and yearn for the tumultuous and unruly days of Abdul Hamid II?"

Locust Infestation and the Russian War

Here is how Great-uncle Abraham describes the famine of 1870 in central Anatolia: "Clouds of locusts devoured everything that was green. Summer pastures on the high plains became barren. That year plants which produced wheat, barley and corn remained stunted and failed to produce the grain we depended on. The leaves of our fruit-bearing trees, having been devoured by the locusts, failed to bear any fruit. During the previous years, our Great-grandfather Ghazar had a very successful business in Talas. Once a year he would travel to Constantinople to buy several rolls of different types of fabric in large quantities. He would later sell these rolls on credit to a commune by the name of *Afshars*, who lived in the area north of Talas. He also owned a flock of sheep and a herd of cattle that grazed in the pastures. That same year, due to the locust infestation his entire herd of livestock perished, because they were unable to find grass to graze on. Within one or two years of this event came another disaster, namely the Russians' attempt to occupy Constantinople. The British joined the Ottomans in the fight against the Russians. Initially due to the famine and later due to the war, our Great-grandfather Ghazar's business failed. Ultimately, he lost everything."

Sent to Merzifon to Learn a Trade

In the aftermath of the locust infestation and the subsequent famine in Talas, on September 2, 1881 Great-uncle Abraham's father Hagop sent him to Merzifon, a city on the eastern coast of the Black Sea, to assist his maternal uncle and great-uncle in their business. He also hoped that he would take this opportunity to learn a new trade. Here is how he describes his life in Merzifon:

"At the time, my Great-uncle Haji Stepan Agha was 75 years old and his son Hagop was 50. They were merchants who sold large quantities of cotton and iron. I was fourteen at the time. I learned their trade and after a while started selling these commodities for them. Their peers respected both of these masters and did not hesitate to consult them when they were confronted with complicated business issues or when they had to settle disputes. They had a private office in *Tas Han*, the well-known large, commercial building of Merzifon. They even taught me how to cook… To tell the truth, I benefited a great deal from their good nature and fame; however, I also encountered certain unusual problems.

"The old man, Haji Stepan Agha was an insomniac who constantly drank Turkish coffee, which he prepared on his brazier. My job was to stay awake at all times and keep his candle lit by cutting its wick every ten minutes with special scissors, so it would generate maximal illumination for him. I stayed with them for four years. The three of us genuinely cared for each other."

In 1883, after living in Merzifon for two years, his father and brothers Kerovpé and Parsegh informed him of their move to Aksaray. They wanted him to leave Merzifon and travel south to join them. The following describes his response:

"When I relayed this message to my Uncle Hagop Agha, it disappointed and saddened him. By now he considered me his son and did not want to see me leave. Hagop Agha told me that if I decided to stay, he would seek a more lucrative job for me and provide me with better living accommodations. However, after some contemplation, he realized he had to respect my decision to return to Aksaray. He gifted me 100 reams of speckled fabric worth 10 gold coins and placed 200 coins of change in my pocket. This was pretty fair, considering that a salary had never been discussed in the past between my father and him. I parted from Hagop Agha on July 22, 1885 with sadness in my heart; it felt as if I was parting from my own father. I detected tears in his eyes as well. The four years I had spent with him had certainly been memorable ones for both of us."

Eventually Hagop Agha's business in Merzifon would stumble as well. His father, Stepan Agha would return to Talas to be with his wife and Hagop Agha would send Great-uncle Abraham to Talas to fetch his own wife and children.

At that young age, Merzifon had made a definite impression on Great-uncle Abraham. He had paid close attention to its demographics, its physical features, and its commerce. Here is how he describes Merzifon:

"At the time 5,000 families lived in Merzifon. Half of the city's population was Muslim and the other half was Armenian. There were about 150-200 Greeks. Merzifon was located at the foot of the Tavshan Mountain where vineyards and gardens with fruit trees were plentiful. Consequently, the city produced substantial quantities of wine. Some owners of wineries annually netted upwards of 20-30-50 and sometimes as much as100 gold coins from this trade."

Merzifon had also impressed Great-uncle Abraham because it had a high concentration of craftsmen. He had noticed that the Muslim craftsmen mostly interweaved speckled towels on their looms. Other craftsmen handcrafted ropes. Still others worked with metals such as copper and iron. Great-uncle remarks: "I was impressed that there was not a single person in town who did not have a craft up his sleeve. There were numerous Armenians in the surrounding towns and cities of Hadji Köy, Amasya, Tokat, and Köprü. Samsun was a harbor on the Black Sea, about two hours away."

Ten years later, Great-uncle Abraham was saddened after hearing the cruel way in which the Armenian population in this *Province of Sebastia* (Sivas) was treated during the Hamidian massacres. Here is what he had to say: "There had been general massacres here [1894-1896], which had cleared the area of a large portion of its Armenian population, killing around 10,000-15,000. Hope for the surviving Armenians would once again return during the early years of the Young Turk revolution. However, the confusion created by World War I during the summer of 1914 presented the perfect opportunity for the Young Turk dictators to permanently eliminate the Armenians. With the deportations from the *Sebastia Province* starting in June 1915, the entire area would soon be denuded of its Armenian population. Not even one in ten Armenians would survive in the area around Merzifon and Amasya."

After leaving Merzifon in 1885, within the next two years Great Uncle Abraham returned to that city twice more to import towels and speckled textiles.

Move from Talas to Aksaray

Up until 1883, my Great-grandmother Melek had remained in Talas with her daughter Sima, while my Great-grandfather Hagop, my Grandfather Kerovpé and my Great-uncle Parsegh had moved further west to Aksaray to start a business and to search for appropriate living quarters for their families. Great-uncle Abraham describes the purchase of their property and the construction of their house in Aksaray in this way:

"In 1898, through Haji Sabri Bey of Konya, we purchased a large property in a central and prized section of the town of Aksaray, with a sizable brook running by throughout the seasons, for 130 gold pieces. We had the land graded and by September of 1899 had two sturdy stone houses built on the property for the sum of 800 gold pieces."

The following is how Great-uncle Abraham describes Aksaray: "By the end of the 19th century, Aksaray was a small town consisting of 2,000 families: 1,700 of these were Muslim, 270 were Armenian and the remaining 30 were Greek. At the time, my Great-grandfather Hagop, my grandfather and uncles saw plenty of potential in Aksaray in the form of business opportunities for the future. Apparently, there were 164 villages in the immediate vicinity of Aksaray, where there was an abundance of fertile land, and where they could plant grains and vegetables and grow fruit trees for commercial purposes. It was in this type of a setting that they first started their business of selling textiles to the residents of Aksaray and its neighboring villages. In time, their family business expanded as its reputation flourished."

A Bride for my Grandfather Kerovpé

From my Great-grandfather Hagop's perspective, it was important for all of his family members to be living in the same town.

Therefore when he went back to Talas to fetch his wife Melek and his daughter Sima, he also thought about my Grandfather Kerovpé. "Let us not leave this town empty-handed. Let's also bring a bride with us from Talas for our son Kerovpé," he reasoned.

Although before leaving for Talas my great-Grandfather had conferred with his son and received his consent, it seems the way in which my Grandfather Kerovpé married my Grandmother Verkin was still quite unconventional. Actually the bride and groom were distantly related to each other, because my grandmother was my Grandfather's paternal Uncle Garabed's granddaughter. Up until the time I was 17 when I left Istanbul for the US, I had the good-fortune of enjoying this grandmother's presence and wise counsel. She was my even-tempered grandmother with the most calming effect on our entire family.

Rather unconventionally, the mother of the bride also visited and stayed with the prospective in laws for an extended time before the wedding, which took place in September of 1892.

On the Way to Lake Elma

As my great-grandfather Hagop's business in Aksaray prospered and expanded, so did the services he provided; for this reason, he needed more help. Soon he was selling not just textiles, but all sorts of consumer staples such as wheat, rye, and even wool. In fact, his business had even diversified into selling flocks of sheep and goats. Wagons of wheat were routinely loaded in Aksaray and transported to Mersin on the Mediterranean coast. For a couple of years, my Great-uncle Parsegh operated as an intermediary in charge of the transportation of their crops, as well as that of other merchants' in and around Aksaray, making sure their harvest would arrive safely in Mersin.

Around the year 1890 it had become necessary for Great-uncle Abraham to travel to a location 15 hours southwest of Adana, called Lake Elma, for the purpose of buying bulls. He initially bought140 bulls, but soon realized he needed 100 more. As he searched for a shepherd, he also realized he needed extra money to cover the cost of the additional bulls. For this, he had to travel to

Mersin. The following is how he relates his amazing experience, which came very close to claiming his life:

"It was a glorious morning in May when I got on my horse to reach Adana. I was going to take the railroad from there to Mersin, to procure the money necessary for the additional bulls. The innkeeper where I was staying suggested that I take a horseman to accompany me. The entire process of my buying and transporting the animals with the shepherd was going to take approximately three months.

"I was feeling quite invincible at the time because I was young, daring, and owned a Martin brand rifle. I thought taking along a horseman would only slow me down; therefore, I decided to go it alone. I left Lake Elma and headed for the town of *Yar Suad*, now called *Jihan* (Seyhan), which was three hours away. I traveled along the scenic river bearing the same name and reached *Missis*. Now I was only six hours away from Adana.

"In the distance, I detected a safe bridge on the river. It was 3 PM when I finally arrived at the bridge and got off my horse. I was hoping to reach Adana by that evening. After feeding my horse some hay and watering him, I hopped back on her. It had been two hours since I had left *Missis*. As I continued riding, I noticed three horsemen advancing toward me. After they got closer, I realized they were Circassians. They appeared to be shady characters.

"Although I realized they might have an ulterior motive, I decided not to deviate from my route. Due to my youth and inexperience, I was unwilling to swallow my pride, even in the presence of imminent danger. Finally our paths crossed. I could see that the horsemen had whips on their backs. I suspected that they were also armed. I later realized their guns were hidden under their whips and were ready to go. In no uncertain terms they shouted out their order at me:

'Do not move!'

"I was terrified, but I tried not to show it. Even though I was taking a very big risk, I reasoned at the time that for me to be robbed by them would feel worse than dying. But there were three of them. I was miserably outnumbered. There was no way I could run them down. I instantly turned my horse around and started galloping as fast as I could. I heard them blasting their orders at me:

'Do not attempt to run away. We will shoot you if you do!'

"As I heard them firing their guns at me, I descended to the fields and brush lower down. I took a moment to check myself; I seemed to be OK. One of their bullets had whizzed by the region of my horse's kidney, bruising his skin. Now I was desperately running away; but the three Circassians were chasing me. I was thankful not to be on higher ground. I tried to be inconspicuous, while making progress amid the lower ploughed fields.

"Thank goodness I had a brave horse who kept on galloping. When I looked back, it seemed with each stride I was distancing myself a little farther from the three horsemen. The ground I was traveling on was soft. It was so soft that at times my horse's feet seemed to get buried in it. But my horse did not let me down.

"After pursuing me for another half hour, which felt like an eternity, the three bandits no longer wanted to waste their time chasing me. They felt compelled to go back. I was saved! That evening when I made it to Adana, it felt more like I had reached paradise.

"That year at *Küpeli Inn*, the owner was Dadour Dadrian from Talas. I procured a place from him. My horse had bled some in his right flank region, but the bleeding had stopped by the time I had reached the inn. Right away, Dadour noticed the blood on my horse. When I told him what had happened, he suggested that we report it to the authorities. I was reluctant because by now the bandits were long gone. Besides, my horse had not sustained any serious injury.

"Early the next morning, I left my horse with the innkeeper and I departed for Mersin on the train. After I procured the amount of money I needed from there, I headed straight back to Adana. When I was running away from the Circassians, I only had an insignificant amount of change; now I had an abundance of money. By now I had also learned that it was best to play it safe; therefore, I sent word to Haji Osman at Elma Lake to send a horseman to accompany me. He sent his nephew and from then on we traveled together. I increased the number of bulls I purchased to 232. After they had grazed sufficiently, with help from the shepherds, we finally made it to Aksaray in 12 days. We knew we could not drive the bulls more than 5-6 hours per day, because we would hurt them if we did.

"After resting in Aksaray for the next two days, we started selling the bulls to the neighboring villages. We were able to sell the 100 pairs of oxen which I had purchased for 4 gold pieces each, for 12 gold pieces. Another 30 were sold for 8-9 gold pieces each. We sold them with the understanding that we would get paid in one and a half years. Half of the money was due at the end of that year in December, and the other half was due in another year. We had to formulate the terms of our sale in this manner because the villagers who were buying from us did not usually have the ready cash available to pay us. Besides, if we got paid on the spot, it would then have been necessary for us to sell the bulls at a far cheaper price. In those days, the villagers were usually quite dependable and generally it was not a difficult task to collect the money from them."

What Great-uncle Abraham does not mention at this point is that, later on during the deportations and the Armenian Genocide of 1915, this mode of transaction would place the Armenian deportees at a great disadvantage, since they would be owed quite a lot of money by the villagers, when the Government of the Young Turks would order them to promptly and permanently leave town.

Great-uncle Abraham's Father-in-Law--Judge Kazanjian

Great-uncle Abraham offers a most complimentary account of his father-in-law, who died in 1887 at age 42. He explains: "Master Haroutioun Kazanjian was a well-respected and honorable Agha, a gentleman who was also hospitable. He was generous to his clients and did not mind entertaining them. He possessed a questioning mind, which came in handy during the long years he served as a judge in the courts. There was no shortage of people arriving at his residence or leaving it, at all hours of the day. Individuals with issues to settle with the government would travel all the way from

Talas and its neighboring villages to seek his counsel. As a rule, he would see to it that food was served to his clients who had traveled the long distances to receive his services. The manner in which he got paid depended on the individual case. He sometimes received money, but on other occasions when he had to settle certain special cases, his clients would bring him rugs."

Sherif Efendi—the Ethical Imam of Aksaray

Up until the 1870s, Great-uncle Abraham remembers Armenians and Turks living in relative harmony. However he notices a development of tenseness in the political and social climate of the Ottoman Empire during the years leading to the Armenian Genocide. This is how he described it: "Upon the urging of the European nations, a new constitution was adopted in 1908 by the Ottoman Empire to give more rights to minorities. In effect, having to take this step increased the fanaticism of the Turkish public, antagonizing them further against the Armenians. As time went on, the situation got worse. As Armenians, we felt that this new freedom bestowed upon us was not substantial, and was in name only. Even though the new congress now had two Armenian representatives, we would often look back with longing, to the days of the cruel Emperor Hamid."

Great-uncle Abraham noted an increase in the general level of dissatisfaction with the government throughout the entire cross-section of the citizenry, which included: distrust, ignorance, fear and misplaced rage. He explains it thus: "It was not just the minorities, such as the Armenians who were dissatisfied with the government; there also were a few Turks who were similarly dissatisfied and wanted to correct the record, because the government had been left in the hands of wicked individuals such as Enver and Talat. Among these judicious individuals was the Imam of Aksaray, Sherif Efendi, who would point the situation to us saying, 'Those higher ups in the government don't have a religion, nor do they believe in the existence of God. They are the real *geavurs* (infidels).' However, as Great-uncle Abraham noted, "The advice of their wise imam would fall on deaf ears and his words would have little effect on the congregation. A fear of the Lord did not exist in them."

It seems throughout the rule of Sultan Hamid II, it was forbidden for Armenians to travel to Constantinople; however, after the adoption of the new constitution, such travel became possible. Great-uncle Abraham is quite aware of the hostility and hatred within the population along religious lines, when he says: "During the Adana Massacre of 1909 and following it, we could almost feel the tension in the air because both sides had started viewing each other as enemies. However, a number of modest and moral Turks existed. In the aftermath of the Hamidian Massacres of 1894-1896, the Muslim religious leader of our town, Sherif Efendi, had lectured from his podium and said:

'Those who have ordered, organized and executed these massacres are all criminals.'"

"Because of this statement of his, certain individuals among the crowd claimed that their imam had betrayed his country. Therefore he was discharged from his duties by Sultan Hamid II, since the sultan had personally been responsible for ordering the massacres. Sometime later because he was such an ethical and well-liked individual, popular demand moved the authorities and Sherif Efendi was asked to resume his duties." Great-uncle Abraham goes on to say, "This ethical imam actually repeated his same definition of "criminality" right after the Adana Massacre of 1909, but who in his congregation was listening?"

Great-uncle Abraham remembers another incident about Imam Sherif Efendi which is equally remarkable:

"In the Bostanlik village of Aksaray, there lived a simple and honest individual by the name of Haji Salih, who used to buy his merchandise from our store. One Thursday he stopped by our store. I saw him take out 14 gold pieces from a blue money bag; he counted them, then he inserted them back into his belt.

'Tomorrow is Friday; *Ziraat Bankasi,* the Agricultural Bank, won't be open; I better deposit the money today; I'll be back,' he said to me and left our store in a hurry. He was back in less than 10 minutes."

'Master Abraham, I must have dropped my money bag. Was my money left here?' "He inquired of me. I explained to him that I saw him insert it into his belt; nevertheless I suggested that we look again. Together we carefully searched our entire store, but it was not there. The poor man left our store empty-handed.

"Three years must have gone-by since this incident. For some time, I had hired a 12-13 year old boy to help me in the store. One day 13 gold pieces were found on him. We asked him where he had gotten them from. After repeated questioning, sometimes amiably and at other times threateningly, four to five days later he confessed that it was the money Haji Salih had lost and said:

'To date, I have spent only one golden coin of that money.'

"From what he confessed, we gathered that as Haji Salih was leaving our store, he had accidentally dropped his money bag in front of our store and when our helper was taking some water to the barbershop next-door, he had found the money bag, but had kept silent about it. We had almost completely forgotten about this incident, since so much time had elapsed.

"Later on that day, I sent word to Haji Salih and late in the afternoon I traveled on horseback to his village to return his money. He was pleased. I requested that he give one golden coin to my helper, which he did; nevertheless, I dismissed him.

"What I really wanted to note was that, right after receiving the money, Haji Salih headed straight to Imam Sherif to relate the incident as it had happened three years ago. As part of his sermon for that Friday, the imam had addressed his congregation in the following manner:

'You at times refer to Christians as *geavurs* and look down at them. However, among them Abraham Lafdjian just located the 14 gold pieces of Haji Salih of Bostanlik that was lost three years ago and personally returned them to him.' "The reason I knew about his sermon was because someone who regularly worshipped in that mosque had stopped by our store that day and had told me about it.

"Later, when the deportations began from our town of Aksaray, the same religious leader was saddened and grieving. He contacted several government authorities and told them:

'I am thoroughly familiar with the Armenians of our town. There are absolutely no treacherous individuals among them.'" Great-uncle Abraham goes on to remark, "However, we realized that since the enforcement of the law had fallen in the hands of wicked individuals, none of his well-meaning statements had done any good."

Construction of the Pasha Hamam (Public Bath)

In the following pages, Great-uncle Abraham describes how he managed the construction of the historic public bath across from their residence, for the people of Aksaray.

"In 1892, I came to know a Batdal Agha who used to shop for yardage from our store in Aksaray, although he lived at an hour's distance from us. I found out that he was originally from Ortaköy in Constantinople. Throughout the years he had continued to maintain an unusually close relationship with the Ottoman Palace. The reason was his older brother Ali, who was initially assigned to the palace as a soldier during the rule of Sultan Mecid. During the course of his service, Ali developed an unusually close friendship with the then teen-age crown prince, Hamid, whom he was employed to supervise. When it was finally time for Ali to leave and return to his hometown of Aksaray, the palace did not wish to permanently discharge him, as he had been such a faithful and competent employee throughout the years. Instead, Ali kept being assigned to increasingly higher ranking positions. After making the pilgrimage to Mecca and earning the title of Haji Ali Pasha, he was ultimately advanced to the post of Interior Minister. Sometime during this interval, he invited his two younger brothers Batdal and Sayid to Constantinople, where they were also bestowed the title of Pasha. In time, Batdal Pasha became a top religious leader and Sayid Pasha an overseer in the Ottoman Palace, necessitating the two brothers to retain a second residence in Ortaköy."

Because there were no schools in Aksaray at the time and only approximately 4% of the population of the Ottoman Empire knew how to read and write, every one of the three brothers had remained illiterate. Nonetheless, in time Batdal Pasha had acquired even more fame as a problem solver for many people. Great-uncle Abraham had noticed that: "whenever an application had to be made in writing, if his stamp of approval appeared on the document, it was almost a guarantee that the project would proceed without delays." Whenever he came to Aksaray, Great-uncle Abraham was his secretary who would read and write his letters; on other occasions, he would travel to Ortaköy in Constantinople to perform the same duties. On one of these occasions when he had gone to Ortaköy, he remembers Batdal Pasha's remark to him:

'If a worthwhile piece of property is ever placed for sale in Aksaray, let me know and we will jointly buy it.'

Buying the Hamam

Apparently, at one time a large public bath for both men and women existed right across from Great-uncle Abraham's newly-constructed house in Aksaray. During an unusually cold and wet winter, when the water level in the nearby river rose to critically high levels, the flood waters collapsed its ceiling and engulfed its interior, completely destroying the structure of the public bath. In time, its appearance deteriorated and became such an eyesore that when the Lafdjians first arrived in Aksaray, people were using the site to dump their garbage. Meanwhile, the heirs who claimed ownership to the property had increased in number and were constantly having disagreements among each other. Additionally, they resented the idea of having to pay a recurring property tax on a defunct business which was not providing them any income. In desperation, they decided to sell the parcel; but so far there had been no takers. Great-uncle Abraham and his brothers must have realized this was the opportunity they were looking for. The following is how Great-uncle Abraham describes their acquisition of the hamam:

"When we first realized that the unsightly property right across from our house was for sale, I wrote to Batdal Pasha in Ortaköy. He wanted me to arrive there right away to discuss the possibility of our jointly buying it."

'If we can be partners and you will accept the responsibility of the construction, I am all for buying it,' he said. "I explained to him that we had a limited amount of capital and if we allocated it all for this purpose, we could not conduct our regular business."

'You shouldn't worry too much about the financial aspect; we'll do something,' he said.

"Five to eight days after my return from Ortaköy, my two brothers and I paid 130 gold pieces to buy part of the title from one of the owners of the property. The entire transaction was completed in a few days when the last remaining owner of the property agreed to sell his title to us for a similar price."

A Deed under Batdal Pasha's Name

Great-uncle Abraham again traveled to Ortaköy for the deed of the property. Batdal Pasha wanted both of their names to appear on the deed, but Great-uncle disagreed: "I was hesitant and wanted only Batdal Pasha's name to appear with the understanding that we jointly owned it. We were a Christian minority in an otherwise Muslim country. We were concerned that the news of our jointly owning the hamam with Batdal Pasha could haunt us in the future. Affluent Turks in Aksaray might write to Haji Ali Pasha at the palace due to jealousy, with questions such as:

'In the presence of so many Turks in Aksaray, why is it that an Armenian is partnering with your brother?'

"Then, Haji Ali Pasha, unaware of our circumstances, would contact his brother, an act that would most likely result in the postponement or the cancelation of the project. Our ulterior motive was not only to improve our immediate neighborhood but also to provide the town's women and youth--Armenians included--a viable alternative to commuting to the existing ancient and dirty public bath in the Turkish district.

"The next time I went to Ortaköy to talk to the Pasha, he was very candid with me: 'Do you know why I am partnering with you?' He asked. 'It is because I trust you more than I trust those Turks in Aksaray,' he told me, in confidentiality. 'After you get the public bath built, since it will be practically next to your home, I know you will always be attentive to its needs and will be able to supervise it,' he pointed out.

"I again reassured him that I would be willing to accept the responsibility of supervising its construction, but I also convinced him that for the time being it would be more appropriate if the deed were registered in the Hall of Records solely under his name. Indeed, after the Pasha, his son Hüseyin, and I returned to Aksaray and paid the fee for the transfer of the title to his name, we started thinking seriously about the construction of the hamam."

The Pasha was elderly and had renal disease. For the treatment of his medical condition, he often traveled either to Konya in central Anatolia or to Constantinople. A short while after he had left for Konya for his routine renal management, the Congressman Ferid Pasha, who later became prime minister, traveled to that city to visit him. During their conversation, Batdal Pasha made a casual reference to the newly-acquired hamam and inquired:

'We bought an old hamam and are planning to get a new one constructed where the old one stands. Do you know of an expert builder who exclusively deals with hamams?'

To this, Ferid Pasha's answer was: 'Efendi (Sir), allow me to find out.' During the congressional session that same day, Ferid Pasha was given the name of the "Master Architect of Hamams, Mgrdich of Akshehir," who had previously built as many as 9-10 hamams and was considered to be the expert in hamam construction. The congressman right away sent a telegram to the governor of Akshehir, asking for Mgrdich. In less than two days Mgrdich had already arrived in Congressman Ferid Pasha's quarters, at which time the congressman contacted Batdal Pasha asking him to come over to meet him. By the time their conversation had concluded, Batdal Pasha had requested Mgrdich to make a special trip to Aksaray to examine the old, dilapidated hamam and to give them his opinion, as well as an estimate of what he thought it would cost to construct a new one. He also instructed Mgrdich to meet with the Lafdjians, to gather all the necessary information, so he could get back to him. Simultaneously, he sent Great-uncle Abraham a letter about Mgrdich's plan to visit Aksaray and meet with them to gather information regarding the hamam he was to construct.

The Construction Begins

A few days later, one late afternoon the Lafdjians noticed the arrival of a carriage in front of their house in Aksaray. When great-uncles Abraham and Parsegh descended to the street, they were greeted by a middle-aged Armenian man in his 50s, who introduced himself as "Master Mgrdich" and a younger man he had brought along with him, no older than 30, whom he introduced as his nephew and assistant Krikor. After an evening's rest, followed by a hearty breakfast the next morning, they inspected the rundown hamam. To great-uncle's surprise, Master Mgrdich's pronouncement on it was rather encouraging:

'Although the hamam's structure is very old, it actually has quite a solid foundation. We can use its present foundation, but we will have to demolish everything else that remains above the ground. Then we can add to the existing foundation and raise the level of the hamam by one meter to build a beautiful new structure with separate men's and women's wings on each side. When completed, it will look picture-perfect,' he reassured them.

After finding out about local sources for stone, lime, and sand, the two also asked Great-uncle Abraham for recommendations for a foreman and workers. Then, on the third day, after receiving a letter from my great-uncle to present to the Pasha, they left Aksaray. Upon their arrival in Konya, Batdal Pasha took them to the palace to Ferid Pasha. Provided that all the expenses would be on Master Mgrdich, he and his committee then negotiated and settled for a price of 750 gold pieces. They signed a contract for Master Mgrdich to begin the project within 15 days.

Deep down Great-uncle Abraham did not think the negotiated price was completely fair to Master Mgrdich and goes on to say: "Since I previously had some familiarity with the construction business, I found the negotiated price a bit too rock-bottom and doubted whether the hamam could be constructed so cheaply. I felt this way because, despite our use of the existing foundation, the overall project still appeared huge. It involved the construction of six chimneys on each side of the building, as well as the installation of marble flooring."

Two weeks later, the Master Builder arrived in their town and brought along five to six workers. The Lafdjians again entertained him, as well as his team of workers, and rented a house for them close to the hamam, where they would rest after work and sleep. It wasn't long before my great-uncles found out that these people cared most of all about their drink of arak, an anise-flavored popular alcoholic drink, and their cigarettes. They were much less particular about their meals and living accommodations. Master Mgrdich had not had any schooling and was illiterate, but he knew his business. When he recited the figures orally, making the calculations in his head, they realized that he was very accurate.

Great-uncle Abraham's Many Responsibilities

Here, Great-uncle Abraham describes how the construction project started on March 20, 1901. "For the duration of the project, this became my primary occupation, because neither the master nor his workers were experienced in purchasing and negotiating. I had to bargain directly with the suppliers, such as the stone mason and the provider of lime, because if it were left to the master, he would simply pay the asking price on the day he needed it. I kept an ongoing account of the prices for the supplies and the wages paid to the workers. As I paid weekly for their services, Master Mgrdich placed his stamp under the amounts paid. Within these guidelines, the project progressed smoothly."

On one occasion when Batdal Pasha came to Aksaray, Great-uncle Abraham requested funds to be forwarded to them from Ali Pasha at the Palace. The Pasha wanted them to do it in writing and said he would place his stamp on the letter. Great-uncle Parsegh wrote the letter as if it was dictated by Batdal Pasha. It said:

'We purchased an old hamam from a renowned section of Aksaray and paid 750 gold pieces for a contract to have it renovated. I have known for some time that my health has been deteriorating. I wanted the hamam to be an investment for my children's financial future. The construction of a hamam being a benevolent effort, we would be appreciative of your help.'

In the past, Haji Ali Pasha had been instrumental in constructing a number of bridges and fountains in many parts of the country, including Aksaray. Fifteen days after the letter was written, 600 gold pieces was wired to them from the palace for this purpose. Two months later, another 300 gold pieces arrived.

At this point in the project, Great-uncle Abraham arrives at the following realization: "By now I had paid over 500 gold pieces to Master Mgrdich and less than half of the project had been completed. I felt I should again travel to Ortaköy and talk to Batdal Pasha. When I arrived there, I explained to him that the expert on hamams Master Mgrdich was not a businessman and that if we spent the money at this rate and our expenditures were not appropriately curbed, we would soon be in debt and there would not be enough funds to complete the hamam."

Batdal Pasha already seemed to be aware of the situation. He said: 'We are not going to let this man lose money. There is no way we can recover from the Palace any expenses above and beyond what was specified in the initial contract. From now on, I ask of you to please handle the finances as much as possible.'

"From then on, we continued working on the project with me controlling the purse strings, and in September of that year the construction of the hamam was completed with the exception of the marble flooring." Previously, for this type of project, Master Mgrdich had gone to Smyrna (Izmir) a couple of times to buy the marble; he insisted on assuming this responsibility. They thought that since he would be passing by his hometown of Akshehir on the way, they should delegate this responsibility to him, since this way he would also have a chance to see his family." After determining the price of the marble from an acquaintance in that business in Beirut, they gave him three money orders worth 150 gold pieces each, and he went on his way.

When Master Mgrdich returned in eighteen days, he had made an arrangement for the marble to be transported by train from Smyrna until Konya, where it would be loaded on the backs of camels to arrive in Aksaray. They installed the black and white marble tiles in a checkerboard style, smoothly sealing the adjoining pieces until they had covered the entire floor of the hamam.

Joint Ownership

Batdal Pasha's chronic kidney disease was familiar to those who knew him. However, it took a sharp turn to the worse around the time of the hamam's completion. In Great-uncle Abraham's words, to be fair to his friend Abraham, Batdal Pasha took the following additional steps: "Realizing that his days were numbered, 45 days before the completion of the hamam, he invited my brother in law Master Misak Houbeserian, as well as my brother Parsegh to the Sari Karaman Village where he lived. He similarly invited Haji Hodja, who was the religious leader of Aksaray, as well as the religious leaders of the neighboring towns and a number of prominent businessmen, numbering around 20-25 in total. They all gathered in his village and enjoyed a meal consisting of two stuffed lambs he had ordered to be served for the occasion. After enjoying the feast, the crowd gathered around his bed when he was ready to address them. He said:

'Look, we and the Lafdjians have jointly bought a hamam in Aksaray and have just about completed its renovation, although for certain reasons its deed is registered solely under my name. After my death, I don't want my children to deny the fact that it was a joint venture. I don't want them to create problems for the Lafdjians and for them to lose the right to their portion of the hamam. I want all of you to be witnesses to this fact.' The Haji Hodja of Aksaray prayed and shortly thereafter, the congregation dispersed.[i]

A short while after this event, even before the plastering of the hamam was completed, Great-uncle Abraham was informed of the death of Batdal Pasha. The news of his passing was telegrammed to Constantinople, since his brother at the Palace would always inquire about his health. Six days after his death, his title of Pasha was bestowed upon Batdal Pasha's son, Hüseyin. A few days later, it was said that when Haji Ali Pasha approached Sultan Hamid II at the Palace, the Sultan remarked:

---

i   Great-uncle Abraham was impressed by the faithfulness, impartiality, and sense of justice of his friend Batdal Pasha.

'Pasha, what is the matter? You look awfully sad.' To this he replied:

'Your Excellency, the brother of your servant has passed away. May the Lord add years to your life, your Excellency.'

Sultan Hamid asked him if he had descendants. When he found out that he had a son, he bestowed Batdal Pasha's title on his son Hüseyin, since the Sultan used to be very fond of Ali Pasha.

Great-uncle Abraham explains: "After the hamam was completed, we leased it for two years for 185 gold pieces. It had become a beautiful hamam. Because it was next to our house, on occasion when it was not occupied, we would go behind the houses to lock the door from inside to have our family members enjoy taking a private bath."

The total cost of the hamam ended up being 1,350 gold pieces. It would have cost twice that amount without its existing solid foundation. It also helped that the cost of the stones, lime, and sand were quite nominal. For Master Mgrdich's services, the Pasha forwarded 30 gold pieces to his family home in Akshehir. However, he and his assistants ate and drank plenty of *arak* in Aksaray. Apparently that was his custom; wherever he built a building, he would not profit much from it, other than for the food and drink he got on the side.

After Batdal Pasha's Demise

Great-uncle Abraham describes the turn of events after Batdal Pasha's passing in the following manner: "After his father's demise and his assuming of the "Pasha" title, Hüseyin frequented Aksaray more often and started questioning why half of the property of the hamam was "being given away to these Armenians." He must have requested a letter to be written to Haji Ali Pasha in Constantinople, giving the author of the letter erroneous information regarding the ownership of the hamam, contradicting what his father had clearly stated.

One day a large, odd-shaped, envelope arrived in the mail, addressed to Great-uncle Abraham. It bore stamps on five different places on the envelope. When he opened it, he could see that it had the signature of the most eminent Imperial Haji Ali. It read:

'During the lifetime of my deceased brother, an old hamam was purchased in Aksaray with your mediation, regarding which it has come to our attention that you have spent a certain amount of money and to which you have devoted your time and labor. Upon my brother's demise, it has been my intention to pass this property's ownership to my nephews. Please receive the approximately 400 gold pieces spent by you from Cherzizade (Hüseyin's wife's parents).

'Regarding your labor, three individuals have been selected to come up with a figure: Kadizade, Cherzizade, and Mousa Efendi. They will determine the appropriate amount you should receive for your time and labor, which Mr. Cherzizade will pay. After receiving this compensation, for my sake, please relinquish all your rights to this property.'

After receiving this document from Constantinople, Great-uncle Abraham said the following to his brother Parsegh: "Our intention in building this hamam in Aksaray was primarily to relieve its residents from having to travel a long distance to the more depressed part of town to take a bath. Secondarily, it was to remove the ugly spectacle and garbage dump that the old hamam had become and ultimately, to improve the value of our property. Since we had succeeded on all three counts, we should just be content with what we got and relinquish our rights. My brother Parsegh did not completely agree with me. Instead, he wrote a letter to Haji Ali Pasha at the Palace bearing both of our signatures, basically to embarrass him. In it he wrote:

'Not long before his demise, your brother Batdal Pasha had organized a special dinner in the presence of a number of religious and civic leaders in the neighborhood, so he could remind everyone of the joint ownership of the hamam shared between him and us. Everyone present that day witnessed his words. If possible, honor Batdal Pasha in the realization of his dream.'

They soon received another letter from Haji Ali Pasha that read: 'We had earlier expressed to you our decision regarding this matter. There will be no changes or additions to what was said earlier on this subject.'

When Great-uncle Abraham received the above letter, this time without communicating with his brother Parsegh, he went and received the 475 gold pieces: 60 for his work on the project and 415 for his expenses.

He had the following to say about Hüseyin Pasha: "As to Hüseyin Pasha, he was so embarrassed that he could not even bear to pass in front of our store. Approximately two years had gone by. In spite of their becoming permanent residents of the town of Aksaray, he and his family had been unable to handle the operation of the hamam. They had left it to a manager who had underwritten excessive expenses. Meanwhile the town's religious leader Haji Hodja and Hüseyin's mother had been constantly reminding him: 'You are not letting your father rest in peace at the cemetery.'

"One evening Hüseyin Pasha came straight to our house. From the way he was acting, I could tell he was somewhat drunk, because if he were not, I don't think he would have ever come. The minute he arrived, he embraced me and said:

'What a huge mistake I made by losing dear friends like you! I felt dissatisfied with what I had and I lied. Please forgive me. The management of the hamam got into the wrong hands and I was faced with many expenses. Even though as a family we are making a decent living, we are unable to sleep at night. I am constantly reminded of my father's words and the fact that I have failed to follow them. This is affecting our entire family and causing us distress. Let half of the hamam again be yours. Take on the management and save us from this pain and suffering,' he begged. "We explained to him that according to the deed, his father and he were the registered owners of the hamam and we took over its management."

The Frigid Winter of 1913

Due to an unusually cold winter in 1913, the river running through Aksaray froze, becoming a solid piece of ice for a depth of at least one meter. During the previous winters, even though the surface water would freeze, some water would continue to run underneath the ice. But this time it was different. Due to the relentless snowfall and the windstorm accompanying it, a lot of snow had accumulated on the river and had kept freezing on it. This forced the newly-arriving waters of the river to flow on the tall sheet of ice during the daytime, and to freeze there at night with the subzero temperatures. Since the river routinely carried a high volume of water from the neighboring mountains, overnight it had suddenly risen to a height of 3-4 meters. As the ice started to melt, it flooded the area and collapsed the foundations and structures of the wooden residences of about 300 families in the vicinity.

Great-uncle Abraham remembers: "My own residence and those of my brothers' were flooded as well, but they were sturdy structures made of stone and they did not collapse. During this natural disaster, all of us had to move out and share living quarters with our neighbors living on higher ground. However, it was not enough that people had to move; their livestock, cows, and mules also had to be transported and provisions had to be made for their sustenance. My brothers moved their furniture to the second story of their house and shared living quarters for ten days with Master Misak Houbeserians, our cousin's family. During these trying times, it was not unusual for three to five families to manage living under the same roof.

"The flood created even a more challenging situation for the Muslim families. This was because according to the guidelines established by their religious leaders, a woman was never to show her face to another member of the opposite sex, other than to her husband. Therefore, to share living quarters with another family was out of the question for them. Meanwhile they had to tend to their animals, to reassure the survival of their livestock.

"After this cold spell, the spring and summer months produced abundant crops and generated a thriving season for business. It was later in 1913 when, with unfaltering trust in the country we lived in, that my two brothers and I bought a number of valuable income properties with the intention of creating a constant stream of revenue for the future. In doing this, we had appreciation in mind as well. It was a wonderful plan, if unforeseen historical events would not so radically alter our lives, as well as those of all Armenians living in Asia Minor."

A 2006 Visit to My Grandparents' Ancestral Home

In 2006, during our "Pilgrimage Tour to Historic Armenia," my husband Greg, my sister Arminé, and I located my paternal grandparents' house in Aksaray. To our surprise and great delight, it was among the rare ancient buildings we could count on our fingers, which were still standing. Since the deportations some ninety one years ago, its basic stone structure had withstood the test of time and utter neglect. Luckily, due to its proximity to the Historic Pasha Hamam--which might be said was my Great-uncle Abraham's informal gift to Aksaray--as well as due to the nearby Seljuk *Medresé,* the Muslim theological school, it had been earmarked by the city of Aksaray for historic preservation. We were able to locate all three of these structures, due to the meticulous descriptions of my Great-uncle Abraham in his memoir.

When I entered the well-insulated kitchen on the ground floor that led to the dining room of my grandparents' house with my husband and sister in the midst of the Central Anatolian smoldering summer heat in July, I did not have any concerns in my mind regarding its safety. It felt cool inside, due to its thick walls and sturdy stone construction. A middle-aged refugee from Kazakhstan, oblivious to the past history of the land, had been living there for the last year with her two young grandchildren and seemed surprised to see us.

In my mind's eye, I could easily picture my Grandmother Verkin laboring in the roomy kitchen, fixing elaborate *dolmas*, stuffed vegetables with meat, parsley, rice, and spices, and cooking them on top of the ever present cast iron stove. I could also picture her kneading some dough on the sturdy, round wooden kitchen table to create medium-thin layers of dough for *manti*, a spiced dumpling filled with ground meat, with her thin wooden rolling pin, for their entire family to enjoy. It felt as if I had suddenly traveled back in time and had taken a peek at their life in Aksaray of almost one hundred years ago. It seemed no one had lived there until recently. However, the second story of their residence did not share the same good fortune. It had not been maintained and was unsafe for us to enter. Its wooden stairwell was hanging loosely, appearing quite precarious from the outside.

Prelude to the Deportations

In January of 1914, certain sealed confidential envelopes arrived from Constantinople, which were addressed to each district and were labeled "red documents." No one was allowed to open them to read their content because it was proclaimed such an act would be punishable by death. These envelopes remained with the administrator of each district for an entire six months, until June 22nd. On that date an order was telegraphed from Constantinople to each district, stating that the envelopes could now be opened. Their message was:

'1st World War has been declared; thus all men ages sixteen through fifty, both Muslim and Christian, are to be conscripted.'

Only the very young and the very old were to be spared. To complicate matters further and cause more apprehension, the government additionally asked each family to remit 45 gold coins. Great-uncle Abraham believed this decision by the government was unreasonable and said: "This was a high price for the deportees to pay, when most people did not have it and when everyone was already facing a frightening and uncertain future. Furthermore, these gold coins would surely have improved their chances of survival during their dangerous odyssey that was shortly to follow. It was especially difficult for my two brothers and me, since we had just completed the payments for our recently acquired properties."

Here, Great-uncle Abraham tries to interpret the political situation of the time: "It should not have taken amazing intelligence on the part of the Turkish leaders to figure out that an alliance with England and France would have been far more reasonable and advantageous for the country than an alliance with Germany and Austria. If that had been the case, the ox presently worth two gold coins would soon have appreciated to fifteen or twenty. Instead, resources and money from Turkey started pouring into Germany, while the population of Ottoman Turkey suffered, many dying of starvation.

According to the historical account, on August 2, 1914, the Ottoman and German governments had signed a treaty of alliance. On October 29, 1914, the Ottoman navy attacked Russian ports on the Black Sea coast, thereby manifesting their participation in World War I on the side of Germany and Austria-Hungary. The Ottoman army concentrated a large part of its troops close to Constantinople and the straits, while the Ottoman Third Army prepared to attack the Suez Canal and the Transcaucasian provinces of the Russian empire. An additional attack was also planned against neutral Persia, while only minor forces were left behind in Iraq. The Ottoman army had not fully recovered from their crushing defeat in the Balkan Wars of 1912-13 yet and needed extensive supplies, meanwhile Enver Pasha, the Ottoman minister of war, miscalculated the relative strength of his forces and entertained dreams of conquests.[1]

The Ottoman attacks failed miserably. By February 1915 the Russians had effectively destroyed the Ottoman Third Army. After defeating the Ottomans in Iraq, the triumphant British troops had advanced onto Baghdad. Similarly in Egypt, after effectively resisting the Ottoman attack on the Suez Canal, they had begun preparations for an attack on Palestine. It seemed obvious that Britain and France had the upper hand. They had already begun to assemble a major fleet at the Dardanelles in what could only be understood as an attempt to seize the straits and the Ottoman capital. Although the Ottoman army had concentrated reinforcements in the area, the general outlook for them seemed to only be turning from bad to worse.

Around this time the situation in the eastern provinces deteriorated markedly and Ottoman forces and administrators turned on the local Armenian population by looting and killing. By the middle of April, the outrages in the area around Lake Van culminated into a full-fledged campaign against the Armenians. In the city of Van, the provincial capital, the Armenian population saw no other way to avoid massacre than to organize a resistance against the Ottoman army by barricading itself in the Armenian town quarter.[2] In other areas of the empire, Armenians and other Christian Ottoman soldiers serving in the Ottoman army were disarmed and ordered to form labor battalions.

Great-uncle Abraham describes some of the difficulties members of the Central Powers faced: "When Germans attacked Belgium, they were bitterly defeated by the French at Marne. This was why the German soldiers could not advance any further in the northwestern direction. Elsewhere in Europe, Russia attacked Austria and Ottoman Turkey, advancing through Erzurum, Van, and Erzincan towards Sivas in eastern Anatolia. Germans were unable to travel through alternate sea routes, because the English and French fleets were the dominant forces at sea.

"In the easternmost provinces of Turkey, when some native Armenians and insurgents from the Van Province assisted the Russian soldiers in an attempt to defeat the Ottoman Turks, it created bitter feelings among them. This was understandable to some degree, but no one could predict they would descend into barbarity, retaliating to the degree that they would behave as wild beasts completely devoid of human compassion," remarks Great-uncle Abraham. The very same large Christian Armenian minority was once [considered] so peaceful and trusted that it was labeled by the sultans "*the millet-I sadika*," meaning, "the loyal nation" in Ottoman Turkish.[3]

What Great-uncle Abraham did not know at the time was that in March 1915, Talat Pasha had given secret oral orders that led to the "removal" and eventually the "annihilation" of the Armenians. Enver and Jemal were complicit, as were many other high-ranking officers.[4]

In April of 1915 the Ottoman Empire passed a decree that their government possessed the right to displace Armenians from their hometowns, individually or collectively as several families residing in a neighborhood and could transplant them wherever the government wished them to live. Even though some news regarding these events circulated at times, it was impossible for the townspeople to communicate with their neighboring provinces to find out what was really happening elsewhere around them, because the distances between towns were considerable and travel most often was by way of the slow donkey. Blaming the war effort as an excuse, even their animals including their horses, were taken away from them. Therefore each town felt quite isolated from its neighbors.

Great-uncle Abraham explains: "It was around this time that 20-25 prominent Armenian residents of Gesaria (Kayseri) were hanged in the public square. It was through the word of mouth that we found out there were many other Armenians who were tortured brutally in the Gesaria jail.

"In Aksaray it was announced that all Armenians had strict orders to turn in their guns and knives to the authorities. If they concealed them and they were later discovered, not only would the guns be confiscated, but their owners would be hanged. Supposedly this regulation had equal bearing on both Christians and Muslims alike. However, it was implemented with the intent of exclusively disarming the Armenians. We are certain of this because the Muslims, who had turned in their guns and knives in the morning, were instructed to return later on in the day to pick them up.

"On June 20, 1915, officials gathered all the Armenian males of Aksaray in the courtyard of the government building, including the 10-12 year old boys. Everyone remained in this courtyard for three days, completely oblivious as to what was in store for them. On the fifth day, the governor had them form lines and asked them to write their names on a piece of paper. After checking their names and cross-examining some of them, it was my father's and my brothers' turn. The governor knew them personally. Since they never had a history of party affiliation in the Armenian community, he allowed them to step aside without questioning them. He later had a confidential conversation with them when he asked them certain questions:

'I am told that there are those among you who have a party affiliation; tell us from now who they are, so that you will not unnecessarily suffer because of them.'

"Since my father and uncles had unpleasant experiences in the past in school and church matters in Talas when they had a party affiliation, from then on they had chosen to remain politically neutral. Therefore, they responded emphatically: 'We do not have anyone in our town with such a party affiliation.'

'Go and pray for the sultan,' said the officials, and for the time being they let everyone return to their homes and families.

Great-uncle remarks: "There was much happiness in the air for the remainder of that day, as though their entire town had been set free."

Deportations from Aksaray Begin

At this point, Great-uncle Abraham's mood becomes more somber: "Ten to twelve days later, the officials once again gathered the Armenian males of our town. This time they sounded more serious and they were more malicious in both their manner and intent. During the previous roundup when we were in the chief of police Mehmed Efendi's office, my father and my two brothers were able to request food to be brought for us from our home. Besides, when it arrived we had been able to share it with the chief of police, even pairing it with *arak*. This time around, things were quite different; no one received any respect, no matter who they were. The officials stuck everyone in the jail, crowding them into a room scarcely large enough for one fourth of the crowd. My father, my two brothers, and I remained in these crowded quarters for an entire day, not knowing what was in store for us."

On the second day, the governor called the priest of Aksaray, Father Kevork, as well as the Protestant Minister, to deliver to them the chilling message: 'The Sultan has ordered that all Armenians with their families and children should leave everything behind and head for Aleppo, Damascus, and Deir el-Zor.' Great-uncle Abraham recalls: "A short while later, a grave-faced Father Kevork, accompanied by the Protestant Minister, was at our door to inform us of the tragedy that was soon to unfold for our people.

"Try to decipher the significance of all this. What does this mean? We are not going a distance of 2-4 hours. How are the old and the very young going to travel? How are we going to procure a means of transportation for everyone? What can we take with us? Everyone was so shell-shocked and confused that they did not know what to do and where to start. The governor was a good man. He tried to slow the bustling gendarmes down with: 'Let these people get ready.' But they had already started inspecting our houses and were stern and demanding: 'Let's go. Hurry up. Aren't you ready to leave your house yet?'

"The townspeople begged the governor to plead with the gendarmes not to put the deportees under extra pressure. But what could the governor do? The orders reaching them from the central government of Enver, Talat, and Jemal were so strict that being permissive could cost the officials their jobs and livelihood.

"Five to ten days later, we realized how fortunate we were compared to most. The gendarmes had driven out Armenians from the neighboring towns of Nigde, Bor, and Nevshehir in an hour or two. Even worse off had been the Armenians of adjacent Kirshehir, because none of them had been spared from the sword."

Great-uncle Abraham continues recalling those unreal days: "Eight days after the general declaration, 40 families left Aksaray. My parents, my two brothers' families, and mine were among the 140 that would leave within another week, around July 17th. The 30 families belonging to the Armenian Protestant faith remained in town. Apparently they were later ordered to settle in a smaller village nearby.

"Throughout this ordeal, the entire Muslim population of the town of Aksaray, as well as that of its villages, hastily headed to the streets to purchase furniture and all kinds of goods at dirt cheap prices from the departing Armenians. Although the locals were purchasing these goods at one fourth of their actual price, it still served a purpose, because in this manner the not so well-to-do ended up with some disposable change in their pockets. They would dearly need this security during their ill-fated journey through the unfamiliar lands they would have to travel, to satisfy its often hostile people. During this ordeal, the so-called "peace keeping force" would constantly be changing with the territory and each group, without exception, would be asking us for gold pieces of different denominations to grant us safe passage through their terrain.

"My father, my brothers, and I bundled our goods into bales and left them for safekeeping with our Muslim and Greek neighbors. This was with the understanding and the wishful thinking that these goods would be returned to us upon our arrival at a future date. Among us the three brothers, there were 41 of these bales. Four years later, when a few members of our family managed to return to Aksaray in an effort to reclaim them, they would be astonished by their unexpected findings, which would teach all of us a valuable lesson regarding mankind.

"The Muslim religious leader of Aksaray, Haji Sherif Efendi kept repeating: 'we know these people of our town; they are very good people.' He even offered to send a telegram to Constantinople, but they cautioned him and said:

'This can prove to be dangerous for you; one religious leader's positive opinion among forty others is not going to make a big difference.'

"In this manner, bidding farewell to our Muslim friends, we left Aksaray with a heavy heart. Sadly, we realized that we were no longer in charge of our destiny and had no idea what the future had in store for us. We left our houses and properties behind with a multitude of carpets and furnishings, the fruits of our hard work and prosperity. We left our barns full of wheat, barley, and hay amounting to 1,000 kg. We also left behind 59 additional bales of wool, very many livestock, and thousands in gold pieces that was owed to us in our business dealings as merchants.

"We had our women and our girls wear colorful dresses so they would be undistinguishable from the Muslim women of the villages. We had them cover their heads to an extent, to mimic their women.

"Our party had 101 oxen and horses. Its total number of live-stock amounted to 450. Later, many people marveled at us that we were so well-prepared. I believe we had a stroke of luck which the majority of the Armenian deportees did not have.

"In trying to relate the events of these times, I have often tried to favor the Turks, giving them the benefit of the doubt. This is because if any part of what I have put down in writing is made public and is interpreted as opposing the Turkish Government, I would face a certain death. I have been afraid to elaborate against the administration, because many an innocent soul was executed by hanging for having done just that.

"In spite of initially receiving some preferential treatment, we were forced to abandon our houses, properties, possessions for an unknown future full of hardships, unsanitary conditions, and suffering due to exhaustion, starvation and illness. This inhumane treatment resulted in the loss of many lives at every corner we turned, whether it was ours or that of another fellow Armenian's whose corpse lay swollen by the side of a dangerous pass he was forced to traverse on foot; it was ultimately too painful for us to bear.

"Leading our ox-cart caravan as the driver was my young nephew Ardashes, as the rest of the drivers followed him on the road to Aleppo."

On the Way to Ulukishla

In time, Great-uncle Abraham's tone becomes even more solemn: "The morally corrupt government had reached an accord with the police force of each town; consequently, at whatever town we arrived, they would demand money from us. The police force was an accomplice to many kidnappings and a significant number of the robberies. We were powerless against them and did not dare resist. If we did, they could easily shoot us to death without having to answer to any legal body."

Two and a half weeks later on August 4th, their caravan arrived at the administrative headquarters of Ulukishla. As my Great-uncle Abraham refers to Ulukishla, his tone becomes gloomier: "This is where our troubles and adversities began. Here we saw gendarmes galloping on horses with guns slung at their sides. The chief of gendarmes in Ulukishla was a man of ill repute, with only hatred in his heart. Also, it was here that we found out the train from Izmit, from the northwest, had brought and dumped a large number of Armenians, mostly girls, many of them brides with only umbrellas in their hands. Too young to know what was in store for them, they were left there with no bed, no cover, and no food. They just had their apparels on them as if they were going to a wedding!"

In 1915, over a third of the population of the *Kaza*, the administrative district, of Izmit was Armenian, numbering over 24,000. Many had moved there from Agn in central Anatolia. It was considered a safe location because it was close to cosmopolitan

Constantinople. Eighteen miles to its northeast was the historic Armenian village of Armash, population 1,500, boasting the only Armenian seminary in western Asia Minor established by Der Khoren of the Patriarchate of Constantinople. Close by was Bardizag, *Bahchecik*, another town with an all-Armenian population of some 10,000 inhabitants. Surrounded by a forest and enjoying a pleasant climate, it had become a resort for the Armenian intellectuals of Constantinople. The seminary was plundered in 1915 and the Armenian population was driven away from these towns.[5] Some of the unfortunate Armenians dumped in Ulukishla by the train from Izmit, and with whom my grandparents and great-uncles crossed paths, most likely belonged to these Armenian towns constituting the Administrative District of Izmit.

Great-uncle explains further about their unfortunate experience in Ulukishla: "Two days before we arrived there, the chief of the gendarmes had an Armenian priest and two other innocent Armenians shot to death for allegedly carrying knives. The previous Armenian families of Izmit were very happy to see us in Ulukishla. We gifted two rugs to the lowly chief of the gendarmes. The 15-20 families from Izmit begged us not to leave them there. We placed their boys and girls in our wagon, but the men had to walk. They were refined city people, merchants, and the like. They were not used to walking long distances, especially in inappropriate shoes. After a while their feet became swollen. During the tortuous stretch of our trip, we gave the ailing folk from Izmit turns riding in our wagon. Our fully-loaded wagons were driven by oxen, which were expected to haul their load for no more than 4-5 hours each day, if they were to remain healthy and strong.

"It had been a few days since we had been traveling on mountainous terrain. On our left were steep hills, forests and towering rocks, and on our right were deep valleys. For us to make it through the mountain pass, we had no choice but to cross these challenging hills. The slightest wrong move on the part of the ox-cart driver could lead to tragic consequences. At times we gave our oxen some relief by encouraging the able-bodied folks to walk part of the way until we reached the summit as the hills climbed into mountains. Through all this, the scorching summer sun was intolerable. Due to overheating, as well as the steep climb, we could hear the oxen panting heavily.

"On our way down, towards the foot of the Taurus Mountains, we faced problems of a different nature, nevertheless equally serious. It was a good thing my older brother Kerovpé's fourteen-year-old son Ardashes managed to restrain the oxen, slowing them down just enough so he could negotiate the sharp turns. Otherwise, our heavy wagon making its way down these dangerous slopes could easily acquire a life of its own and kill the oxen. In this stretch of our saga, we witnessed a number of overturned wagons with the drivers desperately trying to fix their broken wheels to get them going again, while the unlucky passengers watched in despair. Finally crossing the Bozanti Pass, we were on our way to the Cilician plane and the historic town of Tarsus, where St. Paul was born. Here, we bid our fellow Armenians from Izmit farewell and parted from them. I do not know what happened to them after that. There was no end to these types of encounters. I lost count of how many miserable souls I saw on the road under the scorching sun: men, women, and children fallen, exhausted, sick, dead, many stripped of their clothes."

During these somber times, my Great-uncle Abraham and the rest of his extended family still remembered to count their blessings: "This is when we realized that we were the kings of the exiled population. Our tents had beds; we had sacks of flour to make our own bread when it was unavailable, using our own thin iron plates. Before leaving Aksaray, we had also taken the precaution of hiring two men on horseback to accompany and protect us from any attacks and to guard our animals until we reached Aleppo."

Central Station in Osmaniyé

Reaching Osmaniye did not improve Great-uncle Abraham and his family's saga: "As we approached the smoother rolling planes of Adana, the road became easier to handle. We crossed the Seyhan and Ceyhan Rivers and finally arrived at the central station in Osmaniye, 100 miles east of Adana and some 210 miles from where we had originally started in Aksaray. Here, we witnessed a population of 30,000 unlucky and miserable Armenians comprising our humble nation."

In his groundbreaking history of the Armenian Genocide, "The Burning Tigris," Dr. Peter Balakian describes this chilling camp in the following manner: "At times this camp may have held as many as 70,000 deported Armenians. In the camps, the Armenians were attacked by killing squads; women were abducted and raped; and thousands were dying of disease and starvation. "[6] Great-uncle Abraham couldn't help but ask himself the inevitable question: "How can one continue witnessing such suffering and still go on?"

In the end, between a half and two-thirds of the more than two million Armenians living on their historic homeland in the Ottoman Empire were annihilated. The largest body of genocide scholars, the Association of Genocide Scholars of North America, conservatively assess that more than a million Armenians were killed, and probably between 1.2 and 1.3 million. Some historians put the figure at 1.5 million, which spans the period from 1915 to 1922, when the last waves of killing took place.[7]

Finally my grandfather, granduncles and their clan arrived at the center for the exiled population at Katma, which was at a distance of six hours from Aleppo. After having experienced Katma, the following is Great-uncle Abraham's impression: "Here, we found the entire population of our nation. It was such utter confusion and crowding without any identifying markers, that if any member of a family left his tent, he could not find his way back. It was also here that the typhus and the typhoid fevers started because of poor sanitary conditions and lice infestations. Since the tents were in such close proximity to each other, lice travelled freely from tent to tent. Once sickness started, it spread like wildfire. It seemed this was intentional; the government did not want the Armenian population to survive. The miserable existence of the people in Katma, the terrible stink of rotten human waste, the unbearable flies, the unsanitary conditions in the tents, the total confusion families faced in choosing the least of many evils as they sought to find a viable route, will haunt me for the rest of my life."

The government was exiling most Armenians to Raqqa and Deir el-Zor. Columns of women and children at bayonet point had no choice but to head in the direction of the waterless deserts of neighboring Syria; a certain number were to go to Hama, Homs, and Damascus. My grandparents and great-uncles, managed to leave Katma soon, most likely by bribing the local officials.

Aleppo

Starting with the month of September of 1915, Armenians were prevented from entering the city of Aleppo.[8] Great-uncle Abraham expresses his frustration and the hardships they faced in reaching the city of Aleppo: "We wanted to go to Aleppo, but the authorities would not let us. After forty-three days of hardship, and after repeatedly bribing many people, we were allowed to go to the relatively large city of Aleppo along with three other families. At the time the number of Armenian families in this city who had recently arrived, counting us, would only add up to 36. We rented a house on a monthly basis in the Suleymaniyé district. We thought we could be comfortable here, but we were mistaken. The policemen and the administrators of the city would not leave us alone. They kept appearing at our front door and telling us we had to leave. Remaining in this city meant supplying a constant stream of money to many people for an indefinite period." It seems the objective of the triumvirate was to push the deportees into uninhabited terrain in the desert away from Aleppo.

Great-uncle continues: "When we first arrived in Aleppo, we sold thirteen of our animals. The horse carriage that we had purchased for 28 gold pieces would sell only for 4, and the ox-cart purchased for 22 gold pieces would sell for only 3. The rest of our animals would sell for only one or two gold pieces each. I have to admit that we had made it relatively comfortably to Aleppo on account of our animals, our ox cart, and our carriage.

"One day towards the end of our stay in Aleppo, we were all asked to go to a garden. Here, they separated the men from the women with the intent of having the men travel separately from their wives and children. After encountering a great deal of difficulty, we somehow were able to circumvent this fate. It seemed the hardships the deportees faced had robbed them of a good portion of their ability to reason. Unlike our usual selves, we had started to become quite gullible."

To Damascus

At one point it was announced that those headed for Damascus had to procure a ration card. All 36 families from Aksaray went and obtained this document. Three days later these same families were asked to gather at the train station to board the train. Here, Great-uncle Abraham justly expresses his dissatisfaction: "But the train did not arrive that day. On the second day when a freight train finally arrived, it was filthy and was bringing a multitude of sick soldiers from Damascus. My two brothers and I wanted to sweep and clean the two freight trains, since we all had to sit on the bales and on the floor. The local gendarmes prevented us from even partially cleaning the freight train. Here was one more of the unreasonable rules and regulations of the savage government. Not having any other recourse and after having to pay upwards of 19 gold pieces per person, we settled in the filthy freight train and left the hellish city of Aleppo.

"Up to this point we had been able to take preventive measures by always having a spare change of clothing and by laundering our soiled clothes whenever we came across a stream or a lake. During the night we spent on the freight train, we were alarmed when we saw lice traveling freely on our furniture and even on our bodies. But we were defenseless, especially at nights.

"On the second day, even though we had arrived in Damascus, no one was allowed to venture to the city. We had to remain in the immigrants' headquarters at the south end of the city. The chief of police here did not create additional problems for us. After distributing 500 grams of bread to each person, he saw to it that we boarded another train the same day, for which we again had to pay with our own pocket money, to arrive in the lowly town of Daraa, by the railroad station."

When they arrived by the government headquarters, in Daraa, my grandparents and great-uncles were told that they could settle in the villages around this town, as long as they remained at a minimum distance of two hours from the railroad station[ii]. This was a government regulation established specifically with Armenian deportees in mind. The terrain was completely alien to my great uncles and grandparents. The officials asked them to select a village they wanted to settle in. By now all of the deportees were utterly drained of energy as well as intellect and seemed quite confused.

Remté

It was a good thing that Daraa had an accommodating commissioner, Hasan Efendi. My great-uncles and grandfather asked for his advice regarding which village would be the best one for them to settle in. His response was: 'A few days ago they had sent 30-35 families from Konya and we settled them in a village nearby, named Remté. If you would like, you could go there as well.'

A select group representing the 36 families, including my Great-uncle Abraham, visited this village. Their conclusion was: 'Even though Remté is not very clean, none of the villages around the area are any better.'

In 1915, the rail cars were too primitive yet to be able to burn coal and depended on burning wood for fuel, which was transported on the backs of camels. Since camels were the most commonly used mode of transportation in this part of the country, the commissioner of Remté asked the village's camel owners to appropriate 40-50 of their beasts of burden for the 36 families. My grandparents and great-uncles loaded their furniture on the backs of the camels and, while the women and children walked alongside them, they all headed toward Remté. They rented a horse-drawn carriage for my great-grandmother and great-grandfather. Seeing

---

ii   Daraa's other and perhaps more important role in the deportations was that the rails divided here. One of the railroad lines went south to Jerusalem. A second line traveled even further south and more inland into the Arabian Peninsula to Mecca and Medina.

the starved and the dead by the roadside and witnessing thousands
of Armenians wasting away between Aleppo and Damascus, and
hearing about vast numbers having to head towards Deir-El-Zor
had disproportionately depressed the elderly, adversely affecting
their health.

Remté was an Arab village. Its population was made up of
Egyptian peasants. The administrator of the village knew Turkish.
Upon Great-uncle Parsegh's presentation of their documents, he
allocated living quarters for them. To avoid the military draft,
many families had abandoned Remté, moving further inland to
join the Bedouins and had become nomads. The administrator
gave my grandparents and great-uncles the empty mud huts that
the deserters had evacuated.

Great-uncle Abraham describes their living quarters in
Remté thus: "Each mud hut consisted of a dingy dark room with
no windows. It had dirt floors and a single door. If we closed the
door, the inside became practically pitch-black. We had to have a
kerosene lamp on at all times for illumination, but it also subjected
us to an offensive and perhaps hazardous smell." Not having any
other alternative, they settled down and adapted to a life in the
survival mode in these depressing living quarters.

Poor Sanitation

In the words of Great-uncle Abraham, "the locals of this
village were plain people. They had never heard of the word
hygiene." They had extremely low sanitary standards. They
relieved themselves wherever they felt like it, even in the middle of
the street. No rules existed or provisions were made in the village
for some type of a safe sewage disposal system. The mud huts
had wells; however, when it rained, the dirt from the streets also
emptied into these wells along with the rain water and later served
as the primary source of their drinking water.

"None of the Armenian families who were deported here,
including the 35 from Konya, the 34-35 from Afyon Karahisar and
the 10-12 from Adapazari were poor. There were only a few needy
Armenian families whom we felt we ought to help while we lived

in this village. The Arab population was clad in loose-hanging long shirts which covered their entire bodies."

For their drinking water, my grandparents and great-uncles used water from wells in the outskirts of the village, removed from the hub of activity. In spite of this precaution, my grandmother and grandfather soon became gravely ill, having contracted typhus fever earlier from lice in the filthy railway cars. They each would burn with a high fever and in their quest for something cold, they would press their cheeks against the cooler wall of their mud shack. Subsequently the shivers would take over, at which time they could not have enough covers piled on them. They lay in beds in a comatose state in two separate and adjoining mud huts for over three weeks. Negligent government officials knew that the outbreak was not going to die of its own accord, but they did not care. At the end of what felt like an interminable period, my grandmother Verkin--either due to pure chance or to her sensible fighting spirit--miraculously recovered. However, the epidemic claimed the lives of my Grandfather Kerovpé on May 5, 1916, and my Great-grandfather Hagop on September 18, 1916. Great-uncle Abraham offers a detailed account of the high mortality rate the Armenian deportees suffered in this Arab village in the middle of nowhere:

"Roughly a third of the Armenian deportees, 189 out of 672 to be exact, died and were buried in this inhospitable and sparsely populated desert village on the banks of the meager stream Kuruchay. The teacher Shamiram substituted as clergy to administer their last rights and assisted with their burials."

Extended family was a crutch and to some extent a source of comfort. However, it seems from that day on, my fifteen-year-old father Ardashes started feeling personally responsible for his mother's safety, emotional well-being, and financial sustenance. Throughout the seventeen years I lived in Istanbul, I always sensed the existence of a special bond between my father and my grandmother. I believe this closeness helped him later in life to empathize with his clients.

Even though my father's education had formally concluded at the end of first grade in Aksaray in a one room schoolhouse, with personal effort using his ability to reason, he gradually managed to learn to accurately perform the mathematical calculations that would be essential for him in the future for a profession in money-changing. I will always remember him as someone with great regard for education. Unfortunately, after his father's death and on the deportation route, for the immediate and even distant future, further schooling would remain out of the question for him. Much later, when the family settled for a while in Beirut, he was unable to enroll at a school as his cousin, my Great-uncle Abraham's son Onnik (Uncle John), was able to do. This may have influenced his thinking, because many years later when it was time for me and my sister to enroll in high school and college, he felt no financial sacrifice on his part was ever too great, as long as we received the best education available.

An Ordinance

In June 1916 an ordinance from Anatolia made my Great-uncle Abraham feel very uneasy. He expresses his disapproval thus:

"Now, they had also decided that they would interfere in the relationship of man with God, which was totally unacceptable in principle. The government was demanding the members of each family to travel to Daraa to be renamed and reregistered under their new Islamized names. We sent my brother Parsegh, who was our mayor, as well as two other representatives, including Master Ohan, a native of Konya and Master Haroutioun, a native of Afyon Karahisar as our spokesmen, to suggest to the administration in Daraa that because the very old and the very young constituted such a significant portion of our population, it might be simpler for everyone concerned if the government sent their spiritual leader to Remté instead. We made it clear that the residents involved would be more than willing to underwrite the travel expenses of their imam for this purpose. A few days later when he arrived in our village to register us, we couldn't help but greet him with mixed emotions. To our delight, this issue must have soon been forgotten, because during our days in Remté no government official pursued this matter any further."

It seems my great-uncles and the rest of the Armenian families in Remté were quite lucky to have the Islamization issue de-escalate the way it did, because plenty of evidence suggests this not to be the case for many Armenians deported from their homelands in Historic Armenia and forced to travel in a similar southward direction towards Damascus. It caused many of them much anguish and many dilemmas which have continued to the present. According to the research of Dr. Khatchig Mouradian from Clark University, 100 years after the Armenian Genocide, in 2015 the number of Islamized Armenians stands anywhere from one hundred thousand to as high as ten million.[9]

The Threat of the Draft

Soon after the threat of Islamization passed, Great-uncle Abraham describes yet another scare for the deportees: "One day, two gendarmes arrived from Daraa. They said they were sent by the government to gather draft-eligible males between the ages of sixteen and fifty. This was not a good sign, because it reminded us of similar events in the past which had often resulted in the loss of lives. However, we had no choice but to obey. Among our group, a number in excess of fifty males fetched some form of a backpack with supplies; they bid farewell to their wailing wives and young children and left. From the 35 families, only the heads of the households of the Houbeserians, Mutafians, Tombakians, and I were left in Daraa, because we were older than fifty. Naturally we were frightened and all sorts of terrible thoughts crossed our minds, not knowing where our next of kin were being taken and whether they would be shot to death. My younger brother Parsegh accompanied the men as the public official, to find out more about what was going on."

Shortly after arriving in Daraa, Great-uncle Parsegh approached the commander, identified the name of their village and announced to him: 'Sir, we have arrived.'

To this, he responded with: 'I do not understand the logic. There must have been a mistake. You should return back to your previous placements. If we need you, you can always come back here later.'

Great-uncle Abraham goes on to say: "Later on that evening, when the men returned, it was cause for elation in our village. We had thought we had lost them for good. It was a miracle that we were reunited with them again. We thought they were dead and they had somehow made it back to the ranks of the living!"

Hasan Bey

Great-uncle Abraham relates: "In November of 1916, a Circassian gentleman by the name of Hasan Bey arrived in our village from Daraa, who was educated in Constantinople. The Armenian residents of Remté must have initially tried to direct him to the Arab section of the village, until he said: 'I did not come here to settle an issue for the Arabs. I came here to talk about matters that will be important for you.'

They immediately fetched the largest living quarters available. They sent the children to their relatives and accommodated him in a room large and presentable enough to hold the head of each family so they could sit down and listen to what he had to say. A wise neighbor, Master Aram from Yozgat in central Anatolia, thought: 'We need not worry; this man seems to have good intentions. I suspect Armenians are going to be sent to the cities and we seem to be the first village on his list to be given the good news.'

As soon as Hasan Bey started his conversation, Great-uncle Abraham had formed a positive impression and thought what he had to say sounded encouraging: 'I have come to you representing Jemal Pasha. Armenians are educated business people from cities and large towns. Their education and their ability to realize their potential will be wasted in these small villages. I want each family to decide which city they want to live in, including Jaffa, Haifa, Tarabulus (Tripoli, located north of Beirut in Lebanon), Damascus, etc. Damascus has a significant Armenian population and Beirut is very expensive.'

Then he went on to share his views on the politics of the day, saying: 'England is our enemy, and it seems the war will be continuing on for some time. However, be assured that at the time of the final negotiations, it will be England who will be presiding at the peace conference.'

After welcoming Hasan Bey's opinion, Great-uncle Abraham gives his own thoughts on the matter: "It is noteworthy that this Circassian with his limited exposure to world affairs was able to predict better the outcome of the war than the Turkish leaders of ill repute, the Enver and Talat Pashas." [iii 10]

It is obvious that all these different choices of destination pleased but also confused Great-uncle Abraham. He says: "The next morning, after exploring different scenarios of where to immigrate, weighing each one's pros and cons, and after discussing all of this with our fellow deportees from Aksaray, we decided upon Beirut. The reason might have been because we thought the war would end there earlier than in other parts of the world. We also anticipated that we could have more satisfactory professions in that city than anywhere else. Additionally, we reasoned our children would have access to better quality schools there, compared to other cities.

"Hasan Bey seemed somewhat reluctant to send all of the 18 families to Beirut. He repeatedly brought up the very high cost of living in that city and the possibility that our families could starve there. In response to his warning, my brother Parsegh's comment was: 'We have to take our chances. If the local population starves, we will starve with them.'"

Great-uncle Abraham became keenly aware of Hasan Bey's realization that he was dealing with a people with a great deal of inner strength. At the end, concluding that his conversation with the Armenian deportees from Aksaray had been satisfactory, he gave those heading towards Beirut a letter and then left promptly for the next village on his list. Upon their arrival in Daraa, this letter was to be presented to the deportation officer, Mumtaz Bey.

---

iii   Enver Pasha eventually prevailed and he aligned with Germany and Austria-Hungary. Enver admired German militarism and believed it inconceivable that Germany would lose the war.

Ready for Beirut

Great-uncle Abraham explains his brother Parsegh's dealings with Mumtaz Bey thus: "Two days after we had our conversation with Hasan Bey, my younger and more educated brother Parsegh, as well as Masters Ohan and Haroutioun, left for Daraa to meet and converse with Mumtaz Bey to plan for our upcoming transfer to Beirut. Parsegh arrived half an hour earlier than the rest to meet with Mumtaz Bey."

Mumtaz Bey said to him: 'Right now I have been working on the deportation proceedings. I don't want you to return to Remté. I want you to help me with what I am working on.'

To this, Great-uncle Parsegh's reply was: 'Very well, Sir, but our families have to pack and get ready for the road.'

Realizing the urgency Great-uncle Parsegh felt for the Armenian families from Daraa to hit the road, Mumtaz Bey sweetened his offer by allocating two railway cars for them. Somewhat satisfied with this response, Great-uncle Parsegh drafted and forwarded a letter from Daraa to Remté, addressing it to the 18 families who were to depart for Beirut, in which he instructed them to be ready to leave the following day. Later on, when Master Ohan approached Mumtaz Bey with a similar request, he said if his group waited for another five days, he could do the same for them.

The following is how Great-uncle Abraham describes their departure from Remté: "Right after receiving the letter from Daraa, the 18 families which included us, packed and tied our bales and bargained with the village's camel owners for the fee we would have to pay for renting their beasts of burden. Early next morning, we bid farewell to the Arab villagers of Remté and departed from them in the best of terms. However, we realized we could not easily forget the sad memories we were leaving behind, as we were distancing ourselves from this village of mud huts, where sanitation had never been a matter of concern. Meanwhile, the inhabitants of Remté had felt so close to the 18 Armenian families, that a handful of them accompanied us with their livestock all the way to Daraa, to show us how much they valued our friendship. When we finally arrived in Daraa on the backs of the rented camels, we spotted the two railway cars waiting for us at the railroad station. We loaded both trains with our household furniture, cooking utensils and clothing, but, we camped out in tents for the evening."

Mumtaz Bey was unwilling to discharge my Great-uncle Parsegh from his duties, even after the 18 families had arrived in Daraa because Parsegh had lightened his work load considerably for him.

'Maybe you can leave a few days later. I will make the arrangements,' he said to him. To this remark, Great-uncle Parsegh's unhesitating response was:

'I have to be with my boys and wife. I cannot leave them alone.'

As they were leaving Daraa, my great-uncles wanted to gift a rug to Mumtaz Bey, but he declined, saying: 'I cannot accept it; you are deportees.' Thus bidding him farewell, the 18 families departed for Beirut, hoping that from then on, the uphill part of their struggle, in their so far hellish journey, would have been over.

The Railway Car

The engine of the railway car taking the 18 families to Beirut was powered by burning firewood. When it started moving, my great-uncles realized that the ball-bearings of the wheel axles had not been serviced; therefore, the rotating wheels were constantly catching fire. Furthermore, there was not enough grease available to use as lubricant. The two brothers quickly learned to have water on hand in tin cans at all times to extinguish any flames they detected. In Great-uncle Abraham's words:

"We learned to operate the rail engine, because if we didn't, it would catch fire and everything would burn. I have three witnesses to prove this fact, who live in Beirut today: A. Jeknavorian, A. Kitabjian, and M. Dersahagian.

Great-uncle Abraham goes on to tell us of the problems they faced next: "Three days after leaving Daraa, we arrived in Beirut. The governor of Beirut, Azmi Bey, who had been the governor of Konya before, was known for his vulgarity. When my brother Parsegh presented the document allowing us to enter the city, his response was: 'This place is very expensive; I don't see why they have sent you here. There is no bread for people to eat here!' Then he immediately sent a telegram to Daraa, ordering the deportation officer there not to send any further deportees to Beirut. It was due to his telegram that our neighbors in Remté, who were originally from Konya, were not allowed to arrive at the destination of their choice.

"When our extended family first arrived in Beirut, we were taken to Deir Nasira and were offered bread and soup for eighteen days." My Great-uncle Abraham expresses his appreciation for this aid: "I believe it was by virtue of the Lord that we arrived in a clean and orderly place as Deir Nasira, in comparison to the previous filthy and unsanitary village of Remté."

Great-uncle Parsegh's Bold Move

It was just when the governor of Beirut was planning to extricate himself from the responsibility of providing for the deportees by arranging for their departure to a remote location, that a bold but rather risky idea crossed Great-uncle Parsegh's mind: 'I will personally telephone Jemal Pasha in Damascus and tell him that we will not be a burden on the government, provided we are allowed to work.' He reasoned.

When Jemal Pasha heard Great-uncle Parsegh's request, he right away called the governor of Beirut and instructed him: 'Do not send this group of deportees anywhere; just set them free.' Thus, it was with Great-uncle Parsegh's daring move and courage and Jemal Pasha's helpful interference that another disaster was averted and the 18 Armenian deportee families from Aksaray were now allowed to work and rent houses in Beirut.

Life in Beirut

Great-uncle Abraham gives us a brief account of the Armenian community of Beirut as it existed during the first few months of 1917: "At this time, there were about 60-70 Armenian families living in Beirut. There was a small Armenian church with Father Kevork as its pastor. Many of the Armenian deportees would soon venture into the business of baking and pastry making. Among them were the Jeknavorians, who grew truly skilled in this profession and maintained their excellence for many years."

Prior to the deportations when the Lafdjians were living in Aksaray, Great-uncle Abraham's son Onnik (Uncle John) had attended the Jenanian School in Konya. After the family arrived in Beirut in 1917, he benefited from his father's guidance and financial well-being by enrolling at the American University of Beirut. As for my father, he had to worry about making a living for himself, his brother, and his mother since his brother was still in hiding to avoid the draft. In those days, both alternatives--joining the Ottoman army or dodging the draft and subsequently being apprehended--carried extremely high risks.

In an effort to generate some cash, as soon as they were halfway settled, my grandmother Verkin baked bread sticks and hard biscuits for my father to sell in the marketplace, because most of the money they had brought along from Aksaray was exhausted by this time. Within the past two years, a big chunk had disappeared to buy their daily necessities. An even more respectable sum had been spent on bribes and to satisfy the unending demands of the gendarmes of the different towns, starting from the vicinity of Aksaray, all the way to Aleppo. The few gold pieces left were spent on transportation through the rail system, first to get to Daraa and later to Beirut.

The experience of trying to sell his mother's biscuits and bread sticks must have left an indelible mark in my then sixteen-year-old father's memory. A bunch of husky, combative Arab teenagers had tormented him as he was passing through an alley to reach the marketplace. Before he knew what was happening, the bully of the gang had grabbed him from behind. He had lost his balance and fallen to the ground, skinning his right knee and the palms of his hands. Meanwhile, the glass jar containing his baked goods had shattered, scattering its contents all over the alley. During the altercation, the gang members had stolen my father's baked goods before he even had a chance to make it to the marketplace! This traumatic event must have deeply scarred his self-esteem along with some of the other threatening experiences of the deportation years he had tried hard to repress. I happened to know about it because during our sick days as children, my sister and I had heard my Grandmother Verkin allude to it, in between her fairy tales.

Soon after arriving in Beirut, another misfortune would hit Great-uncle Abraham and his wife. Here he discusses this sad event and its repercussions for his entire family: "On March 25, 1917 our twenty year old son, Haroutiun died unexpectedly of typhus fever. Once again, his loss shook up our entire family. We had expected the darkest days of the deportation to be over by now. However, it reminded us once again of the painful consequences we were still suffering from having traveled and lived in primitive and unsanitary conditions, which exposed us to lice and other germs. It seems we were still being reminded of our vulnerability shaped by history, dislocation and disease. In hindsight, it was a good thing my wife and I were religious, because our faith helped alleviate the heavy emotional burden of this tragedy. It helped us come to terms with events over which we realized we had no control."

An Attempt to Make a Living

This is Great-uncle Abraham's description of how he made a living in Beirut: "I rented a store in a strategic location in the business district of the city. The war was still raging in many parts of the Ottoman Empire; consequently, the ordinary flour used in making bread had shot up in price. One kilogram cost as much as two and a half gold pieces. I bought and sold all sorts of commodities in this store. Also because of the war, commerce with Europe by way of the Mediterranean had come to a standstill. However, people still needed clothes, beds, and comforters. I bought these essentials wholesale and sold them to the public, charging retail prices which were not outrageous and yet offered me a favorable profit margin.

"There was a lot of demand for cotton and a healthy profit could easily be made by selling this commodity. Armenian immigrants from Aleppo, Hama, and Homs would buy the cotton and spin it to produce the preferred product, linen. I would buy 100-200 kilograms of cotton, paying anywhere 20-60 in the local currency and could usually sell it for 70-80. It was a thriving business because I only paid 36 Turkish liras annually for rent and did not have to worry about a down payment or a security deposit for the store, because most of the population at the time consisted of military deserters and leaving the country would not even cross their minds. I continued this profitable business until the end of World War I.

"The government employed my brother Parsegh in Beirut as a court clerk for the Turkish-speaking population. Because of his position as a court official, he also had the additional unexpected benefit of receiving food rations from the government, which he often shared with the rest of his extended family members.

"I had an Arab assistant by the name of Abu Halil, because I needed someone who was fluent in Arabic and also familiar with the local rules and regulations. I was lucky to have Abu Halil both as this expert and also because he was willing to accept what I could pay him for his services."

Behiyé's House

Abu Halil had a Muslim neighbor lady, Behiyé, who every ten days would purchase substantial quantities of good quality cotton from Great-uncle Abraham to later sell it in Hama. One day, Abu Halil informed him that Behiyé was planning to sell her house. 'You should buy it,' he said.

Great-uncle Abraham's answer to him was: "What are we going to do with it? We own a stately house and many investment properties, including parcels of land in our own country. A few days later, he repeated it again. He was a wise man with a good instinct about the changes the future was about to bring. He kept saying to me: 'Beirut is an important port. You cannot compare property here with that in Anatolia,' but again, I mostly ignored his suggestion."

Businesses in Beirut would close down at noontime on Saturdays, to reopen their doors again on Monday mornings. That very Sunday, Abu Halil insisted that Great-uncle Abraham visit him at his home. He went there with his son Onnik. Being a generous host, he had ordered a large variety of dishes to serve them. Since Behiyé was his neighbor, after dinner he wanted the three of them to take a walk towards her house to converse with her in person.

Behiyé's house was on a quiet street on the road to Damascus, not far from the tramway. They had to ascend six stone stairs to get to her front door. It had four bedrooms with a fairly large-sized family-room, a kitchen, and a bathroom. It boasted a set of charming gardens both in front and in the back. Her serene garden in the back had an assortment of trees and a small pool. These are Great-uncle Abraham's words describing the conversation between Abu Halil, Behiye and him: "While we sat by the pool, Behiyé served us Turkish coffee. Abu Halil, who knew Turkish, proceeded to translate for us. He explained to Behiyé that I was his friend and was inquiring about the price of her house. She said she wanted 600 liras, but I was hesitant. Her final proposal through Abu Halil, as our intermediary and translator, was for 500 liras, which was 75-80 golden coins. I told her we would think it over and let her know. Deep down, I knew we had more than the necessary funds at the time to buy this house."

In the evening, Great-uncle Abraham discussed the prospect of their buying Behiyé's neat little house in Beirut with his younger brother Parsegh. However, his brother was reluctant: 'We are immigrants; we don't know what our fate will be tomorrow. Someday in the future, that sum may be just what we may need to prevent our kids from starving,' he said.

Due to his familiarity with the law and the arbitration process, Great-uncle Parsegh must have also realized that the purchase of a house by an Armenian immigrant from a Muslim woman might not legally pass muster. Another factor prompting Parsegh to be unwilling to even consider the reasonable asking price may have been his somber mood at the time, since he had just lost his one and-a-half-year old son Kevork to typhus fever and was still grieving.

Deep down, Great-uncle Abraham must have really wanted to take the chance to buy Behiyé's house, because he keeps mentioning it in the following fashion: "There were ways of purchasing this property with the help of a reputable friend such as Abu Halil. We could have purchased it in his name and later converted it into mine. What was really in the way was our thinking that we owned a great residence and enviable properties in Anatolia. In spite of the overwhelming problems we had experienced and atrocities we had witnessed within the last three years, we still continued to have trust in the integrity of the Turkish people. We had lived in close quarters with them, in adjoining neighborhoods for many years, and had gotten to know a number of trustworthy Turkish businessmen."

Our Last Error

World War I ended in November 1918 with Germany and the Ottoman Turks losing the war. Right around then, Great-uncle Abraham's sister's son-in-law Haigazun, who was a merchant, arrived in Beirut to purchase rolls of wholesale textile. During this trip, he also paid a visit to them and was rather direct in asking Great-uncle Abraham the following question: 'Since business is so much better in Anatolia, why do you insist on staying in Beirut?'

Other relatives, especially his brother-in-law Dikran Kazanjian, had similar opinions. When the initial deadly wave of deportations from Aksaray had started in July 1915, the Kazanjians had been allowed to remain in Aksaray a while longer, because they belonged to the Protestant faith. However, in less than a year, the Young Turks had applied their unforgiving rules to them as well. Later, the Kemalist movement had necessitated their move to Konya[iv]. Initially, Armenians in Konya were fortunate to have a benevolent governor, who saved the lives of many deportees, until the triumvirate of Talat, Enver, and Jemal Pashas replaced him with an Armenophobic one.

---

iv Konya was a city in central Anatolia which was home to 25,000 Armenians in 1915 and was also the burial ground of Rumi, the leader of a milder sect of Islam, *Mevlevis*, to which the "Whirling Dervishes" also belonged.

In late 1918, Great-uncle Abraham mentions the following communication with his brother-in-law Dikran Kazanjian, who at the end of WWI had established a sizable business in Konya as a money changer: *"Dikran wrote to me several times recommending that we return back to Aksaray. He kept insisting: 'Continuing to stay in Beirut is a big mistake.'*

"My brother Parsegh and I weighed these recommendations, along with the Ottoman Turks' loss of WWI. We thought that since we still owned substantial properties and investments in Aksaray, with the potential of a steady stream of income, it did not make sense to keep residing in a foreign city and country. Therefore, trusting the evaluation of my relatives, I sold that gem of a store in Beirut on Sersok for only twelve and-a-half golden coins. Then, we gathered our belongings and accompanied my brother Parsegh's family, as well as that of my deceased brother Kerovpé's, including his widow and his two sons Ardashes and Dikran, and got ready to head north towards Mersin, on the southern coast of Turkey."

Arrival in Mersin

This is where Great-uncle Abraham is surprised to see such a changed Mersin and Adana: "After an initial delay due to illness in the family, we took a French warship from Beirut and, around midnight in May of 1919, we arrived in Mersin, our fourth homeland. It was here that we observed a spectacle that was hard for us to believe. Both Mersin and Adana were full of Armenians! It was as if they had become an Armenian Cilicia. The Turks were so afraid of the Armenians that they avoided venturing out of their homes at night! Shortly after we met in Mersin with my brother Parsegh, in the spacious house he had rented for our extended family, we tried to evaluate the political situation to the best of our ability."

News in general, including that of sudden political changes, traveled at a snail's pace in those days in Anatolia. For this reason, by the beginning of the summer of 1919, neither one of my great-uncles had an inkling about the sudden progress of the nationalist insurgent hero Mustafa Kemal Atatürk, who had declared himself the new leader of the Turks. After his sudden progress in northern Anatolia, especially in the Black Sea region, he was reclaiming the formerly lost lands of the Ottoman Empire. Meanwhile, each one of my great-uncles was busy on the Mediterranean coast of Turkey in Mersin, trying to accomplish a different task. In Great-uncle Abraham's words:

"My brother Parsegh took along with him my brother-in-law Misak Kazanjian, as well as my deceased brother Kerovpé's son, Dikran, and headed straight towards our hometown of Aksaray, leaving me as the only adult male in Mersin in charge of our extended family. Meanwhile, we left my son Onnik behind in Beirut, after enrolling him at the American University of Beirut."

Returning to Aksaray

Four years after being on the deportation route, when Great-uncle Parsegh returned to his hometown of Aksaray with his nephew Dikran and Great-uncle Abraham's brother-in-law Misak, they were greeted royally both by the town's unskilled laborers as well as by its genteel citizens. They respected them and held many feasts and celebrations in their honor.

As to the recovery of the family possessions entrusted to local families for safekeeping, that was a different story…The extended family had designated Misak for this demanding task. Great-uncles Parsegh and Abraham had written to him at the end of WWI in November 1918, providing specific information about the number of bales and their contents; they had also supplied him with a list of the names and addresses of the residents of Aksaray and its neighboring towns who had accepted the responsibility of being their custodians. The family had reasoned that since the bales had presumably remained untouched for four full years, they should be fetched before moths got to them. 'Please ask for them; unpack them; sell them. Then mail us the proceeds, whatever you are able to get for them,' was the family's request from Misak.

However, when Misak contacted the various custodians of the bales, they showed him only a few, most of which had already been unpacked with the choice articles missing. 'Here it is,' they said with indifference, presenting him with a number amounting to less than one fourth of the total number of bales.

He especially remembers Mustafa Zade of Hisar: "That lowly man did not even show Misak a single bale out of the twelve he had accepted from us for safekeeping," deplored Great-uncle Abraham. But Misak also reported a few pleasant surprises to him, which rekindled his trust in mankind and led Great-uncle Abraham to make the following positive remarks:

"In the town of Chimeli, we had left 224 golden coins worth of merchandise with Master Haji Seuleuk. When he was asked to sell them, he promptly complied and returned the exact amount he had received for them on the day of the transaction. To the same individual, we had also entrusted gold jewelry, pearls, watches, and gold chains, as well as the furniture of our two houses. He returned the fair value of everything to Misak, without any compromises. It is hard to believe that there can be so much disparity in morals and honesty from one man to the next..."

Thinking that the family was shortly to move back to Aksaray, Great-uncle Parsegh had asked the governor of Damascus, who had rented their houses to the government in their absence, to collect the rent and arrange for the houses' evacuation. These were necessary steps, because during the war, their residence in Aksaray had been converted into a makeshift hospital; its playroom had become a telegram center; and its large farm had become the stable for the principality.

Upon arriving in Aksaray, Great-uncle Parsegh had been able to receive the rent that was due. The townspeople had also sent letters to the neighboring *Mutlubatimiz* villages, which were owned by my great-uncles, informing the tenants: 'The Lafdjians have returned from the deportations. Since they were among our prominent and valued citizens, you should remit whatever amount you owed them. We were treated with kindness and humanity by these people; therefore we want to please them by making sure we pay our debts.'

Additionally, there were four villages in *Alevi Saratli* referred to as *Lafdjian's villages*. Great-uncle Parsegh went to these villages, where he was to collect 186 gold coins. The villagers gave him 169 gold coins; they entertained him for three days and told him that those who owed the remaining 17 gold coins were out of town at the time. However, they promised him they would collect the money and deliver it to him. Great-uncle Abraham describes the villagers' response to his brother's homecoming as "wonderful and well beyond our expectations."

Sevastopol

Around this time in 1919, Great-uncle Abraham's brother-in-law, Dikran Kazanjian, who lived in Konya, was headed to Constantinople with his family with the intention of ultimately immigrating to the United States. Meanwhile, after returning from Aksaray, his brother-in-law Misak Kazanjian, his nephew Dikran Lafdjian and his sister's son-in-law Haigazoun Cherkezian had become business partners and had started traveling by sea from Constantinople as merchants and money-changers. Here is how Great-uncle Abraham describes a most ambitious business venture on their part and his involvement in it:

"The three had reasoned that it would be profitable for them to export textiles by weight to Sevastopol on the northern Black Sea coast, since this Russian city still remained accessible by sea. They asked me to partner with them by financially contributing to their capital so they could have a larger inventory. The idea seemed reasonable at the time, but I must not have been fully aware of the seriousness of the political crisis in Russia at the time."

At the end of WWI, military experts mistakenly anticipated a short conflict for Russia. But the strains of a prolonged war had placed the blame on the czarist regime of Nicolas II, forcing him to abdicate. As provincial governments took over, they did not do much better. Opposition to the war grew in the country as Bolsheviks seized the moment, riding chaos into power and withdrawing from the European war altogether. Soon they would fight a vicious civil war which at the end would strengthen their dominance and seal the country's bitter fate for decades to come.[11]

Great-uncle Abraham goes on to relate the fate of his relatives in Sevastopol: "A short while after the three reached

Sevastopol, Russian Civil War broke out in the wake of the 1917 Russian Revolution. The city had become the scene of brutal fighting between the Czarist, Bolshevik, and anarchist forces. Following the Bolshevik victory, Sevastopol became part of the Russian Soviet Socialist Republic. Meanwhile, the Russian ruble was devalued. Although the local government in Sevastopol eventually agreed to pay for their textiles in equivalent freight-carloads of wheat to arrive in Constantinople, instead of in denominations of the devalued Russian ruble, they had to go through a prolonged negotiation process. By the time an understanding was reached that their textiles were worth 124 freight carloads of wheat, the war and the intensifying Bolshevik Revolution had made it unsafe for the three to remain in Sevastopol any longer. Therefore, after the shipment of 29 freight carloads of wheat to Constantinople, they had to relinquish their rights for the remaining 95. They abandoned their rolls of textile in Sevastopol and fled to Constantinople on the first available ship, realizing that they were lucky just to have escaped out of there alive."

Leaving Cilicia

Great-uncle Abraham goes on to relate the rest of their odyssey: "While all the above unexpected scenarios were unfolding, one after the other in the different provinces of the Ottoman Empire and its neighboring countries, my wife Gül Dudu and I were on the Mediterranean coast of Mersin, in Cilicia, with my two brothers' families. My brother Parsegh was alone in Aksaray; my brother-in-law Misak and my nephew Dikran were in Constantinople, and Misak's family was in Konya, in central Anatolia.

This is when the generally positive and confident mood of Great-uncle Abraham becomes noticeably somber, as he reminisces: "Who would think that the government of Kemal would come into being and the defeated Turks would once again rise from the ashes? We could not have imagined this scenario even in our wildest dreams and neither could anyone else. However, it happened and with it came a reversal of fortune for us, bringing about a sharp decline in our family's financial well-being. We would end up losing all of what we owned: our great properties and our guaranteed incomes.

"Four days after visiting my brother-in-law in Konya when I finally arrived in Mersin, I found out I had received a telegram from my brother Parsegh in Aksaray informing me that he had workers loading large quantities of wheat on the backs of camels, some of which had already left town and were headed for Mersin. Due to his isolated location in Aksaray in central Anatolia, he must have been unsuspecting and unaware of the latest political developments resulting in the Kemalists' growing strength, since he had been deprived of all contact with the neighboring precincts. Unfortunately, only very few of these camels would safely reach Mersin. Instead, on the way to their destination, they would be intercepted by the Kemalist forces around Eregli.

"This sudden change in the political environment resulted in the Kemalist government's rise to power and prohibiting land travel throughout Anatolia. This ban would confine my brother Parsegh to Aksaray, making it impossible for him to join his wife and children for what would end up being an unbelievably long period of eight years. Had I not left Konya for Mersin in time, I probably would have been in a similar predicament; furthermore, there would have been no adult male in charge of our extended family in Mersin."

At the end of WWI, the Allies' initial gains were reversed in the lands of the Ottoman Empire in Anatolia. These developments resulted from the Allies' own greed, their unreasonable delays in negotiating, and their inability to agree upon a fair partitioning of the lands of the collapsing Ottoman Empire among themselves. Also, a major factor in this disagreement was Iraqi oil, since it was one of the prizes of the war. Eventually a compromise would be reached, whereby the American and British oil companies would divide the Iraqi oil.[12] While the allies continued their unending arguments with each other, behind the scenes, the Turkish insurgent leader Mustafa Kemal tirelessly conspired with Italy, France, and Russia, acquired their weapons, gained experience, and emerged as a triumphant commander.

A solemn Great-uncle Abraham remarks: "Sadly, we found out that in November 1920, the French had already signed a treaty with the Kemalist government, promising them they would vacate Cilicia in two months to return it to the Turks. This news completely devastated the already crushed surviving Armenians, as they had already suffered the pain of the deportations and the Genocide of 1915. They hoped that since the Ottoman Turks had lost the war, Armenians would now be able to resettle in Cilicia, and, with hard work, could perhaps make up their losses in a few years. However in the interim, France had become unwilling and unable to help the Armenians of Cilicia as earlier pledged, and instead promised the region to Turkey. This decision on France's part once again placed the 100,000 Armenians of this area under the Turkish yoke, which by now to Armenians was worse than death. Their only remaining recourse was to emigrate.

"We are still suffering the consequences of this emigration. Furthermore, even though our family traveled together during the deportations, in the end we would all scatter to different parts of the world: Beirut, Constantinople, United States, Canada, South America, Romania, Greece, and Armenia." Today just three million Armenians live in Armenia. [During the period 1915-1922] The Armenian population in the Ottoman Empire dropped from about two million to fewer than 500,000. Most historians call this subtraction the modern world's first genocide.[13]

The Nightmare in Mersin

Although Great-uncle Abraham manages to remain relatively calm and collected throughout his memoir, his mood becomes noticeably somber as he, along with the rest of the Armenians from Anatolia, faces the extraordinary dilemma in Mersin: "I cannot begin to describe how difficult and bothersome this unavoidable necessity to emigrate became for our people. Armenians from everywhere started to pour into Mersin to get passports. There was not a single person who was well-informed about what was going on. Only those involved in this crisis could fully comprehend the difficulties we faced and how hastily we had to make the serious decisions that would impact not only our lives but also those of the generations to come.

"First and foremost, we hoped that we were making the right decision regarding where to emigrate. Secondly, just like me, countless other Armenians from Cilicia were waiting at the quay in long lines to buy their tickets for the ships to take them to the country where they thought they would face the least number of complications. Meanwhile, they hoped they could come up with the necessary funds and that the ship would have enough room for their entire family. Once these important matters were addressed, they had to wait for the tender to take them to their ship, not to mention the problems they would encounter once they were on it.

"While I was holding in my hand what I thought was the right amount of money to buy our tickets, it would take me exactly five hours to actually manage to get them. With my elderly mother next to me at this hour of torment, my family, my brothers' families, and the family of Master Misak Houbeserian were all looking up to me for guidance. This was not because I was any more knowledgeable in helping them, but because I was the only available adult male relative whom they felt they could trust.

"Around this time, my brother-in-law Misak and my nephew Dikran had to travel to Iskenderun as part of their money-changing business and were to board a ship in Mersin for this purpose. I felt responsible to confer with them before making the final decisions for their families. Since we all thought at the time that it was unlikely that the British would leave Constantinople, and because it would be easier for us to find orderly and high-quality schools in that city to educate the next generation, and since plenty of houses were available for rent there, we decided that Constantinople would be the destination of my two brothers' families, as well as that of the Houbeserians. As for my family, since my son Onnik was attending the American University of Beirut at the time, and since my daughter Nver and son-in law Armenag Cherkezian had already left for Beirut, it made sense for that city to be our destination as well.

"Four days later when Misak and Dikran returned from Iskenderun, we had my brothers' and Misak Houbeserian's families board the ship to take them to Constantinople; subsequently, we returned to Beirut."

The Rapid Transformation of Beirut

Great-uncle Abraham cannot believe his eyes when he sees Beirut again: "It had been only one and a half years since we had last lived in this city. When we arrived there, we realized that it had changed drastically during that short period. There were hardly any houses available now in the city for us to rent. My son-in-law, having arrived there five days earlier, had managed to rent a house with four bedrooms to accommodate us all for 120 gold pieces. We used to live in a perfect house with five bedrooms and a bath facing the Mediterranean for one fourth of that price… However, what was most painful for me was to find out what had happened to the price of my previous store in the Sersok Marketplace, which I had sold a year and a half ago for 12 gold pieces. It was now worth 500 Egyptian gold pieces, whose value had by now appreciated even more against the Turkish currency. Having to pay such an inflated price for a store, in addition to a newly required huge security deposit, after having moved four times already and having witnessed so much suffering and injustice was too much for me to bear. I was heart-broken and had lost my previous enthusiasm for work.

"There were plenty of additional reasons for my feeling so dejected. In 1920, before we left Mersin, the Marash and Hadjin massacres had already occurred, in which the survivors of the Armenian Genocide, who returned to southeastern Anatolia to claim their previous properties, were slaughtered. Through the grapevine, we heard that Hadjin was in ruins and that orphans were roaming its streets. During our stay in Mersin, we had received the news that the Greeks had been defeated in Anatolia by the Turks and that they were fleeing. Later in 1922, an unimaginable carnage would unfold in and around Smyrna, today's Izmir: Hundreds of thousands of terrified Armenian and Greek refugees had been pouring to Smyrna to what they thought until then was a safe, Christian city. Mustafa Kemal and his Turkish army would soon arrive there. The Turkish soldiers would start a fire in the Armenian Quarter which would quickly spread and engulf the entire city, with the exception of its Turkish Quarter, until it would become unrecognizable. During this catastrophe, countless Armenian and Greek refugees would be trapped in the city and be raped, burned, starved, and killed as they attempted to make it to the quay to escape the fire. Meanwhile, French, British, Italian, and American warships sat still in the harbor, just watching, because they did not want to alienate the Turks. What an unlucky nation we Armenians must have been that lady luck never smiled on us…"

Family Scattered Throughout the World

Great-uncle Abraham relates the rest of his family's story thus: "In 1922, our son Onnik (Uncle John) graduated from the American University of Beirut. My wife and I were hoping that he could find a desirable job in and around Beirut. At the time, my son-in-law Armenag was employed by the travel industry. Because of his familiarity with the English language, Onnik also started his first job in this profession by accompanying Armenian emigrants from the Middle East for the first leg of their journey to Marseille, France; then he would take them north to Cherbourg to help them with all the necessary transactions so they could board the ship that would take them to New York harbor.

"After repeating this trip several times with the emigrants, he must have made up his mind to settle in the U.S., himself. Early in June of 1923 he wrote to us from Le Havre, France, disclosing this plan. At the time, his mother and I felt apprehensive about his decision for a number of reasons. Most importantly, although he was 23, he was still quite inexperienced, and would be completely on his own during the entire venture. Another reason for our concern was that those who had successfully emigrated, had applied to the U.S. embassy earlier, and were already on a quota list; additionally, someone from the U.S. most likely had vouched for them. Onnik had met none of these requirements. His next communication to us was a short letter from Le Havre, France, which said:

'Look for my telegram nine days beyond the date of my letter for news of my safe arrival in the United States.'

At this point, Great-uncle Abraham philosophizes thus: "If a young chick manages to fly away from the family nest for the first time would he ever return? Meanwhile, in spite of the elapsing of several years, the gloomy and unjust events I had witnessed within the past several years continued to make their presence felt in my soul, giving me the survivor's guilt, crushing my enthusiasm and depressing my energy level, ultimately reminding me of my advancing age. For the above reasons, since at the time my wife and I did not have any major expenses and I was getting on in years, I became reluctant to start a new business, unless it was absolutely necessary. We have been able to live comfortably by being somewhat frugal and also because my son has regularly forwarded some money to us from the U.S.; I thank the Lord for all of this.

"If someone asked me how I felt as a father under my present circumstances, the following is how I would respond: If my son were close by at the time and I could have counseled him so he could have benefited from my experiences, including my mistakes, things might have turned out better for him. I regret that at the time of his departure in 1923, the political situation in the Middle East, in the lands that at one time belonged to the Ottoman Empire had precluded a constructive conversation between father and son. Therefore, all I can do now from so far away is to pray that the Lord will guide him and that he will be happy and well. Although my wife traveled to the U.S. and saw Onnik in 1933, so far I have not, even though my yearning for him has not diminished through the years. After he became a U.S. citizen, he sent documents to his mother and me, stating that he has vouched for us to become U.S. residents. Throughout the years, he has not forgotten us and has written to us regularly.

"I have worked hard throughout my life and have enjoyed times of prosperity. Then, again, I have lived through and survived the torment of the deportation to the Syrian Desert and have witnessed the suffering and death of countless innocent countrymen and relatives of mine, during a genocide that I relive in my memory practically every day.

"After some 70 years, I can no longer find the drive and vigor in me to propel me to the other end of the world to be with my children. The more I think about it, the more I envision myself as an orphan in an unfamiliar land, with a language incomprehensible to me; therefore, I have abandoned the idea of immigrating to the United States. However, I will never give up hope that one day the world will be a more peaceful place to live in and that my children will come and visit me. I wish them and their loved ones continued success."

Great-Uncle Abraham's Epic Poem

(I wrote this poem favoring the Turks since part of my writing is detrimental to the government and if discovered by them, I would be punished outright because they would hang the innocent; how dare I talk against the government?)

1914 (1330)

During this world's mournful years
All the nations came out in the open arena
All wearing soldiers' war uniforms.

A storm was unleashed from Bosnia-Sarajevo Palace
Not looking out for Serbia, the little victim,
Assassinated heir to the throne and his wife.
Austria became agitated.

Hostile vagabond's first victim,
The prince
Bullet hit both, at once
They fell as ordered by God's will.

Austria could not tolerate this
Anew it demanded a high price,
Wanted Serbia to be annexed.
All Slavic countries became angry.

Russia wanted to get involved
To protect Serbia's interests.
Became impossible to reconcile,
Quickly threw problem into the arena.

Conquering Germans having noticed this
Being Austria's ally,
Having confidence in their 42inch cannons,
Instantly hoisted their proud flag.
(At that time Germany owned 42inch cannons. Being allies
of Turkey, I had to praise the Germans.)

Seeing this, French became alarmed
They quickly realized the menace;
They blocked the road to Belgium
Too bad that "the flames had reached the eaves."
(The matter had gotten out of hand.)

Instigator the English, pursuing profit,
Noticing a big challenger against them
Having destroyed large and small nations in the past,
Began to provoke the world.

During this period our Turkey thought
Since the danger became recognized
Intent of the nation became obvious,
For our safety, war was to ensue.

Our deportation was proclaimed
The army of the Ottoman Empire was invited.
Heroically rushing towards war;
Let there be light! Calipha and Rabbini.

(Extol higher powers.)
(Let the reader comprehend...)

Italians said they were neutral
Their allies trusted them.
Nine months they were in preparation
Their plans were crooked.
(The Italians were Germany's allies before.)

At this point the Balkans were only ones left,
This penetrated their brains (affected their thinking)
These small countries were in reflection,
I wonder what the final decision would be.

At the end Bulgaria was left,
Thought a lot, but made a miraculous decision
Got together a mobilization force and went to war.
This made Russia very upset.

Now the world got all mixed up
Torpedoes collided with each other
Flowing blood reached the Danube,
Rockets killing the mothers' children.

Refugee's Ballad

At this instant while we were
Our nation's respected soldiers,
Their families were after dry bread.
Unimaginable deportations started.

Those remaining, while thinking
And working on complimenting,
Thought possible while sacrificing,
Began to realize it outside of their expectations.

However additional miseries started,
Many cities had been emptied before it came to us.
We did not know what affairs this country got into,
In July we felt the "winter" season.

On August 4th we left the country
We bid good bye to some of our neighbors.
Those that cared about us we left them disconsolate.
What a sad day those travels started!

Let's make the voyage straight through
Let's go to Ulukishla kaza (district).
Hate the gendarme commander
The difficulties of the road started here.

We passed from Bozanti to Tarsus and Adana
Foreign regions not that fortunate,
No remedy on any subject.
Told to hurry-up, rushing started.

We passed by Ceyhan and Seyhan Rivers,
Osmaniye town center we reported,
Thirty thousand individuals we observed
My God, what an impoverished nation, chaos had started.

Bloody Gorge, Infidels' Mountain, what roads!
Difficult, forested, very steep hills,
Here and there fallen and miserable souls.
Astounded, how can you tolerate all this?

We arrived at huge center, Katma.
We found the entire population amassed here.
Those separated from the tents could not be found
Typhoid-typhus sicknesses started.

After forty three days of difficult travel
We saw the big city of Aleppo.
We thought we should be comfortable here
However the stress and misery started here.

For those entering this city money had no value
Those who were thought to be smart were not.
Casualties increased without limit
Digging ditches for burial started.
(Everyone lost their minds
They were giving money to
Those who said "we can keep you here"
However there was no work to be found.)

Multitude of people were sent to Rakka
Those who left kept looking back
As if we looked like we were remaining there;
At the end suddenly our evacuation started.

Having permits we separated.
We were placed on the Damascus train,
We were packed like sardines in the wagons.
The train started towards Damascus.
(We had gotten a permit to go to Damascus.)

Entering the sacred soil of Damascus
Gradually the train slowed down,
We could not see the city well
The train started to move again.

Eventually we came to the last stop, Daraa.
We found a good top commissar
We got deported to Remté village district
A little bit of comfort started here.

We survived well this travel
But let's not pass over the difficulties.
In this location, three thousand hungry families
Started thinking and looking for bread.

Now consider this nation
Wonder, mercy, kindness, generosity,
Prayers of dependents of Reshat Mehmet.
Assistance of honorable Jemal Pasha.
For centuries we will hate Talaat
The bloody killer of million individuals.

Abraham H. Lafdjian
(Translated by Gregory Ketabgian)

(Endnotes)

1 Kaiser, Hilmar in collaboration with Luther and Nancy Eskijian, *At the Crossroads of Der Zor*. London: Gomidas Institute, 2002, pp. 6-7.

2 Ibid p.8

3 Salopek, Paul, "A Century Later Slaughter Still Haunts Turkey and Armenia" *National Geographic, April 2016.*

4 Rogan, Eugene, "The Fall of the Ottomans" *The Wall Street Journal,* Sept 5, 2015. Part C.

5 Hovannisian, Richard, Koker, Osman, "*Armenian Communities of Asia Minor*" (with Post Card Collection of O.C. Calumeno), Costa Mesa: Mazda, 2014, pp. 238-239.

6 Balakian, Peter, *The Burning Tigris*. New York: Harper Collins, 2003, p.192.

7 Ibid p.196

8 Kaiser, Hilmar in collaboration with Luther and Nancy Eskijian, *At the Crossroads of Der Zor.* London: Gomidas Institute, 2002, p.23.

9 Mouradian, Khatchig, "*Un-Hiding the Past: Myth-Making and the "Hidden Armenians" of Turkey.*" Clark University, Lecture @ Cal State University, Northridge, Jan 31, 2015.

10   Louis, Roger, "End of the Caliphate" *The Wall Street Journal, Sept 5, 2015, Part C.*

11   Hay,William Anthony, "The Twilight of Empire" *The Wall Street Journal.* Aug 29, 2015, Part C.

12   Ureneck, Lou, *The Great Fire.* New York: Harper Collins, 2015, p.246.

13   Salopek, Paul, "A Century Later Slaughter Still Haunts Turkey and Armenia" *National Geographic*, April, 2016.

EPILOGUE

The United States Has Been Good to Us

Not a day passes without my uttering a heartfelt "thank you" to the United States for enabling us, its citizens, institutions and media to lead authentic, free and ethical lives. I get disheartened when I read about the recent takeover by the Turkish government of the *Zaman* and *Cumhuriyet,* two newspapers with significant circulation in Turkey, the arrest of their publishers and prominent journalists on their editorial staff, in an attempt to silence critical media and opposition voices.

As a member of an ethnic minority, my generation has made more headway in the United States without undue interference from the government at unpredictable intervals, as had been the case in Turkey when I lived there with my family during my first seventeen years. This country's fairness to its citizens and its caring for their safety has given me a chance to be more relaxed and productive. By behaving in this manner, am I perhaps putting tradition and culture on the back burner?

I am so thankful that freedom is part of the law of the land here. As for opportunities, they still abound, although one has to be willing to work harder to take advantage of them. Somewhat disappointing is the fact that even here in the United States, cultural peculiarities are difficult for some people to tolerate. I realize the United States has always been a melting pot of cultures and that I do not have to be of only one ancestry to fit in. Furthermore, in contrast to my former homeland, I do not have to live in constant fear of one sort or other: deportation, punishment, or even death because I do not belong to that particular ancestry.

As the years have gone by, I have increasingly realized the important role history has played in our lives. Even my most cautious father, who could not breathe a word to me and my sister about the history of our people while we lived in Turkey, made it a priority of his to remember the past as soon as he was ready to set foot in this country. At great risk to him and my mother, he made sure to bring that special box which contained Great-uncle Abraham's memoir from Istanbul and convinced me I should translate it, to keep the memory of our past alive. He must have realized, "Memories not shared are history lost forever."

Acknowledgments

I owe a great deal to the help of friends and relatives who made this memoir possible. My friend Gail Tager, "The Honorary Armenian," early on underscored the importance of remembering and recording the past to make it available for the generations to come. Reading my memoir in its early form and encouraging me to go on, she has an important role both in its genesis and fruition. So does Maggie Mangassarian Goschin, since she has been a bottomless source of energy and encouragement through the entire process, as well as a supplier of rare books I would otherwise have been unable to find. I am thankful to my sister Armine Garboushian for filling in the blanks as necessary throughout the entire process, but particularly regarding our maternal grandparents' years in Kastamonu, as well as for supplying the pertinent detail of the two years our parents spent in Istanbul, when I was no longer living in that city. Another important contribution of hers was urging me to have a dialogue with my mother's only surviving cousin, Silva Ghazarian in France, who gave me her eyewitness account of Stalin's repression her family had suffered, along with my uncle's family. I am grateful that on our 2007 Armenia trip when we visited my cousin Armen, he was willing to share some of these same events with me involving his parents. Subsequently, his son Hovig was most helpful in being the communicator between us to fill in any details I may have previously missed. Our trip to Historic Armenia led by Dr. Garbis Der Yeghiayan in 2006, which included a side-trip to the childhood home of my father and grandparents, awakened in me the desire to proceed with the memoir. I am similarly thankful to my husband's cousin Jesse Matossian for his research, which included the Caltech files, regarding information on my father's cousin Jacob Lafdjian. I have also benefited from a conversation with a late cousin, Rose Jemelian, who confirmed for me certain facts during Jacob's early years in the U.S., which my father had previously shared with me.

I thank my friend Aida Bedrosian for her detailed eyewitness account as an eight-year-old during the Cyprus Crisis in Ortaköy, as

354

well as Serj Bulanikian for guiding me and keeping me abreast on this unfortunate historical event we had both experienced. Similarly I am indebted to my friend Arpie Dalian for sharing with me both her father's unwarranted incarceration in 1973 in Istanbul, as well as his neighbor Mr.Chilinguirian's amusing eyewitness account of a sleepless night spent on the Island of Kinali, both of which reveal what Armenians had to endure physically and psychologically during times of crisis in Turkey. I am also thankful to Dikran Dalian for his time and effort in helping me on the subject of Halide Edib Adivar. I am equally indebted to another friend and distant relative Hilda Parunyan for sharing with me her experience with her Turkish History teacher in Yesayan High School in Istanbul, as well as to her mother Sona Tuncer, for enlightening me regarding my maternal grandfather's mandatory departure to Askale as part of a labor battalion.

From the beginning all the way to its completion, my husband Dr. Gregory Ketabgian worked just as hard on this project as I did, be it in the area of research, maps, genealogy, and the translation of great-uncle's epic poem, formatting, design or the formulation of the front cover. He also spent countless hours reading over my drafts, coming up with constructive criticism and ideas. I also am most grateful that on her trip to California, our daughter Dr. Tamara Ketabgian, presently professor of Victorian English in Beloit College in Wisconsin, devoted a number of days of her busy schedule to edit my memoir to make it more readable. I learned a great deal from her corrections. I also wish to thank my daughter Dr. Ani Ketabgian for her interest in this project and for her thoughtfulness in providing me with well-chosen books that inspired me to go on. I could always depend on our youngest daughter Lena Ketabgian to respond to my technical needs on an emergency basis. I am grateful for that, as well as in her interest in the memoir.

About the Author

Alice Lafdjian Ketabgian was born and raised in Istanbul, Turkey and is a descendent of Genocide Survivors. She received her childhood education from Aramyan Ounchiyan elementary school in Kadiköy, followed by a high school education at Üsküdar Amerikan Kiz Lisesi in Üsküdar.

Upon arrival in Southern California in 1962, she attended La Verne College for two years and transferred to UCLA to receive an M.S. in Human Physiology from the School of Medicine in 1968. When her youngest child was two and a half, she started attending Cal State LA in the evenings, eventually completing the requirements for a registered dietitian. After initially functioning as a clinical dietitian in her husband Dr. Ketabgian's internal medicine office for a number of years, she became the office manager and functioned in that capacity for the following 25 years until their retirement in 2004.

With a newly-revived interest in Armenian history and literature, she translated *Anneannem* of Fethiye Çetin to English in 2006 (unpublished). An account of her Pilgrimage to Historic Armenia was published in the *Armenian Observer* the same year.

356

Lafdjian Family Tree (Partial)

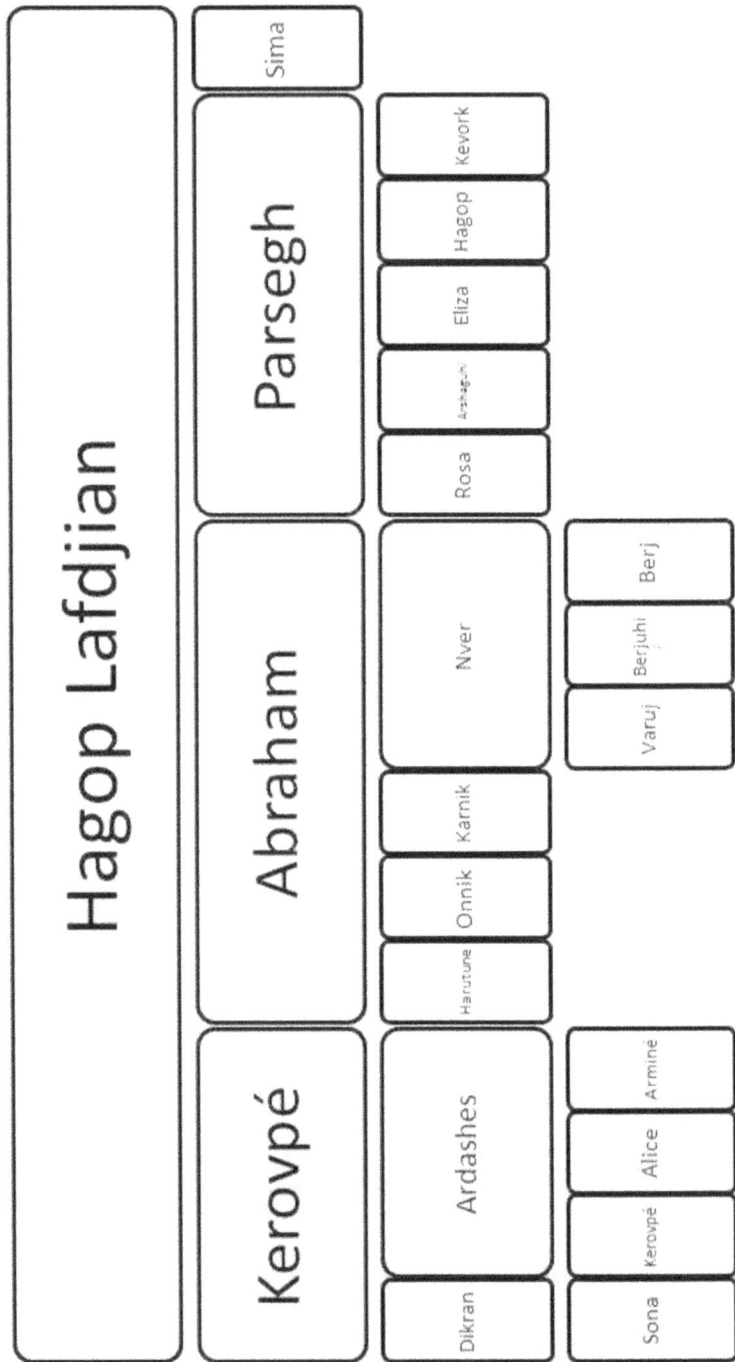

Hagop Lafdjian

Sima

Parsegh
- Rosa
- Arshagun
- Eliza
- Hagop
- Kevork

Abraham
- Harutune
- Onnik
- Karnik
- Nver
  - Varuj
  - Berjuhi
  - Berj

Kerovpé
- Dikran
- Ardashes
  - Sona
  - Kerovpé
  - Alice
  - Arminé

Stepanyan Family Tree (Partial)

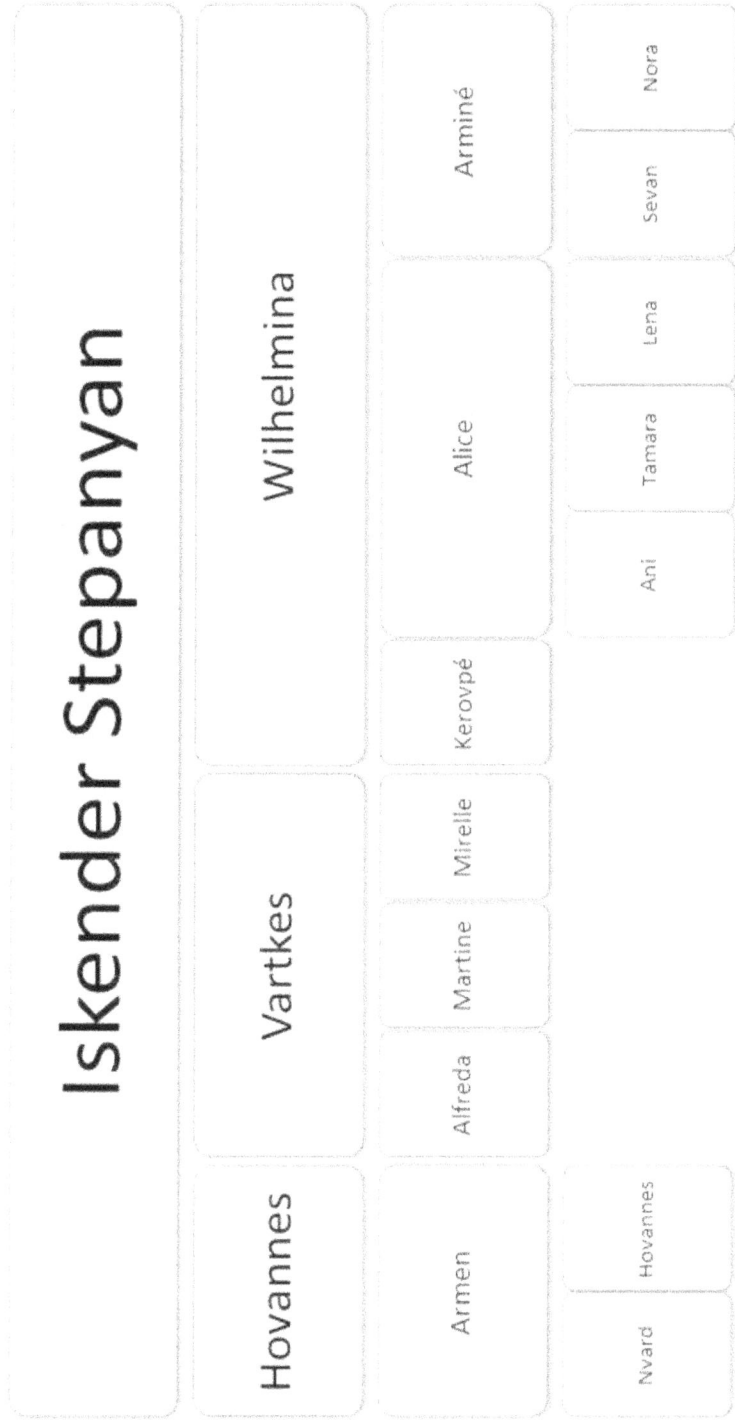

Iskender Stepanyan

- **Hovannes**
- **Vartkes**
  - Alfreda
  - Martine
  - Mirelle
  - Kerovpé
- **Wilhelmina**
  - Alice
    - Ani
    - Tamara
    - Lena
    - Sevan
    - Nora
  - Arminé

- Armen
  - Nvard
  - Hovannes

www.ingramcontent.com/pod-product-compliance
Lightning Source LLC
Chambersburg PA
CBHW021213090426
42740CB00006B/210